BEVERLY HILLS PUBLIC LIBRARY
3 5048 00702 4209

D1017490

Something That Will Surprise the World

ALSO BY SUSAN DUNN

Jefferson's Second Revolution: The Election Crisis of 1800 and the Triumph of Republicanism (2004)

George Washington (with James MacGregor Burns, 2004)

The Social Contract and *The First and Second Discourses,* by Jean-Jacques Rousseau (ed., 2002)

The Three Roosevelts: Patrician Leaders Who Transformed America (with James MacGregor Burns, 2001)

Sister Revolutions: French Lightning, American Light (1999)

Diversity and Citizenship: New Challenges for American Nationhood (ed., with Gary J. Jacobsohn, 1996)

The Deaths of Louis XVI: Regicide and the French Political Imagination (1994)

Something That Will Surprise the World

The Essential Writings of the

Founding Fathers

Selected and edited with an Introduction by

Susan Dunn

A Member of the Perseus Books Group
New York

Published by Basic Books,
A Member of the Perseus Books Group

Books published by Basic Books are available at special discounts for bulk purchases in the United States by corporations, institutions, and other organizations. For more information, please contact the Special Markets Department at the Perseus Books Group, 11 Cambridge Center, Cambridge MA 02142, or call (617) 252-5298 or (800) 255-1514, or e-mail special.markets@perseusbooks.com.

Designed by Brent Wilcox
Set in 10.75 point New Caledonia

Library of Congress Cataloging-in-Publication Data
Something that will surprise the world : the essential writings of the founding fathers / edited by Susan Dunn.
p. cm.
Includes bibliographical references and index.
ISBN-13: 978-0-465-01779-9
ISBN-10: 0-465-01779-7
1. United States—Politics and government—1775–1783—Sources. 2. United States—Politics and government—1783–1809—Sources. 3. United States—Politics and government—1809–1817—Sources. 4. Statesmen—United States—Archives. 5. Presidents—United States—Archives. I. Dunn, Susan, 1945– .
E302.1.S66 2006
973.4092'2—dc22

2006009003

06 07 08 / 10 9 8 7 6 5 4 3 2 1

Contents

Foreword

BY JOSEPH J. ELLIS

During the past decade there has been a discernible surge of interest in the Founding Fathers. An electromagnetic field has always surrounded the founding generation, which is one reason we have felt obliged to capitalize and mythologize those "present at the creation." But until recently the tendency has been to keep our distance from them, admire them from afar, treat them like icons carved in granite on Mount Rushmore or encased in marble on the Mall or the Tidal Basin. Like the patriarchs of the Old Testament, they have been revered but distant presences, figures who remain in the middle distance of our memory, like statues in the mist.

The recent surge of interest in the founders has tended to defy the iconic stereotype, blow away the mist, transform the marble into flesh and blood. It has given us flawed founders. The founders have become more interesting as they have become more human. As their foibles and imperfections have become more evident, or should we say self-evident, instead of becoming disappointed we have found them more interesting. In that sense they are more like us, and therefore have more to teach us.

It is not clear why the founders have rather suddenly become fashionable. On the one hand, the magisterial editions of their papers, begun in most cases in the middle of the twentieth century, have been marching forward at a stately pace and have now produced a massive body of evidence previously unavailable to scholars. On the other hand, most of the recent work, especially books that have enjoyed a wide readership, has not been written by professional historians. Whether it is David McCullough's biography of John Adams, Ron Chernow's portrait of Alexander Hamilton, or Walter Isaacson's depiction of Benjamin Franklin, in each case the author works outside the groves of academe. There are exceptions, of course. (And I am pleased to be one of them.) But the huge readership currently fascinated with the founders is not being served by card-carrying historians.

Indeed, the agenda of the academy remains resolutely focused elsewhere, on the ordinary rather than the extraordinary, on the periphery rather than the center, on the inarticulate rather than the articulate. As a general rule, the founders are either studiously ignored or contemptuously condemned as the deadest, whitest males in American history. And like the conversations among policy wonks inside the beltway, what scholars refer to as academic discourse remains an in-house affair largely unintelligible to the broader public.

And so the emergence of a sizable audience for serious books about the revolutionary generation—an audience that has begun to rival the longstanding popular interest in the Civil War—is an unusual phenomenon. It has not trickled down from academe, but rather bubbled up from below where ordinary readers live. There is a genuine appetite out there in the land for work on the men, not the myths, who founded the nation in which we all still live. The obvious question becomes: Why?

Based on my own experience responding to questions from audiences who represent this readership, there is a profound sense of despair with our modern-day political culture, a deep-felt conviction that we have somehow created a political process at the national level almost designed to eliminate excellence and leadership. Why, they ask, must we choose between George Bush and John Kerry, when in 1800 they got to choose between John Adams and Thomas Jefferson? We might call this mode of thinking "enlightened nostalgia," for it is rooted in a once-upon-a-time mentality that, truth be told, is not quite fair to the present generation of political leaders, who lack access to Mount Rushmore. Being first gives the founders an incalculable advantage. As Ralph Waldo Emerson so nicely put it, "They saw God face to face; we can only see Him second-hand."

And yet, there is an enlightened dimension to this modern-day nostalgia. For the revolutionary generation did discover the political values and invent the political institutions under which the American republic still functions. In that sense we are still living their legacy, and it behooves us to understand how it is that we reside in the oldest and most successful republican experiment in world history. Not only that, the ideas and institutions created by the revolutionary generation have enjoyed global success, having destroyed the monarchical dynasties of the nineteenth century and then vanquished the totalitarian despotism of the twentieth, just as Thomas Jefferson predicted they would.

Within the American political universe, the founding era produced the "big bang" that has radiated its energies and implications right up to the present. If history is an argument without end, in American history the founders framed the argument that we are still having about our rights and responsibilities as citizens, about the proper relationship between individual rights and national security, about the role of religion in a secular state, about the tension between the twin goals of freedom and equality.

The founders, in effect, set the mold, and we go back to them, for the same reason that they went back to the Greek and Roman classics. They are, in fact, our American classics, the primal version and original intentions of our ongoing experiment to reconcile the competing imperatives that have fascinated and bedeviled political philosophers since Aristotle. They began the conversation we are still having.

So neither nostalgic nor celebratory motives by themselves can fully explain the surge of interest in the founders. For once you go back to meet them, in Emerson's terms, "face to face," you discover, whatever your original reasons for making the trip, people more palpable than icons, more complicated than mythical cartoons, often improvising at the edge of catastrophe, but ultimately defining the abiding shape of the republic we still inhabit. Since we can presume there was nothing special in the water back then, and that these men, collectively and individually, had no direct access to God's will, and since miraculous explanations are generally regarded as inadmissible in the scholarly world, the obvious question then becomes: How did they do it?

The answer, or perhaps answers, can be found in the pages that follow, where the editor, Susan Dunn, has made a deft and judicious selection of letters and documents from the five most prominent founders. It is somewhat baffling, especially given the surge of interest in the founders, that a collection of this sort has not appeared earlier. To my knowledge, the only previous attempt to provide an introduction to the founders' own words that spans the entire collective, not just one or two figures, is the book by Adrienne Koch entitled *The American Enlightenment*, which has been out of print for over thirty years.

Here they are, then, in all their throbbing intensity, personal quirks, marvelous detachment, temporary enthusiasms, brilliant inspirations, abiding jealousies, human doubts, final regrets. These pages allow you to enter the conversation at its formative stage. Do so with the confidence that it is, at last, safe to get to know them as they really were.

Introduction

BY SUSAN DUNN

From dusty, colorless paintings, they look down at us with distant, indifferent eyes, waxen faces, grim mouths tightly set. No signs of warmth. No smiles. They look embalmed.

But what if, behind those impassive, expressionless masks, there was more? Ferocious ambition. Steadfast courage. Radical ideas. Penetrating intelligence. Buoyant idealism. Steely self-control. Repressed desires. Bruised egos. Volatile tempers.

Thirteen backwater, sparsely populated colonies, remote from the great metropolises of Europe, produced an astounding galaxy of revolutionary leaders—Washington, Hamilton, Adams, Jefferson, Madison—who stood at the head of a remarkable array of talented men at every level in society and in domains from politics to diplomacy and journalism.

Together they fought a successful war of independence against the mightiest power on earth, created an enduring constitution for their new nation, established stable representative institutions and a system of adversarial political parties, and set the stage for economic development and growing prosperity.

Their collective leadership—their boldness, their daring, their brilliance, their freshness of vision—would never be surpassed in American history. Nor would it be equaled elsewhere in the world. Too often, revolutionary movements—in France, Russia, China, Algeria, Iran, Cuba, and elsewhere—met with a dismal fate: suppression of individual rights, outlawing of dissent and opposition, suspension of constitutions, violence, purges, despotism, totalitarianism.

Why were the American founders able to succeed when the leaders of so many other revolutionary movements failed? How can we explain the genius of their collective leadership?

On the surface, they appeared reluctant to lead. "I beg it may be remembered by every Gentleman in the room," said George Washington when he appeared before the Continental Congress to accept command of the Continental Army in 1775, that "I do not think myself equal to the command I am honored with." Toward the end of the war, in 1782, he angrily reprimanded Colonel Lewis Nicola for urging him to declare himself king of the United States. And when the war was over, he gave up military power gladly, relieved to return to his "vine and fig tree." A few years later, he balked at attending the Constitutional Convention in Philadelphia, yielding only at the last minute to the entreaties of friends. Nor was he eager to govern the new republic as its first president. Before his inauguration, he confessed that he felt like "a culprit who is going to the place of his execution."[1] He seemed to want nothing more than to resign from power—one historian termed him a "virtuoso of resignations."[2]

"Every day confirms me in the intention of renouncing public life," Alexander Hamilton wrote to his young wife in 1781. "Let others waste their time and their tranquillity in a vain pursuit of power and glory; be it my object to be happy in a quiet retreat with my better angel."[3] John Adams assured his son John Quincy that he was "very indifferent" to the outcome of the presidential election of 1796 when he ran against Thomas Jefferson, "really, truly and sincerely."[4] Should he lose, he told his wife, Abigail, he would retire from public life without a complaint, without the smallest dread of private life.[5] Perhaps he was a "fool," he mused, to serve at all.[6]

Jefferson hardly expressed more enthusiasm about life in the political arena. Public service and private misery were inextricably linked, he explained, adding, "I have not the vanity to count myself among those whom the state would think worth oppressing with perpetual service." Shouldn't one's personal happiness come first? "If we are made in some degree for others," he wrote, "yet in a greater are we made for ourselves."[7] In 1794, after resigning as secretary of state from Washington's cabinet, Jefferson proclaimed that he would not give up retirement "for the empire of the universe."[8]

And yet, time after time, Jefferson dutifully descended from his mountaintop, embarking on long sojourns in Williamsburg, Philadelphia, Richmond, Paris, New York, and Washington, playing leading roles in the political life of colonial Virginia, revolutionary America, and finally, the

United States. He understood fully the leadership obligations of a man of his social class and intellect. "Hold on then, my dear friend," he urged James Madison in 1794 upon learning that Madison might withdraw from public life. "I do not see . . . a greater affliction than the fear of your retirement; but this must not be, unless to a more splendid & a more efficacious post."[9] Their professed dislike of public life and longing to return to their families, estates, and law practices notwithstanding, the leaders of the revolutionary generation never doubted that the responsibility to lead their communities and their nation fell to them.

Not yet a democracy, eighteenth-century America was a socially stratified society at the top of which stood an elite class of educated gentlemen. Men like Washington, Jefferson, Madison, and Adams, who were born into prominent families, took their social rank seriously, accepting its responsibilities as well as its privileges. Public service was their duty, required of them by their position in society.[10]

And indeed they piled up decades of public service, schooling themselves in every aspect of politics. George Washington: member of the Virginia House of Burgesses, delegate to the Continental Congress, commander in chief of the Continental Army, president of the Constitutional Convention in 1787, first president of the United States. Alexander Hamilton: aide to General George Washington, member of the New York state legislature, delegate to the Constitutional Convention, secretary of the treasury. John Adams: Massachusetts legislator, delegate to the Continental Congress, commissioner to France, minister to Great Britain, vice president and then president of the United States. Thomas Jefferson: member of the Virginia House of Burgesses, delegate to the Continental Congress, governor of Virginia, minister to France, secretary of state, vice president, president. James Madison: member of the Virginia Council of State, delegate to both the Continental Congress and the Constitutional Convention, member of the House of Representatives, secretary of state, president.

Was their service to the nation little more than grudging, dutiful acquiescence to their sense of responsibility? Not exactly. For if we peel away the mantra of groans about public life and professions of burning desire to return to vines and fig trees, another picture emerges: These were men of vast ambition.

"Reputation ought to be the perpetual subject of my Thoughts, and Aim of my Behavior," wrote the twenty-four-year-old John Adams. He reproached himself for not coming up with a silver bullet, a quick fix for instant renown. "Why have I not Genius to start some new Thought. Some thing that will *surprize the World.* New, grand, wild, yet regular thought that may raise me *at once* to fame."[11] Adams had more on his mind than disinterested public service: He was a young man on the make.

So was Alexander Hamilton. "My ambition is prevalent," he wrote at the green age of fourteen. Without family or fortune to sustain him, Hamilton vowed to rise above the low condition of a shipping clerk in the West Indies, admitting, "I . . . would willingly risk my life tho' not my Character to exalt my Station."[12] Wishing to "act a conspicuous part"[13] in the Revolution, he was elated to serve as George Washington's aide.

Washington easily understood Hamilton's ambition. As a young man he too had been driven, first for acceptance into the elite world of Virginia's great families, families like the Fairfaxes into which his older half brother had married. "It is in their power," he realized, "to be very serviceable upon many occasion's to us, as *young beginner's.*"[14]

But Washington's ambition was not limited to social climbing: He wanted, above all, recognition on the public stage. "The chief part" of his happiness, he candidly admitted, was "the esteem and notice" of his country. As a young lieutenant colonel, he longed for proof that the leaders of the British army held him in higher esteem than the "*common run* of provincial officers." Not even the official statement of gratitude that he and his troops received from the House of Burgesses in 1754 satisfied his hunger for recognition.[15] So off he went that same year, traveling on horseback from Virginia to Boston—in vain—to request a royal commission from the acting commander in chief of British forces in America. A year later, he journeyed to Philadelphia with the same request—and the same result.[16] How could he cement his reputation and honor? How could he and the men of his generation "surprize the World" and achieve the notice and fame they craved?

"You and I, my dear friend, have been sent into life at a time when the greatest lawgivers of antiquity would have wished to live," wrote John Adams in 1776. "How few of the human race have ever enjoyed an opportunity of making an election of government . . . for themselves or their children!"[17] Adams had discovered the key to the reputation he longed for: Revolution. The American struggle for freedom from British rule presented the opportunity to participate in events of world-historical importance: not only a revolutionary war of independence but, even more important, the founding and consolidation of a republic—the first extended and diverse one in history. If the men of the revolutionary generation succeeded, fame—no, immortality—would be theirs. "Those who establish republics or kingdoms," Niccolò Machiavelli had remarked three hundred years earlier, would forever receive the praise of historians. They would be rescued from the oblivion that is man's fate.[18]

Fame and a life of distinguished service to the country were so inextricably linked in the minds of the American founders that any political leader who seemed unconcerned with recognition and applause was suspect—for such a person was probably motivated only by self-interest, unrestrained by a moral code. "Mr. Burr has never appeared solicitous for fame," commented Alexander Hamilton about his hated rival, "& that great Ambition unchecked by . . . the love of Glory, is an unruly Tyrant who never can keep long in a course which good men will approve."[19] Though self-interest could not be expected to vanish, the quest for glory and reputation implied the fusion of personal ambition and public service. Love of fame, the historian Douglass Adair wrote, transformed the desire for self-aggrandizement and personal reward into a "golden concern" for public service.[20] Machiavelli would have agreed. "A well-regulated republic," he wrote, "should open the way to public honors to those who seek reputation by means that are conducive to the public good."[21] It was a win-win situation: The nation won, and so did its leaders.

Were the founders, then, simply crass and calculating "transactional" leaders, exchanging great deeds for fame? Hardly. They knew well that far more was at stake than their own egos and lives. Revolutionary idealism electrified John Adams. "I am well aware of the toil, and blood, and treasure that it will cost us to maintain this Declaration [of Independence]," Adams wrote on July 3, 1776, to his wife, Abigail. "Yet, through all the gloom, I can see the rays of ravishing light and glory."[22]

George Washington recognized that he and his soldiers in the Continental Army were fighting for "all that is dear and valuable in Life." When he looked back on his service for the British in the French and Indian Wars of the 1750s, Washington realized that the cause he had fought for had been merely "the usual contest of Empire and Ambition," tangential to the "general interest" of society and to the welfare of the people. In such a war, the "conscience of a soldier" had so little at stake that he could "properly insist," as he had, to the point of obsession, "upon his claims of Rank, and extend his pretensions even to Punctilio."[23] But the American Revolution was a different kind of conflict. Indeed, its leaders ardently committed their lives, honor, and fortunes in a war, as Washington wrote, not only for "the happiness of my own countrymen, but that of mankind in general."[24]

Still, neither the desire for fame nor revolutionary passion is sufficient to explain the founders' astonishing success. Nor is their public service, the long years of crucial experience in the give-and-take of everyday politics.

On the contrary, especially in times of ferment, turbulence, and great historical transformations, experience can have only limited value. Men of experience understand the system and play by the rules, but in the 1770s and 1780s, those rules were changing.

Ideas and vision are the motor of history. Experience, along with an understanding of the past, could instruct people as to what systems of government would *not* work, James Madison pointed out, but seldom did historical precedents offer lessons for the future. On the contrary, they "furnish no other light than that of beacons," Madison wrote, "which give warning of the course to be shunned, without pointing out that which ought to be pursued."[25] To shape their political future, people had no choice but to turn to their rational faculties, their knowledge of political theory and Enlightenment thought, and their own imaginations. "Much is to be hoped from the progress of reason," he wrote, "and if any thing is to be hoped, every thing ought to be tried."[26] The idea of embarking on untried paths ignited Madison's imagination. "I can see no danger," he said at the Virginia ratifying convention, "in submitting to practice an experiment which seems to be founded on the best theoretic principles."[27]

The "glory" of the Americans, according to Madison, was that they had not "suffered a blind veneration for antiquity, for custom."[28] On the contrary, in their provincial colonies on the margins of the British Empire, far from the sophisticated cities of Europe, Americans could indulge their creativity, profiting from the intellectual freedom their isolation bestowed. "Remote from all other aid," Jefferson wrote, "we are obliged to invent and to execute; to find means within ourselves, and not to lean on others."[29] In remarkable feats of self-invention, Americans theorized about freedom and equality, deliberated on a social contract for a large and diverse population, devised guarantees for individual rights and liberties, fashioned a plan to harmonize state governments and a national union, and created almost from scratch a constitution and representative political institutions. In *Federalist* No. 1, Hamilton celebrated the Constitution as the product of "reflection and choice."[30] The Framers had charted a path, Madison excitedly wrote, that had "no parallel in the annals of human society."[31] He even called Americans the first free people to choose their own form of government since "the creation of the world."[32]

But the genius of the founders was that, while they were men of learning and vision, they also had enough practical experience in politics to understand just how far ideas and theories should be taken. Madison was not just a scholar and a thinker, commented one admiring contemporary; he was also a "profound politician."[33] The uniqueness of the founding period, wrote historian Gordon S. Wood, was that "ideas and power, intellectualism and politics, came together—indeed were one with each other—in a way never again duplicated in American history."[34]

Like Madison, Jefferson welcomed fresh political theories. "I am never afraid of the issue," he wrote, "where reason is left free to exert her force."[35] He admired the new political theories of the Enlightenment that gave "a full scope to reason" to "strike out truths as yet unperceived and unacknowledged."[36] Exhilarated by the prospect of perpetual change, Jefferson had the electrifying perception that "the earth belongs always to the living generation."[37] In a letter to Madison, he expressed his hope that every generation, not just his own, would possess the freedom and creative energy to renew society. The logic of his argument led him to conclude that all laws and constitutions should naturally expire after nineteen years, the life span of a generation.

Jefferson's radical theory took Madison aback. Attempting to calm his friend's enthusiasm, Madison suggested that the stability and well-being of society require continuity between generations. "There seems then to be a foundation in the nature of things," Madison wrote in his usual understated manner, "in the relation which one generation bears to another." Of course, people had the right to abolish a government that was utterly defective, but Madison expressed reservations about a proliferation of alterations and innovations that overwhelmed a people's traditions and customs. "Would not a Government so often revised," he asked Jefferson, "become too mutable to retain those prejudices in its favor which antiquity inspires, and which are perhaps a salutary aid to the most rational Government in the most enlightened age?"[38] Madison's goal was government founded on reason, but, he added prudently, "the most rational government will not find it a superfluous advantage to have the prejudices of the community on its side."[39]

For his part, Alexander Hamilton appreciated the value of ideas, but he was even warier of them than Madison. Just as the French Revolution was heating up, an alarmed Hamilton warned the Marquis de Lafayette that its leaders had no practical experience in politics to rein in their wild, impractical ideas. "I dread the reveries of your Philosophic politicians," he wrote.[40] Governments needed a more stable foundation than the "ebullitions" of philosophers.[41] Experience, Hamilton concluded, was "the least fallible guide of human opinions."[42]

"Let every sluice of knowledge be opened," John Adams wrote in 1765, when Great Britain imposed a tax on printed matter, inhibiting communication, the very means of knowledge.[43] But he was less ebullient when that sluice was opened in France. French philosophers, he sneered, were not only "totally destitute of Common Sense," but set history on a backward course.[44] "They rent and tore the whole garment to pieces and left not one whole thread in it."[45] Adams loved ideas, but, unlike Jefferson, he usually preferred those of the past, discovering in antiquity "eternal, unchangeable truth."[46]

Less pessimistic and more forward-looking than Adams, George Washington intuitively recognized the need for both fresh Enlightenment ideas and practical experience. He hailed the eighteenth-century revolutionary era because it wedded the wisdom of political philosophers with that of working legislators. It was a period, he wrote, "when . . . the researches of the human mind, after social happiness, [and] the Treasures of knowledge, acquired by the labours of Philosophers, Sages and Legislatures . . . are laid open for our use, and their collected wisdom may be happily applied in the Establishment of our forms of Government."[47]

Washington also grasped that the middle ground between theory and experience was *experiment.* "The preservation of the sacred fire of liberty, and the destiny of the Republican model of Government," Washington told his rapt listeners at his inauguration as president in 1789, were deeply and finally "staked on the *experiment* entrusted to the hands of the American people." In 1789, the outcome of that experiment was still uncertain, but Washington was hopeful that "wisdom . . . aided by experience" would bring the new government "as near to perfection as any human institution ever approximated." It would not be an easy ride. He would be confronted with vociferous critics of his administration's policies, a burgeoning opposition party, and even citizen rebellions. But the young republic rode out the storms, and in 1796, in his Annual Message to Congress, a satisfied Washington could congratulate his fellow citizens "on the success of the experiment" they had conducted together.[48]

Abstract blueprints for the wholesale overhaul and restructuring of society plunged revolutionary movements in France, China, and Russia into violence, repression, and totalitarianism. But Americans avoided that turbulence by submitting their theories to the test of experience. The founders inspired American citizens and energized politics—the mundane routine of compromises, brokered deals, and incremental changes—by holding up lofty principles and idealistic visions. But they also moderated those visions by injecting them with strong doses of prudence and transactional leadership.

"His passions were naturally strong," Thomas Jefferson commented about George Washington, "but his reason, generally, stronger."[49] Although the political ideas and the practical political experience of the founders were central to the American revolutionary project, perhaps even more crucial to the success of their movement was their *character.*

The founders mastered the art of self-mastery.

They had strong tempers, but their self-control was even stronger. They artfully staged themselves as gentlemen-citizens, the embodiment of self-restraint and public service, determined to earn the esteem of both their social equals and their superiors. One lived one's life under the gaze of others. What mattered, Washington emphasized to his young nephew in a letter of avuncular advice, was how one appeared "in the *eyes of judicious men.*"[50] So crucial was the estimation of the world and so defining were the watchful, judgmental eyes of others that one learned to internalize their gaze and behave, even in private, as if one were performing in public—or in a hall of mirrors. "Whenever you are to do a thing," Jefferson wrote to his nephew Peter Carr, "tho' it can never be known but to yourself, ask yourself how you would act if all the world were *looking at you* and act accordingly."[51]

But how can a young man with no experience know how to behave well? How can he trust that his judgment is good and his behavior restrained? Jefferson knew that a young person could not be expected always to be wise and prudent, but he also knew that he could learn from others how to play the part. By choosing exceptionally distinguished men as role models, one could pattern one's behavior after theirs and also imagine oneself performing before their judging eyes. "Under temptations & difficulties," Jefferson explained in a letter to his grandson, "I would ask myself what would Dr. Small, Mr. Wythe, Peyton Randolph do in this situation? What course in it will insure me their approbation? . . . Knowing the even & dignified line they pursued, I could never doubt for a moment which of two courses would be in character for them." The steady practice of this "self-cathechising habit," Jefferson assured his grandson, would lead him to the "prudent selection & steady pursuits of what is right." The "role" one played would eventually grow indistinguishable from—it would become—one's own moral character.[52]

The unusual self-restraint that the founders cultivated earned them the respect of "judicious men." But it had a far greater importance, for the founders' moderation is the final element that explains the success of their revolutionary enterprise. Alexander Hamilton believed that the ultimate outcome of the American Revolution would depend on the self-restraint of the victors. After independence was won, when the New York legislature demanded summary legal action against Americans who had remained loyal to Great Britain during the war, Hamilton tried to dissuade the legislators from punishing a whole class of people. The spirit of the American

Revolution, he reminded them, "cherishes legal liberty, holds the rights of every individual sacred, condemns or punishes no man without regular trial." Although "nothing is more common than for a free people, in times of heat and violence, to gratify momentary passions," he underscored that "the dangerous consequences of this power are manifest."[53]

Too bad that the radical leaders of the French Revolution, who would indulge in just the kind of vindictiveness and summary group punishments that Hamilton had warned against, could not appreciate American-style self-restraint. "I would say that great moderation should be used," General Washington advised his young friend Lafayette in 1788, when confrontation between the French parliament and King Louis XVI seemed imminent. "I caution you . . . against running into extremes."[54] But five years later, showing none of Washington's or Hamilton's restraint, radical revolutionaries in France would proceed, with utter contempt for legal process, to guillotine en masse their political adversaries, dooming their Revolution, their republic, and themselves.

The moderation of the American founders assured a spirit of tolerance in the young nation. Open to the reasoning and arguments of others—of adversaries as well as friends, they laid the foundation for an open society and a free marketplace of ideas. Should he "set up [his] judgment as the standard of perfection?" Washington wrote in his draft notes for his first inaugural speech. "And shall I arrogantly pronounce that whosoever differs from me, must discern the subject through a distorting medium, or be influenced by some nefarious design?"[55] Washington wished to return to the theme of tolerance in his Farewell Address. "Infallibility not being the attribute of Man," he wrote in the draft of that address, "we ought to be cautious in censuring the opinions and conduct of one another."[56]

One of the qualities Jefferson prized most in himself was, similarly, his patience—if not receptivity—for the ideas of others. "When I hear another express an opinion, which is not mine," Thomas Jefferson wrote to his grandson, "I say to myself, He has a right to his opinion, as I to mine; why should I question it. His error does me no injury, and shall I become a Don Quixot to bring all men by force of argument, to one opinion?"[57]

The founders would need every ounce of their toleration for the opinions of others, for, during the first decades of the republic, they would agree on little.

During the War of Independence, the years of the Confederation, and the summer of the Constitutional Convention, they had worked mostly in harmony. James Madison even commented that, in the remarkable concord that reigned in Philadelphia in 1787, he almost discerned "a finger of that Almighty hand."[58] But such harmony was not to be expected of citizens and politicians of the new federal union, unless there were some extreme crisis and overwhelming sense of shared purpose.[59] Indeed, the American *constitutional consensus,* in the words of one historian, presented "an invitation to conflict,"[60] an agreement to disagree. What the founders had not expected was conflict that would split apart Washington's own cabinet.

Washington had wanted an inclusive administration that could profit from the talents of the nation's greatest men. His strategy was to encourage his cabinet members to express their views and then to decide the course to be pursued.[61] For a while, they worked harmoniously and productively together, drawing on one another's strengths and abilities. But deep ideological fault lines slashed through the cabinet, straining the president's patience. Hamilton and Jefferson were "daily pitted in the cabinet like two cocks," Jefferson later recalled.

They disagreed about almost everything: Hamilton's plan for the national government to assume the revolutionary debts of the states; his plan for the Bank of the United States, which would fund large industrial and infrastructure projects; his Report on Manufactures, which proposed a variety of subsidies to encourage the development of industry. Hamilton wanted to strengthen the power of the national government, hoping that the power of the states would wither, whereas Jefferson defended states' rights, darkly warning against "consolidation" and "monarchy." They disagreed about the French Revolution, with Jefferson cheering his revolutionary brethren while Hamilton condemned the "atrocious depravity" of the radicals who were beheading their political enemies.[62] They disagreed about a proclamation of American neutrality in the conflicts that embroiled Europe. They disagreed about the treaty that John Jay negotiated with Great Britain. Madison and Jefferson accused Hamilton and his allies of constituting a party that was "partial to the opulent," while they desired government for the people.[63]

Above all, they disagreed about their visions for the new nation. Hamilton envisaged a powerful military-industrial state that would "baffle all the combinations of European jealousy to restrain our growth," dictating a new balance of power in the world.[64] "We are the embryo of a great empire," he wrote in 1795.[65] Jefferson, who believed that government should be moral rather than merely powerful, envisaged a self-contained, backwater, agrarian and mercantile nation that, in the short run, tolerated slavery. In other words, the republic he wanted to establish, as Henry Adams commented, "was an enlarged Virginia."

The ideological abyss between these two brilliant, powerful men deeply disturbed President Washington; he improbably hoped that Hamilton and Jefferson might find grounds for compromise, settling on a "middle course."[66] His greatest fear was that political parties might emerge from their deepening and spreading contention. Throughout his presidency, Washington had stressed the theme of unity, hoping to banish dissension simply by governing in what he considered to be the interest of all. National unity, he reminded Americans in his Farewell Address, was "a main Pillar in the Edifice of your real independence, the support of your tranquillity at home, your peace abroad, of your safety, of your prosperity, of that very Liberty which you so highly prize."

It was not surprising that Washington would see parties as a political disease that would weaken that pillar. They enabled "cunning, ambitious and unprincipled men," he wrote in his Farewell Address, to subvert the power of the people and to "usurp for themselves the reins of Government." The ultimate danger of parties, he ominously warned, was that they could provoke such "disorders and miseries" that men would be forced to seek order and security "in the absolute power of an individual," that is, in despotism.

Washington was hardly alone in condemning parties. James Madison criticized "the pestilential influence of party animosities."[67] Jefferson, too, spoke out against parties. "If I could not go to heaven but with a party," he quipped in 1789, "I would not go there at all."[68] And Adams execrated parties, contending that they would not "permit Improvements to be made. As soon as one Man hints at an improvement, his Rival . . . misconstrues it, misrepresents it, ridicules it, insults it, and persecutes it."[69]

And yet, out of the disagreements between Hamilton and Jefferson emerged not only healthy, creative, vital debate but two rival political parties: the Federalist Party championed by Hamilton and the Republican Party organized in Congress in the 1790s by Madison and led to victory in the presidential election of 1800 by Jefferson. Although those parties were shaped more by events than by a conscious plan, the creation of a party system and its ultimate acceptance and absorption into the political culture was the final crowning achievement of the Founding Fathers. "No free Country," James Madison would observe in the 1820s, "has ever been without parties, which are a natural offspring of Freedom."[70] There would be no repressive "one-party democracy" in America, no guillotines to behead the opposition, no gulags to hold dissidents indefinitely in cold storage. Instead there would be an open, inclusive, dynamic political arena—especially after women and African Americans secured the right to vote.

Courageous, ambitious, rational, creative, dedicated, experienced, moderate, tolerant: Were the Founding Fathers perfect? Well . . .

If Americans did not forcefully assert their rights against arbitrary British rule, George Washington indignantly wrote in 1774, they would become "tame & abject Slaves as the Blacks we Rule over with such arbitrary Sway."[71] Slavery: the most deplorable form of human degradation. And yet, even though Washington, Jefferson, and Madison agreed that all men were created equal and that nothing was more important than life, liberty, and the pursuit of happiness, they not only condoned slavery but bought, bred, and bargained away slaves.

In private, Washington expressed his hopes that "slavery in this Country may be abolished by slow, sure, and imperceptible degrees."[72] But when, against the advice of James Madison, the House of Representatives turned away two antislavery petitions in 1790, concluding that the federal government had no jurisdiction in matters pertaining to slavery, Washington expressed relief that the issue had "at length been put to sleep." Discussions of slavery, he judged, had been "mal-apropos." More vital to the survival of the young republic, he felt, was "a spirit of accommodation."[73] Doubtless Washington intuited—correctly—that debates on slavery could explode into union-shattering conflict. Although he possessed the unusual benevolence—and concern for his eternal reputation—to free his slaves upon his death, or upon the death of Martha, his wife, should she outlive him, during the years of his presidency and retirement he made no public pronouncements against slavery.

"The whole commerce between master and slave," Jefferson had written in 1787 in his *Notes on the State of Virginia,* consisted of "the most unremitting despotism on the one part, and degrading submission on the other." He did not doubt that slavery was evil. "I tremble for my country when I reflect that God is just," Jefferson wrote, adding that "his justice cannot sleep for ever."[74] But although he had fought to exclude slavery entirely from the trans-Appalachian west in 1784, he took a different stand in 1820. Then he bitterly opposed the Missouri Compromise, which prohibited the spread of slavery into states north of the line 36°30', the northern boundary of Arkansas. Appalled by the intrusion of the national government into the affairs of the states, Jefferson deemed it more urgent to rescue the republic from "monarchical" federalism than to rescue blacks—and the nation itself—from the abomination of slavery. That year, he came up with his own proposal for ending slavery: Slave owners would "give up all born after a certain day . . . that these should be placed under the guardianship of the State, and sent at a proper age to S. Domingo."[75] Unable to imagine a just, biracial society, he devised a scheme that was as impractical as it was morally inadequate. At a loss for a solution, an elderly Jefferson finally abdicated any leadership of the problem, announcing his "abandonment of the subject."[76]

Did the founders do better in protecting the rights and lands of American Indians? Although President Jefferson extolled native Americans for their "ardent love of liberty and independence," he nevertheless exhorted them to renounce their "reverence for the customs of their ancestors" and instead adapt to a settled, agricultural way of life.[77] His administration continued to buy up the lands of Indians and plan for their removal to the far west. Indians, he wrote, "will in time either incorporate with us as citizens of the U.S. or remove beyond the Mississippi."[78] Those who refused to sell their land to the government and resisted the advance of settlers would find themselves crushed by the likes of Major General Andrew Jackson, the future president.

"Remember the ladies," Abigail Adams had hopefully written to her husband in 1776.[79] But neither he nor any of the men of the revolutionary generation took any steps to secure an equal education for women or to help them advance toward some semblance of equal rights. "A plan of female education has never been a subject of systematic contemplation with me," Jefferson admitted to a friend.[80] When his secretary of the treasury, Albert Gallatin, audaciously suggested that a few women might be recruited for some minor positions in his department, Jefferson stonily replied, "The appointment of a woman to office is an innovation for which the public is not prepared, nor am I."[81] Case closed.

"The will of the majority is in all cases to prevail," Jefferson had exuberantly declared in his inaugural address in 1801. There would always be "absolute acquiescence in the decisions of the majority," he told the rapt crowd, adding two provisos: that the will of the majority be "reasonable" in order to be "rightful," and that the "minority possess their equal rights, which equal law must protect." But not only were the founders resolutely unresponsive to the basic needs of the numerical majority of Americans—blacks and women combined—they did not even recognize them as members of the minority. The "will of the majority" and protection of the rights of the minority apparently referred only to white male property-owners.

Perhaps it was not surprising that the founders blinded themselves or were indifferent to the fact that the majority of the inhabitants of the United

States went unrepresented in the government, for the design of the Constitution itself reflected their basic dread of the majority—as well as their fear of a tyrannical despot. The most dangerous threat to the stability of the republic, Madison had stressed in his *Federalist* essays of 1787 and 1788, lay in a majority of citizens who could tyrannize individuals and minorities and infringe upon their rights. To counter such a possibility, Madison, Hamilton, Washington, and the other men present at the Constitutional Convention (Jefferson was in Paris and Adams in London) devised a system of checks and balances as a way to fragment authority and prevent a concentration of power. Power would be divided not only between the states and the national government but also within the national government itself. It would be institutionally split, Madison wrote, "between different bodies of men, who might watch and check each other."[82]

The greatest—perhaps the only—strength of the people lies in their sheer numbers, in their ability to mobilize tens of thousands or hundreds of thousands of voters in elections. But the Framers designed the Constitution to impede popular power by breaking it up, not only through separated institutions but through separated elections as well. Madison's blueprint for government required so many various methods for choosing senators, representatives, and the president and so many carefully staggered elections that the branches of government would ultimately represent distinct and, most likely, conflicting majorities, thereby thwarting the power and thrust of the real majority of voters.

But Madison's political thought would change. Only a few years after composing *Federalist* No. 10, in which he had discussed the importance of blocking the majority and strengthening the rights of minority groups, he came to believe that the most serious problem in American government was not majority rule but rather *minority* rule. In a series of newspaper articles that he wrote anonymously for the *National Gazette* in 1791 and 1792, he argued that a wealthy, privileged minority—Hamilton's Federalists—controlled the government and shaped its policies to the detriment of the vast majority of citizens.

"The vital principle of republican government," Madison would write in 1833, "is the *lex majoris partis,* the will of the majority." Criticism of majority government "strikes at the root of Republicanism." In a striking shift from his earlier principles, Madison, at age eighty-two, in response to South Carolina's move to unilaterally nullify federal laws, now unequivocally demanded protection of the *majority* and of its ability to wield power. It was clearly a greater injustice, he suggested, to frustrate a majority of citizens than to frustrate a minority of them.

But Madison realized that the anti-majoritarian thrust of the Constitution, which he himself had helped to design so meticulously, would be virtually impossible to foil. The *numerical* majority, he explained, even though it had "justice on its side," could easily be thwarted by the "constitutional majority," which had, on its side, checks and balances, staggered elections, veto traps, and other minority-empowering devices. And to this fundamental injustice he could offer no real remedy.[83]

Scarred by monarchical abuses of power, fearful of the "mob" and the unruly "people," and wanting stability, not energy, in government, the Framers had designed a brilliant Constitution for Americans—and especially for well-educated, wealthy, and self-protective eighteenth-century gentlemen like themselves.

Who were the Founding Fathers? Above all, they were "thinking revolutionaries."[84] They theorized about government and political institutions; they pondered the problem of factions and parties; they reflected on education and religion; they intellectualized about progress and change. Their lives centered around *ideas.* They read, they meditated, they imagined, they questioned, they debated—and, above all, they wrote. They revealed themselves and the truth of their lives in their thoughts and their words.

How much did they write? There are thirty-nine volumes of the writings of George Washington, edited by John Fitzpatrick. *The Papers of Alexander Hamilton,* edited by Harold C. Syrett, weigh in at twenty-seven volumes. The first thirty-one volumes published by the Thomas Jefferson Papers project at Princeton University cover his writings only up to the year 1800. How many more volumes will be needed for the writings of the last twenty-six years of his life? The twenty-two volumes of the James Madison Papers reach 1813—twenty-three more years to go. The team compiling and editing the John Adams Papers at the Harvard University Press has published twelve volumes that go up to 1782: Forty-four years of Adams's writings remain to be published. The founders took care to preserve their writings, knowing, hoping that we would read their words, understand them, learn from them, judge them.

This book contains many of their most important letters, speeches, and essays. Here you will find the founders, in the present tense of their lives, unfiltered, unscripted by a narrator, unshaped by a story line. Read their words, and they will tell you who they are.

GEORGE WASHINGTON
1732–1799

Introduction

On a warm summer day in July 1796, standing on the steps of the west door to his home at Mount Vernon, Washington spoke to some friends about a subject dear to his heart: a national university, a university of the United States. It would be his gift to his country. Although he had designated land for it in the new federal city and had personally offered a substantial endowment, leaders in Congress had displayed little interest in his plan.

And yet, what better way to symbolize the new federal union than with a university sponsored by the republic itself? It was a vision colored by the college education Washington never had and by the military education he did have. Recalling his years fighting as a young man, Washington especially remembered experiences of community and fraternity—the fraternity of men who sleep, hope, obey, fight, and die together. "A century in the ordinary intercourse, would not have accomplished what the Seven years association in Arms did," he wrote. The new university would similarly offer its students communion—in learning. "Young men from different parts of the United States," he added, "would be assembled together, & would by degrees discover that here was not that cause for those jealousies and prejudices which one part of the Union had imbibed against another part."[1]

That generous, expansive national perspective was Washington's most precious gift to the nation. Although some Americans (especially Virginians) resented the strong national government, supported states' rights, dwelled on the sectional differences between North and South, and toyed with the idea of disunion, Washington's commitment to the American nation—and to the unity of that nation—never wavered. As commander in chief, as retired general, as president of the Constitutional Convention, and especially as the first president of the United States, he incarnated the national idea.

Still, if they had been told that this elitist southerner with aristocratic tendencies would come to represent a revolutionary nation as well as the aspirations of reformers around the world, many of the people who knew and admired Washington in the early 1760s might have been surprised. After the Stamp Act of 1765, he indeed underwent a sea change. Eager to defend "the liberty which we have derived from our Ancestors" against the "lordly Masters in Great Britain,"[2] he organized, with his friend George Mason, a boycott of British goods and contemplated the possibility of armed confrontation with Great Britain.[3] In 1775, he was the obvious choice to head the continental army: A Virginian commander in chief leading Massachusetts volunteers immediately transformed the troops into a truly national force. Even before the colonies declared war or independence, they would have in Washington a national leader.

Especially as president, Washington intuitively grasped that he would have to fulfill a symbolic as well as a political function. As the head of government, he would immerse himself in day-to-day politics. But as the emblematic head of state, he would have to stand above politics, providing unifying leadership and embodying the values of American society, the American *character.* "I glory in the character of Washington because I know him to be an exemplification of the American character," John Adams had written in 1785.[4]

What constituted the persona—the character and values—that the president would project onto his waiting, receptive country? His virtue, his integrity, courage, and political skill were well known and widely admired—as were his cool reserve and dignity. But there was something else that he wished to embody and communicate to Americans, something stunningly modern: respect for human reason and a belief in human happiness. Indeed, the young republic, he wrote in 1788, had just presented to the world the "Novel and astonishing Spectacle" of a people deliberating "calmly on what form of government will be most conducive to their happiness."[5]

What kind of happiness did he have in mind? "Happiness & splendour,"[6] he underscored, had little in common. Happiness meant the collective satisfaction of virtuous and reasonable citizens who enjoy equal rights, live in a well-ordered society, and benefit from improvements in their lives. "I think I see a *path,* as clear and as direct as a ray of light," Washington wrote to Lafayette in 1789. "Nothing but harmony, honesty, industry and frugality are necessary to make us a great and happy people."[7] Happiness was more than just a goal: It was the essential *obligation* of government.

As the head of the infant republic, Washington had a stupendous task cut out for him: He would have to establish an energetic, powerful executive branch of government, foster citizens' loyalty to the new nation and respect for its laws, create an economically sound environment for commerce and industry, and protect America from European aggression, while at the same time relating somehow to the desires of average Americans for freedom, equality, and happiness. It was a high-wire act—and he succeeded brilliantly.

Still, by 1792, the job had taken a toll on the sixty-year-old president. Bone tired, he informed his closest advisers that he wished to retire from the presidency at the end of his first term in office. In unison, they all voiced alarm. In the present "unsettled condition" of the young government, Madison told him, "no possible successor" could perform as well in the presidency.[8] "The confidence of the whole union is centered in you," Jefferson added. "North & South will hang together, if they have you to hang on."[9] "The greatest evil, that could befall the country at the present juncture," Hamilton concurred, would be Washington's retirement from politics.[10]

Resigned to his fate, the indispensable Father of the country served out his two terms in office. And then, after a lifetime of public service, he finally took the long journey home.

THE WRITINGS OF GEORGE WASHINGTON

Rules of Civility & Decent Behaviour in Company and Conversation

[1747]*

1. Every action in company ought to be with some sign of respect to those present.

4. In the presence of others sing not to yourself with a humming noise, nor drum with your fingers or feet.

6. Sleep not when others speak, sit not when others stand, speak not when you should hold your peace, walk not when others stop.

14. Turn not your back to others, especially in speaking; jog not the table or desk on which another reads or writes; lean not on any one.

18. Read no letters, books, or papers in company; but when there is a necessity for doing it, you must ask leave. Come not near the books or writings of any one so as to read them, unless desired, nor give your opinion of them unasked; also, look not nigh when another is writing a letter.

19. Let your countenance be pleasant, but in serious matters somewhat grave.

22. Show not yourself glad at the misfortune of another, though he were your enemy.

29. When you meet with one of greater quality than yourself, stop and retire, especially if it be at a door or any strait place, to give way for him to pass.

33. They that are in dignity, or in office, have in all places precedency; but whilst they are young they ought to respect those that are their equals in birth, or other qualities, though they have no public charge.

35. Let your discourse with men of business be short and comprehensive.

39. In writing, or speaking, give to every person his due title, according to his degree and the custom of the place.

40. Strive not with your superiors in argument, but always submit your judgment to others with modesty.

44. When a man does all he can, though it succeeds not well, blame not him that did it.

46. Take all admonitions thankfully, in what time or place soever given; but afterwards, not being culpable, take a time or place convenient to let him know it that gave them.

---

*Washington probably copied these rules from a seventeenth-century translation by Francis Hawkins of a 1595 Jesuit book, *Bienséance de la Conversation entre les Hommes*.—Editor.

47. Mock not, nor jest at any thing of importance; break no jests that are sharp-biting, and if you deliver any thing witty, and pleasant, abstain from laughing thereat yourself.

48. Wherein you reprove another be unblamable yourself; for example is more prevalent than precepts.

49. Use no reproachful language against any one, neither curse, nor revile.

52. In your apparel, be modest, and endeavour to accommodate nature, rather than to procure admiration; keep to the fashion of your equals, such as are civil and orderly with respect to times and places.

54. Play not the peacock, looking every where about you to see if you be well decked, if your shoes fit well, if your stockings sit neatly, and clothes handsomely.

56. Associate yourself with men of good quality, if you esteem your own reputation, for it is better to be alone, than in bad company.

58. Let your conversation be without malice or envy, for it is a sign of a tractable and commendable nature; and in all causes of passion, admit reason to govern.

61. Utter not base and frivolous things amongst grave and learned men; nor very difficult questions or subjects among the ignorant; nor things hard to be believed.

64. Break not a jest where none takes pleasure in mirth; laugh not aloud, nor at all without occasion. Deride no man's misfortune, though there seem to be some cause.

65. Speak not injurious words neither in jest nor earnest; scoff at none, although they give occasion.

66. Be not forward, but friendly and courteous; the first to salute, hear, and answer; and be not pensive when it is a time to converse.

67. Detract not from others, neither be excessive in commending.

69. If two contend together take not the part of either unconstrained, and be not obstinate in your own opinion; in things indifferent be of the major side.

70. Reprehend not the imperfections of others, for that belongs to parents, masters, and superiors.

71. Gaze not on the marks or blemishes of others, and ask not how they came. What you may speak in secret to your friend, deliver not before others.

72. Speak not in an unknown tongue in company, but in your own language, and that as those of quality do, and not as the vulgar; sublime matters treat seriously.

73. Think before you speak, pronounce not imperfectly, nor bring out your words too hastily, but orderly and distinctly.

74. When another speaks, be attentive yourself, and disturb not the audience. If any hesitate in his words, help him not, nor prompt him without being desired; interrupt him not, nor answer him, till his speech be ended.

77. Treat with men at fit times about business, and whisper not in the company of others.

85. In company of these of higher quality than yourself speak not till you are asked a question; then stand upright put off your hat and answer in few words. [. . .]

To Colonel William Fitzhugh

BELVOIR, NOVEMBER 15TH 1754.

Dear Sir,

I was favored with your letter from Rousby Hall, of the 4th instant. It demands my best acknowledgments for the particular marks of esteem you have expressed therein, and for the kind assurances of his Excellency Governor Sharpe's good wishes towards me. I also thank you, and sincerely, Sir, for your friendly intention of making my situation easy, if I return to the service; and do not doubt, could I submit to the terms, that I should be as happy under your command in the absence of the General, as under any gentleman's whatever. But I think the disparity between the present offer of a company and my former rank too great to expect any real satisfaction or enjoyment in a corps, where I once did, or thought I had a right to, command; even if his Excellency had power to suspend the orders received in the Secretary of War's letter; which, by the by, I am very far from thinking he either has, or will attempt to do, without fuller instructions than I believe he has; especially, too, as there has been a representation of this matter by Governour Dinwiddie, and, I believe, the Assembly of this State. We have advices that it was received before Demmarree obtained his letter.

All that I presume the General *can* do, is, to prevent the different corps from interfering, which will occasion the duty to be done by corps, instead of detachments; a very inconvenient way, as is found by experience.

You make mention in your letter of my continuing in the service, and retaining my Colonel's commission. This idea has filled me with surprise; for, if you think me capable of holding a Commission, that has neither rank or emolument annexed to it, you must entertain a very contemptible opinion of my weakness, and believe me to be more empty than the Commission itself.

Besides, Sir, if I had time, I could enumerate many good reasons, that forbid all thoughts of my returning; and which to you, or any other, would, upon the strictest scrutiny, appear to be well founded. I must be reduced to a very low command, and subjected to that of many, who have acted as my inferior officers. In short, every captain, bearing the King's Commission, every half-pay officer, or others appearing with such commission, would rank before me. For these reasons I choose to submit to the loss of health, which I have, however, already sustained (not to mention the effects) and the fatigue I have undergone in our first efforts, than subject myself to the same inconveniences, and run the risk of a second disappointment.

I shall have the consolation of knowing, that I have opened the way, when the smallness of our numbers exposed us to the attacks of a superior enemy; that I have hitherto stood the heat and brunt of the day, and escaped untouched in time of extreme danger; and that I have the thanks of my country, for the services I have rendered it.

It shall not sleep in silence, my having received information that those peremptory orders from home, which you say could not be dispensed with, for reducing the regiments into Independent Companies, were generated, hatched and brought from Will's Creek. Ingenuous treatment and plain dealing I at least expected. It is to be hoped the project will answer; it shall meet with my acquiescence in every thing except personal services. I herewith enclose Governour Sharpe's letter, which I beg you will return to him, with my acknowledgments for the favour he intended me. Assure him, Sir, as you truly may, of my reluctance to quit the service, and of the pleasure I should have received in attending his fortunes. Also inform him, that it was to obey the call of honour, and the advice of my friends, I declined it, and not to gratify any desire I had to leave the military line.

My inclinations are strongly bent to arms.

The length of this, and the small room I have left, tell me how necessary it is to conclude; which I will do, as you always shall find

Truly and sincerely your most humble servant

To Sally Cary Fairfax

FORT CUMBERLAND AT WILLES CREEK,
7TH OF JUNE 1755.

Dear Madam:

When I had the pleasure to see you last, you express'd an Inclination to be informed of my safe arrival at Camp with the charge that was entrusted to my care; but at the same time desir'd it might be communicated in a Letter to some body of your acquaintance. This I took as a Gentle rebuke and polite manner of forbidding my corrisponding with you and conceive this opinion is not illy founded when I reflect that I have hither to found it impracticable to engage one moment of your attention. If I am right in this I hope you will excuse my present presumption and lay the imputation to elateness at my successful arrival. If on the contrary these are fearfull apprehensions only, how easy is it to remove my suspicion, enliven my Spirits, and make me happier than the Day is long, by honouring me with a corrispondance which you did once partly promise.

Please to make my Complts. to Miss Hannah, and to Mr. Bryan to whom I shall do myself the pleasure of writing so soon as I hear he is return'd from Westmoreland.

I am Madam Your most Obedt & most Hble Servt

To Robert Dinwiddie

FORT LOUDOUN, SEPTEM. 17TH 1757.

Honble. Sir,

A letter of the 22d ultimo, from Captain Peachy, came to my hands the other day, contents as follows (here was inserted the letter). I shou'd take it infinitely kind, if your Honor would please to inform me, whether a report of this nature was ever made to you; and, in that case, who was the author of it?

It is evident, from a variety of circumstances, and especially from the change in your Honor's conduct towards me, that some person, as well inclined to detract, but better skilled in the art of detraction, than the author of the above stupid scandal, has made free with my character. For I cannot suppose, that malice so absurd, so barefaced, so diametrically opposite to truth, to common policy, and, in short, to every thing but villainy, as the above is, *could* impress you with so ill an opinion of my honor and honesty!

If it be possible, that Colonel Corbin—(for my belief is staggered, not being conscious of having given the least cause to any one, much less to that gentleman, to reflect so grossly,) I say, if it be possible, that Colonel Corbin could descend so low as to be the propagator of this story, he must either be vastly ignorant in the state of affairs in this county at *that time;* or else he must suppose, that the whole body of inhabitants had combined with me, in executing the deceitful fraud. Or why did they, almost to a man, forsake their dwellings in the greatest terror and confusion; so that, while one half of them sought shelter in paltry forts, (of their own building,) the other fled to the adjacent counties for refuge, numbers of them even to Carolina, from whence they have never returned?

These are facts well known; but not better known, than that these wretched people, while they lay pent up in forts, destitute of the common support of life (having in their precipitate flight forgotten, or were unable rather to secure, any kind of necessaries,) did dispatch messengers of their own (thinking I had not represented their miseries in the piteous manner they deserved), with addresses to your Honor and the Assembly, praying relief. And did I ever send any alarming account, without also sending the original papers, (or the copies,) which gave rise to it?

That I have foibles, and perhaps many of them, I shall not deny. I should esteem myself, as the world also would, vain and empty, were I to arrogate perfection.

Knowledge in military matters is to be acquired by practice and experience only; and, if I have erred, great allowance should be made for my errors for want of it—unless those errors should appear to be willful; and then, I conceive it would be more generous to charge me with my faults, and let me stand or fall according to evidence, than to stigmatize me behind my back.

It is uncertain in what light my services may have appeared to your Honor; but this I know, and it is the highest consolation I am capable of feeling; that no man, that ever was employed in a public capacity, has endeavoured to discharge the trust reposed in him with greater honesty, and more zeal for the country's interest, than I have done; and if there is any person living, who can say with justice, that I have offered any intentional wrong to the public, I will chearfully submit to the most ignominious punishment, that an injured people ought to inflict! On the other hand, it is hard to have my character arraigned, and my actions condemned, without a hearing.

I must therefore again beg in *more plain,* and in very *earnest terms,* to know if Colonel Corbin has taken the liberty of representing my character to your Honor with such ungentlemanly freedom as the letter implies? Your condescension herein will be acknowledged, as a singular favor done your Honor's most obedient, humble servant.

To Sally Cary Fairfax

CAMP AT FORT CUMBERLAND,
12TH SEPTR 1758.

Dear Madam,

Yesterday I was honored with your short but very agreeable favor of the first inst. How joyfully I catch at the happy occasion of renewing a corrispondance which I feared was disrelished on your part, I leave to time, that never failing expositor of all things, and to a monitor equally faithful in my own breast, to testify. In silence I now express my joy; silence, which in some cases, I wish the present, speaks more intelligably than the sweetest eloquence.

If you allow that any honor can be derived from my opposition to our present system of management, you destroy the merit of it entirely in me by attributing my anxiety to the animating prospect of possessing Mrs. Custis, when—I—need not name it.—guess yourself.—Should not my own Honor and country's welfare be the excitement? 'Tis true, I profess myself a votary to love. I acknowledge that a lady is in the case, and further I confess that this lady is known to you. Yes, Madame, as well as she is to one who is too sensible of her charms to deny the Power whose influence he feels and must ever submit to. I feel the force of her amiable beauties in the recollection of a thousand tender passages that I could wish to obliterate, till I am bid to revive them. But experience, alas! sadly reminds me how impossible this is, and evinces an opinion which I have long entertained, that there is a Destiny which has the control of our actions, not to be resisted by the strongest efforts of Human Nature.

You have drawn me, dear Madam, or rather I have drawn myself, into an honest confession of a simple Fact. Misconstrue not my meaning;—'tis obvious—doubt it not, nor expose it. The world has no business to know the object of my Love, declared in this manner to—you, when I want to conceal it. One thing above all things in this world I wish to know, and only one person of your acquaintance can solve me that, or guess my meaning. But adieu to this till happier times, if I ever shall see them. The hours at present are melancholy dull. Neither the rugged toils of war, nor the gentler conflict of A_____ B_____s, is in my choice. I dare believe you are as happy as you say. I wish I was happy also. Mirth, good humor, ease of mind, and—what else?—cannot fail to render you so and consummate your wishes. [. . .]

I cannot easily forgive the unseasonable haste of my last express, if he deprived me thereby of a single word you intended to add. The time of the present messenger is, as the last might have been, entirely at your disposal. I cant expect to hear from my friends more than this once before the fate of the expedition will some how or other be determined. I therefore beg to know when you set out for Hampton, and when you expect to return to Belvoir again. And I should be glad also to hear of your speedy departure, as I shall thereby hope for your return before I get down. The disappointment of seeing your family would give me much concern. From any thing I can yet see 'tis hardly possible to say when we shall finish. I dont think there is a probability of it till the middle of November. Your letter to

Captain Gist I forwarded by a safe hand the moment it came to me. His answer shall be carefully transmitted.

Col. Mercer, to whom I delivered your message and compliments, joins me very heartily in wishing you and the Ladies of Belvoir the perfect enjoyment of every happiness this world affords. Be assured that I am, Dr Madam with the most unfeigned regard, Yr most Obedient & Most Obliged Hble Srvt.

N.B. Many accidents happening (to use a vulgar saying) between the Cup and the Lip, I choose to make the Exchange of Carpets myself, since I find you will not do me the honour to accept mine.

To Robert Cary & Company

MOUNT VERNON, 20TH SEPTEMBER 1765.

Gentn

[. . .] It appears pretty evident to me from the prices I have generally got for my Tobacco in London, & from some other concomitant Circumstances, that it only suits the Interest of a few particular Gentlemen to continue their consignments of this commodity to that place, while others shoud endeavour to substitute some other Article in place of Tobacco, and try their success therewith. In order thereto you woud do me a singular favour in advising of the general price one might expect for good Hemp in your Port watered & prepared according to Act of Parliament, with an estimate of the freight, & all other Incident charges pr Tonn that I may form some Idea of the profits resulting from the growth—I shoud be very glad to know at the sametime how rough & undressd Flax has generally, and may probably sell; for this year I have made an Essay in both, and altho. I suffer pretty considerably by the attempt, owing principally to the severity of the Drougth, & my inexperience in the management I am not altogether discouraged from a further prosecution of the Scheme provided I find the Sales with you are not clogd with too much difficulty and expence.

The Stamp Act, imposed on the Colonies by the Parliament of Great Britain engrosses the conversation of the speculative part of the Colonists, who look upon this unconstitutional method of Taxation as a direful attack upon their Liberties, & loudly exclaim against the violation—What may be the result of this (I think I may add) ill Judgd measure, and the late restrictions of our Trade and other Acts to Burthen us, I will not undertake to determine; but this I think may be said—that the advantages accruing to the Mother Country will fall far short of the expectation's of the Ministry; for certain it is, that the whole produce of our labour hitherto has centred in Great Britain—what more can they desire? and that all Taxes which contribute to lessen our Importation of British Goods must be hurtful to the Manufacturers of them, and to the Common Weal—The Eyes of our People (already beginning to open) will perceive, that many of the Luxuries which we have heretofore lavished our Substance to Great Britain for can well be dispensed with whilst the Necessaries of Life are to be procurd (for the most part) within ourselves—This consequently will introduce frugality; and be a necessary stimulation to Industry—Great Britain may then load her Exports with as Heavy Taxes as She pleases but where will the consumption be? I am apt to think no Law or usage can compel us to barter our money or Staple Commodities for their Manufacturies, if we can be supplied within ourselve upon the better Terms—nor will her Traders dispose of them without a valuable consideration and surety of Pay—where then lyes the utility of these Measures?

As to the Stamp Act taken in a single and distinct view; one, & the first bad consequence attending of it I take to be this—our Courts of Judicature will be shut up, it being morally impossible under our present Circumstances that the Act of Parliament can be complied with, were we ever so willing to enforce the execution; for not to say, which alone woud be sufficient, that there is not money to pay the Stamps there are many other Cogent Reasons to prevent it and if a stop be put to our Judicial proceedings it may be left to yourselves, who have such large demands upon the Colonies, to determine, who is to suffer most in this event—the Merchant, or the Planter. [. . .]

To George Mason

MOUNT VERNON, 5TH APRIL 1769.

Dear Sir,

Herewith you will receive a letter and sundry papers, which were forwarded to me a day or two ago by Dr. Ross of Bladensburg. I transmit them with the greater pleasure, as my own desire of knowing your sentiments upon a matter of this importance exactly coincides with the Doctor's inclinations.

At a time, when our lordly Masters in Great Britain will be satisfied with nothing less than the deprivation of American freedom, it seems highly necessary that something should be done to avert the stroke, and maintain the liberty which we have derived from our Ancestors. But the manner of doing it, to answer the purpose effectually, is the point in question.

That no man should scruple, or hesitate a moment, to use a–ms in defence of so valuable a blessing, on which all the good and evil of life depends, is clearly my opinion. Yet a–ms, I would beg leave to add, should be the last resource, the *dernier resort.* Addresses to the throne, and remonstrances to Parliament, we have already, it is said, proved the inefficacy of. How far, then, their attention to our rights and privileges is to be awakened or alarmed, by starving their trade and manufactures, remains to be tried.

The northern colonies, it appears, are endeavoring to adopt this scheme. In my opinion it is a good one, and must be attended with salutary effects, provided it can be carried pretty generally into execution. But how far it is practicable to do so, I will not take upon me to determine. That there will be difficulties attending the execution of it every where, from clashing interests, and selfish, designing men, (ever attentive to their own gain, and watchful of every turn, that can assist their lucrative views, in preference to every other consideration) cannot be denied; but in the Tobacco Colonies, where the trade is so diffused, and in a manner wholly conducted by factors for their principals at home, these difficulties are certainly enhanced, but I think not insurmountably increased, if the gentlemen in their several counties will be at some pains to explain matters to the people, and stimulate them to a cordial agreement to purchase none but certain enumerated articles out of any of the stores after such a period, nor import nor purchase any themselves. This, if it did not effectually withdraw the factors from their importations, would at least make them extremely cautious in doing it, as the prohibited goods could be vended to none but the non-associators, or those who would pay no regard to their association; both of whom ought to be stigmatized, and made the objects of public reproach.

The more I consider a Scheme of this sort, the more ardently I wish success to it, because I think there are private as well as public advantages to result from it,—the former certain, however precarious the other may prove. For in respect to the latter, I have always thought, that by virtue of the same power, (for here alone the authority derives) which assumes the right of taxation, they may attempt at least to restrain our manufactories, especially those of a public nature; the same equity and justice prevailing in the one case as the other, it being no greater hardship to forbid my manufacturing, than it is to order me to buy goods of them loaded with duties, for the express purpose of raising a revenue. But as a measure of this sort would be an additional exertion of arbitrary power, we cannot be worsted, I think, by putting it to the test.

On the other hand, that the Colonies are considerably indebted to Great Britain, is a truth universally acknowledged. That many families are reduced almost, if not quite, to penury and want from the low ebb of their fortunes, and estates daily selling for the discharge of debts, the public papers furnish but too many melancholy proofs of, and that a scheme of this sort will contribute more effectually than any other I can devise to emerge the country from the distress it at present labors under, I do most firmly believe, if it can be generally adopted. And I can see but one set of people (the merchants excepted,) who will not, or ought not, to wish well to the Scheme, and that is those who live genteelly and hospitably on clear estates. Such as these were they, not to consider the valuable object in view, and the good of others, might think it hard to be curtailed in their living and enjoyments. For as to the penurious man, he saves his money and he saves his credit, having the best plea for doing that, which before, perhaps, he had the most violent struggles to refrain from doing. The extravagant and expensive man has the same good plea to retrench his expences. He is thereby furnished with a pretext to live within bounds, and embraces it. Prudence dictated economy to him before, but his resolution was too weak to put it in practice; For how can I, *says he,* who have lived in such and such a manner, change my method? I am ashamed to do it, and, besides, such an alteration in the system of my living will create suspicions of the decay in my fortune, and such a thought the world must not harbour. I will e'en continue my course: till at last the course discontinues the estate, a sale of it being the consequence of his perseverance in error. This I am satisfied is the way, that many, who have set out in the wrong track, have reasoned, till ruin stares them in the face. And in respect to the poor and needy man, he is only left in the same situation that he was found,—better, I might say, because, as he judges from comparison, his condition is amended in proportion as it approaches nearer to those above him.

Upon the whole, therefore, I think the Scheme a good one, and that it ought to be tried here, with such alterations as the exigency of our circumstances renders absolutely necessary. But how, and in what manner to begin the work, is a matter worthy of consideration, and whether it can be attempted with propriety or efficacy (further than a communication of sentiments to one another,) before May, when the Court and Assembly will meet in Williamsburg, and a uniform plan can be concerted, and sent into the different counties to operate at the same time and in the same manner every where, is a thing I am somewhat in doubt upon, and should be glad to know your opinion of. I am Dr Sir Your most Obt humble Servant.

To Bryan Fairfax

MOUNT VERNON, JULY 20TH, 1774.

Dear Sir,

[. . .] That I differ very widely from you, in respect to the mode of obtaining a repeal of the acts so much and so justly complained of, I shall not hesitate to acknowledge; and that this difference in opinion may probably proceed from the different constructions we put upon the conduct and intention of the ministry may also be true; but, as I see nothing, on the one hand, to induce a belief that the Parliament would embrace a favorable opportunity of repealing acts, which they go on with great rapidity to pass, and in order to enforce their Tyrannical System; and, on the other, observe, or think I observe, that government is pursuing a regular plan at the expense of law and justice to overthrow our Constitutional Rights and liberties, how can I expect any redress from a measure, which has been ineffectually tried already? For, Sir, what is it we are contending against? Is it against paying the duty of three pence per pound on tea because burthensome? No, it is the Right only, we have all along disputed, and to this end we have already petitioned his Majesty in as humble and dutiful manner as subjects could do. Nay, more, we applied to the House of Lords and House of Commons in their different legislative capacities, setting forth, that, as Englishmen, we could not be deprived of this essential and valuable part of our Constitution. If, then, as the fact really is, it is against the right of taxation that we now do, and, (as I before said,) all along have contended, why should they suppose an exertion of this power would be less obnoxious now than formerly? And what reasons have we to believe that they would make a second attempt, whilst the same sentiments filled the breast of every American, if they did not intend to enforce it if possible?

The conduct of the Boston people could not justify the rigor of their measures, unless there had been a requisition of payment and refusal of it; nor did that measure require an act to deprive the government of Massachusetts Bay of their Charter, or to exempt offenders from trial in the place where offences were committed, as there was not, nor could not be, a single instance produced to manifest the necessity of it. Are not all these things self evident proofs of a fixed and uniform plan to tax us? If we want further proofs, do not all the debates in the House of Commons serve to confirm this? And has not General Gage's conduct since his arrival, (in stopping the address of his Council, and publishing a proclamation more becoming a Turkish bashaw, than an English governor and declaring it treason to associate in any manner by which the commerce of Great Britain is to be affected,) exhibited an unexampled testimony of the most despotic system of tyranny, that ever was practised in a free government? In short, what further proofs are wanted to satisfy one of the designs of the ministry, than their own acts, which are uniform and plainly tending to the same point, nay, if I mistake not, avowedly to fix the right of taxation? What hope then from petitioning, when they tell us that now or never is the time to fix the matter? Shall we, after this, whine and cry for relief, when we have already tried it in vain? Or shall we supinely sit and see one province after another fall a sacrifice to despotism? If I was in any doubt, as to the right which the Parliament of Great Britain had to tax us without our consents, I should most heartily coincide with you in opinion, that to petition, and petition only, is the proper method to apply for relief; because we should then be asking a favor, and not claiming a right, which, by the law of nature and our Constitution, we are, in my opinion, indubitably entitled to. I should even think it criminal to go further than this, under such an idea; but none such I have. I think the Parliament of Great Britain hath no more right to put their hands into my pocket, without my consent, than I have to put my hands into yours for money; and this being already urged to them in a firm, but decent manner, by all the Colonies, what reason is there to expect any thing from their justice?

As to the Resolution for addressing the throne, I own to you, Sir, I think the whole might as well have been expunged. I expect nothing from the measure, nor should my voice have accompanied it, if the non-Importation Scheme was intended to be retarded by it; for I am convinced, as much as I am of my existence, that there is no relief but in their distress; and I think, at least I hope, that there is publick virtue enough left among us to deny ourselves every thing but the bare necessaries of life to accomplish this end. This we have a right to do, and no power upon earth can compel us to do otherwise, till they have first reduced us to the most abject state of Slavery that ever was designed for mankind. The stopping our exports would, no doubt, be a shorter cut than the other to effect this purpose; but if we owe money to Great Britain, nothing but the last necessity can justify the non-payment of it; and, therefore, I have great doubts upon this head, and wish to see the other method first tried, which is legal and will facilitate these payments.

I cannot conclude without expressing some concern, that I should differ so widely in sentiments from you, in a matter of such great moment and general import; and should much distrust my own judgment upon the occasion, if my nature did not recoil at the thought of submitting to measures, which I think subversive of every thing that I ought to hold dear and valuable, and did I not find, at the same time, that the voice of mankind is with me.

I must apologize for sending you so rough a sketch of my thoughts upon your letter. When I looked back, and saw the length of my own, I could not, as I am also a good deal hurried at this time, bear the thoughts of making off a fair copy. I am, &c.

Address to the Continental Congress

JUNE 16, 1775

Mr. President,

Though I am truly sensible of the high honor done me in this appointment, yet I feel great distress from a consciousness that my abilities and military experience may not be equal to the extensive and important trust. However, as the Congress desire it, I will enter upon the momentous duty and exert every power I possess in their service and for support of the glorious cause. I beg they will accept my most cordial thanks for this distinguished testimony of their approbation.

But lest some unlucky event should happen unfavourable to my reputation, I beg it may be remembered by every gentleman in the room, that I this day declare with the utmost sincerity I do not think myself equal to the command I am honored with.

As to pay, Sir, I beg leave to assure the Congress, that as no pecuniary consideration could have tempted me to accept this arduous employment at the expence of my domestic ease and happiness, I do not wish to make any profit from it. I will keep an exact account of my expenses. Those I doubt not they will discharge, and that is all I desire.

To Mrs. Martha Washington

PHILADELPHIA, JUNE 18TH 1775.

My Dearest,

I am now set down to write to you on a subject, which fills me with inexpressible concern, and this concern is greatly aggravated and increased, when I reflect upon the uneasiness I know it will give you. It has been determined in Congress, that the whole army raised for the defence of the American cause shall be put under my care, and that it is necessary for me to proceed immediately to Boston to take upon me the command of it.

You may believe me, my dear Patsy, when I assure you, in the most solemn manner, that, so far from seeking this appointment, I have used every endeavor in my power to avoid it, not only from my unwillingness to part with you and the family, but from a consciousness of its being a trust too great for my capacity, and that I should enjoy more real happiness in one month with you at home, than I have the most distant prospect of finding abroad, if my stay was to be seven times seven years. But as it has been a kind of destiny, that has thrown me upon this service, I shall hope that my undertaking of it is designed to answer some good purpose. You might, and I suppose did perceive, from the tenor of my letters, that I was apprehensive I could not avoid this appointment, as I did not even pretend to intimate when I should return. That was the case. It was utterly out of my power to refuse this appointment, without exposing my character to such censures, as would have reflected dishonor upon myself, and given pain to my friends. This, I am sure, could not, and ought not, to be pleasing to you, and must have lessened me considerably in my own esteem. I shall rely, therefore, confidently on that Providence, which has heretofore preserved and been bountiful to me, not doubting but that I shall return safe to you in the fall. I shall feel no pain from the toil or the danger of the campaign; my unhappiness will flow from the uneasiness I know you will feel from being left alone. I therefore beg of you to summon your whole fortitude and resolution and pass your time as agreeably as possible. Nothing will give me so much sincere satisfaction as to hear this, and to hear it from your own pen. [. . .] My earnest and ardent desire is, that you would pursue any plan that is most likely to produce content, and a tolerable degree of tranquillity as it must add greatly to my uneasy feelings to hear that you are dissatisfied and complaining at what I really could not avoid.

As life is always uncertain, and common prudence dictates to every man the necessity of settling his temporal concerns, whilst it is in his power, and whilst the mind is calm and undisturbed, I have, since I came to this place (for I had not time to do it before I left home) got Colonel Pendleton to draft a will for me, by the directions which I gave him, which will I now enclose. The provision made for you in case of my death will, I hope, be agreeable. [. . .]

I shall add nothing more at present as I have several letters to write, but to desire that you will remember me to Milly and all friends, and to assure you that I am, with the most unfeigned regard, my dear Patsy, your affectionate.

To Lund Washington

COL. MORRIS'S, ON THE HEIGHTS
OF HARLEM, 30 SEPTEMBER, 1776.

Dear Lund,

Your letter of the 18th, which is the only one received and unanswered, now lies before me. The amazement which you seem to be in at the unaccountable measures which have been adopted by _____ would be a good deal increased if I had time to unfold the whole system of their management since this time twelve months. I do not know how to account for the unfortunate steps which have been taken but from that fatal idea of conciliation which prevailed so long—fatal, I call it, because from my soul I wish it may prove so, though my fears lead me to think there is too much danger of it. This time last year I pointed out the evil consequences of short enlistments, the expenses of militia, and the little dependence that was to be placed in them. I assured _____ that the longer they delayed raising a standing army, the more difficult and chargeable would they find it to get one, and that, at the same time that the militia would answer no valuable purpose, the frequent calling them in would be attended with an expense, that they could have no conception of. Whether, as I have said before, the unfortunate hope of reconciliation was the cause, or the fear of a standing army prevailed, I will not undertake to say; but the policy was to engage men for twelve months only. The consequence of which, you have had great bodies of militia in pay that never were in camp; you have had immense quantities of provisions drawn by men that never rendered you one hour's service (at least usefully), and this in the most profuse and wasteful way. Your stores have been expended, and every kind of military destroyed by them; your numbers fluctuating, uncertain, and forever far short of report—at no one time, I believe, equal to twenty thousand men fit for duty. At present our numbers fit for duty (by this day's report) amount to 14,759, besides 3,427 on command, and the enemy within stone's throw of us. It is true a body of militia are again ordered out, but they come without any conveniences and soon return. I discharged a regiment the other day that had in it fourteen rank and file fit for duty only, and several that had less than fifty. In short, such is my situation that if I were to wish the bitterest curse to an enemy on this side of the grave, I should put him in my stead with my feelings; and yet I do not know what plan of conduct to pursue. I see the impossibility of serving with reputation, or doing any essential service to the cause by continuing in command, and yet I am told that if

I quit the command inevitable ruin will follow from the distraction that will ensue. In confidence I tell you that I never was in such an unhappy, divided state since I was born. To lose all comfort and happiness on the one hand, whilst I am fully persuaded that under such a system of management as has been adopted, I cannot have the least chance for reputation, nor those allowances made which the nature of the case requires; and to be told, on the other, that if I leave the service all will be lost, is, at the same time that I am bereft of every peaceful moment, distressing to a degree. But I will be done with the subject, with the precaution to you that it is not a fit one to be publicly known or discussed. If I fall, it may not be amiss that these circumstances be known, and declaration made in credit to the justice of my character. And if the men will stand by me (which by the by I despair of), I am resolved not to be forced from this ground while I have life; and a few days will determine the point, if the enemy should not change their plan of operations; for they certainly will not—I am sure they ought not—to waste the season that is now fast advancing, and must be precious to them. I thought to have given you a more explicit account of my situation, expectation, and feelings, but I have not time. I am wearied to death all day with a variety of perplexing circumstances—disturbed at the conduct of the militia, whose behavior and want of discipline has done great injury to the other troops, who never had officers, except in a few instances, worth the bread they eat. My time, in short, is so much engrossed that I have not leisure for corresponding, unless it is on mere matters of public business.

I therefore in answer to your last Letter of the 18th shall say

With respect to the chimney, I would not have you for the sake of a little work spoil the look of the fireplaces, tho' that in the parlor must, I should think, stand as it does; not so much on account of the wainscotting, which I think must be altered (on account of the door leading into the new building,) as on account of the chimney piece and the manner of its fronting into the room. The chimney in the room above ought, if it could be so contrived, to be an angle chimney as the others are: but I would not have this attempted at the expence of pulling down the partition.—The chimney in the new room should be exactly in the middle of it—the doors and every thing else to be exactly answerable and uniform—in short I would have the whole executed in a masterly manner.

You ought surely to have a window in the gable end of the new cellar (either under the Venitian window, or one on each side of it).

Let Mr. Herbert know that I shall be very happy in getting his brother exchanged as soon as possible, but as the enemy have more of our officers than we of theirs, and some of ours have been long confined (and claim ye right of being first exchanged,) I do not know how far it may be in my power at this time, to comply with his desires.

Remember me to all our neighbors and friends, particularly to Colo. Mason, to whom I would write if I had time to do it fully and satisfactorily. Without this, I think the correspondence on my part would be unavailing—

I am with truth and sincerity, Dr Lund yr affect'e friend.

To Lund Washington

FALLS OF DELAWARE, SOUTH SIDE, 10TH DECR 1776.

Dear Lund,

[. . .] I wish to Heaven it was in my power to give you a more favorable account of our situation than it is. Our numbers, quite inadequate to the task of opposing that part of the army under the command of General Howe, being reduced by sickness, desertion, and political deaths (on and before the first instant, and having no assistance from the militia), were obliged to retire before the enemy, who were perfectly well informed of our situation, till we came to this place, where I have no idea of being able to make a stand, as my numbers, till joined by the Philadelphia militia, did not exceed three thousand men fit for duty. Now we may be about five thousand to oppose Howes whole army, that part of it excepted which sailed under the command of Gen. Clinton. I tremble for Philadelphia. Nothing, in my opinion, but Gen. Lee's speedy arrival, who has been long expected, though still at a distance (with about three thousand men), can save it. We have brought over and destroyed all the boats we could lay our hands on upon the Jersey shore for many miles above and below this place; but it is next to impossible to guard a shore for sixty miles, with less than half the enemy's numbers; when by force or strategem they may suddenly attempt a passage in many different places. At present they are encamped or quartered along the other shore above and below us (rather this place, for we are obliged to keep a face towards them) for fifteen miles. [. . .]

DECR 17TH TEN MILES ABOVE THE FALLS.

[. . .] I have since moved up to this place, to be more convenient to our great and extensive defence of this river. Hitherto, by our destruction of the boats, and vigilance in watching the fords of the river above the falls (which are now rather high), we have prevented them from crossing; but how long we shall be able to do it God only knows, as they are still hovering about the river. And if every thing else fails, will wait till the 1st of January, when there will be no other men to oppose them but militia, none of which but those from Philadelphia, mentioned in the first part of the letter, are yet come (though I am told some are expected from the back counties). When I say none but militia, I am to except the Virginia regiments and the shattered remains of Smallwoods, which, by fatigue, want of clothes, &c., are reduced to nothing—Weedons, which was the strongest, not having more than between one hundred and thirty and forty men fit for duty, the rest being in the hospitals. The unhappy policy of short enlistments and a dependence upon militia will, I fear, prove the downfall of our cause, though early pointed out with an almost prophetic spirit.

Our cause has also received a severe blow in the captivity of Gen. Lee. Unhappy man! Taken by his own imprudence, going three or four miles from his own camp, and within twenty of the enemy, notice of which by a rascally Tory was given a party of light horse seized him in the morning after travelling all night, and carried him off in high triumph and with every mark of indignity, not even suffering him to get his hat or sartout coat. The troops that were under his command are not yet come up with us, though I think they may be expected to-morrow. A large part of the Jerseys have given every proof of disaffection that a people can do, and this part of Pennsylvania are equally inimical. In short, your imagination can scarce extend to a situation more distressing than mine. Our only dependence now is upon the speedy enlistment of a new army. If this fails us, I think the game will be pretty well up, as, from disaffection and want of spirit and fortitude, the inhabitants, instead of resistance, are offering submission and taking protection from Gen. Howe in Jersey. [. . .] I am &c.

To George Clinton

HEAD-QUARTERS VALLEY FORGE, FEBRUARY 16, 1778.

Dear Sir,

It is with great reluctance I trouble you on a subject, which does not properly fall within your province; but it is a subject that occasions me more distress, than I have felt since the commencement of the war; and which loudly demands the most zealous exertions of every person of weight and authority, who is interested in the success of our affairs; I mean the present dreadful situation of the army for want of provisions, and the miserable prospects before us with respect to futurity. It is more alarming, than you will probably conceive; for, to form a just idea, it were necessary to be on the spot. For some days past, there has been little less than a famine in camp. A part of the army has been a week without any kind of flesh, and the rest three or four days. Naked and starving as they are, we cannot enough admire the incomparable patience and fidelity of the soldiery, that they have not been ere this excited by their sufferings to a general mutiny and dispersion. Strong symptoms, however, of discontent have appeared in particular instances; and nothing but the most active efforts every where can long avert so shocking a catastrophe.

Our present sufferings are not all. There is no foundation laid for any adequate relief hereafter. All the magazines provided in the States of New Jersey, Pennsylvania, Delaware, and Maryland, and all the immediate, additional supplies they seem capable of affording, will not be sufficient to support the army more than a month longer, if so long. Very little has been done to the eastward, and as little to the southward; and whatever we have a right to expect from those quarters must necessarily be very remote, and is, indeed, more precarious than could be wished. When the fore-mentioned supplies are exhausted, what a terrible crisis must ensue, unless all the energy of the continent shall be exerted to provide a timely remedy.

Impressed with this idea, I am, on my part, putting every engine at work, that I can possibly think of, to prevent the fatal consequences, we have so great reason to apprehend. I am calling upon all those, whose stations and influence enable them to contribute their aid upon so important an occasion; and, from your well known zeal, I expect every thing within the compass of your power, and that the abilities and resources of the State over which you preside will admit. I am sensible of the disadvantages it labors under, from having been so long the scene of war, and that it must be exceedingly drained by the great demands to which it has been subject. But, though you may not be able to contribute materially to our relief, you can perhaps do something towards it; and any assistance, however trifling in itself, will be of great moment at so critical a juncture, and will conduce to the keeping of the army together, till the commissary's department can be put upon a better footing, and effectual measures concerted to secure a permanent and competent supply. What methods you can take, you will be the best judge of; but, if you can devise any means to procure a quantity of cattle, or other kind of flesh, for the use of this army, to be at camp in the course of a month, you will render a most essential service to the common cause. I have the honor to be, &c.

To Lund Washington

MIDDLE BROOK, FEBRUARY 24, 1779.

Dear Lund: I wrote to you by the last post, but in so hasty a manner as not to be so full and clear as the importance of the subject might require. In truth, I find myself at a loss to do it to my own satisfaction in this hour of more leisure and thought, because it is a matter of much importance and requires a good deal of judgment and foresight to time things in such a way as to answer the purposes I have in view.

The advantages resulting from the sale of my negroes, I have very little doubt of; because, as I observed in my last, if we should ultimately prove unsuccessful (of which I am under no apprehension unless it falls on us as a punishment for our want of public, and indeed private virtue) it would be a matter of very little consequence to me, whether my property is in Negroes, or loan office Certificates, as I shall neither ask for, nor expect any favor from his most gracious Majesty, nor any person acting under his authority; the only points therefore for me to consider, are, first, whether it would be most to my interest, in case of a fortunate determination of the present contest, to have negroes, and the Crops they will make; or the sum they will now fetch and the interest of the money. And, secondly, the critical moment to make this sale.

With respect to the first point (if a negro man will sell at, or near one thousand pounds, and woman and children in proportion) I have not the smallest doubt on which side the balance, placed in the scale of interest, will preponderate: My scruples arise from a reluctance in offering these people at public vendue, and on account of the uncertainty of timeing the sale well. In the first case, if these poor wretches are to be held in a state of slavery, I do not see that a change of masters will render it more irksome, provided husband and wife, and Parents and children are not separated from each other, which is not my intentions to do. And with respect to the second, the judgment founded in a knowledge of circumstances, is the only criterion for determining when the tide of depreciation is at an end; for like the flux and reflux of the water, it will no sooner have got to its full ebb or flow, but an immediate turn takes place, and every thing runs in a contrary direction. To hit this critical moment then, is the point; and a point of so much nicety, that the longer I reflect upon the subject, the more embarrassed I am in my opinion; for if a sale takes place while the money is in a depreciating state, that is, before it has arrived at the lowest ebb of depreciation; I shall lose the difference, and if it is delayed, 'till some great and important event shall give a decisive turn in favor of our affairs, it may be too late. Notwithstanding, upon a full consideration of the whole matter; if you have done nothing in consequence of my last letter, I wou'd have you wait 'till you hear further from me on this subject. I will, in the meanwhile, revolve the matter in my mind more fully, and may possibly be better able to draw some more precise conclusions than at present, while you may be employed in endeavouring to ascertain the highest prices Negroes sell at, in different parts of the Country, where, and in what manner it would be best to sell them, when such a measure is adopted, (which I think will very likely happen in the course of a few months.)

Inclosed is my Bond for conveyance of the Land purchased of the Ashfords &c. It is as well drawn as I can do it, and I believe it to be effectual.

To James Warren

MIDDLEBROOK, MARCH 31, 1779.

Dear Sir:

[. . .] Our conflict is not likely to cease so soon as every good man would wish. The measure of iniquity is not yet filled; and, unless we can return a little more to first principles, and act a little more upon patriotic grounds, I do not know when it will, or what may be the issue of the contest. Speculation, Peculation, Engrossing, forestalling, with all their concomitants, afford too many melancholy proofs of the decay of public virtue, and too glaring instances of its being the interest and desire of too many, who would wish to be thought friends, to continue the war.

Nothing, I am convinced, but the depreciation of our currency, proceeding in a great measure from the foregoing causes, aided by stockjobbing and party dissensions, has fed the hopes of the Enemy and kept the B. arms in America to this day. They do not scruple to declare this themselves, and add, that we shall be our own conquerors. Cannot our common country Am. possess virtue enough to disappoint them? Is the paltry consideration of a little dirty pelf to individuals to be placed in competition with the essential rights and liberties of the present generation, and of millions yet unborn? Shall a few designing men, for their own aggrandizement, & to gratify their own avarice, overset the goodly fabric we have been rearing at the expence of so much time, blood, & treasure? And shall we at last become the victims of our own abominable lust of gain? Forbid it Heaven! Forbid it all & every State in the Union! by enacting & enforcing efficacious laws for checking the growth of these monstrous evils, & restoring matters in some degree to the pristine state they were in at the commencement of the war.

Our cause is noble. It is the cause of mankind! and the danger to it is to be apprehended from ourselves. Shall we slumber and sleep, then, while we should be punishing those miscreants, who have brot. these troubles upon us, & who are aimg. to continue us in them; while we should be striving to fill our battalions, & devising ways and means to appreciate the currency, on the credit of wch. every thing depends? I hope not. Let vigorous measures be adopted; not to limit the prices of articles, for this I believe is inconsistent with the very nature of things, and impracticable in itself; but to punish speculators, forestallers, & extortioners, and above all to sink the money by heavy taxes, to promote public & private economy, Encourage manufactures &c. Measures of this sort, gone heartily into by the several States, would strike at once at the root of all our evils, & give the coup de grace to British hope of subjugating this continent, either by their arms or their arts. The first, as I have before observed, they acknowledge is unequal to the task; the latter I am sure will be so, if we are not lost to every thing that is good & virtuous.

A little time now must unfold in some degree the enemy's designs. Whether the state of affairs in Europe will permit them to augment their army with more than recruits for the Regiments now on the continent, and therewith make an active and vigorous campaign; or whether, with their Florida & Canadian force, they will aid & abet the Indians in ravaging our western Frontier, while their shipg. with detachments, harass, (and if they mean to prosecute the predatory war, threatened by administration through their commissioners) burn, & destroy our sea coast; or whether, contrary to expectation, they should be more disposed to negotiate than to either, is more than I can determine. The latter will depend very much upon their apprehensions from the court of Spain, & expectations of foreign aid & powerful alliances. At present we seem to be in a chaos. But this cannot last long, as I suppose the ultimate determination of the British court will be developed at the meeting of Parliament after the hollidays.

Mrs. Washington joins me in cordial wishes & best respects to Mrs. Warren. She would have done herself the pleasure of writing, but the present conveyance was sudden. I am, with sincere esteem and regard, dear Sir, &c.

To Colonel Lewis Nicola

NEWBURGH, MAY 22, 1782.

Sir,

With a mixture of great surprise and astonishment, I have read with attention the sentiments you have submitted to my perusal. Be assured, Sir, no occurrence in the course of the war has given me more painful sensations, than your information of there being such ideas existing in the army, as you have expressed, and I must view with abhorrence and reprehend with severity. For the present the communicatn. of them will rest in my own bosom, unless some further agitation of the matter shall make a disclosure necessary.

I am much at a loss to conceive what part of my conduct could have given encouragement to an address, which to me seems big with the greatest mischiefs, that can befall my Country. If I am not deceived in the knowledge of myself, you could not have found a person to whom your schemes are more disagreeable. At the same time, in justice to my own feelings, I must add, that no man possesses a more sincere wish to see ample justice done to the army than I do; and, as far as my powers and influence, in a constitutional way, extend, they shall be employed to the utmost of my abilities to effect it, should there be any occasion. Let me conjure you, then, if you have any regard for your Country, concern for yourself or posterity, or respect for me, to banish these thoughts from your mind, and never communicate, as from yourself or any one else, a sentiment of the like nature. With esteem, I am.

Circular Letter Addressed to the Governors of All the States on Disbanding the Army

HEAD-QUARTERS, NEWBURGH, JUNE 8, 1783.

Sir,

The great object, for which I had the honor to hold an appointment in the service of my country, being accomplished, I am now preparing to resign it into the hands of Congress, and to return to that domestic retirement, which, it is well known, I left with the greatest reluctance; a retirement for which I have never ceased to sigh, through a long and painful absence, and in which (remote from the noise and trouble of the world) I meditate to pass the remainder of life, in a state of undisturbed repose. But before I carry this resolution into effect, I think it a duty incumbent on me to make this my last official communication; to congratulate you on the glorious events which Heaven has been pleased to produce in our favor; to offer my sentiments respecting some important subjects, which appear to me to be intimately connected with the tranquillity of the United States; to take my leave of your Excellency as a public character; and to give my final blessing to that country, in whose service I have spent the prime of my life, for whose sake I have consumed so many anxious days and watchful nights, and whose happiness, being extremely dear to me, will always constitute no inconsiderable part of my own.

Impressed with the liveliest sensibility on this pleasing occasion, I will claim the indulgence of dilating the more copiously on the subjects of our mutual felicitation. When we consider the magnitude of the prize we contended for, the doubtful nature of the contest, and the favorable manner in which it has terminated, we shall find the greatest possible reason for gratitude and rejoicing. This is a theme that will afford infinite delight to every benevolent and liberal mind, whether the event in contemplation be considered as the source of present enjoyment or the parent of future happiness; and we shall have equal occasion to felicitate ourselves on the lot which Providence has assigned us, whether we view it in a natural, a political, or moral point of light.

The citizens of America, placed in the most enviable condition, as the sole lords and proprietors of a vast tract of continent, comprehending all the various soils and climates of the world, and abounding with all the necessaries and conveniences of life, are now, by the late satisfactory pacification, acknowledged to be possessed of absolute freedom and independency. They are, from this period, to be considered as the actors on a most conspicuous theatre, which seems to be peculiarly designated by Providence for the display of human greatness and felicity. Here they are not only surrounded with every thing, which can contribute to the completion of private and domestic enjoyment; but Heaven has crowned all its other blessings, by giving a fairer opportunity for political happiness, than any other nation has ever been favored with. Nothing can illustrate these observations more forcibly, than a recollection of the happy conjuncture of times and circumstances, under which our republic assumed its rank among the nations. The foundation of our empire was not laid in the gloomy age of ignorance and superstition; but at an epocha when the rights of mankind were better understood and more clearly defined, than at any former period, the researches of the human mind after social happiness have been carried to a great extent; the treasures of knowledge, acquired by the labors of philosophers, sages, and legislators, through a long succession of years, are laid open for our use, and their collected wisdom may be happily applied in the establishment of our forms of government. The free cultivation of letters, the unbounded extension of commerce, the progressive refinement of manners, the growing liberality of sentiment, and, above all, the pure and benign light of Revelation, have had a meliorating influence on mankind and increased the blessings of society. At this auspicious period, the United States came into existence as a nation; and, if their citizens should not be completely free and happy, the fault will be entirely their own. [. . .]

To James Warren

MOUNT VERNON, OCTR 7TH 1785.

Dear Sir,

The assurances of your friendship, after a silence of more than six years, are extremely pleasing to me. Friendship, formed under the circumstances that ours commenced are not easily eradicated; and I can assure you, that mine has undergone no diminution. Every occasion, therefore, of renewing it will give me pleasure, and I shall be happy at all times to hear of your welfare.

The war, as you have very justly observed, has terminated most advantageously for America, and a large and glorious field is presented to our view; but I confess to you freely, my dear Sir, that I do not think we possess wisdom or justice enough to cultivate it properly. Illiberality, jealousy, and local policy mix too much in all our public councils for the good government of the Union. In a word, the confederation appears to me to be little more than an empty sound, and Congress a nugatory body, their ordinances being little attended to.

To me it is a solecism in politics, indeed it is one of the most extraordinary things in nature, that we should confederate for national purposes, and yet be afraid to give the rulers thereof who are the creatures of our making, appointed for a limited and short duration, and who are amenable for every action—recallable at any moment—and subject to all the evils they may be instrumental in producing, sufficient powers to order and direct the affairs of that nation.

By such policy as this the wheels of government are clogged, and our brightest prospects, and that high expectation, which was entertained of us by the wondering world, is turned into astonishment; and from the high ground on which we stood, we are descending into the valleys of confusion and darkness.

That we have it in our power to become one of the most respectable nations upon earth, admits not, in my humble opinion, of a doubt, if we would but pursue a wise, just, and liberal policy towards one another, and would keep good faith with the rest of the world. That our resources are ample and increasing, none can deny; but, whilst they are grudgingly applied, or not applied at all, we give a vital stab to public faith, and must sink into contempt in the eyes of Europe.

It has long been a speculative question among philosophers and wise men, whether foreign commerce is of advantage to any country; that is, whether the luxury, effeminacy, and corruption which are introduced by it, are counterbalanced by the conveniences and wealth of which it is productive. But the right decision of this question is of very little importance to us. We have abundant reason to be convinced, that the spirit of trade, which pervades these States, is not to be restrained. It behoves us then to establish upon just principles; and this, any more than other matters of national concern, cannot be done by thirteen heads differently constructed. The necessity, therefore, of a controlling power is obvious; and why it should be withheld is beyond my comprehension. [. . .]

[. . .] Mrs. Washington offers compliments and best wishes to Mrs Warren, to which be pleased to add those of, dear Sir, Yr Most Obedt Hble Servt

To James Madison

MOUNT VERNON, 5TH NOVR 1786.

My dear Sir,

I thank you for the communications in your letter of the 1st instant. The decision of the House on the question respecting a paper emission is portentous, I hope, of an auspicious session. It may certainly be classed with the important questions of the present day, and merited the serious consideration of the Assembly. Fain would I hope, that the great and most important of all objects, the *federal government*, may be considered with that calm and deliberate attention, which the magnitude of it so loudly calls for at this critical moment.

Let prejudices, unreasonable jealousies, and local interest, yield to reason and liberality. Let us look to our national character, and to things beyond the present period. No morn ever dawned more favorably than ours did; and no day was ever more clouded than the present! Wisdom and good examples are necessary at this time to rescue the political machine from the impending storm. Virginia has now an opportunity to set the latter, and has enough of the former, I hope, to take the lead in promoting this great and arduous work. Without an alteration in our political creed, the superstructure we have been seven years raising, at the expence of so much blood and treasure, must fall. We are fast verging to anarchy and confusion. [. . .]

[. . .] The consequences of a lax or inefficient government are too obvious to be dwelt on. Thirteen sovereignties pulling against each other, and all tugging at the federal head, will soon bring ruin on the whole; whereas a liberal and energetic Constitution, well guarded and closely watched to prevent encroachments, might restore us to that degree of respectability and consequence, to which we had a fair claim and the brightest prospect of attaining. With sentiments of very great esteem and regard

I am, Dear Sir, &c.

Diary Entry

MONDAY, SEPTEMBER 17, 1787.

Met in Convention, when the Constitution received the unanimous assent of 11 States and Colo. Hamilton's from New York (the only delegate from thence in Convention), and was subscribed to by every member present, except Govr. Randolph and Colo. Mason from Virginia, & Mr. Gerry from Massachusetts.

The business being thus closed, the members adjourned to the City Tavern, dined together, and took a cordial leave of each other—after which I returned to my lodgings, did some business with, and received the papers from the Secretary of the Convention, and retired to meditate on the momentous wk. which had been executed, after not less than five, for a large part of the time six and sometimes 7 hours sitting every day, Sundays & the ten days adjournment to give a Comee. opportunity & time to arrange the business for more than four months.

To the Marquis de Lafayette

MOUNT VERNON, APRIL 28, 1788.

[. . .] The Conventions of six States only have as yet accepted the new Constitution. No one has rejected it. It is believed that the Convention of Maryland, which is now in session, and that of South Carolina, which is to assemble on the 12th of May, will certainly adopt it. It is also since the elections of members of the Convention have taken place in this State, more generally believed, that it will be adopted here, than it was before those elections were made. There will, however, be powerful and eloquent speeches on both sides of the question in the Virginia Convention; but as Pendleton, Wythe, Blair, Madison, Jones, Nicholas, Innis, and many other of our first characters, will be advocates for its adoption, you may suppose the weight of abilities will rest on that side. Henry and

Mason are its great adversaries. The governor, if he approves it at all, will do it feebly. [. . .]

[. . .] Now, although it is not to be expected, that every individual, in Society, will or can be brought to agree upon what is exactly the best form of government, yet there are many things in the Constitution, which only need to be explained, in order to prove equally satisfactory to all parties. For example, there was not a member of the convention, I believe, who had the least objection to what is contended for by the Advocates for a *Bill of Rights* and *Trial by Jury*. The first, where the people evidently retained every thing, which they did not in express terms give up, was considered nugatory, as you will find to have been more fully explained by Mr. Wilson and others; and, as to the second, it was only the difficulty of establishing a mode, which should not interfere with the fixed modes of any of the States, that induced the Convention to leave it as a matter of future adjustment.

There are other points in which opinions would be more likely to vary. As for instance, on the ineligibility of the same person for president, after he should have served a certain course of years. Guarded so effectually as the proposed constitution is, in respect to the prevention of bribery and undue influence in the choice of president, I confess I differ widely myself from Mr. Jefferson and you, as to the necessity or expediency of rotation in that appointment. The matter was fairly discussed in the Convention, and to my full convictions, though I cannot have time or room to sum up the argument in this letter. There cannot in my judgment be the least danger, that the president will by any practicable intrigue ever be able to continue himself one moment in office, much less perpetuate himself in it, but in the last stage of corrupted morals and political depravity; and even then, there is as much danger that any other species of domination would prevail. Though, when a people shall have become incapable of governing themselves, and fit for a master, it is of little consequence from what quarter he comes. Under an extended view of this part of the subject, I can see no propriety in precluding ourselves from the services of any man, who on some great emergency shall be deemed universally most capable of serving the public.

In answer to the observations you make on the probability of my election to the presidency, knowing me as you do, I need only say, that it has no enticing charms and no fascinating allurements for me. However, it might not be decent for me to say I would refuse to accept, or even to speak much about an appointment, which may never take place; for, in so doing, one might possibly incur the application of the moral resulting from that fable, in which the fox is represented as inveighing against the sourness of the grapes, because he could not reach them. All that it will be necessary to add, my dear Marquis, in order to show my decided predilection is, that, (at my time of life and under my circumstances,) the increasing infirmities of nature and the growing love of retirement do not permit me to entertain a wish beyond that of living and dying an honest man on my own farm. Let those follow the pursuits of ambition and fame, who have a keener relish for them, or who may have more years in store for the enjoyment.

Mrs. Washington, while she requests that her best compliments may be presented to you, joins with me in soliciting that the same friendly and affectionate memorial of our constant remembrance and good wishes may be made acceptable to Madame de Lafayette and the little ones. I am, &c.

P. S. May 1st. Since writing the foregoing letter, I have received authentic accounts that the Convention of Maryland has ratified the new Constitution by a majority of 63 to 11.

To George Steptoe Washington

MOUNT VERNON, 23D MARCH 1789.

Dear George,

As it is probable I shall soon be under the necessity of quitting this place, and entering once more into the bustle of publick life, in conformity to the voice of my Country and the earnest entreaties of my friends, however contrary it is to my own desires or inclinations; I think it incumbent on me as your Uncle and friend, to give you some advisory hints, which if properly attended to, will, I conceive, be found very useful to you in regulating your conduct and giving you respectability not only at present but through every period of life.

You have now arrived to that age when you must quit the trifling amusements of a boy, and assume the more dignified manners of a man. At this crisis your conduct will attract the notice of those who are about you; and as the first impressions are generally the most lasting, your doings now may mark the leading traits of your character through life. It is therefore, absolutely necessary, if you mean to make any figure upon the Stage, that you should take the first steps right. What these steps are and what general line is to be pursued to lay the foundation of an honorable and happy progress, is the part of age and experience to point out. This I shall do, as far as in my power with the utmost chearfulness; and, I trust, that your own good sense will shew you the necessity of following it.

The first and great object with you at present is to acquire, by industry and application, such knowledge as your situation enables you to obtain, as will be useful to you in life. In doing this two other important objects will be gained besides the acquisition of knowledge—namely a habit of industry, and a disrelish of that profusion of money and dissipation of time which are ever attendant upon idleness. I do not mean by a close application to your studies that you should never enter into those amusements which are suited to your age and station. They may be made to go hand in hand with each other, and used in their proper seasons, will ever be found to be a mutual assistance to each other. But what amusements are to be taken, and when, is the great matter to be attended to—your own judgement, with the advice of your *real* friends who may have an opportunity of a personal intercourse with you can point out the particular manner in which you may *best* spend your moments of relaxation, much better than I can at a distance.—One thing, however, I would strongly impress upon you, viz: that when you have leisure to go into company that it should always be of the best kind that the place you are in will afford; by this means you will be constantly improving your manners and cultivating your mind while you are relaxing from your books; and good company will always be found much less expensive than bad. You cannot offer, as an excuse for not using it, that you cannot gain admission there, or that you have not a proper attention paid you in it, this is an apology made only, by those whose manners are disgusting, or whose character is exceptionable; neither of which, I hope will ever be said of you.

I cannot enjoin too strongly upon you a due observance of economy and frugality: As you well know yourself, the present state of your property and finances will not admit of any unnecessary expense. The article of clothing is *now* one of the chief expenses you will incur; and in this, I fear, you are not so economical as you should be. Decency and cleanliness will always be the first object in the dress of a judicious and sensible man. A conformity to the prevailing fashion in a certain degree is necessary—but it does not follow from thence that a man should always get a new coat, or other clothes, upon every trifling change in the mode, when, perhaps he has two or three very good ones by him. A person who is anxious to be a leader of the fashion, or one of the first to follow it, will certainly appear in the eyes of judicious men, to have nothing better than a frequent change of dress to recommend him to notice. I would always wish you to appear sufficiently decent to entitle you to admission into any company, where you may be,—but I cannot too strongly enjoin it upon you—and your own knowledge must convince you of the truth of it—that you should be as little expensive in this respect as you properly can—You should always keep some clothes to wear to church, or on particular occasions, which should not be worn every day. This can be done without any additional expense; for whenever it is necessary to get new clothes, those which have been kept for particular occasions will then come in as every day ones, unless they should be of a superior quality to the new. What I have said with respect to clothes will apply perhaps more pointedly to Lawrence than to you,—and as you are much older than he is, and more capable of judging of the propriety of what I have here observed, you must pay attention to him, in this respect, and see that he does not wear his clothes improperly or extravagantly.

Much more might be said to you, as a young man, upon the necessity of paying due attention to the moral virtues; but this may, perhaps, more properly be the subject of a future letter when you are about to enter into the world. If you comply with the advice herein given, to pay a diligent attention to your studies, and employ your time of relaxation in proper company, you will find but few opportunities and little inclination, while you continue at an Academy, to enter into those scenes of vice and dissipation which too often present themselves to youth in every place, and particularly in towns. If you are determined to neglect your books, and plunge into extravagance and dissipation nothing that I can now say would prevent it,—for you must be employed, and if it is not in pursuit of those things profitable, it must be in pursuit of those which are destructive.

As your time of continuing with Mr. Hanson expires the last of this month and I understand that Doctor Craik has expressed an inclination to take you and Lawrence to board with him, I shall know his determination respecting the matter. [. . .] Should you or Lawrence therefore behave in such a manner as to occasion any complaints being made to me, you may depend upon losing that place which you now have in my affections, and any future hope you may have from me. But if, on the contrary, your conduct is such as to merit my regard you may always depend upon the warmest attachment and sincere regard of

Your affectionate friend and Uncle.

To Henry Knox

MOUNT VERNON, APRIL 1ST 1789

My dear Sir,

The mail of the 30th brought me your favor of the 23d, by which, and the regular information you have had the goodness to transmit of the state of things in New York, I feel myself very much obliged, and thank you accordingly.

I feel for those members of the new Congress, who hitherto have given an unavailing attendance at the theatre of business. For myself the delay may be compared to a reprieve; for in confidence I can assure *you,* (with the *world* it would obtain *little credit,*) that my movements to the chair of government will be accompanied by feelings not unlike those of a culprit, who is going to the place of his execution; so unwilling am I, in the evening of a life nearly consumed in public cares, to quit a peaceful abode for an ocean of difficulties, without that competency of political skill, abilities, and inclination, which are necessary to manage the helm. I am sensible that I am embarking the voice of my countrymen and a good name of my own, on this voyage; but what returns will be made for them, Heaven alone can foretell. Integrity and firmness is all I can promise. These, be the voyage long or short, shall never forsake me, although I may be deserted by all men; for of the consolations, which are to be derived from these, under any circumstances, the world cannot deprive me. With best wishes for Mrs Knox, & sincere friendship for yourself—I remain Your affectionate

First Inaugural Address

APRIL 30, 1789.

Fellow Citizens of the Senate and of the House of Representatives,

Among the vicissitudes incident to life, no event could have filled me with greater anxieties, than that of which the notification was transmitted by your order, and received on the 14th day of the present month. On the one hand, I was summoned by my country, whose voice I can never hear but with veneration and love, from a retreat which I had chosen with the fondest predilection, and, in my flattering hopes, with an immutable decision, as the asylum of my declining years; a retreat which was rendered every day more necessary as well as more dear to me, by the addition of habit to inclination, and of frequent interruptions in my health to the gradual waste committed on it by time. On the other hand, the magnitude and difficulty of the trust, to which the voice of my country called me, being sufficient to awaken in the wisest and most experienced of her citizens a distrustful scrutiny into his qualifications, could not but overwhelm with despondence one, who, inheriting inferior endowments from nature, and unpractised in the duties of civil administration, ought to be peculiarly conscious of his own deficiencies. In this conflict of emotions, all I dare aver is, that it has been my faithful study to collect my duty from a just appreciation of every circumstance by which it might be affected. All I dare hope is, that, if in executing this task, I have been too much swayed by a grateful remembrance of former instances, or by an affectionate sensibility to this transcendent proof of the confidence of my fellow-citizens; and have thence too little consulted my incapacity as well as disinclination for the weighty and untried cares before me; my error will be palliated by the motives which misled me, and its consequences be judged by my country with some share of the partiality in which they originated.

Such being the impressions under which I have, in obedience to the public summons, repaired to the present station, it would be peculiarly improper to omit, in this first official act, my fervent supplications to that Almighty Being, who rules over the universe, who presides in the councils of nations, and whose providential aids can supply every human defect, that his benediction may consecrate to the liberties and happiness of the people of the United States a government instituted by themselves for these essential purposes, and may enable every instrument employed in its administration to execute with success the functions allotted to his charge. In tendering this homage to the Great Author of every public and private good, I assure myself that it expresses your sentiments not less than my own; nor those of my fellow-citizens at large, less than either. No people can be bound to acknowledge and adore the invisible hand, which conducts the affairs of men, more than the people of the United States. Every step, by which they have advanced to the character of an independent nation, seems to have been distinguished by some token of providential agency. And, in the important revolution just accomplished in the system of their united government, the tranquil deliberations and voluntary consent of so many distinct communities, from which the event has resulted, cannot be compared with the means by which most governments have been established, without some return of pious gratitude along with an humble anticipation of the future blessings which the past seem to presage. These reflections, arising out of the present crisis, have forced themselves too strongly on my mind to be suppressed. You will join with me, I trust, in thinking that there are none, under the influence of which the proceedings of a new and free government can more auspiciously commence.

By the article establishing the executive department, it is made the duty of the President "to recommend to your consideration such measures as he shall judge necessary and expedient." The circumstances, under which I now meet you, will acquit me from entering into that subject farther than to refer you to the great constitutional charter under which we are assembled; and which, in defining your powers, designates the objects to which your attention is to be given. It will be more consistent with those circumstances, and far more congenial with the feelings which actuate me, to substitute, in place of a recommendation of particular measures, the tribute that is due to the talents, the rectitude, and the patriotism, which adorn the characters selected to devise and adopt them. In these honorable qualifications I behold the surest pledges, that as, on one side, no local prejudices or attachments, no separate views or party animosities, will misdirect the comprehensive and equal eye, which ought to watch over this great assemblage of communities and interests; so, on another, that the foundations of our national policy will be laid in the pure and immutable principles of private morality, and the pre-eminence of a free government be exemplified by all the attributes, which can win the affections of its citizens, and command the respect of the world.

I dwell on this prospect with every satisfaction, which an ardent love for my country can inspire; since there is no truth more thoroughly established, than that there exists in the economy and course of nature an indissoluble union between virtue and happiness, between duty and advantage, between the genuine maxims of an honest and magnanimous policy, and the solid rewards of public prosperity and felicity; since we ought to be no less persuaded that the propitious smiles of Heaven can never be expected on a nation that disregards the eternal rules of order and right, which Heaven itself has ordained; and since the preservation of the sacred fire of liberty, and the destiny of the republican model of government, are justly considered as *deeply*, perhaps as *finally* staked, on the experiment intrusted to the hands of the American people.

Besides the ordinary objects submitted to your care, it will remain with your judgment to decide, how far an exercise of the occasional power delegated by the fifth article of the Constitution is rendered expedient at the present juncture by the nature of objections which have been urged against the system, or by the degree of inquietude which has given birth to them. Instead of undertaking particular recommendations on this subject, in which I could be guided by no lights derived from official opportunities, I shall again give way to my entire confidence in your discernment and pursuit of the public good; for I assure myself, that, whilst you carefully avoid every alteration, which might endanger the benefits of a united and effective government, or which ought to await the future lessons of experience; a reverence for the characteristic rights of freemen, and a regard for the public harmony, will sufficiently influence your deliberations on the question, how far the former can be more impregnably fortified, or the latter be safely and advantageously promoted.

To the preceding observations I have one to add, which will be most properly addressed to the House of Representatives. It concerns myself, and will therefore be as brief as possible. When I was first honored with a call into the service of my country, then on the eve of an arduous struggle for its liberties, the light in which I contemplated my duty required, that I should renounce every pecuniary compensation. From this resolution I have in no instance departed. And being still under the impressions which produced it, I must decline as inapplicable to myself any share in the personal emoluments, which may be indispensably included in a permanent provision for the executive department; and must accordingly pray, that the pecuniary estimates for the station in which I am placed may, during my continuance in it, be limited to such actual expenditures as the public good may be thought to require.

Having thus imparted to you my sentiments, as they have been awakened by the occasion which brings us together, I shall take my present leave; but not without resorting once more to the benign Parent of the human race, in humble supplication, that, since he has been pleased to favor the American people with opportunities for deliberating in perfect tranquillity, and dispositions for deciding with unparalleled unanimity on a form of government for the security of their union and the advancement of their happiness; so his divine blessing may be equally *conspicuous* in the enlarged views, the temperate consultations, and the wise measures, on which the success of this government must depend.

To John Adams

MAY 10, 1789.

The President of the United States wishes to avail himself of your sentiments on the following points.

1st Whether a line of conduct, equally distant from an association with all kinds of company on the one hand and from a total seclusion from Society on the other, ought to be adopted by him? and, in that case, how is it to be done?

2d What will be the least exceptionable method of bringing any system, which may be adopted on this subject, before the Public and into use?

3d Whether, after a little time, one day in every week will not be sufficient for receiving visits of Compliment?

4th Whether it would tend to prompt impertinent applications & involve disagreeable consequences to have it known, that the President will, every

Morning at 8 Oclock, be at leisure to give Audiences to persons who may have business with him?

5th Whether, when it shall have been understood that the President is not to give general entertainment in the manner the Presidents of Congress have formerly done, it will be practicable to draw such a line of discrimination in regard to persons, as that Six, eight or ten official characters (including in the rotation the members of both Houses of Congress) may be invited informally or otherwise to dine with him on the days fixed for receiving Company, without exciting clamours in the rest of the Community?

6th Whether it would be satisfactory to the Public for the President to make about four great entertainmts in a year on such great occasions as—the Anniversary of the Declaration of Independence, the Alliance with France—the Peace with Great Britain—the Organization of the general government: and whether arrangements of these two last kinds could be in danger of diverting too much of the Presidents time from business, or of producing the evils which it was intended to avoid by his living more recluse than the Presidents of Congress have heretofore lived.

7th Whether there would be any impropriety in the Presidents making informal visits—that is to say, in his calling upon his Acquaintances or public Characters for the purposes of sociability or civility—and what (as to the form of doing it) might evince these visits to have been made in his private character, so as that they might not be construed into visits from the President of the United States? and in what light would his appearance *rarely* at *Tea* parties be considered?

8th Whether, during the recess of Congress, it would not be advantageous to the interests of the Union for the President to make the tour of the United States, in order to become better acquainted with their principal Characters & internal Circumstances, as well as to be more accessible to numbers of well-informed persons, who might give him useful informations and advices on political subjects?

9th If there is a probability that either of the arrangements may take place, which will eventually cause additional expenses, whether it would not be proper that these ideas should come into contemplation, at the time when Congress shall make a permanent provision for the support of the Executive.

Remarks

On the one side no augmentation can be effected in the pecuniary establishment which shall be made, in the first instance, for the support of the

Executive—on the other, all monies destined to that purpose beyond the actual expenditures, will be left in the Treasury of the United States or sacredly applied to the promotion of some national objects.

Many things which appear of little importance in themselves and at the beginning, may have great and durable consequences from their having been established at the commencement of a new general Government. It will be much easier to commence the administration, upon a well adjusted system built on tenable grounds, than to correct errors or alter inconveniences after they shall have been confirmed by habit. The President in all matters of business & etiquette, can have no object but to demean himself in his public character, in such a manner as to maintain the dignity of Office, without subjecting himself to the imputation of superciliousness or unnecessary reserve. Under these impressions, he asks for your candid and undisguised opinions.

To Catharine Macaulay Graham

NEW YORK, JANY 9TH 1790.

Madam,

Your obliging letter dated in October last has been received, and, as I do not know when I shall have more leisure than at present to throw together a few observations in return for yours, I take up my pen to do it by this early occasion.

In the first place I thank you for your congratulatory sentiments on the event, which has placed me at the head of the American government, as well as for the indulgent partiality, which it is to be feared, however, may have warped your judgment too much in my favor. But you do me no more than justice in supposing, that, if I had been permitted to indulge my first and fondest wish, I should have remained in a private station.

Although neither the present age nor posterity may possibly give me full credit for the feelings, which I have experienced on this subject, yet I have a consciousness that nothing short of an absolute conviction of duty could ever have brought me upon the scenes of public life again. The establishment of our new government seemed to be the last great experiment for promoting human happiness by a reasonable compact in civil society. It was to be in the first instance, in a considerable degree, a government of accommodation as well as a government of laws. Much was to be done by *prudence,* much by *conciliation,* much by *firmness.* Few, who are not philosophical spectators, can realize the difficult and delicate part, which a man in my situation had to act. All see, and most admire, the glare which hovers round the external trappings of elevated office. To me there is nothing in it beyond the lustre, which may be reflected from its connexion with a power of promoting human felicity.

In our progress towards political happiness my station is new, and, if I may use the expression, I walk on untrodden ground. There is scarcely an action, whose motives may not be subject to a double interpretation. There is scarcely any part of my conduct, which may not hereafter be drawn into precedent. Under such a view of the duties inherent to my arduous office, I could not but feel a diffidence in myself on the one hand, and an anxiety for the community, that every new arrangement should be made in the best possible manner, on the other. If, after all my humble but faithful endeavors to advance the felicity of my country and mankind, I may indulge a hope that my labors have not been altogether without success, it will be the only real compensation I can receive in the closing scenes of life.

On the actual situation of this country under its new government, I will, in the next place, make a few remarks. That the government, though not absolutely perfect, is one of the best in the world, I have little doubt. I always believed, that an unequivocally free and equal representation of the people in the legislature, together with an efficient and responsible executive, were the great pillars on which the preservation of American freedom must depend. It was indeed next to a miracle, that there should have been so much unanimity in points of such importance among such a number of citizens, so widely scattered, and so different in their habits in many respects, as the Americans were. Nor are the growing unanimity and increasing good will of the citizens to the government less remarkable, than favorable circumstances. So far as we have gone with the new government, (and it is completely organized and in operation,) we have had greater reason, than the most sanguine could expect, to be satisfied with its success. Perhaps a number of accidental circumstances have concurred with the real effects of the government to make the people uncommonly well pleased with their situation and prospects. The harvests of wheat have been remarkably good, the demand for that article from abroad is great, the increase of commerce is visible in every port, and the number of new manufactures introduced in one year is astonishing. I have lately made a tour through the Eastern States. I found the country in a great degree recovered from the ravages of war; the Towns flourishing, and the people delighted with a government instituted by themselves, and for their own good. The same facts I have also reason to believe, from good authority, exist in the Southern States.

By what I have just observed, I think you will be persuaded, that the ill-boding politicians, who prognosticated that America would never enjoy any fruits from her independence, and that she would be obliged to have recourse to a foreign power for protection, have at least been mistaken. I shall sincerely rejoice to see, that the American Revolution has been productive of happy consequences on both sides of the Atlantic. The renovation of the French constitution is indeed one of the most wonderful events in the history of mankind, and the agency of the Marquis de Lafayette in a high degree honorable to his character. My greatest fear has been, that the nation would not be sufficiently cool and moderate in making arrangements for the security of that liberty, of which it seems to be fully possessed.

[. . .] I am with great regard, &c.

To the Hebrew Congregation in Newport, Rhode Island

AUGUST 18, 1790

Gentlemen

While I receive, with much satisfaction, your Address replete with expressions of affection and esteem; I rejoice in the opportunity of assuring you, that I shall always retain a grateful remembrance of the cordial welcome I experienced in my visit to Newport, from all classes of Citizens.

The reflection on the days of difficulty and danger which are past is rendered the more sweet, from a consciousness that they are succeeded by days of uncommon prosperity and security. If we have wisdom to make the best use of the advantages with which we are now favored, we cannot fail, under the just administration of a good Government, to become a great and a happy people.

The Citizens of the United States of America have a right to applaud themselves for having given to mankind examples of an enlarged and liberal policy: a policy worthy of imitation. All possess alike liberty of conscience and immunities of citizenship. It is now no more that toleration is spoken of, as if it was by the indulgence of one class of people, that another enjoyed the exercise of their inherent natural rights. For happily the Government of the United States, which gives to bigotry no sanction, to persecution no assistance requires only that they who live under its protection should demean themselves as good citizens, in giving it on all occasions their effectual support.

It would be inconsistent with the frankness of my character not to avow that I am pleased with your favorable opinion of my Administration, and fervent wishes for my felicity. May the Children of the Stock of Abraham, who dwell in this land, continue to merit and enjoy the good will of the other Inhabitants; while every one shall sit in safety under his own vine and figtree, and there shall be none to make him afraid. May the father of all mercies scatter light and not darkness in our paths, and make us all in our several vocations useful here, and in his own due time and way everlastingly happy.

Third Annual Message to Congress

OCTOBER 25, 1791

Fellow-Citizens of the Senate and House of Representatives:

I meet you upon the present occasion with the feelings, which are naturally inspired by a strong impression of the prosperous situation of our common country, and by a persuasion equally strong, that the labors of the present session which has just commenced will, under the guidance of a spirit no less prudent than patriotic, issue in measures conducive to the stability and increase of national prosperity.

Numerous as are the providential blessings, which demand our grateful acknowledgments, the abundance, with which another year has again rewarded the industry of the husbandman, is too important to escape recollection.

Your own observations, in your respective situations, will have satisfied you of the progressive state of agriculture, manufactures, commerce, and navigation. In tracing their causes, you will have remarked, with particular pleasure, the happy effects of that revival of confidence, public as well as private, to which the Constitution and Laws of the United States have so eminently contributed; and you will have observed, with no less interest, new and decisive proofs of the increasing reputation and credit of the nation. But you, nevertheless, cannot fail to derive satisfaction from the confirmation of these circumstances, which will be disclosed in the several official communications, that will be made to you in the course of your deliberations.

The rapid subscriptions to the Bank of the United States, which completed the sum allowed to be subscribed in a single day, is among the striking and pleasing evidences which present themselves, not only of confidence in the Government, but of resource in the community.

In the interval of your recess, due attention has been paid to the execution of the different objects, which were specially provided for by the laws and resolutions of the last session.

Among the most important of these, is the defence and security of the western frontiers. To accomplish it on the most humane principles was a primary wish.

Accordingly, at the same time that treaties have been provisionally concluded, and other proper means used to attach the wavering, and to confirm in their friendship the well-disposed tribes of Indians, effectual measures have been adopted to make those of a hostile description sensible, that a pacification was desired upon terms of moderation and justice.

These measures having proved unsuccessful, it became necessary to convince the refractory of the power of the United States to punish their depredations. Offensive operations have, therefore, been directed; to be conducted, however, as consistently as possible with the dictates of humanity. Some of these have been crowned with full success, and others are yet depending. The expeditions, which have been completed, were carried on, under the authority and at the expense of the United States, by the militia of Kentucky; whose enterprise, intrepidity, and good conduct are entitled to peculiar commendation.

Overtures of peace are still continued to the deluded tribes, and considerable numbers of individuals belonging to them have lately renounced all further opposition, removed from their former situations, and placed themselves under the immediate protection of the United States.

It is sincerely to be desired, that all need of coercion in future may cease; and that an intimate intercourse may succeed, calculated to advance the happiness of the Indians, and to attach them firmly to the United States.

In order to this, it seems necessary, that they should experience the benefits of an impartial dispensation of justice; that the mode of alienating their lands, the main source of discontent and war, should be so defined and regulated as to obviate imposition, and, as far as may be practicable, controversy concerning the reality and extent of the alienations which are made; that commerce with them should be promoted under regulations tending to secure an equitable deportment towards them, and that such rational experiments should be made for imparting to them the blessings of civilization, as may from time to time suit their condition; that the executive of the United States should be enabled to employ the means, to which the Indians have been long accustomed, for uniting their immediate interests with the preservation of peace; and that efficacious provision should be made for inflicting adequate penalties upon all those, who, by violating their rights, shall infringe the treaties and endanger the peace of the Union.

A system corresponding with the mild principles of religion and philanthropy towards an unenlightened race of men, whose happiness materially depends on the conduct of the United States, would be as honorable to the national character as conformable to the dictates of sound policy.

The powers specially vested in me by the act laying certain duties on distilled spirits, which respect the subdivisions of the districts into surveys, the appointment of officers, and the assignment of compensations, have likewise been carried into effect. In a matter, in which both materials and experience were wanting to guide the calculation, it will be readily conceived, that there must have been difficulty in such an adjustment of the rates of compensation, as would conciliate a reasonable competency with a proper regard to the limits prescribed by the law. It is hoped that the circumspection, which has been used, will be found in the result to have secured the last of the two objects; but it is probable, that, with a view to the first, in some instances a revision of the provision will be found advisable.

The impressions, with which this law has been received by the community, have been, upon the whole, such as were to be expected among enlightened and well-disposed citizens, from the propriety and necessity of the measure. The novelty, however, of the tax, in a considerable part of the United States, and a misconception of some of its provisions, have given occasion in particular places to some degree of discontent. But it is satisfactory to know, that this disposition yields to proper explanations and more just apprehensions of the true nature of the law. And I entertain a full confidence, that it will, in all, give way to motives, which arise out of a just sense of duty and a virtuous regard to the public welfare.

If there are any circumstances in the law, which, consistently with its main design, may be so varied as to remove any well-intentioned objections that may happen to exist, it will consist with a wise moderation to make the proper variations. It is desirable, on all occasions, to unite with a steady and firm adherence to constitutional and necessary acts of government, the fullest evidence of a disposition, as far as may be practicable, to consult the wishes of every part of the community, and to lay the foundations of the public administration in the affections of the people.

Pursuant to the authority contained in the several acts on that subject, a district of ten miles square, for the permanent seat of the government of the United States, has been fixed, and announced by proclamation; which district will comprehend lands on both sides of the river Potomac, and the towns of Alexandria and George Town. A city has also been laid out agreeably to a plan which will be placed before Congress; and, as there is a prospect, favored by the rate of sales which have already taken place, of ample funds for carrying on the necessary public buildings, there is every expectation of their due progress. [. . .]

To James Madison

MOUNT VERNON, MAY 20TH 1792.

My dear Sir,

As there is a possibility if not a probability, that I shall not see you on your return home;—or, if I should see you that it may be on the road and under circumstances which will prevent my speaking to you on the subject we last conversed upon; I take the liberty of committing to paper the following thoughts, and requests.

I have not been unmindful of the sentiments expressed by you in the conversations just alluded to:—on the contrary I have again, and again revolved them with thoughtful anxiety; but without being able to dispose my mind to a longer continuation in the office I now have the honor to hold.—I therefore still look forward to the fulfilment of my fondest and most ardent wishes to spend the remainder of my days (which I cannot expect will be many) in ease and tranquillity.

Nothing short of conviction that my deriliction of the Chair of Government (if it should be the desire of the people to continue me in it) would involve the Country in serious disputes respecting the chief Magestrate, and the disagreeable consequences which might result therefrom in the floating and divided opinions which seem to prevail at present, could, in any wise, induce me to relinquish the determination I have formed: and of this I do not see how any evidence can be obtained previous to the Election. My vanity, I am sure is not of that cast to allow me to view the subject in this light.

Under these impressions then, permit me to reiterate the request I made to you at our last meeting—namely, to think of the proper time, and the best mode of announcing the intention; and that you would prepare the latter.—In revolving this subject myself, my judgment has always been embarrassed.—On the one hand, a previous declaration to retire, not only carries with it the appearance of vanity and self-importance, but it may be construed into a Manœuvre to be invited to remain.—And on the other hand, to say nothing, implys consent; or, at any rate, would leave the matter in doubt; and to decline afterwards might be deemed as bad, and uncandid.

I would fain carry my request to you farther than is asked above, although I am sensible that your compliance with it must add to your trouble; but as the recess may afford you leizure, and I flatter myself you have dispositions to oblige me, I will, without apology, desire (if the measure in itself should strike you as proper, and likely to produce public good, or private honor) that you would turn your thoughts to a Valedictory address from me to the public, expressing in plain and modest terms, that having been honored with the Presidential chair, and to the best of my abilities contributed to the organization and administration of the government—that having arrived at a period of life when the private walks of it, in the shade of retirement, becomes necessary and will be most pleasing to me;—and the spirit of the government may render a rotation in the elective officers of it more congenial with their ideas of liberty and safety, that I take my leave of them as a public man; and in bidding them adieu (retaining no other concern than such as will arise from fervent wishes for the prosperity of my Country) I take the liberty at my departure from civil, as I formerly did at my military exit to invoke a continuation of the blessings of Providence upon it, and upon all those who are the supporters of its interests, and the promoters of harmony, order and good government.

That to impress these things it might, among other things be observed, that we are *all* the children of the same country—a country great and rich in itself—capable and promising to be, as prosperous and as happy as any the annals of history have ever brought to our view—That our interest, however deversified in local and smaller matters, is the same in all the great and essential concerns of the Nation.—That the extent of our Country—the diversity of our climate and soil—and the various productions of the States consequent of both, are such as to make one part not only convenient, but perhaps indispensably necessary to the other part;—and may render the whole (at no distant period) one of the most independant in the world.—That the established government being the work of our own hands, with the seeds of amendment engrafted in the Constitution, may by wisdom, good dispositions, and mutual allowances; aided by experience, bring it as near to perfection as any human institution ever approximated; and therefore, the only strife among us ought to be, who should be foremost in facilitating and finally accomplishing such great and desirable objects; by giving every possible support, and cement to the Union.—That however necessary it may be to keep a watchful eye over public servants, and public measures, yet there ought to be limits to it; for suspicions unfounded, and jealousies too lively, are irritating to honest feeling; and oftentimes are productive of more evil than good.

To enumerate the various subjects which might be introduced into such an Address would require thought; and to mention them to you would be unnecessary, as your own judgment will comprehend *all* that will be proper; whether to touch, specifically, any of the exceptionable parts of the Constitution may be doubted.—All I shall add therefore at present, is, to beg the favor of you to consider—1st. the propriety of such an address.—2d. if approved, the several matters which ought to be contained in it—and

3d. the time it should appear: that is, whether at the declaration of my intention to withdraw from the service of the public—or to let it be the closing act of my administration—which will end with the next session of Congress (the probability being that that body will continue sitting until March,) when the House of Representatives will also dissolve.

'Though I do not wish to hurry you (the cases not pressing) in the execution of either of the publications beforementioned, yet I should be glad to hear from you generally on both—and to receive them in time, if you should not come to Philadelphia until the session commences, in the form they are finally to take.—I beg leave to draw your attention also to such things as you shall conceive fit subjects for communication on that occasion; and noting them as they occur that you would be so good as to furnish me with them in time to be prepared, and engrafted with others for the opening of the session. With very sincere and affectionate regard, I am—ever Yours

To Thomas Jefferson

MOUNT VERNON, AUGT 23D. 1792.

My dear Sir,

[. . .] How unfortunate, and how much is it to be regretted [. . .] that, while we are encompassed on all sides with avowed enemies and insidious friends, internal dissentions should be harrowing and tearing our vitals. The last, to me, is the most serious, the most alarming, and the most afflicting of the two; and, without more charity for the opinions and acts of one another in governmental matters, or some more infallible criterion by which the truth of speculative opinions, before they have undergone the test of experience, are to be forejudged, than has yet fallen to the lot of fallibility, I believe it will be difficult, if not impracticable, to manage the reins of government, or to keep the parts of it together; for if, instead of laying our shoulders to the machine after measures are decided on, one pulls this way and another that, before the utility of the thing is fairly tried, it must inevitably be torn asunder; and in my opinion the fairest prospect of happiness and prosperity, that ever was presented to man, will be lost perhaps for ever!

My earnest wish and my fondest hope, therefore, is, that instead of wounding suspicions and irritable charges, there may be liberal allowances, mutual forbearances, and temporizing yieldings *on all sides.* Under the exercise of these, matters will go on smoothly, and, if possible, more prosperously. Without them, every thing must rub; the wheels of government will clog; our enemies will triumph, and, by throwing their weight into the disaffected scale, may accomplish the ruin of the goodly fabric we have been erecting.

I do not mean to apply this advice, or these observations, to any particular person or character. I have given them in the same general terms to other officers of the government—because the disagreements, which have arisen from difference of opinions, and the attacks, which have been made upon almost all the measures of government, and most of its executive officers, have for a long time past filled me with painful sensations, and cannot fail, I think, of producing unhappy consequences at home and abroad. [. . .]

[. . .] With sincere esteem and friendship, I am, always, Your affectionate.

To Alexander Hamilton [Private]

MOUNT VERNON, AUGT. 26TH. 1792.

My dear Sir,

[. . .] Differences in political opinions are as unavoidable, as, to a certain point, they may perhaps be necessary; but it is to be regretted, exceedingly, that subjects cannot be discussed with temper on the one hand, or decisions submitted to without having the motives, which led to them, improperly implicated on the other; and this regret borders on chagrin, when we find that men of abilities, zealous patriots, having the same *general* objects in view, and the same upright intentions to prosecute them, will not exercise more charity in deciding on the opinions and actions of one another. When matters get to such lengths, the natural inference is, that both sides have strained the cords beyond their bearing, and that a middle course would be found the best, until experience shall have pointed out the right mode, or (which is not to be expected, because it is denied to mortals) there shall be some *infallible* rule by which we could fore judge events.

Having premised these things, I would fain hope, that liberal allowances will be made for the political opinions of one another; and, instead of those wounding suspicions, and irritating charges, with which some of our Gazettes are so strongly impregnated, and cannot fail, if persevered in, of pushing matters to extremity, and thereby tear the machine asunder, that there might be mutual forbearances and temporizing yieldings *on all sides.* Without these, I do not see how the reins of government are to be managed, or how the Union of the States can be much longer preserved.

How unfortunate would it be, if a fabric so goodly, erected under so many providential circumstances, and in its first stages having acquired such respectability, should, from diversity of sentiments, or internal obstructions to some of the acts of government (for I cannot prevail on myself to believe, that these measures are as yet the deliberate acts of a determined party), should be harrowing our vitals in such a manner as to have brought us to the verge of dissolution. Melancholy thought! But, at the same time that it shows the consequences of diversified opinions, when pushed with too much tenacity, it exhibits evidence also of the necessity of accommodation, and of the propriety of adopting such healing measures as may restore harmony to the discordant members of the Union, and the governing powers of it.

I do not mean to apply this advice to any measures, which are passed, or to any character in particular. I have given it in the same *general* terms to other officers of the government. My earnest wish is, that balsam may be poured into *all* the wounds, which have been given, to prevent them from gangrening, and from those fatal consequences, which the community may sustain if it is withheld. The friends of the Union must wish this. Those, who are not, but wish to see it rended, will be disappointed, and all things, I hope, will go well.

[. . .] You may be assured of the sincere and affectionate regard of Yours. [. . .]

To Thomas Jefferson

MOUNT VERNON, APRIL 12 1793.

Dear Sir,

Your letter of the 7th was brought to me by the last post.

War having actually commenced between France and Great Britain, it behoves the government of this country to use every means in it's power to prevent the citizens thereof from embroiling us with either of those powers, by endeavoring to maintain a strict neutrality. I therefore require, that you will give the subject mature consideration, that such measures as shall be deemed most likely to effect this desirable purpose may be adopted without delay; for I have understood, that vessels are already designated as privateers, and preparing accordingly.

Such other measures as may be necessary for us to pursue against events, which it may not be in our power to avoid or control, you will also think of, and lay them before me at my arrival in Philadelphia; for which place I shall set out to-morrow, but will leave it to the advices, which I may receive to-night by the post, to determine whether it is to be by the most direct route, or by the one I proposed to have come, that is, by Reading, the canals between the rivers of Pennsylvania, Harrisburg, Carlisle, &c. With very great esteem and regard, I am, Dear Sir, Your mo: hble Servt.

To Thomas Jefferson

PHILADELPHIA, JANUARY 1, 1794.

Dear Sir,

I yesterday received, with sincere regret, your resignation of the office of Secretary of State. Since it has been impossible to prevail upon you to forego any longer the indulgence of your desire for private life, the event, however anxious I am to avert it, must be submitted to.

But I cannot suffer you to leave your station without assuring you, that the opinion, which I had formed of your integrity and talents, and which dictated your original nomination, has been confirmed by the fullest experience; and that both have been eminently displayed in the discharge of your duty.

Let a conviction of my most earnest prayers for your happiness accompany you in your retirement; and while I accept, with the warmest thanks, your solicitude for my welfare, I beg you to believe that I always am, dear Sir, &c.

To Henry Lee [Private]

GERMANTOWN, AUGUST 26, 1794.

Dear Sir,

Your favor of the 17th came duly to hand, and I thank you for its communications. As the insurgents in the western counties of this State are resolved, (as far as we have yet been able to learn from the commissioners, who have been sent among them,) to persevere in their rebellious conduct until what they call the excise law is repealed, and acts of oblivion and amnesty are passed, it gives me sincere consolation amidst the regret, with which I am filled by such lawless and outrageous conduct, to find by your letter above mentioned, that it is held in general detestation by the good people of Virginia, and that you are disposed to lend your *personal* aid to subdue this spirit, and to bring those people to a proper sense of their duty.

On this latter point I shall refer you to letters from the War office, and to a private one from Colonel Hamilton, (who, in the absence of the Secretary of War, superintends the *military* duties of that department,) for my sentiments on this occasion.

It is with equal pride and satisfaction I add, that, as far as my information extends, this insurrection is viewed with universal indignation and abhorrence, except by those who have never missed an opportunity by side blows or otherwise to aim their shafts at the general government; and even among these there is not a spirit hardy enough yet *openly* to justify the daring infractions of law and order; but by palliatives are attempting to suspend all proceedings against the insurgents, until Congress shall have decided on the case, thereby intending to gain time, and if possible to make the evil more extensive, more formidable, and of course more difficult to counteract and subdue.

I consider this insurrection as the first *formidable* fruit of the Democratic Societies, brought forth, I believe, too prematurely for their own views, which may contribute to the annihilation of them.

That these societies were instituted by the *artful and designing* members (many of their body I have no doubt mean well, but know little of the real plan,) primarily to sow the seeds of jealousy and distrust among the people of the government, by destroying all confidence in the administration of it, and that these doctrines have been budding and blowing ever since, is not new to any one, who is acquainted with the characters of their leaders, and has been attentive to their manœuvres. I early gave it as my opinion to the confidential characters around me, that, if these societies were not counteracted, (not by prosecutions, the ready way to make them grow stronger,) or did not fall into disesteem from the knowledge of their origin, and the views with which they had been instituted by their father, Genet, for purposes well known to the government, that they would shake the government to its foundation. Time and circumstances have confirmed me in this opinion; and I deeply regret the probable consequences, not as they will affect me personally, for I have not long to act on this theatre, and sure I am that not a man amongst them can be more anxious to put me aside, than I am to sink into the profoundest retirement, but because I see, under a display of popular and fascinating guises, the most diabolical attempts to destroy the best fabric of human government and happiness, that has ever been presented for the acceptance of mankind.

A part of the plan for creating discord is, I perceive, to make me say things of others, and others of me, which have no foundation in truth. The first, in many instances I *know* to be the case; and the second I believe to be so. But truth or falsehood is immaterial to them, provided their objects are promoted.

Under this head may be classed, I conceive, what it is reported I have said of Mr. Henry, and what Mr. Jefferson is reported to have said of me; on both of which, particularly the first, I mean to dilate a little. [. . .]

With respect to the words said to have been uttered by Mr. Jefferson, they would be enigmatical to those, who are acquainted with the characters about me, unless supposed to be spoken ironically; and in that case they are too injurious to me, and have too little foundation in truth, to be ascribed to him. There could not be the trace of doubt on his mind of predilection in mine towards Great Britain or her politics, unless, (which I do not believe,) he has set me down as one of the most deceitful and uncandid men living; because, not only in private conversations between ourselves on this subject, but in my meetings with the confidential servants of the public, he has heard me often, when occasions presented themselves, express very different sentiments, with an energy that could not be mistaken by *any one* present.

Having determined, as far as lay within the power of the executive, to keep this country in a state of neutrality, I have made my public conduct accord with the system; and, whilst so acting as a public character, consistency and propriety as a private man forbid those intemperate expressions in favor of one nation, or to the prejudice of another, which many have indulged themselves in, and I will venture to add, to the embarrassment of government, without producing any good to the country. With very great esteem, &c.

To John Jay

PHILADELPHIA, AUGUST 30, 1794.

My dear Sir,

Your letter of the 23d of June from London, and the duplicate, have both been received; and your safe arrival after so short a passage gave sincere pleasure, as well on private as on public account, to all your friends in this country; and to none in a greater degree, I can venture to assure you, than it did to myself. [. . .]

[. . .] All the difficulties we encounter with the Indians, their hostilities, the murders of helpless women and innocent children along our frontiers, results from the conduct of the Agents of Great Britain in this country. In vain is it then for its administration *in Britain* to disavow having given orders, which will warrant such conduct, whilst their Agents go unpunished; whilst we have a thousand corroborating circumstances, and indeed almost as many evidences, some of which cannot be brought forward, to prove that they are seducing from our alliance, and endeavoring to remove over the line, tribes that have hitherto been kept in peace and friendship with us, at a heavy expence, and who have no cause of complaint, except pretended ones of their creating; whilst they keep in a state of irritation the tribes, who are hostile to us, and are instigating those who know little of us or we of them, to unite in the war against us; and whilst it is an undeniable fact, that they are furnishing the whole with arms, ammunition, clothing, and even provisions, to carry on the war; I might go further, and, if they are not much belied, add men also, in disguise.

Can it be expected, I ask, so long as these things are known in the United States, or at least firmly believed, and suffered with impunity by Great Britain, that there ever will or can be any cordiality between the two countries? I answer, NO! And I will undertake, without the gift of prophecy, to predict, that it will be impossible to keep this country in a state of amity with Great Britain long, if the posts are not surrendered. A knowledge of these being *my* sentiments would have little weight, I am persuaded, with the British administration, nor perhaps with the nation, in effecting the measure; but both may rest satisfied, that, if they want to be in peace with this country, and to enjoy the benefits of its trade &ca. to give up the posts is the only road to it. Withholding them, and the consequences we feel at present continuing, war will be inevitable.

This letter is written to you in extreme haste, whilst the papers respecting this subject I am writing on are copying at the Secretary of States office, to go by express to New York, for a vessel which we have just heard sails to-morrow. You will readily perceive, therefore, I had no time for digesting, and as little for correcting it. I shall only add, that you may be assured always of the sincere friendship and affection of yours, &c.

To Eleanor Parke Custis

PHILADELPHIA, JANUARY 16, 1795.

Dear Nellie:

Your letter, the receipt of which I am now acknowledging, is written correctly and in fair characters, which is an evidence that you command, when you please, a fair hand. Possessed of these advantages, it will be your own fault if you do not avail yourself of them, and attention being paid to the choice of your subjects, you can have nothing to fear from the malignancy of criticism, as your ideas are lively, and your descriptions agreeable. Let me touch a little now on your Georgetown ball, and happy, thrice happy, for the fair who were assembled on the occasion, that there was a man to spare; for had there been 79 ladies and only 78 gentlemen, there might, in the course of the evening, have been some disorder among the caps; notwithstanding the apathy which *one* of the company entertains for the "*youth*" of the present day, and her determination "never to give herself a moment's uneasiness on account of any of them." A hint here; men and women feel the same inclinations towards each other *now* that they always have done, and which they will continue to do until there is a new order of things, and *you,* as others have done, may find, perhaps, that the passions of your sex are easier raised than allayed. Do not therefore boast too soon or too strongly of your insensibility to, or resistance of, its powers. In the composition of the human frame there is a good deal of inflammable matter, however dormant it may lie for a time, and like an intimate acquaintance of yours, when the torch is put to it, *that* which is *within you* may burst into a blaze; for which reason and especially too, as I have entered upon the chapter of advices, I will read you a lecture drawn from this text.

Love is said to be an involuntary passion, and it is, therefore, contended that it cannot be resisted. This is true in part only, for like all things else, when nourished and supplied plentifully with aliment, it is rapid in its progress; but let these be withdrawn and it may be stifled in its birth or much stinted in its growth. For example, a woman (the same may be said of the other sex) all beautiful and accomplished, will, while her hand and heart are undisposed of, turn the heads and set the circle in which she moves on fire. Let her marry, and what is the consequence? The madness *ceases* and all is quiet again. Why? not because there is any diminution in the charms of the lady, but because there is an end of hope. Hence it follows, that love may and therefore ought to be under the guidance of reason, for although we cannot avoid first impressions, we may assuredly place them under guard; and my motives for treating on this subject are to show you, while you remain Eleanor Parke Custis, spinster, and retain the resolution to love with moderation, the propriety of adhering to the latter resolution, at least until you have secured your game, and the way by which it may be accomplished.

When the fire is beginning to kindle, and your heart growing warm, propound these questions to it. Who is this invader? Have I a competent knowledge of him? Is he a man of good character; a man of sense? For, be assured, a sensible woman can never be happy with a fool. What has been his walk in life? Is he a gambler, a spendthrift, or drunkard? Is his fortune sufficient to maintain me in the manner I have been accustomed to live, and my sisters do live, and is he one to whom my friends can have no reasonable objection? If these interrogatories can be satisfactorily answered, there will remain but one more to be asked, that, however, is an important one. Have I sufficient ground to conclude that his affections are engaged by me? Without this the heart of sensibility will struggle against a passion that is not reciprocated—delicacy, custom, or call it by what epithet you will, having precluded all advances on your part. The declaration, without the *most indirect* invitation of yours, must proceed from the man, to render it permanent and valuable, and nothing short of good sense and an easy unaffected conduct can draw the line between prudery and coquetry. It would be no great departure from truth to say, that it rarely happens otherwise than that a thorough-paced coquette dies in celibacy, as a punishment for her attempts to mislead others, by encouraging looks, words, or actions, given for no other purpose than to draw men on to make overtures that they may be rejected.

This day, according to our information, gives a husband to your elder sister, and consummates, it is to be presumed, her fondest desires. The dawn with us is bright, and propitious, I hope, of her future happiness, for a full measure of which she and Mr. Law have my earnest wishes. Compliments and congratulations on this occasion, and best regards are presented to your mamma, Dr. Stuart and family; and every blessing, among which a good husband when you want and deserve one, is bestowed on you by yours, affectionately.

To Alexander Hamilton [Private]

MOUNT VERNON, 29TH JULY 1795.

My dear Sir,

Your letters of the 20th and 21st Instt. found me at this place, after a hot and disagreeable ride.

As the measures of the government respecting the treaty were taken before I left Philadelphia, something more imperious than has yet appeared, must turn up to occasion a change.—Still, it is very desirable to ascertain, if possible, after the paroxysm of the fever is a little abated, what the real temper of the people is, concerning it; for at present the cry against the Treaty is like that against a mad-dog; and every one, in a manner, seems engaged in running it down.—

That it has received the most tortured interpretation, and that the writings against it (which are very industriously circulated) are pregnant of the most abominable mis-representations, admits of no doubt;—yet, there are to be found, so far as my information extends, many well disposed men who conceive, that in the settlement of *old* disputes, a proper regard to reciprocal justice does not appear in the Treaty; whilst others, also well enough affected to the government, are of opinion that to have had *no* commercial treaty would have been better for this country than the restricted one, agreed to; in as much, say they, the nature of our Exports and imports (without any extra, or violent measures) would have forced or led to a more adequate intercourse between the two nations without any of those shackles which the treaty has imposed. In a word, that as our *exports* consist chiefly of *provisions* and *raw materials,* which to the manufacturers in G. Britain, and to their Islands in the West Indies, affords employment and food; they must have had them on *our* terms, if they were not to be obtained on their *own;* whilst the *imports* of this country, offers the best mart for their fabrics; and of course, is the principal support of their manufacturers; but the string which is most played on, because it strikes with most force the popular ear, is the violation, as they term it, of our engagements with France; or in other words the predilection shown by that instrument to G. Britain at the expence of the French nation.

The consequences of which are more to be apprehended than any, which are likely to flow from other causes, as ground of opposition; because, whether the fact is, in *any* degree true or not, it is the interest of the French (whilst the animosity, or jealousies between the two nations exist) to avail themselves of such a spirit to keep *us* and *G. Britain* at variance; and they will in my opinion accordingly do it.—To what *length* their policy may induce them to carry matters, is too much in embryo at this moment to decide:—but I predict much embarrassment to the government therefrom—and in my opinion, too much pains cannot be taken by those who speak, or write, in favor of the treaty, to place this matter in its true light.—

I have seen with pleasure, that a writer in one of the New York papers under the signature of Camillus, has promised to answer,—or rather to defend the treaty—which has been made with G. Britain.—To judge of this work from the first number, which I have seen, I auger well of the performance and shall expect to see the subject handled in a clear, distinct and satisfactory manner:—but if measures are not adopted for its dissemination a few only will derive lights from the knowledge or labor of the author; whilst the opposition pieces will spread their poison in all directions; and Congress, more than probable, will assemble with the unfavorable impressions of their constituents. The difference of conduct between the friends and foes of order and good government, is in nothing more striking than that the latter are always working like bees, to distil their poison;

whilst the former, depending often times *too much* and *too long* upon the sense and good dispositions of the people to work conviction, neglect the means of effecting it.

With sincere esteem & regard I am, your Affecte.

To Thomas Jefferson

MOUNT VERNON, JULY 6, 1796.

Dear Sir,

When I inform you, that your letter of the 19th ultimo went to Philadelphia and returned to this place before it was received by me, it will be admitted, I am persuaded, as an apology for my not having acknowledged the receipt of it sooner.

If I had entertained any suspicions before, that the queries, which have been published in Bache's paper, proceeded from you, the assurances you have given of the contrary would have removed them; but the truth is, I harboured none. I am at no loss to conjecture from what source they flowed, through what channel they were conveyed, and for what purpose they and similar publications appear. They were known to be in the hands of Mr. Parker in the early part of the last session of Congress. They were shown about by Mr. Giles during the session, and they made their public exhibition about the close of it.

Perceiving and probably hearing, that no abuse in the Gazettes would induce me to take notice of anonymous publications against me, those, who were disposed to do me *such friendly offices,* have embraced without restraint every opportunity to weaken the confidence of the people; and, by having the *whole* game in their hands, they have scrupled not to publish things that do not, as well as those which do exist, and to mutilate the latter, so as to make them subserve the purposes which they have in view.

As you have mentioned the subject yourself, it would not be frank, candid, or friendly to conceal, that your conduct has been represented as derogatory from that opinion *I* had conceived you entertained of me; that, to your particular friends and connexions you have described, and they have denounced, me as a person under a dangerous influence; and that, if I would listen *more* to some *other* opinions, all would be well. My answer invariably has been, that I had never discovered any thing in the conduct of Mr. Jefferson to raise suspicions in my mind of his insincerity; that, if he would retrace my public conduct while he was in the administration, abundant proofs would occur to him, that truth and right decisions were the *sole* objects of my pursuit; that there were as many instances within his *own* knowledge of my having decided *against* as *in favor* of the opinions of the person evidently alluded to; and, moreover, that I was no believer in the infallibility of the politics or measures of *any man living.* In short, that I was no party man myself, and the first wish of my heart was, if parties did exist, to reconcile them.

To this I may add, and very truly, that, until within the last year or two, I had no conception that parties would or even could go the length I have been witness to; nor did I believe until lately, that it was within the bounds of probability, hardly within those of possibility, that, while I was using my utmost exertions to establish a national character of our own, independent, as far as our obligations and justice would permit, of every nation of the earth, and wished, by steering a steady course, to preserve this country from the horrors of a desolating war, that I should be accused of being the enemy of one nation, and subject to the influence of another; and, to prove it, that every act of my administration would be tortured, and the grossest and most insidious mis-representations of them be made, by giving one side *only* of a subject, and that too in such exaggerated and indecent terms as could scarcely be applied to a Nero, a notorious defaulter, or even to a common pickpocket. But enough of this. I have already gone further in the expression of my feelings than I intended. [. . .]

Mrs. Washington begs you to accept her best wishes, and with very great esteem, &c.

To Alexander Hamilton [Private]

PHILADELPHIA, 1ST. SEPTR. 1796

My dear Sir,

About the middle of last week I wrote to you; and that it might escape the eye of the inquisitive (for some of my letters have lately been pried into), I took the liberty of putting it under a cover to Mr. Jay.

Since then, revolving on the paper that was enclosed therein, on the various matters it contained, and on the just expression of the advice or recommendation which was given in it, I have regretted that another subject (which in my estimation is of interesting concern to the well-being of this country) was not touched upon also;—I mean education *generally,* as one of the surest means of enlightening and giving just ways of thinking to our citizens, but particularly the establishment of a university; where the youth from *all parts* of the United States might receive the polish of erudition in the arts, sciences, and belles-lettres; and where those who were disposed to run a political course might not only be instructed in the theory and principles, but (this seminary being at the seat of the general government) where the legislature would be in session half the year, and the interests and politics of the nation of course would be discussed, they would lay the surest foundation for the practical part also.

But that which would render it of the highest importance, in my opinion, is, that the juvenal period of life, when friendships are formed, and habits established, that will stick by one; the youth or young men from different parts of the United States would be assembled together, & would by degrees discover that there was not that cause for those jealousies and prejudices which one part of the Union had imbibed against another part:—of course, sentiments of more liberality in the general policy of the country would result from it. What but the mixing of people from different parts of the United States during the war rubbed off these impressions? A century in the ordinary intercourse, would not have accomplished what the Seven years association in Arms did; but that ceasing, prejudices are beginning to revive again, and never will be eradicated so effectually by any other means as the intimate intercourse of characters in early life,—who, in all probability, will be at the head of the councils of this country in a more advanced stage of it. [. . .]

Let me pray you, therefore to introduce a section in the address expressive of these sentiments, and recommendatory of the measure, without any mention, however, of my proposed personal contribution to the plan.

Such a section would come in very properly after the one which relates to our religious obligations, or in a preceding part, as one of the recommendatory measures to counteract the evils arising from geographical discriminations. With affectionate regard, I am always Yours

Farewell Address

UNITED STATES, SEPTEMBER 19, 1796.

Friends, and Fellow-Citizens: The period for a new election of a Citizen, to Administer the Executive government of the United States, being not far distant, and the time actually arrived, when your thoughts must be employed in designating the person, who is to be cloathed with that important trust, it appears to me proper, especially as it may conduce to a more distinct expression of the public voice, that I should now apprise you of the resolution I have formed, to decline being considered among the number of those, out of whom a choice is to be made.

I beg you, at the same time, to do me the justice to be assured, that this resolution has not been taken, without a strict regard to all the considerations appertaining to the relation, which binds a dutiful citizen to his country, and that, in with drawing the tender of service which silence in my situation might imply, I am influenced by no diminution of zeal for your future interest, no deficiency of grateful respect for your past kindness; but am supported by a full conviction that the step is compatible with both.

The acceptance of, and continuance hitherto in, the office to which your Suffrages have twice called me, have been a uniform sacrifice of inclination to the opinion of duty, and to a deference for what appeared to be your desire. I constantly hoped, that it would have been much earlier in my power, consistently with motives, which I was not at liberty to disregard, to return to that retirement, from which I had been reluctantly drawn. The strength of my inclination to do this, previous to the last Election, had even led to the preparation of an address to declare it to you; but mature reflection on the then perplexed and critical posture of our Affairs with foreign Nations, and the unanimous advice of persons entitled to my confidence, impelled me to abandon the idea.

I rejoice, that the state of your concerns, external as well as internal, no longer renders the pursuit of inclination incompatible with the sentiment of duty, or propriety; and am persuaded whatever partiality may be retained for my services, that in the present circumstances of our country, you will not disapprove my determination to retire.

The impressions, with which I first undertook the arduous trust, were explained on the proper occasion. In the discharge of this trust, I will only say, that I have, with good intentions, contributed towards the Organization and Administration of the government, the best exertions of which a very fallible judgment was capable. Not unconscious, in the outset, of the inferiority of my qualifications, experience in my own eyes, perhaps still more in the eyes of others, has strengthened the motives to diffidence of myself; and every day the encreasing weight of years admonishes me more and more, that the shade of retirement is as necessary to me as it will be welcome. Satisfied that if any circumstances have given peculiar value to my services, they were temporary, I have the consolation to believe, that while choice and prudence invite me to quit the political scene, patriotism does not forbid it.

In looking forward to the moment, which is intended to terminate the career of my public life, my feelings do not permit me to suspend the deep acknowledgment of that debt of gratitude wch. I owe to my beloved country, for the many honors it has conferred upon me; still more for the stedfast confidence with which it has supported me; and for the opportunities I have thence enjoyed of manifesting my inviolable attachment, by services faithful and persevering, though in usefulness unequal to my zeal. If benefits have resulted to our country from these services, let it always be remembered to your praise, and as an instructive example in our annals, that, under circumstances in which the Passions agitated in every direction were liable to mislead, amidst appearances sometimes dubious, viscissitudes of fortune often discouraging, in situations in which not unfrequently want of Success has countenanced the spirit of criticism, the constancy of your support was the essential prop of the efforts, and a guarantee of the plans by which they were effected. Profoundly penetrated with this idea, I shall carry it with me to my grave, as a strong incitement to unceasing vows that Heaven may continue to you the choicest tokens of its beneficence; that your Union and brotherly affection may be perpetual; that the free constitution, which is the work of your hands, may be sacredly maintained; that its Administration in every department may be stamped with wisdom and Virtue; that, in fine, the happiness of the people of these States, under the auspices of liberty, may be made complete, by so careful a preservation and so prudent a use of this blessing as will acquire to them the glory of recommending it to the applause, the affection, and adoption of every nation which is yet a stranger to it.

Here, perhaps, I ought to stop. But a solicitude for your welfare, which cannot end but with my life, and the apprehension of danger, natural to that solicitude, urge me on an occasion like the present, to offer to your solemn contemplation, and to recommend to your frequent review, some sentiments; which are the result of much reflection, of no inconsiderable observation, and which appear to me all important to the permanency of your felicity as a People. These will be offered to you with the more freedom, as you can only see in them the disinterested warnings of a parting friend, who can possibly have no personal motive to biass his counsel. Nor can I forget, as an encouragement to it, your endulgent reception of my sentiments on a former and not dissimilar occasion.

Interwoven as is the love of liberty with every ligament of your hearts, no recommendation of mine is necessary to fortify or confirm the attachment.

The Unity of Government which constitutes you one people is also now dear to you. It is justly so; for it is a main Pillar in the Edifice of your real independence, the support of your tranquillity at home, your peace abroad, of your safety, of your prosperity, of that very Liberty which you so highly prize. But as it is easy to foresee, that from different causes and from different quarters, much pains will be taken, many artifices employed, to weaken in your minds the conviction of this truth; as this is the point in your political fortress against which the batteries of internal and external enemies will be most constantly and actively (though often covertly and insidiously) directed, it is of infinite moment, that you should properly estimate the immense value of your national Union to your collective and individual happiness; that you should cherish a cordial, habitual and immoveable attachment to it; accustoming yourselves to think and speak of it as of the Palladium of your political safety and prosperity; watching for its preservation with jealous anxiety; discountenancing whatever may suggest even a suspicion that it can in any event be abandoned, and indignantly frowning upon the first dawning of every attempt to alienate any portion of our Country from the rest, or to enfeeble the sacred ties which now link together the various parts.

For this you have every inducement of sympathy and interest. Citizens by birth or choice, of a common country, that country has a right to concentrate your affections. The name of AMERICAN, which belongs to you, in your national capacity, must always exalt the just pride of Patriotism, more than any appellation derived from local discriminations. With slight shades of difference, you have the same Religion, Manners, Habits and political Principles. You have in a common cause fought and triumphed together. The independence and liberty you possess are the work of joint councils, and joint efforts; of common dangers, sufferings and successes.

But these considerations, however powerfully they address themselves to your sensibility are greatly outweighed by those which apply more immediately to your Interest. Here every portion of our country finds the most commanding motives for carefully guarding and preserving the Union of the whole.

The *North,* in an unrestrained intercourse with the *South,* protected by the equal Laws of a common government, finds in the productions of the latter, great additional resources of Maratime and commercial enterprise and precious materials of manufacturing industry. The *South* in the same Intercourse, benefitting by the Agency of the *North,* sees its agriculture grow and its commerce expand. Turning partly into its own channels the seamen of the *North,* it finds its particular navigation envigorated; and while it contributes, in different ways, to nourish and increase the general mass of the National navigation, it looks forward to the protection of a Maratime strength, to which itself is unequally adapted. The *East,* in a like intercourse with the *West,* already finds, and in the progressive improvement of interior communications, by land and water, will more and more find a valuable vent for the commodities which it brings from abroad, or manufactures at home. The *West* derives from the *East* supplies requisite to its growth and comfort, and what is perhaps of still greater consequence, it must of necessity owe the *secure* enjoyment of indispensable *outlets* for its own productions to the weight, influence, and the future Maritime strength of the Atlantic side of the Union, directed by an indissoluble community of Interest as *one Nation*. Any other tenure by which the *West* can hold this essential advantage, whether derived from its own seperate strength, or from an apostate and unnatural connection with any foreign Power, must be intrinsically precarious.

While then every part of our country thus feels an immediate and particular Interest in Union, all the parts combined cannot fail to find in the united mass of means and efforts greater strength, greater resource, proportionably greater security from external danger, a less frequent interruption of their Peace by foreign Nations; and, what is of inestimable value! they must derive from Union an exemption from those broils and Wars between themselves, which so frequently afflict neighbouring countries, not tied together by the same government; which their own rivalships alone would be sufficient to produce, but which opposite foreign alliances, attachments and intriegues would stimulate and imbitter. Hence likewise they will avoid the necessity of those overgrown Military establishments, which under any form of Government are inauspicious to liberty, and which are to be regarded as particularly hostile to Republican Liberty: In this sense it is, that your Union ought to be considered as a main prop of your liberty, and that the love of the one ought to endear to you the preservation of the other.

These considerations speak a persuasive language to every reflecting and virtuous mind, and exhibit the continuance of the UNION as a primary object of Patriotic desire. Is there a doubt, whether a common government can embrace so large a sphere? Let experience solve it. To listen to mere speculation in such a case were criminal. We are authorized to hope that a proper organization of the whole, with the auxiliary agency of governments for the respective Sub divisions, will afford a happy issue to the experiment. 'Tis well worth a fair and full experiment With such powerful and obvious motives to Union, affecting all parts of our country, while experience shall not have demonstrated its impracticability, there will always be reason, to distrust the patriotism of those, who in any quarter may endeavor to weaken its bands.

In contemplating the causes wch. may disturb our Union, it occurs as matter of serious concern, that any ground should have been furnished for characterizing parties by *Geographical* discriminations: *Northern* and *Southern; Atlantic* and *Western;* whence designing men may endeavour to excite a belief that there is a real difference of local interests and views. One of the expedients of Party to acquire influence, within particular districts, is to misrepresent the opinions and aims of other Districts. You cannot shield yourselves too much against the jealousies and heart burnings which spring from these misrepresentations. They tend to render Alien to each other those who ought to be bound together by fraternal affection. The Inhabitants of our Western country have lately had a useful lesson on this head. They have seen, in the Negociation by the Executive, and in the unanimous ratification by the Senate, of the Treaty with Spain, and in the universal satisfaction at that event, throughout the United States, a decisive proof how unfounded were the suspicions propagated among them of a policy in the General Government and in the Atlantic States unfriendly to their Interests in regard to the MISSISSIPPI. They have been witnesses to the formation of two Treaties, that with G: Britain and that with Spain, which secure to them every thing they could desire, in respect to our Foreign relations, towards confirming their prosperity. Will it not be their wisdom to rely for the preservation of these advantages on the UNION by wch. they were procured? Will they not henceforth be deaf to those advisers, if such there are, who would sever them from their Brethren and connect them with Aliens?

To the efficacy and permanency of Your Union, a Government for the whole is indispensable. No Alliances however strict between the parts can be an adequate substitute. They must inevitably experience the infractions and interruptions which all Alliances in all times have experienced. Sensible of this momentous truth, you have improved upon your first essay, by the adoption of a Constitution of Government, better calculated than your former for an intimate Union, and for the efficacious management of your common concerns. This government, the offspring of our own choice uninfluenced and unawed, adopted upon full investigation and mature deliberation, completely free in its principles, in the distribution of its powers, uniting security with energy, and containing within itself a provision for its own amendment, has a just claim to your confidence and your support. Respect for its authority, compliance with its Laws, acquiescence in its measures, are duties enjoined by the fundamental maxims of true Liberty. The basis of our political systems is the right of the people to make and to alter their Constitutions of Government. But the Constitution which at any time exists, 'till changed by an explicit and authentic act of the whole People, is sacredly obligatory upon all. The very idea of the power and the right of the

People to establish Government presupposes the duty of every Individual to obey the established Government.

All obstructions to the execution of the Laws, all combinations and Associations, under whatever plausible character, with the real design to direct, controul counteract, or awe the regular deliberation and action of the Constituted authorities are distructive of this fundamental principle and of fatal tendency. They serve to organize faction, to give it an artificial and extraordinary force; to put in the place of the delegated will of the Nation, the will of a party; often a small but artful and enterprizing minority of the Community; and, according to the alternate triumphs of different parties, to make the public administration the Mirror of the ill concerted and incongruous projects of faction, rather than the organ of consistent and wholesome plans digested by common councils and modefied by mutual interests. However combinations or Associations of the above description may now and then answer popular ends, they are likely, in the course of time and things, to become potent engines, by which cunning, ambitious and unprincipled men will be enabled to subvert the Power of the People, and to usurp for themselves the reins of Government; destroying afterwards the very engines which have lifted them to unjust dominion.

Towards the preservation of your Government and the permanency of your present happy state, it is requisite, not only that you steadily discountenance irregular oppositions to its acknowledged authority, but also that you resist with care the spirit of innovation upon its principles however specious the pretexts. One method of assault may be to effect, in the forms of the Constitution, alterations which will impair the energy of the system, and thus to undermine what cannot be directly overthrown. In all the changes to which you may be invited, remember that time and habit are at least as necessary to fix the true character of Governments, as of other human institutions; that experience is the surest standard, by which to test the real tendency of the existing Constitution of a country; that facility in changes upon the credit of mere hypotheses and opinion exposes to perpetual change, from the endless variety of hypotheses and opinion: and remember, especially, that for the efficient management of your common interests, in a country so extensive as ours, a Government of as much vigour as is consistent with the perfect security of Liberty is indispensable. Liberty itself will find in such a Government, with powers properly distributed and adjusted, its surest Guardian. It is indeed little else than a name, where the Government is too feeble to withstand the enterprises of faction, to confine each member of the Society within the limits prescribed by the laws and to maintain all in the secure and tranquil enjoyment of the rights of person and property.

I have already intimated to you the danger of Parties in the State, with particular reference to the founding of them on Geographical discriminations. Let me now take a more comprehensive view, and warn you in the most solemn manner against the baneful effects of the Spirit of Party, generally.

This spirit, unfortunately, is inseperable from our nature, having its root in the strongest passions of the human Mind. It exists under different shapes in all Governments, more or less stifled, controuled, or repressed; but, in those of the popular form it is seen in its greatest rankness and is truly their worst enemy.

The alternate domination of one faction over another, sharpened by the spirit of revenge natural to party dissention, which in different ages and countries has perpetrated the most horrid enormities, is itself a frightful despotism. But this leads at length to a more formal and permanent despotism. The disorders and miseries, which result, gradually incline the minds of men to seek security and repose in the absolute power of an individual: and sooner or later the chief of some prevailing faction more able or more fortunate than his competitors, turns this disposition to the purposes of his own elevation, on the ruins of Public Liberty.

Without looking forward to an extremity of this kind (which nevertheless ought not to be entirely out of sight) the common and continual mischiefs of the spirit of Party are sufficient to make it the interest and the duty of a wise People to discourage and restrain it.

It serves always to distract the Public Councils and enfeeble the Public administration. It agitates the Community with ill founded jealousies and false alarms, kindles the animosity of one part against another, foments occasionally riot and insurrection. It opens the door to foreign influence and corruption, which find a facilitated access to the government itself through the channels of party passions. Thus the policy and the will of one country, are subjected to the policy and will of another.

There is an opinion that parties in free countries are useful checks upon the Administration of the Government and serve to keep alive the spirit of Liberty. This within certain limits is probably true, and in Governments of a Monarchical cast Patriotism may look with endulgence, if not with favour, upon the spirit of party. But in those of the popular character, in Governments purely elective, it is a spirit not to be encouraged. From their natural tendency, it is certain there will always be enough of that spirit for every salutary purpose. And there being constant danger of excess, the effort ought to be, by force of public opinion, to mitigate and assuage it. A fire not to be quenched; it demands a uniform vigilance to prevent its bursting into a flame, lest instead of warming it should consume.

It is important, likewise, that the habits of thinking in a free Country should inspire caution in those entrusted with its administration, to confine themselves within their respective Constitutional spheres; avoiding in the exercise of the Powers of one department to encroach upon another. The spirit of encroachment tends to consolidate the powers of all the departments in one, and thus to create whatever the form of government, a real despotism. A just estimate of that love of power, and proneness to abuse it, which predominates in the human heart is sufficient to satisfy us of the truth of this position. The necessity of reciprocal checks in the exercise of political power; by dividing and distributing it into different depositories, and constituting each the Guardian of the Public Weal against invasions by the others, has been evinced by experiments ancient and modern; some of them in our country and under our own eyes. To preserve them must be as necessary as to institute them. If in the opinion of the People, the distribution or modification of the Constitutional powers be in any particular wrong, let it be corrected by an amendment in the way which the Constitution designates. But let there be no change by usurpation; for though this, in one instance, may be the instrument of good, it is the customary weapon by which free governments are destroyed. The precedent must always greatly overbalance in permanent evil any partial or transient benefit which the use can at any time yield.

Of all the dispositions and habits which lead to political prosperity, Religion and morality are indispensable supports. In vain would that man claim the tribute of Patriotism, who should labour to subvert these great Pillars of human happiness, these firmest props of the duties of Men and citizens. The mere Politician, equally with the pious man ought to respect and to cherish them. A volume could not trace all their connections with private and public felicity. Let it simply be asked where is the security for property, for reputation, for life, if the sense of religious obligation *desert* the oaths, which are the instruments of investigation in Courts of Justice? And let us with caution indulge the supposition, that morality can be maintained without religion. Whatever may be conceded to the influence of refined education on minds of peculiar structure, reason and experience both forbid us to expect that National morality can prevail in exclusion of religious principle.

'Tis substantially true, that virtue or morality is a necessary spring of popular government. The rule indeed extends with more or less force to every species of free Government. Who that is a sincere friend to it, can look with indifference upon attempts to shake the foundation of the fabric?

Promote then as an object of primary importance, Institutions for the general diffusion of knowledge. In proportion as the structure of a government gives force to public opinion, it is essential that public opinion should be enlightened.

As a very important source of strength and security, cherish public credit. One method of preserving it is to use it as sparingly as possible: avoiding occasions of expence by cultivating peace, but remembering also that timely disbursements to prepare for danger frequently prevent much greater disbursements to repel it; avoiding likewise the accumulation of debt, not only by shunning occasions of expence, but by vigorous exertions in time of Peace to discharge the Debts which unavoidable wars may have occasioned, not ungenerously throwing upon posterity the burthen which we ourselves ought to bear. The execution of these maxims belongs to your Representatives, but it is necessary that public opinion should cooperate. To facilitate to them the performance of their duty, it is essential that you should practically bear in mind, that towards the payment of debts there must be Revenue; that to have Revenue there must be taxes; that no taxes can be devised which are not more or less inconvenient and unpleasant; that the intrinsic embarrassment inseperable from the selection of the proper objects (which is always a choice of difficulties) ought to be a decisive motive for a candid construction of the Conduct of the Government in making it, and for a spirit of acquiescence in the measures for obtaining Revenue which the public exigencies may at any time dictate.

Observe good faith and justice towds. all Nations. Cultivate peace and harmony with all. Religion and morality enjoin this conduct; and can it be that good policy does not equally enjoin it? It will be worthy of a free, enlightened, and, at no distant period, a great Nation, to give to mankind the magnanimous and too novel example of a People always guided by an exalted justice and benevolence. Who can doubt that in the course of time and things the fruits of such a plan would richly repay any temporary advantages wch. might be lost by a steady adherence to it? Can it be, that Providence has not connected the permanent felicity of a Nation with its virtue? The experiment, at least, is recommended by every sentiment which ennobles human Nature. Alas! is it rendered impossible by its vices?

In the execution of such a plan nothing is more essential than that permanent, inveterate antipathies against particular Nations and passionate attachments for others should be excluded; and that in place of them just and amicable feelings towards all should be cultivated. The Nation, which indulges towards another an habitual hatred, or an habitual fondness, is in some degree a slave. It is a slave to its animosity or to its affection, either of which is sufficient to lead it astray from its duty and its interest. Antipathy in one Nation against another, disposes each more readily to offer insult and injury, to lay hold of slight causes of umbrage, and to be haughty and intractable, when accidental or trifling occasions of dispute occur. Hence frequent collisions, obstinate envenomed and bloody contests. The Nation, prompted by illwill and resentment sometimes impels to War the Government, contrary to the best calculations of policy. The Government sometimes participates in the national propensity, and adopts through passion what reason would reject; at other times, it makes the animosity of the Nation subservient to projects of hostility instigated by pride, ambition and other sinister and pernicious motives. The peace often, sometimes perhaps the Liberty, of Nations has been the victim.

So likewise, a passionate attachment of one Nation for another produces a variety of evils. Sympathy for the favourite nation, facilitating the illusion of an imaginary common interest, in cases where no real common interest exists, and infusing into one the enmities of the other, betrays the former into a participation in the quarrels and Wars of the latter, without adequate inducement or justification: It leads also to concessions to the favourite Nation of priviledges denied to others, which is apt doubly to injure the Nation making the concessions; by unnecessarily parting with what ought to have been retained; and by exciting jealousy, ill will, and a disposition to retaliate, in the parties from whom eql. priviledges are withheld: And it gives to ambitious, corrupted, or deluded citizens (who devote themselves to the favourite Nation) facility to betray, or sacrifice the interests of their own country, without odium, sometimes even with popularity; gilding with the appearances of a virtuous sense of obligation a commendable deference for public opinion, or a laudable zeal for public good, the base or foolish compliances of ambition corruption or infatuation.

As avenues to foreign influence in innumerable ways, such attachments are particularly alarming to the truly enlightened and independent Patriot. How many opportunities do they afford to tamper with domestic factions, to practice the arts of seduction, to mislead public opinion, to influence or awe the public Councils! Such an attachment of a small or weak, towards a great and powerful Nation, dooms the former to be the satellite of the latter.

Against the insidious wiles of foreign influence, (I conjure you to believe me fellow citizens) the jealousy of a free people ought to be *constantly* awake; since history and experience prove that foreign influence is one of the most baneful foes of Republican Government. But that jealousy to be useful must be impartial; else it becomes the instrument of the very influence to be avoided, instead of a defence against it. Excessive partiality for one foreign nation and excessive dislike of another, cause those whom they actuate to see danger only on one side, and serve to veil and even second the arts of influence on the other. Real Patriots, who may resist the intrigues of the favourite, are liable to become suspected and odious; while its tools and dupes usurp the applause and confidence of the people, to surrender their interests.

The Great rule of conduct for us, in regard to foreign Nations is in extending our commercial relations to have with them as little *political* connection as possible. So far as we have already formed engagements let them be fulfilled, with perfect good faith. Here let us stop.

Europe has a set of primary interests, which to us have none, or a very remote relation. Hence she must be engaged in frequent controversies, the causes of which are essentially foreign to our concerns. Hence therefore it must be unwise in us to implicate ourselves, by artificial ties, in the ordinary vicissitudes of her politics, or the ordinary combinations and collisions of her friendships, or enmities:

Our detached and distant situation invites and enables us to pursue a different course. If we remain one People, under an efficient government, the period is not far off, when we may defy material injury from external annoyance; when we may take such an attitude as will cause the neutrality we may at any time resolve upon to be scrupulously respected; when belligerent nations, under the impossibility of making acquisitions upon us, will not lightly hazard the giving us provocation; when we may choose peace or war, as our interest guided by our justice shall Counsel.

Why forego the advantages of so peculiar a situation? Why quit our own to stand upon foreign ground? Why, by interweaving our destiny with that of any part of Europe, entangle our peace and prosperity in the toils of European Ambition, Rivalship, Interest, Humour or Caprice?

'Tis our true policy to steer clear of permanent Alliances, with any portion of the foreign world. So far, I mean, as we are now at liberty to do it, for let me not be understood as capable of patronising infidility to existing engagements (I hold the maxim no less applicable to public than to private affairs, that honesty is always the best policy). I repeat it therefore, let those engagements be observed in their genuine sense. But in my opinion, it is unnecessary and would be unwise to extend them.

Taking care always to keep ourselves, by suitable establishments, on a respectably defensive posture, we may safely trust to temporary alliances for extraordinary emergencies.

Harmony, liberal intercourse with all Nations, are recommended by policy, humanity and interest. But even our Commercial policy should hold an equal and impartial hand: neither seeking nor granting exclusive favours or preferences; consulting the natural course of things; diffusing and deversifying by gentle means the streams of Commerce, but forcing nothing; establishing with Powers so disposed; in order to give to trade a stable course, to define the rights of our Merchants, and to enable the Government to support them; conventional rules of intercourse, the best that present circumstances and mutual opinion will permit, but temporary, and liable to be from time to time abandoned or varied, as experience and circumstances shall dictate; constantly keeping in view, that 'tis folly in one Nation to look for disinterested favors from another; that it must pay with a portion of its Independence for whatever it may accept under that character; that by such acceptance, it may place itself in the condition of having given equivalents for nominal favours and yet of being reproached with ingratitude for not giving more. There can be no greater error than to expect, or calculate upon real favours from Nation to Nation. 'Tis an illusion which experience must cure, which a just pride ought to discard.

In offering to you, my Countrymen these counsels of an old and affectionate friend, I dare not hope they will make the strong and lasting impression, I could wish; that they will controul the usual current of the passions, or prevent our Nation from running the course which has hitherto marked the Destiny of Nations: But if I may even flatter myself, that they may be productive of some partial benefit, some occasional good; that they may now and then recur to moderate the fury of party spirit, to warn against the mischiefs of foreign Intriegue, to guard against the Impostures of pretended patriotism; this hope will be a full recompence for the solicitude for your welfare, by which they have been dictated.

How far in the discharge of my Official duties, I have been guided by the principles which have been delineated, the public Records and other evidences of my conduct must Witness to You and to the world. To myself, the assurance of my own conscience is, that I have at least believed myself to be guided by them.

In relation to the still subsisting War in Europe, my Proclamation of the 22d. of April 1793 is the index to my Plan. Sanctioned by your approving voice and by that of Your Representatives in both Houses of Congress, the spirit of that measure has continually governed me; uninfluenced by any attempts to deter or divert me from it.

After deliberate examination with the aid of the best lights I could obtain I was well satisfied that our Country, under all the circumstances of the case, had a right to take, and was bound in duty and interest, to take a Neutral position. Having taken it, I determined, as far as should depend upon me, to maintain it, with moderation, perseverence and firmness.

The considerations, which respect the right to hold this conduct, it is not necessary on this occasion to detail. I will only observe, that according to my understanding of the matter, that right, so far from being denied by any of the Belligerent Powers has been virtually admitted by all.

The duty of holding a Neutral conduct may be inferred, without any thing more, from the obligation which justice and humanity impose on every Nation, in cases in which it is free to act, to maintain inviolate the relations of Peace and amity towards other Nations.

The inducements of interest for observing that conduct will best be referred to your own reflections and experience. With me, a predominant motive has been to endeavour to gain time to our country to settle and mature its yet recent institutions, and to progress without interruption, to that degree of strength and consistency, which is necessary to give it, humanly speaking, the command of its own fortunes.

Though in reviewing the incidents of my Administration, I am unconscious of intentional error, I am nevertheless too sensible of my defects not to think it probable that I may have committed many errors. Whatever they may be I fervently beseech the Almighty to avert or mitigate the evils to which they may tend. I shall also carry with me the hope that my Country will never cease to view them with indulgence; and that after forty five years of my life dedicated to its Service, with an upright zeal, the faults of incompetent abilities will be consigned to oblivion, as myself must soon be to the Mansions of rest.

Relying on its kindness in this as in other things, and actuated by that fervent love towards it, which is so natural to a Man, who views in it the native soil of himself and his progenitors for several Generations; I anticipate with pleasing expectation that retreat, in which I promise myself to realize, without alloy, the sweet enjoyment of partaking, in the midst of my fellow Citizens, the benign influence of good Laws under a free Government, the ever favourite object of my heart, and the happy reward, as I trust, of our mutual cares, labours and dangers.

To James McHenry [Private]

MOUNT VERNON, APRIL 3, 1797.

Dear Sir,

Your letter of the 24th ultimo has been duly received, and I thank you for the information given in it. Let me pray you to have the goodness to communicate to me occasionally such matters, as are interesting and not contrary to the rules of your official duty to disclose. We get so many details in the Gazettes, and of such different complexions, that it is impossible to know what credence to give to any of them.

The conduct of the French government is so much beyond calculation, and so unaccountable upon any principle of justice, or even of that sort of policy, which is familiar to plain understandings, that I shall not *now* puzzle my brains in attempting to develope the motives of it.

We got home without accident, and found the roads drier and better than I ever travelled them at that season of the year. The attentions we met with on our journey were very flattering, and to some, whose minds are differently formed from mine, would have been highly relished; but I avoided in every instance, where I had any previous knowledge of the intention, and could by earnest entreaties prevail, all parade and escorts. Mrs. Washington took a violent cold in Philadelphia, which hangs upon her still; but it is not as bad as it did.

I find myself in the situation nearly of a new beginner; for, although I have not houses to build (except one, which I must erect for the accommodation and security of my military, civil, and private papers, which are voluminous and may be interesting), yet I have not one or scarcely any thing else about me, that does not require considerable repairs. In a word, I am already surrounded by joiners, masons, and painters &ca &ca. and such is my anxiety to get out of their hands, that I have scarcely a room to put a friend into, or to set in myself, without the music of hammers, or the odoriferous smell of paint. [. . .]

Mrs. Washington and Miss Custis thank you for your kind remembrance of them, and join in best regards for Mrs. McHenry and yourself, with, dear Sir, etc.

To Lawrence Lewis

MOUNT VERNON, AUGUST 4, 1797.

Dear Sir: Your letter of the 24th ulto has been received, and I am sorry to hear of the loss of your servant; but it is my opinion these elopements will be MUCH MORE, before they are LESS frequent: and that the persons making them should never be retained, if they are recovered, as they are sure to contaminate and discontent others. I wish from my soul that the Legislature of this State could see the policy of a gradual Abolition of Slavery; It would prevt. much future mischief. [. . .]

To Sally Cary Fairfax

MOUNT VERNON, MAY 16, 1798.

My Dear Madam,

Five and twenty years, nearly, have passed away, since I have considered myself as the permanent resident at this place, or have been in a situation to endulge myself in a familiar intercourse with my friends by letter or otherwise.

During this period, so many important events have occurred, and such changes in men and things have taken place, as the compass of a letter would give you but an inadequate idea of. None of which events, however, nor all of them together, have been able to eradicate from my mind the recollection of those happy moments, the happiest in my life, which I have enjoyed in your company.

Worn out in a manner by the toils of my past labor, I am again seated under my Vine and Fig tree, and wish I could add, that there are none to make us afraid; but those, whom we have been accustomed to call our good friends and allies, are endeavouring, if not to make us afraid, yet to despoil us of our property, and are provoking us to acts of self-defence, which may lead to war. What will be the result of such measures, time, that faithful expositor of all things, must disclose. My wish is to spend the remainder of my days, which cannot be many, in rural amusements, free from those cares from which public responsibility is never exempt.

Before the war, and even while it existed, although I was eight years from home at one stretch, except the *en passant visits* made to it on my march to and from the siege of Yorktown, I made considerable additions to my dwelling house, and alterations in my offices and gardens; but the dilapidation occasioned by time, and those neglects, which are co-extensive with the absence of proprietors, have occupied as much of my time within the last twelve months in repairing them, as at any former period in the same space; and it is matter of sore regret, when I cast my eyes towards Belvoir, which I often do, to reflect, that the former inhabitants of it, with whom we lived in such harmony and friendship, no longer reside there, and that the ruins can only be viewed as the memento of former pleasures. Permit me to add, that I have wondered often, your nearest relations being in this country, that you should not prefer spending the evening of your life among them, rather than close the sublunary scene in a foreign country, numerous as your acquaintances may be, and sincere as the friendships you may have formed.

A century hence, if this country keeps united (and it is surely its policy and interest to do it), will produce a city, though not as large as London, yet of a magnitude inferior to few others in Europe, on the banks of the Potomac, where one is now establishing for the permanent seat of the government of the United States, between Alexandria and Georgetown, on the Maryland side of the river; a situation not excelled, for commanding prospect, good water, salubrious air, and safe harbour, by any in the world; and where elegant buildings are erecting and in forwardness for the reception of Congress in the year 1800.

Alexandria, within the last seven years, since the establishment of the general government, has increased in buildings, in population, in the improvement of its streets by well executed pavements, and in the extension of its wharves, in a manner of which you can have very little idea. This show of prosperity, you will readily conceive, is owing to its commerce. The extension of *that trade* is occasioned, in a great degree, by the opening of the inland navigation of the Potomac River, now cleared to Fort Cumberland, upwards of two hundred miles, and by a similar attempt to accomplish the like up the Shenandoah, one hundred and fifty miles more. In a word, if this country can steer clear of European politics, stand firm on its bottom, and be wise and temperate in its government, it bids fair to be one of the greatest and happiest nations in the world.

Knowing that Mrs. Washington is about to give an account of the changes, which have happened in the neighbourhood and in our own family, I shall not trouble you with a repetition of them. [. . .]

To John Adams, President of the United States

MOUNT VERNON, JULY 13, 1798.

Dear Sir,

I had the honor, on the evening of the 11th instant, to receive from the hands of the Secretary of War your favor of the 7th, announcing that you had, with the advice and consent of the Senate, appointed me "Lieutenant General and Commander in Chief of all the Armies raised or to be raised for the Service of the United States."

I cannot express how greatly affected I am at this new proof of public confidence, and the highly flattering manner in which you have been pleased to make the communication; at the same time I must not conceal from you my earnest wish, that the choice had fallen on a man less declined in years, and better qualified to encounter the usual vicissitudes of war.

You know, Sir, what calculations I had made relative to the probable course of events on my retiring from Office, and the determination I had consoled myself with, of closing the remnant of my days in my present peaceful abode. You will, therefore, be at no loss to conceive and appreciate the sensations I must have experienced, to bring my mind to any conclusion that would pledge me, at so late a period of life, to leave Scenes I sincerely love, to enter upon the boundless field of public action, incessant trouble, and high responsibility.

It was not possible for me to remain ignorant of, or indifferent to, recent transactions. The conduct of the Directory of France towards our Country, their insidious hostility to its government, their various practices to withdraw the affections of the People from it, the evident tendency of their arts and those of their Agents to countenance and invigorate opposition, their disregard of solemn treaties and the laws of nations, their war upon our defenceless commerce, their treatment of our Minister of Peace, and their demands amounting to tribute, could not fail to excite in me corresponding sentiments with those my countrymen have so generally expressed in their affectionate addresses to you. Believe me, Sir, no one can more cordially approve of the wise and prudent measures of your Administration. They ought to inspire universal confidence, and will no doubt, combined with the state of things, call from Congress such laws and means, as will enable you to meet the full force and extent of the crisis.

Satisfied, therefore, that you have sincerely wished and endeavored to avert war, and exhausted to the last drop the cup of reconciliation, we can with pure hearts appeal to Heaven for the justice of our cause, and may confidently trust the final result to that kind Providence, who has heretofore and so often signally favored the people of these United States.

Thinking, in this manner, and feeling how incumbent it is upon every person of every description to contribute at all times to his countrys welfare, and especially in a moment like the present, when every thing we hold dear is so seriously threatened, I have finally determined to accept the Commission of Commander in Chief of the Armies of the United States; with the reserve only, that I shall not be called into the field until the Army is in a situation to require my presence, or it becomes indispensable by the urgency of circumstances.

In making this reservation I beg it to be understood, that I do not mean to withhold any assistance to arrange and organize the Army, which you may think I can afford. I take the liberty also to mention, that I must decline having my acceptance considered as drawing after it any immediate charge upon the public, or that I can receive any emoluments annexed to the appointment, before entering into a Situation to incur expence.

The Secretary of War being anxious to return to the seat of Government, I have detained him no longer than was necessary to a full communication upon the several points he had in charge. With very great respect and consideration, I had the honor, &c.

The Will of George Washington

In the name of God amen.

I GEORGE WASHINGTON of Mount Vernon, a citizen of the United States and lately President of the same do make ordain and declare this Instrument, which is written with my own hand and every page thereof subscribed with my name to be my last Will & Testament, revoking all others.

Imprimus. All my debts, of which there are but few, and none of magnitude, are to be punctually and speedily paid, and the legacies hereinafter bequeathed are to be discharged as soon as circumstances will permit, and in the manner directed.

ITEM. To my dearly beloved wife, Martha Washington I give and bequeath the use, profit and benefit of my whole Estate, real and personal, for the term of her natural life, except such parts thereof as are specially disposed of hereafter: My improved lot in the Town of Alexandria, situated on Pitt and Cameron Streets, I give to her & her heirs forever, as I also do my household and kitchen furniture of every sort and kind, with the liquors and groceries which may be on hand at the time of my decease, to be used and disposed of as she may think proper.

ITEM. Upon the decease of wife it is my Will and desire, that all the Slaves which I hold in *my own right* shall receive their freedom—To emancipate them during her life, would tho earnestly wished by me, be attended with such insuperable difficulties, on account of their intermixture by marriages with the Dower Negroes as to excite the most painful sensations—if not disagreeable consequences from the latter while both descriptions are in the occupancy of the same proprietor; it not being in my power under the tenure by which the Dower Negroes are held to manumit them—And whereas among those who will receive freedom according to this devise there may be some who from old age, or bodily infirmities & others who on account of their infancy, that will be unable to support themselves, it is my Will and desire that all who come under the first and second description shall be comfortably clothed and fed by my heirs while they live and that such of the latter description as have no parents living, or if living are unable, or unwilling to provide for them, shall be bound by the Court until they shall arrive at the age of twenty five years, and in cases where no record can be produced whereby their ages can be ascertained, the Judgment of the Court upon its own view of the subject shall be adequate and final.—The negroes thus bound are (by their Masters and Mistresses) to be taught to read and write and to be brought up to some useful occupation, agreeably to the Laws of the Commonwealth of Virginia, providing for the support of orphan and other poor children. And I do hereby expressly forbid the sale or transportation out of the said Commonwealth of any Slave I may die possessed of, under any pretence, whatsoever. And I do moreover most pointedly, and most solemnly enjoin it upon my Executors hereafter named, or the survivors of them to see that *this* clause respecting Slaves and every part thereof be religiously fulfilled at the Epoch at which it is directed to take place without evasion neglect or delay, after the crops which may then be on the ground are harvested, particularly as it respects the aged and infirm; Seeing that a regular and permanent fund be established for their support so long as there are subjects requiring it; not trusting to the uncertain provisions to be made by individuals.—And to my Mulatto man, William (calling himself William Lee) I give immediate freedom or if he should prefer it (on account of the accidents which have befallen him and which have rendered him incapable of walking or of any active employment) to remain in the situation he now is, it shall be optional in him to do so—In either case however I allow him an annuity of thirty dollars during his natural life which shall be independent of the victuals and cloaths he has been accustomed to receive; if he chuses the last alternative, but in full with his freedom, if he prefers the first, and this I give him as a testimony of my sense of his attachment to me and for his faithful services during the Revolutionary War.

ITEM—To the Trustees, (Governors or by whatsoever other name they may be designated) of the Academy in the Town of Alexandria, I give and bequeath, in Trust, Four thousand dollars, or in other words twenty of the shares which I hold in the Bank of Alexandria towards the support of a Free School, established at, and annexed to the said Academy for the purpose of educating such orphan children, or the children of such other poor and indigent persons as are unable to accomplish it with their own means, and who in the judgment of the Trustees of the said Seminary, are best entitled to the benefit of this donation—The aforesaid twenty shares I give and bequeath in perpetuity—the dividends only of which are to be drawn for and applied by the said Trustees for the time being, for the uses above mentioned, the stock to remain entire and untouched, unless indications of a failure of the said Bank should be so apparent or discontinuance thereof should render a removal of this fund necessary; in either of these cases the amount of the stock here devised is to be vested in some other bank or public institution whereby the interest may with regularity and certainty be drawn and applied as above.—And to prevent misconception, my meaning is, and is hereby declared to be that these twenty shares are in lieu of and not in addition to the Thousand pounds given by a missive letter some years ago in consequence whereof an annuity of fifty pounds has since been paid towards the support of this institution. [. . .]

ALEXANDER HAMILTON
1755–1804

Introduction

Aggressively seizing the initiative, George Washington's thirty-four-year-old secretary of the treasury drafted reports and proposals on public credit, a national bank, and manufacturing. Disdaining incremental change, Alexander Hamilton's goal was nothing less than transforming the country's economic and industrial landscape purposefully, radically, and lastingly.

He was not going to let a little matter like the Constitution get in his way. The Constitution had given full control for fiscal and commercial matters to Congress, but Hamilton reversed the intention of the Framers, determined to empower the executive branch. "Energy in the executive is a leading character in the definition of good government," he had written in *Federalist* No. 70. "It is essential to the protection of the community against foreign attacks: It is not less essential to the steady administration of the laws, to the protection of property [and] to the security of liberty." Unlike so many sleepy and stagnant administrations in the nineteenth century, Washington's government, thanks to Hamilton, bubbled over with innovation, experimentation, and controversy.

Hamilton's Report on Public Credit was a typically imaginative initiative—a plan for the new federal government to establish its credit-worthiness by assuming the nation's revolutionary debts as well as the debts of the states. "A national debt," he had commented in 1781, is "a national blessing."[1]

The most controversial of Hamilton's ideas was his proposal for a national bank. The Bank of the United States would service the national debt, assist in collecting taxes, and make loans to major private enterprises and to the government itself, and the Bank's certificates of indebtedness would circulate as a kind of supplementary currency. At the heart of the plan was a marriage of government and private bankers: Hamilton's aim was to fund major infrastructure and industrial projects while giving wealthy businessmen a vested interest in the nation's political and financial strength.

Hamilton presented his Report on Manufactures in response to Congress's request for a plan to promote industry and free the United States from dependence on other nations for essentials, especially military supplies. After almost two years of evaluating the nation's capacities and needs, Hamilton in December 1791 unveiled his plan to guarantee the nation's industrial power for decades to come. No believer in laissez-faire economics, which he impatiently dismissed as a "wild speculative paradox,"[2] Hamilton called for the government to regulate, plan, and stimulate economic development. He proposed governmental support and subsidies for business, awards for inventions, a variety of internal improvements, such as interstate roads and canals, and the encouragement of the immigration of manufacturers and workmen—and he coldly approved making women and children more "useful" by adding them to the labor force in factories.

Whereas Washington had begun his presidency with a gentle vision of a prosperous, peaceful, educated nation, Hamilton had grander things in mind. History had taught him that republics were not pacific; on the contrary, they were no less addicted than monarchies to war. "No government could give us tranquility and happiness at home," he had declared at the Constitutional Convention, "which did not possess sufficient stability and strength to make us respectable abroad."[3]

Hamilton excelled in a series of hard-nosed and innovative policies. But was something missing from his agenda? In the hundreds of pages he wrote, he rarely, if ever, acclaimed or even mentioned the ideals of the Revolution; he never demonstrated that his programs would further the welfare of average citizens; he never bothered to refute the impression that he distrusted democracy. On the contrary, a pervasive fear of the turbulence of the people colored his attitude toward politics. His imagination was ignited, not by the prospect of helping ordinary Americans pursue happiness, but rather by the idea of increasing the power and prestige of the state itself. And a state modeled on Great Britain at that! "We think in English," Hamilton had famously said, encapsulating his admiration more for the might of the empire than for a common language.[4]

Hamilton despised the democratic and egalitarian trends that were transforming American politics and that, in 1801, ushered his political adversaries, Jefferson and Madison, into office. Was it this shift in the political landscape that unnerved and repelled him, or was it a more personal and lacerating disillusionment with life that led him to confess to his friend Gouverneur Morris in 1802, "This American world was not made for me."

Longing to "withdraw from the Scene,"[5] he had begun construction of a new house in northern Manhattan. "A garden, you know," he wrote to another friend, "is a very useful refuge of a disappointed politician."[6]

"Our real Disease," he wrote on the very eve of his death, "is DEMOCRACY."[7] That same evening, he feebly argued that he had to go through with his duel with Aaron Burr in order to retain "the ability to be in future useful [. . .] in those crises of our public affairs."[8] But surely he realized that there could be no useful role in America for an adversary of the people—or for the man who had sabotaged his party's own candidate, John Adams, in the election of 1800. "General Hamilton *hated* republican government," Morris later commented in a lengthy examination of his friend's politics. "He never failed on every occasion to advocate the excellence of, and avow his attachment to, monarchical government."[9]

Turning his back on the modern world that he and his generation had helped to create, the most brilliant, rational, hard-nosed, and innovative of the founders bowed to the feudal code of knightly honor and ceded his fate to a game of chance.

THE WRITINGS OF ALEXANDER HAMILTON

To Edward Stevens

ST CROIX NOVEMR. 11TH 1769

Dear Edward

This just serves to acknowledge receipt of yours per Capt. Lowndes, which was delivered me yesterday. The truth of Capt. Lightbourn & Lowndes information is now verified by the presence of your father and sister, for whose safe arrival I pray; and that they may convey that satisfaction to your soul that must naturally flow from the sight of absent friends in health; and shall, for news this way, refer you to them. As to what you say respecting your having soon the happiness of seeing us all, I wish for an accomplishment of your hopes, provided they are concomitant with your welfare; otherwise not; though I doubt whether I shall be present or not, for, to confess my weakness, Ned, my ambition is prevalent, so that I contemn the grovelling and condition of a clerk or the like, to which my fortune, etc. condemns me, and would willingly risk my life though not my character to exalt my station. Im confident, Ned, that my youth excludes me from any hopes of immediate preferment; nor do I desire it; but I mean to prepare the way for futurity. Im no philosopher you see and may jusly said to build castles in the air; my folly makes me ashamed, and I beg you'll conceal it; yet Neddy we have seen such schemes successful when the projector is constant. I shall conclude saying, I wish there was a war. I am Dr Edward Yours

P.S. I this morning received yours by William Smith, and am pleased to see you give such close application to study.

To Gouverneur Morris

HEADQUARTERS, MORRISTOWN, MAY 19, 1777

Dear Sir:

I this moment received the favor of your letter of the 16th instant.

I partly agree and partly disagree with you respecting the deficiencies of your Constitution. That there is a want of vigor in the executive, I believe, will be found true. To determine the qualifications proper for the chief executive magistrate requires the deliberate wisdom of a select assembly, and cannot be safely lodged with the people at large. That instability is inherent in the nature of popular governments I think very disputable; unstable democracy, is an epithet frequently in the mouths of politicians; but I believe that from a strict examination of the matter—from the records of history, it will be found that the fluctuation of governments in which the popular principle has borne a considerable sway, have proceeded from its being compounded with other principles;—and from its being made to operate in an improper channel. Compound governments, though they may be harmonious in the beginning, will introduce distinct interests, and these interests will clash, throw the State into convulsions, and produce a change or dissolution. When the deliberative or judicial powers are vested wholly or partly in the collective body of the people, you must expect error, confusion, and instability. But a representative democracy, where the right of election is well secured and regulated, and the exercise of the legislative, executive, and judiciary authorities is vested in select persons, chosen *really* and not *nominally* by the people, will, in my opinion, be most likely to be happy, regular, and durable. That the complexity of your Legislature will occasion delay and dilatoriness, is evident, and I fear may be attended with a much greater evil;—as expedition is not very material *in making* laws, especially when the government is well digested and matured by time. The evil I mean is, that in time your Senate, from the very name, and from the mere circumstance of its being a separate member of the Legislature, will be liable to degenerate into a body purely aristocratical.

And I think the danger of an abuse of power from a simple legislative would not be very great, in a government where the equality and fulness of popular representation is so wisely provided for as in yours. On the whole, though I think there are the defects intimated, I think your government far the best that we have yet seen, and capable of giving long and substantial happiness to the people. Objections to it should be suggested with great caution and reserve. [. . .]

To John Laurens

[MORRISTOWN, NEW JERSEY,] JANY 8T. [1780]

I had written the enclosed and was called off. Some ruffian hand has treated it in the manner you see. I have no time to copy it. I shall take up the story where I left it.

Another reason for believing the destination is your way, is that Governor Martin and divers others refugees of Georgia South and North Carolina are said to have gone in the fleet. You will have a busy time; acquit yourselves well. We hope however that some late violent winds will drown them all on their way. There is no other military news.

Believe me my Dr Laurens I am not insensible of the first mark of your affection in recommending me to your friends for a certain commission. However your partiality may have led you to overrate my qualifications that very partiality must endear you to me; and all the world will allow that your struggles and scruples upon the occasion deserve the envy of men of vertue. I am happy you placed the matter upon the footing you did, because I hope it will ultimately engage you to accept the appointment. Had it fallen to my lot, I should have been flattered by such a distinction but I should have felt all your embarrassments.

Of this however I need have no apprehension. Not one of the four in nomination but would stand a better chance than myself; and yet my vanity tells me they do not all merit a preference. But I am a stranger in this country. I have no property here, no connexions. If I have talents and integrity, (as you say I have) these are justly deemed very spurious titles in these enlightened days, when unsupported by others more solid; and were it not for your example, I should be inclined in considering the composition of a certain body, to suppose that three fourths of them are mortal enemies to the first and three fourths of the other fourth have a laudable contempt for the last.

Adieu God preserve and prosper you

I have strongly sollicited leave to go to the Southward. It could not be refused; but arguments have been used to dissuade me from it, which however little weight they may have had in my judgment gave law to my feelings. I am chagrined and unhappy but I submit. In short Laurens I am disgusted with every thing in this world but yourself and *very* few more honest fellows and I have no other wish than as soon as possible to make a brilliant exit. 'Tis a weakness; but I feel I am not fit for this terrestreal Country.

All the Lads embrace you. The General sends his love. Write to him as often as you can.

To Elizabeth Schuyler

AUGUST 1780

Impatiently My Dearest have I been expecting the return of your father to bring me a letter from my charmer with the answers you have been good enough to promise me to the little questions asked in mine by him. I long to see the workings of my Betseys heart, and I promise my self I shall have ample gratification to my fondness in the sweet familiarity of her pen. She will there I hope paint me her feelings without reserve—even in those tender moments of pillowed retirement, when her soul abstracted from every other object, delivers itself up to Love and to me—yet with all that delicacy which suits the purity of her mind and which is so conspicuous in whatever she does.

It is now a week my Betsey since I have heard from you. In that time I have written you twice. I think it will be adviseable in future to number our letters, for I have reason to suspect they do not all meet with fair play. This is number one.

Meade just comes in and interrupts me by sending his love to you. He tells you he has written a long letter to his widow asking her opinion of the propriety of quitting the service; and that if she does not disapprove it, he will certainly take his final leave after the campaign. You see what a fine opportunity she has to be enrolled in the catalogue of heroines, and I dare say she will set you an example of fortitude and patriotism. I know too you have so much of the Portia in you, that you will not be out done in this line by any of your sex, and that if you saw me inclined to quit the service of your country, you would dissuade me from it. I have promised you, you recollect, to conform to your wishes, and I persist in this intention. It remains with you to show whether you are a *Roman* or an *American wife*.

Though I am not sanguine in expecting it, I am not without hopes this Winter will produce a peace and then you must submit to the mortification of enjoying more domestic happiness and less fame. This I know you will not like, but we cannot always have things as we wish.

The affairs of England are in so bad a plight that if no fortunate events attend her this campaign, it would seem impossible for her to proceed in the war. But she is an obstinate old dame, and seems determined to ruin her whole family, rather than to let Miss America go on flirting it with her new lovers, with whom, as giddy young girls often do, she eloped in contempt of her mothers authority. I know you will be ready to justify her conduct and to tell me the ill treatment she received was enough to make any girl of spirit act in the same manner. But I will one day cure you of these refractory notions about the right of resistance, (of which I foresee you will be apt to make a very dangerous application), and teach you the great advantage and absolute necessity of implicit obedience.

But now we are talking of times to come, tell me my pretty damsel have you made up your mind upon the subject of housekeeping? Do you soberly relish the pleasure of being a poor mans wife? Have you learned to think a home spun preferable to a brocade and the rumbling of a waggon wheel to the musical rattling of a coach and six? Will you be able to see with perfect composure your old acquaintances flaunting it in gay life, tripping it along in elegance and splendor, while you hold an humble station and have no other enjoyments than the sober comforts of a good wife? Can you in short be an Aquileia and chearfully plant turnips with me, if fortune should so order it? If you cannot my Dear we are playing a comedy of all in the wrong, and you should correct the mistake before we begin to act the tragedy of the unhappy couple.

I propose you a set of new questions my lovely girl; but though they are asked with an air of levity, they merit a very serious consideration, for on their being resolved in the affirmative stripped of all the colorings of a fond imagination our happiness may absolutely depend. I have not concealed my circumstances from my Betsey; they are far from splendid; they may possibly even be worse than I expect, for every day brings me fresh proof of the knavery of those to whom my little affairs are entrusted. They have already filed down what was in their hands more than one half, and I am told they go on diminishing it, 'till I *fear* they will reduce it below my *former fears.* An indifference to property enters into my character too much, and what affects me now as my Betsey is concerned in it, I should have laughed at or not thought of at all a year ago. But I have thoroughly examined my own heart. Beloved by you, I can be happy in any situation, and can struggle with every embarrassment of fortune with patience and firmness. I cannot however forbear entreating you to realize our union on the dark side and satisfy, without deceiving yourself, how far your affection for me can make you happy in a privation of those elegancies to which you have been accustomed. If fortune should smile upon us, it will do us no harm to have been prepared for adversity; if she frowns upon us, by being prepared, we shall encounter it without the chagrin of disappointment. Your future rank in life is a perfect lottery; you may move in an exalted you may move in a very humble sphere; the last is most probable; examine well your heart. And in doing it, dont figure to yourself a cottage in romance, with the spontaneous bounties of nature courting you to enjoyment. Dont imagine yourself a shepherdess, your hair embroidered with flowers a crook in your hand tending your flock under a shady tree, by the side of a cool fountain, your faithful shepherd sitting near and entertaining you with gentle tales of love. These are pretty dreams and very apt to enter into the heads of lovers when they think of a connection without the advantages of fortune. But they must not be indulged. You must apply your situation to real life, and think how you should feel in scenes of which you may find examples every day. So far My Dear Betsey as the tenderest affection can compensate for other inconveniences in making your estimate, you cannot give too large a credit for this article. My heart overflows with every thing for you, that admiration, esteem and love can inspire. *I would this moment give the world to be near you only to kiss your sweet hand.* Believe what I say to be truth and imagine what are my feelings when I say it. Let it awake your sympathy and let our hearts melt in a prayer to be soon united, never more to be separated.

Adieu loveliest of your sex

Instead of inclosing your letter to your father I inclose his to you because I do not know whether he may not be on his way here. If he is at home he will tell you the military news. If he has set out for camp, you may open and read my letters to him. The one from Mr. Mathews you will return by the first opportunity.

To James Duane

LIBERTY POLE, NEW JERSEY, SEPT. 3D 1780

Dr. Sir

Agreeably to your request and my promise I sit down to give you my ideas of the defects of our present system, and the changes necessary to save us from ruin. They may perhaps be the reveries of a projector rather than the sober views of a politician. You will judge of them, and make what use you please of them.

The fundamental defect is a want of power in Congress. It is hardly worth while to show in what this consists, as it seems to be universally acknowleged, or to point out how it has happened, as the only question is how to remedy it. It may however be said that it has originated from three causes—an excess of the spirit of liberty which has made the particular states show a jealousy of all power not in their own hands; and this jealousy has led them to exercise a right of judging in the last resort of the measures recommended by Congress, and of acting according to their own opinions of their propriety or necessity, a diffidence in Congress of their own powers, by which they have been timid and indecisive in their resolutions, constantly making concessions to the states, till they have scarcely left themselves the shadow of power; a want of sufficient means at their disposal to answer the public exigencies and of vigor to draw forth those means; which have occasioned them to depend on the states individually to fulfil their engagements with the army, and the consequence of which has been to ruin their influence and credit with the army, to establish its dependence on each state separately rather than *on them,* that is rather than on the whole collectively.

It may be pleaded, that Congress had never any definitive powers granted them and of course could exercise none—could do nothing more than recommend. The manner in which Congress was appointed would warrant, and the public good required, that they should have considered themselves as vested with full power *to preserve the republic from harm.* They have done many of the highest acts of sovereignty, which were always chearfully submitted to—the declaration of independence, the declaration of war, the levying an army, creating a navy, emitting money, making alliances with foreign powers, appointing a dictator &c. &c.—all these implications of a complete sovereignty were never disputed, and ought to have been a standard for the whole conduct of Administration. Undefined powers are discretionary powers, limited only by the object for which they were given—in the present case, the independence and freedom of America. The confederation made no difference; for as it has not been generally adopted, it had no operation. But from what I recollect of it, Congress have even descended from the authority which the spirit of that act gives them, while the particular states have no further attended to it than as it suited their pretensions and convenience. It would take too much time to enter into particular instances, each of which separately might appear inconsiderable; but united are of serious import. I only mean to remark, not to censure.

But the confederation itself is defective and requires to be altered; it is neither fit for war, nor peace. The idea of an uncontrolable sovereignty in each state, over its internal police, will defeat the other powers given to Congress, and make our union feeble and precarious. [. . .]

The confederation gives the states individually too much influence in the affairs of the army; they should have nothing to do with it. The entire formation and disposal of our military forces ought to belong to Congress. It is an essential cement of the union; and it ought to be the policy of Congress to des(troy) all ideas of state attachments in the army and make it look up wholly to them. [. . .]

I shall now propose the remedies, which appear to me applicable to our circumstances, and necessary to extricate our affairs from their present deplorable situation.

The first step must be to give Congress powers competent to the public exigencies. This may happen in two ways, one by resuming and exercising the discretionary powers I suppose to have been originally vested in them for the safety of the states and resting their conduct on the candor of their country men and the necessity of the conjuncture: the other by calling immediately a convention of all the states with full authority to conclude finally upon a general confederation, stating to them beforehand explicity the evils arising from a want of power in Congress, and the impossibily of supporting the contest on its present footing, that the delegates may come possessed of proper sentiments as well as proper authority to give to the meeting. Their commission should include a right of vesting Congress with the whole or a proportion of the unoccupied lands, to be employed for the purpose of raising a revenue, reserving the jurisdiction to the states by whom they are granted.

The first plan, I expect will be thought too bold an expedient by the generality of Congress; and indeed their practice hitherto has so rivetted the opinion of their want of power, that the success of this experiment may very well be doubted.

I see no objection to the other mode, that has any weight in competition with the reasons for it. The Convention should assemble the 1st of November next, the sooner, the better; our disorders are too violent to admit of a common or lingering remedy. The reasons for which I require them to be vested with plenipotentiary authority are that the business may suffer no delay in the execution, and may in reality come to effect. A convention may agree upon a confederation; the states individually hardly ever will. We must have one at all events, and a vigorous one if we mean to succeed in the contest and be happy hereafter. As I said before, to engage the states to comply with this mode, Congress ought to confess to them plainly and unanimously the impracticability of supporting our affairs on the present footing and without a solid coercive union. I ask that the Convention should have a power of vesting the whole or a part of the unoccupied land in Congress, because it is necessary that body should have some property as a fund for the arrangements of finance; and I know of no other kind that can be given them.

The confederation in my opinion should give Congress complete sovereignty; except as to that part of internal police, which relates to the rights of property and life among individuals and to raising money by internal taxes. It is necessary, that every thing, belonging to this, should be regulated by the state legislatures. Congress should have complete sovereignty in all that relates to war, peace, trade, finance, and to the management of foreign affairs, the right of declaring war of raising armies, officering, paying them, directing their motions in every respect, of equipping fleets and doing the same with them, of building fortifications arsenals magazines &c. &c., of making peace on such conditions as they think proper, of regulating trade, determining with what countries it shall be carried on, granting indulgencies laying prohibitions on all the articles of export or import, imposing duties granting bounties & premiums for raising exporting importing and applying to their own use the product of these duties, only giving credit to the states on whom they are raised in the general account of revenues and expences, instituting Admiralty courts &c., of coining money, establishing banks on such terms, and with such privileges as they think proper, appropriating funds and doing whatever else relates to the operations of finance, transacting every thing with foreign nations, making alliances offensive and defensive, treaties of commerce, &c. &c. [. . .]

And why can we not have an American bank? Are our monied men less enlightened to their own interest or less enterprising in the persuit? I believe the fault is in our government which does not exert itself to engage them in such a scheme. It is true, the individuals in America are not very rich, but this would not prevent their instituting a bank; it would only prevent its being done with such ample funds as in other countries. Have they not sufficient confidence in the government and in the issue of the cause? Let the Government endeavour to inspire that confidence, by adopting the measures I have recommended or others equivalent to them. [. . .]

The first step to establishing the bank will be to engage a number of monied men of influence to relish the project and make it a business. [. . .]

If a Convention is called the minds of all the states and the people ought to be prepared to receive its determinations by sensible and popular writings, which should conform to the views of Congress. There are epochs in human affairs, when *novelty* even is useful. If a general opinion prevails that the old way is bad, whether true or false, and this obstructs or relaxes the operation of the public service, a change is necessary if it be but for the sake of change. This is exactly the case now. 'Tis an universal sentiment that our present system is a bad one, and that things do not go right on this account. The measure of a Convention would revive the hopes of the people and give a new direction to their passions, which may be improved in carrying points of substantial utility. The Eastern states have already pointed out this mode to Congress; they ought to take the hint and anticipate the others.

And, in future, My Dear Sir, two things let me recommend, as fundamental rules for the conduct of Congress—to attach the army to them by every motive, to maintain an air of authority (not domineering) in all their measures with the states. The manner in which a thing is done has more influence than is commonly imagined. Men are governed by opinion; this opinion is as much influenced by appearances as by realities; if a Government appears to be confident of its own powers, it is the surest way to inspire the same confidence in others; if it is diffident, it may be certain, there will be a still greater diffidence in others, and that its authority will not only be distrusted, controverted, but contemned.

I wish too Congress would always consider that a kindness consists as much in the manner as in the thing: the best things done hesitatingly and with an ill grace lose their effect, and produce disgust rather than satisfaction or gratitude. [. . .]

To George Washington

NOVEMBER 22, 1780.

Dear Sir:

Some time last fall, when I spoke to your Excellency about going to the southward, I explained to you candidly my feelings with respect to military reputation, and how much it was my object to act a conspicuous part in some enterprise that might perhaps raise my character as a soldier above mediocrity. You were so good as to say you would be glad to furnish me with an occasion. When the expedition to Staten Island was afoot, a favorable one seemed to offer. There was a battalion without a field officer, the command of which, I thought, as it was accidental, might be given to me without inconvenience. I made an application for it through the Marquis, who informed me of your refusal on two principles—one, that the giving me a whole battalion might be a subject of dissatisfaction; the other, that if any accident should happen to me, in the present state of your family, you would be embarrassed for the necessary assistance.

The project you now have in contemplation affords another opportunity. I have a variety of reasons that press me to desire ardently to have it in my power to improve it. I take the liberty to observe that the command may now be proportioned to my rank, and that the second objection ceases to operate, as, during the period of establishing our winter-quarters, there will be a suspension of material business; besides which, my peculiar position will, in any case, call me away from the army in a few days, and Mr. Harrison may be expected back early next month. My command may consist of one hundred and fifty or two hundred men, composed of fifty men of Major Gibbes' corps, fifty from Col. Meigs' regiment, and fifty or a hundred more from the light infantry; Major Gibbes to be my major. The hundred men from here may move on Friday morning towards _____, which will strengthen the appearances for Staten Island, to form a junction on the other side of the Passaic.

I suggest this mode to avoid the complaints that might arise from composing my party wholly of the light infantry, which might give umbrage to the officers of that corps, who, on this plan, can have no just subject for it.

The primary idea may be, if circumstances permit, to attempt with my detachment Bayard's Hill. Should we arrive early enough to undertake it, I should prefer it to any thing else, both for the brilliancy of the attempt in itself and the decisive consequences of which its success would be productive. If we arrive too late to make this eligible (as there is reason to apprehend), my corps may form the van of one of the other attacks; and Bayard's Hill will be a pretext for my being employed in the affair, on a supposition of my knowing the ground, which is partly true. I flatter myself, also, that my military character stands so well in the army as to reconcile the officers in general to the measure. All circumstances considered, I venture to say any exceptions which might be taken would be unreasonable.

I take this method of making the request to avoid the embarrassment of a personal explanation. I shall only add that, however much I have the matter at heart, I wish your Excellency entirely to consult your own inclination, and not, from a disposition to oblige me, to do any thing that may be disagreeable to you. It will, nevertheless, make me singularly happy if your wishes correspond with mine.

To Philip Schuyler

HEAD QUARTERS, NEW WINDSOR, FEBY 18, 81.

My Dear Sir:

Since I had the pleasure of writing you last, an unexpected change has taken place in my situation. I am no longer a member of the General's family. This information will surprise you, and the manner of the change will surprise you more. Two days ago, the General and I passed each other on the stairs. He told me he wanted to speak to me. I answered that I would wait upon him immediately. I went below, and delivered Mr. Tilghman a letter to be sent to the commissary, containing an order of a pressing and interesting nature.

Returning to the General, I was stopped on the way by the Marquis de La Fayette, and we conversed together about a minute on a matter of business. He can testify how impatient I was to get back, and that I left him in a manner which, but for our intimacy, would have been more than abrupt. Instead of finding the General, as is usual, in his room, I met him at the head of the stairs, where, accosting me in an angry tone, "Colonel Hamilton," said he, "you have kept me waiting at the head of the stairs these ten minutes. I must tell you, sir, you treat me with disrespect." I replied, without petulancy, but with decision: "I am not conscious of it, sir; but since you have thought it necessary to tell me so, we part." "Very well, sir," said he, "if it be your choice," or something to this effect, and we separated. I sincerely believe my absence, which gave so much umbrage, did not last two minutes.

In less than an hour after, Tilghman came to me in the General's name, assuring me of his great confidence in my abilities, integrity, usefulness, etc., and of his desire, in a candid conversation, to heal a difference which could not have happened but in a moment of passion. I requested Mr. Tilghman to tell him—1. That I had taken my resolution in a manner not to be revoked. 2. That, as a conversation could serve no other purpose than to produce explanations, mutually disagreeable, though I certainly would not refuse an interview if he desired it, yet I would be happy if he would permit me to decline it. 3. That, though determined to leave the family, the same principles which had kept me so long in it would continue to direct my conduct towards him when out of it. 4th. That, however, I did not wish to distress him, or the public business, by quitting him before he could derive other assistance by the return of some of the gentlemen who were absent. 5. And that, in the mean time, it depended on him to let our behavior to each other be the same as if nothing had happened. He consented to decline the conversation, and thanked me for my offer of continuing my aid in the manner I had mentioned.

Thus we stand. I wait Mr. Humphrey's return from the Eastward and may be induced to wait the return of Mr. Harrison from Virginia.

I have given you so particular a detail of our difference from the desire I have to justify myself in your opinion. Perhaps you may think I was precipitate in rejecting the overture made by the General to an accommodation. I assure you, my dear sir, it was not the effect of resentment; it was the deliberate result of maxims I had long formed for the government of my own conduct.

I always disliked the office of an Aide de camp as having in it a kind of personal dependence. I refused to serve in this capacity with two Major Generals at an early period of the war. Infected however with the enthusiasm of the times, an idea of the General's character which experience taught me to be unfounded overcame my scruples, and induced me to *accept his invitation* to enter into his family.

I believe you know the place I held in the General's confidence and counsels, which will make it the more extraordinary to you to learn that for three years past I have felt no friendship for him and have professed none.

The truth is, our dispositions are the opposites of each other, and the pride of my temper would not suffer me to profess what I did not feel. Indeed, when advances of this kind have been made to me on his part, they were received in a manner that showed at least that I had no desire to court them, and that I wished to stand rather upon a footing of military confidence than of private attachment.

You are too good a judge of human nature not to be sensible how this conduct in me must have operated on a man to whom all the world is offering incense. With this key you will easily unlock the present mystery.

At the end of the war I may say many things to you concerning which I shall impose upon myself till then an inviolable silence.

The General is a very honest man. His competitors have slender abilities, and less integrity. His popularity has often been essential to the safety of America, and is still of great importance to it. These considerations have influenced my past conduct respecting him, and will influence my future. I think it is necessary he should be supported.

His estimation in your mind, whatever may be its amount, I am persuaded has been formed on principles which a circumstance like this cannot materially affect; but if I thought it could diminish your friendship for him, I should almost forego the motives that urge me to justify myself to you. I wish what I have said to make no other impression than to satisfy you I have not been in the wrong. It is also said in confidence, as a public knowledge of the breach would, in many ways, have an ill effect. It will probably be the policy of both sides to conceal it, and cover the separation with some plausible pretext. I am importuned by such of my friends as are privy to the affair, to listen to a reconciliation; but my resolution is unalterable.

As I cannot think of quitting the army during the war, I have a project of re-entering into the artillery, by taking Lieutenant-Colonel Forrest's place, who is desirous of retiring on half-pay. I have not, however, made up my mind upon this head, as I should be obliged to come in the youngest Lieutenant-Colonel instead of the eldest, which I ought to have been by natural succession, had I remained in the corps; and, at the same time, to resume studies relative to the profession, which, to avoid inferiority, must be laborious.

If a handsome command in the campaign in the light infantry should offer itself, I shall balance between this and the artillery. My situation in the latter would be more solid and permanent: but as I hope the war will not last long enough to make it progressive, this consideration has the less force. A command for the campaign would leave me the winter to prosecute studies relative to my future career in life. With respect to the former, I have been materially the worse for going into his family.

I have written to you on this subject with all the freedom and confidence to which you have a right and with an assurance of the interest you take in all that concerns me.

Very sincerely & Affectionately

To Robert Morris

APRIL 30, 1781.

Sir:

I was among the first who were convinced that an administration by single men was essential to the proper management of the affairs of this country. I am persuaded now it is the only resource we have to extricate ourselves from the distresses which threaten the subversion of our cause. It is palpable that the people have lost all confidence in our public councils; and it is a fact, of which I dare say you are as well apprised as myself, that our friends in Europe are in the same disposition. I have been in a situation that has enabled me to obtain a better idea of this than most others; and I venture to assert that the Court of France will never give half the succors to this country, while Congress holds the reins of administration in their own hands, which they would grant, if these were entrusted to individuals of established reputation, and conspicuous for probity, abilities, and fortune. [. . .]

To me it appears evident that an executive ministry, composed of men with the qualifications I have described, would speedily restore the credit of government abroad and at home—would induce our allies to greater exertions in our behalf—would inspire confidence in moneyed men in Europe, as well as in America, to lend us those sums of which it may be demonstrated we stand in need, from the disproportion of our national wealth to the expenses of the war. [. . .]

[. . .] 'T is by introducing order into our finances—by restoring public credit—not by gaining battles, that we are finally to gain our object. 'T is by putting ourselves in a condition to continue the war—not by temporary, violent, and unnatural efforts to bring it to a decisive issue, that we shall, in reality, bring it to a speedy and successful one. In the frankness of truth I believe, sir, you are the man best capable of performing this great work.

In expectation that all difficulties will be removed, and that you will ultimately act on terms you approve, I take the liberty to submit to you some ideas relative to the objects of your department. I pretend not to be an able financier; it is a part of administration which has been least in my way, and, of course, has least occupied my inquiries and reflections. Neither have I had leisure or materials to make accurate calculations. I have been obliged to depend on memory for important facts, for want of the authorities from which they are drawn. With all these disadvantages, my plan must necessarily be crude and defective; but if it may be a basis for something more perfect, or if it contains any hints that may be of use to you, the trouble I have taken myself, or may give you, will not be misapplied. At any rate, the confidence I have in your judgment assures me that you will receive with pleasure communications of this sort: if they contain anything useful, they will promote your views and the public benefit; if not, the only evil is the trouble of reading them; and the best informed will frequently derive lights, even from reveries of projectors and quacks. There is scarcely any plan so bad as not to have something good in it. I trust mine to your candor without further apology; you will at least do justice to my intention.

The first step towards determining what ought to be done in the finances of this country, is to estimate, in the best manner we can, its capacity for revenue; and the proportion between what it is able to afford, and what it stands in need of, for the expenses of its civil and military establishments. There occur to me two ways of doing this: 1st. By examining what proportion the revenues of other countries have borne to their stock of wealth, and applying the rule to ourselves, with proper allowance for the difference of circumstances. 2d. By comparing the result of this rule with the product of taxes in those States which have been the most in earnest in taxation. The reason for having recourse to the first method is, that our own experience of our faculties in this respect has not been sufficiently clear, or uniform, to admit of a certain conclusion: so that it will be more satisfactory to judge of them by a general principle, drawn by the example of other nations, compared with what we have effected ourselves, than to rely entirely upon the latter.

The nations with whose wealth and revenues we are best acquainted, are France, Great Britain, and the United Provinces. The real wealth of a nation, consisting in its labor and commodities, is to be estimated by the sign of that wealth—its circulating cash. There may be times when, from particular accidents, the quantity of this may exceed or fall short of a just representative; but it will turn again to a proper level, and in the general course of things, maintain itself in that state. [. . .]

To [. . .] give individuals ability and inclination to lend in any proportion to the wants of government, a plan must be devised which, by incorporating their means together and uniting them with those of the public, will, on the foundation of that incorporation and union, erect a mass of credit that will supply the defect of moneyed capital, and answer all the purposes of cash; a plan which will offer adventurers immediate advantages, analogous to those they receive by employing their money in trade, and eventually greater advantages; a plan which will give them the greatest security the nature of the case will admit for what they lend; and which will not only advance their own interest and secure the independence of their country, but, in its progress, have the most beneficial influence upon its future commerce, and be a source of national strength and wealth.

I mean the institution of a NATIONAL BANK. This I regard, in some shape or other, as an expedient essential to our safety and success; unless, by a happy turn of European affairs, the war should speedily terminate in a manner upon which it would be unwise to reckon. There is no other that can give to government that extensive and systematic credit which the defect of our revenues makes indispensably necessary to its operations.

The longer it is delayed the more difficult it becomes. Our affairs grow every day more relaxed and more involved; public credit hastens to a more irretrievable catastrophe; the means for executing the plan are exhausted in partial and temporary efforts. [. . .]

In the present system of things, the health of a State, particularly a commercial one, depends on a due quantity and regular circulation of cash, as much as the health of an animal body depends upon the due quantity and regular circulation of the blood. There are indisputable indications that we have not a sufficient medium; and what we have is in continual fluctuation. The only cure to our public disorders, is to fix the value of the currency we now have, and increase it to a proper standard, in a species that will have the requisite stability.

The error of those who would explode paper money altogether, originates in not making proper distinctions. Our paper was, in its nature, liable to depreciation, because it had no funds for its support, and was not upheld by private credit. The emissions under the resolution of March, '80, have partly the former advantage, but are destitute of the latter, which is equally essential. No paper credit can be substantial, or durable, which has no funds, and which does not unite, immediately, the interest and influence of the moneyed men, in its establishment and preservation. A credit begun on this basis, will, in process of time, greatly exceed its funds: but this requires time and a well-settled opinion in its favor. 'T is in a national bank, alone, that we can find the ingredients to constitute a wholesome, solid, and beneficial credit. [. . .]

A national debt, if it is not excessive, will be to us a national blessing. It will be a powerful cement of our Union. It will also create a necessity for keeping up taxation to a degree which, without being oppressive, will be a spur to industry, remote as we are from Europe, and shall be from danger. It were otherwise to be feared our popular maxims would incline us to too great parsimony and indulgence. We labor less now than any civilized nation of Europe; and a habit of labor in the people is as essential to the health and vigor of their minds and bodies, as it is conducive to the welfare of the state. We ought not to suffer our self-love to deceive us in a comparison upon these points.

I have spun out this letter to a much greater length than I intended. To develop the whole connection of my ideas on the subject, and place my plan in the clearest light, I have indulged myself in many observations which might have been omitted. I shall not longer intrude upon your patience than to assure you of the sincere sentiments of esteem with which I have the honor to be,

Sir, your most obedient and humble servant,

A Second Letter from Phocion

APRIL 1784

In a first formation of a government the society may multiply its precautions as much, and annex as many conditions to the enjoyment of its rights, as it shall judge expedient; but when it has once adopted a constitution, that constitution must be the measure of its discretion, in providing for its own safety, and in prescribing the conditions upon which its privileges are to be enjoyed. If the constitution declares that persons possessing certain qualifications shall be entitled to certain rights, while that constitution remains in force, the government which is the mere creature of the constitution, can divest no citizen, who has the requisite qualifications, of his corresponding rights. [. . .]

The right of a government to prescribe the conditions on which its privileges shall be enjoyed, is bounded with respect to those who are already included in the compact, by its original conditions; in admitting strangers it may add new ones; but it cannot without a breach of the social compact deprive those, who have been once admitted of their rights, unless for some declared cause of forfeiture authenticated with the solemnities required by the subsisting compact.

The rights too of a republican government are to be modified and regulated by the principles of such a government. These principles dictate, that no man shall lose his rights without a hearing and conviction, before the proper tribunal; that previous to his disfranchisement, he shall have the full benefit of the laws to make his defence; and that his innocence shall be presumed till his guilt has been proved. These with many other maxims, never to be forgotten in any but tyrannical governments, oppose the aims of those who quarrel with the principles of Phocion.

Cases indeed of extreme necessity are exceptions to all general rules; but these only exist, when it is manifest the safety of the community is in imminent danger. Speculations of possible danger never can be justifying causes of departures from principles on which in the ordinary course of things all private security depends—from principles which constitute the essential distinction between free and arbitrary governments.

When the advocates for legislature discriminations are driven from one subterfuge to another, their last resting place is—that this is a new case, the case of a revolution. Your principles are all right say they, in the ordinary course of society, but they do not apply to a situation like ours. This is opening a wilderness, through all the labyrinths of which, it is impossible to pursue them: The answer to this must be, that there are principles eternally true and which apply to all situations; such as those that have been already enumerated—that we are not now in the midst of a revolution but have happily brought it to a successful issue—that we have a constitution formed as a rule of conduct—that the frame of our government is determined and the general principle of it is settled—that we have taken our station among nations have claimed the benefit of the laws which regulate them, and must in our turn be bound by the same laws—that those eternal principles of social justice forbid the inflicting punishment upon citizens, by an abridgement of rights, or in any other manner, without conviction of some specific offence by regular trial and condemnation—that the constitution we have formed makes the trial by jury the only proper mode of ascertaining the delinquencies of individuals—that legislative discriminations, to supersede the necessity of inquiry and proof, would be an usurpation on the judiciary powers of the government, and a renunciation of all the maxims of civil liberty—that by the laws of nations and the rules of justice, we are bound to observe the engagements entered into on our behalf, by that power which is invested with the constitutional prerogative of treaty—and that the treaty we have made in its genuine sense, ties up the hands of government from any species of future prosecution or punishment, on account of the part taken by individuals in the war. [. . .]

Happily, for us, in this country, the position is not to be controverted; that the constitution is the creature of the people; but it does not follow that they are not bound by it, while they suffer it to continue in force; nor does it follow, that the legislature, which is, on the other hand, a creature of the constitution, can depart from it, on any presumption of the contrary sense of the people.

The constitution is the compact made between the society at large and each individual. The society therefore, cannot without breach of faith and injustice, refuse to any individual, a single advantage which he derives under that compact, no more than one man can refuse to perform his agreement with another. If the community have good reasons for abrogating the old compact, and establishing a new one, it undoubtedly has a right to do it; but until the compact is dissolved with the same solemnity and certainty with which it was made, the society, as well as individuals, are bound by it.

All the authority of the legislature is delegated to them under the constitution; their rights and powers are there defined; if they exceed them, 'tis a treasonable usurpation upon the power and majesty of the people; and by the same rule that they may take away from a single individual the rights he claims under the constitution, they may erect themselves into perpetual dictators. The sense of the people, if urged in justification of the measure, must be considered as a mere pretext; for that sense cannot appear to them in a form so explicit and authoritative, as the constitution under which they act; and if it could appear with equal authenticity, it could only bind, when it had been preceded by a declared change in the form of government.

The contrary doctrine serves to undermine all those rules, by which individuals can know their duties and their rights, and to convert the government into a government of *will* not of *laws.*

The Federalist, *No. 1*

OCTOBER 27, 1787

To the People of the State of New York:

After an unequivocal experience of the inefficiency of the subsisting federal government, you are called upon to deliberate on a new Constitution for the United States of America. The subject speaks its own importance; comprehending in its consequences nothing less than the existence of the UNION, the safety and welfare of the parts of which it is composed, the fate of an empire in many respects the most interesting in the world. It has been frequently remarked that it seems to have been reserved to the people of this country, by their conduct and example, to decide the important question, whether societies of men are really capable or not of establishing good government from reflection and choice, or whether they are forever destined to depend for their political constitutions on accident and force. If there be any truth in the remark, the crisis at which we are arrived may with propriety be regarded as the era in which that decision is to be made; and a wrong election of the part we shall act may, in this view, deserve to be considered as the general misfortune of mankind.

This idea will add the inducements of philanthropy to those of patriotism, to heighten the solicitude which all considerate and good men must feel for the event. Happy will it be if our choice should be directed by a judicious estimate of our true interests, unperplexed and unbiassed by considerations not connected with the public good. But this is a thing more ardently to be wished than seriously to be expected. The plan offered to our deliberations affects too many particular interests, innovates upon too many local institutions, not to involve in its discussion a variety of objects foreign to its merits, and of views, passions and prejudices little favorable to the discovery of truth.

Among the most formidable of the obstacles which the new Constitution will have to encounter may readily be distinguished the obvious interest of a certain class of men in every State to resist all changes which may hazard a diminution of the power, emolument, and consequence of the offices they hold under the State establishments; and the perverted ambition of another class of men, who will either hope to aggrandize themselves by the confusions of their country, or will flatter themselves with fairer prospects of elevation from the subdivision of the empire into several partial confederacies than from its union under one government.

It is not, however, my design to dwell upon observations of this nature. I am well aware that it would be disingenuous to resolve indiscriminately the opposition of any set of men (merely because their situations might subject them to suspicion) into interested or ambitious views. Candor will oblige us to admit that even such men may be actuated by upright intentions; and it cannot be doubted that much of the opposition which has made its appearance, or may hereafter make its appearance, will spring from sources, blameless at least, if not respectable—the honest errors of minds led astray by preconceived jealousies and fears. So numerous indeed and so powerful are the causes which serve to give a false bias to the judgment, that we, upon many occasions, see wise and good men on the wrong as well as on the right side of questions of the first magnitude to society. This circumstance, if duly attended to, would furnish a lesson of moderation to those who are ever so much persuaded of their being in the right in any controversy. And a further reason for caution, in this respect, might be drawn from the reflection that we are not always sure that those who advocate the truth are influenced by purer principles than their antagonists. Ambition, avarice, personal animosity, party opposition, and many other motives not more laudable than these, are apt to operate as well upon those who support as those who oppose the right side of a question. Were there not even these inducements to moderation, nothing could be more ill-judged than that intolerant spirit which has, at all times, characterized political parties. For in politics, as in religion, it is equally absurd to aim at making proselytes by fire and sword. Heresies in either can rarely be cured by persecution.

And yet, however just these sentiments will be allowed to be, we have already sufficient indications that it will happen in this as in all former cases of great national discussion. A torrent of angry and malignant passions will be let loose. To judge from the conduct of the opposite parties, we shall be led to conclude that they will mutually hope to evince the justness of their opinions, and to increase the number of their converts by the loudness of their declamations and the bitterness of their invectives. An enlightened zeal for the energy and efficiency of government will be stigmatized as the offspring of a temper fond of despotic power and hostile to the principles of liberty. An over-scrupulous jealousy of danger to the rights of the people, which is more commonly the fault of the head than of the heart, will be represented as mere pretence and artifice, the stale bait for popularity at the expense of the public good. It will be forgotten, on the one hand, that jealousy is the usual concomitant of love, and that the noble enthusiasm of liberty is apt to be infected with a spirit of narrow and illiberal distrust. On the other hand, it will be equally forgotten that the vigor of government is essential to the security of liberty; that, in the contemplation of a sound and well-informed judgment, their interest can never be separated; and that a dangerous ambition more often lurks behind the specious mask of zeal for the rights of the people than under the forbidding appearance of zeal for the firmness and efficiency of government. History will teach us that the former has been found a much more certain road to the introduction of despotism than the latter, and that of those men who have overturned the liberties of republics, the greatest number have begun their career by paying an obsequious court to the people; commencing demagogues, and ending tyrants.

In the course of the preceding observations, I have had an eye, my fellow-citizens, to putting you upon your guard against all attempts, from whatever quarter, to influence your decision in a matter of the utmost moment to your welfare, by any impressions other than those which may result from the evidence of truth. You will, no doubt, at the same time, have collected from the general scope of them, that they proceed from a source not unfriendly to the new Constitution. Yes, my countrymen, I own to you that, after having given it an attentive consideration, I am clearly of opinion it is your interest to adopt it. I am convinced that this is the safest course for your liberty, your dignity, and your happiness. I affect not reserves which I do not feel. I will not amuse you with an appearance of deliberation when I have decided. I frankly acknowledge to you my convictions, and I will freely lay before you the reasons on which they are founded. The consciousness of good intentions disdains ambiguity. I shall not, however, multiply professions on this head. My motives must remain in the depository of my own breast. My arguments will be open to all, and may be judged of by all. They shall at least be offered in a spirit which will not disgrace the cause of truth.

I propose, in a series of papers, to discuss the following interesting particulars:—*The utility of the UNION to your political prosperity—The insufficiency of the present Confederation to preserve that Union—The necessity of a government at least equally energetic with the one proposed, to the attainment of this object—The conformity of the proposed Constitution to the true principles of republican government—Its analogy to your own State constitution*—and lastly, *The additional security which its adoption will afford to the preservation of that species of government, to liberty, and to property.*

In the progress of this discussion I shall endeavor to give a satisfactory answer to all the objections which shall have made their appearance, that may seem to have any claim to your attention.

It may perhaps be thought superfluous to offer arguments to prove the utility of the UNION, a point, no doubt, deeply engraved on the hearts of the great body of the people in every State, and one, which it may be imagined, has no adversaries. But the fact is, that we already hear it whispered in the private circles of those who oppose the new Constitution, that the thirteen States are of too great extent for any general system, and that we must of necessity resort to separate confederacies of distinct portions of the whole.* This doctrine will, in all probability, be gradually propagated, till it has votaries enough to countenance an open avowal of it. For nothing can

*The same idea, tracing the arguments to their consequences, is held out in several of the late publications against the New Constitution.

be more evident, to those who are able to take an enlarged view of the subject, than the alternative of an adoption of the new Constitution or a dismemberment of the Union. It will therefore be of use to begin by examining the advantages of that Union, the certain evils, and the probable dangers, to which every State will be exposed from its dissolution. This shall accordingly constitute the subject of my next address.

PUBLIUS.

The Federalist, *No. 70*

MARCH 15, 1788

To the People of the State of New York:

There is an idea, which is not without its advocates, that a vigorous Executive is inconsistent with the genius of republican government. The enlightened well-wishers to this species of government must at least hope that the supposition is destitute of foundation; since they can never admit its truth, without at the same time admitting the condemnation of their own principles. Energy in the executive is a leading character in the definition of good government. It is essential to the protection of the community against foreign attacks: It is not less essential to the steady administration of the laws, to the protection of property against those irregular and high-handed combinations which sometimes interrupt the ordinary course of justice, to the security of liberty against the enterprises and assaults of ambition, of faction, and of anarchy. Every man the least conversant in Roman story, knows how often that republic was obliged to take refuge in the absolute power of a single man, under the formidable title of Dictator, as well against the intrigues of ambitious individuals who aspired to the tyranny, and the seditions of whole classes of the community whose conduct threatened the existence of all government, as against the invasions of external enemies who menaced the conquest and destruction of Rome.

There can be no need, however, to multiply arguments or examples on this head. A feeble Executive implies a feeble execution of the government. A feeble execution is but another phrase for a bad execution; and a government ill executed, whatever it may be in theory, must be, in practice, a bad government.

Taking it for granted, therefore, that all men of sense will agree in the necessity of an energetic Executive, it will only remain to inquire, what are the ingredients which constitute this energy? How far can they be combined with those other ingredients which constitute safety in the republican sense? And how far does this combination characterize the plan which has been reported by the convention?

The ingredients which constitute energy in the Executive are, first, unity; secondly, duration; thirdly, an adequate provision for its support; fourthly, competent powers.

The ingredients which constitute safety in the republican sense are, first, a due dependence on the people; secondly, a due responsibility.

Those politicians and statesmen who have been the most celebrated for the soundness of their principles and for the justice of their views, have declared in favor of a single Executive and a numerous legislature. They have, with great propriety, considered energy as the most necessary qualification of the former, and have regarded this as most applicable to power in a single hand; while they have, with equal propriety, considered the latter as best adapted to deliberation and wisdom, and best calculated to conciliate the confidence of the people and to secure their privileges and interests.

That unity is conducive to energy will not be disputed. Decision, activity, secrecy, and despatch will generally characterize the proceedings of one man in a much more eminent degree than the proceedings of any greater number; and in proportion as the number is increased, these qualities will be diminished.

This unity may be destroyed in two ways: either by vesting the power in two or more magistrates of equal dignity and authority; or by vesting it ostensibly in one man, subject, in whole or in part, to the control and cooperation of others, in the capacity of counsellors to him. Of the first, the two Consuls of Rome may serve as an example; of the last, we shall find examples in the constitutions of several of the States. New York and New Jersey, if I recollect right, are the only States which have intrusted the executive authority wholly to single men.* Both these methods of destroying the unity of the Executive have their partisans; but the votaries of an executive council are the most numerous. They are both liable, if not to equal, to similar objections, and may in most lights be examined in conjunction.

The experience of other nations will afford little instruction on this head. As far, however, as it teaches any thing, it teaches us not to be enamoured of plurality in the Executive. We have seen that the Achæans, on an experiment of two Prætors, were induced to abolish one. The Roman history

*New-York has no council except for the single purpose of appointing to offices; New-Jersey has a council, whom the governor may consult. But I think from the terms of the constitution their resolutions do not bind him.

records many instances of mischiefs to the republic from the dissensions between the Consuls, and between the military Tribunes, who were at times substituted for the Consuls. But it gives us no specimens of any peculiar advantages derived to the state from the circumstance of the plurality of those magistrates. That the dissensions between them were not more frequent or more fatal, is matter of astonishment, until we advert to the singular position in which the republic was almost continually placed, and to the prudent policy pointed out by the circumstances of the state, and pursued by the Consuls, of making a division of the government between them. The patricians engaged in a perpetual struggle with the plebeians for the preservation of their ancient authorities and dignities; the Consuls, who were generally chosen out of the former body, were commonly united by the personal interest they had in the defence of the privileges of their order. In addition to this motive of union, after the arms of the republic had considerably expanded the bounds of its empire, it became an established custom with the Consuls to divide the administration between themselves by lot—one of them remaining at Rome to govern the city and its environs, the other taking the command in the more distant provinces. This expedient must, no doubt, have had great influence in preventing those collisions and rivalships which might otherwise have embroiled the peace of the republic.

But quitting the dim light of historical research, attaching ourselves purely to the dictates of reason and good sense, we shall discover much greater cause to reject than to approve the idea of plurality in the Executive, under any modification whatever.

Wherever two or more persons are engaged in any common enterprise or pursuit, there is always danger of difference of opinion. If it be a public trust or office, in which they are clothed with equal dignity and authority, there is peculiar danger of personal emulation and even animosity. From either, and especially from all these causes, the most bitter dissensions are apt to spring. Whenever these happen, they lessen the respectability, weaken the authority, and distract the plans and operations of those whom they divide. If they should unfortunately assail the supreme executive magistracy of a country, consisting of a plurality of persons, they might impede or frustrate the most important measures of the government, in the most critical emergencies of the state. And what is still worse, they might split the community into the most violent and irreconcilable factions, adhering differently to the different individuals who composed the magistracy.

Men often oppose a thing, merely because they have had no agency in planning it, or because it may have been planned by those whom they dislike.

But if they have been consulted, and have happened to disapprove, opposition then becomes, in their estimation, an indispensable duty of self-love. They seem to think themselves bound in honor, and by all the motives of personal infallibility, to defeat the success of what has been resolved upon contrary to their sentiments. Men of upright, benevolent tempers have too many opportunities of remarking, with horror, to what desperate lengths this disposition is sometimes carried, and how often the great interests of society are sacrificed to the vanity, to the conceit, and to the obstinacy of individuals, who have credit enough to make their passions and their caprices interesting to mankind. Perhaps the question now before the public may, in its consequences, afford melancholy proofs of the effects of this despicable frailty, or rather detestable vice, in the human character.

Upon the principles of a free government, inconveniences from the source just mentioned must necessarily be submitted to in the formation of the legislature; but it is unnecessary, and therefore unwise, to introduce them into the constitution of the Executive. It is here too that they may be most pernicious. In the legislature, promptitude of decision is oftener an evil than a benefit. The differences of opinion, and the jarrings of parties in that department of the government, though they may sometimes obstruct salutary plans, yet often promote deliberation and circumspection, and serve to check excesses in the majority. When a resolution too is once taken, the opposition must be at an end. That resolution is a law, and resistance to it punishable. But no favorable circumstances palliate or atone for the disadvantages of dissension in the executive department. Here, they are pure and unmixed. There is no point at which they cease to operate. They serve to embarrass and weaken the execution of the plan or measures to which they relate, from the first step to the final conclusion of it. They constantly counteract those qualities in the Executive which are the most necessary ingredients in its composition,—vigor and expedition, and this without any counterbalancing good. In the conduct of war, in which the energy of the Executive is the bulwark of the national security, every thing would be to be apprehended from its plurality.

It must be confessed that these observations apply with principal weight to the first case supposed—that is, to a plurality of magistrates of equal dignity and authority, a scheme, the advocates for which are not likely to form a numerous sect; but they apply, though not with equal, yet with considerable weight to the project of a council, whose concurrence is made constitutionally necessary to the operations of the ostensible Executive. An artful cabal in that council would be able to distract and to enervate the whole system of administration. If no such cabal should exist, the mere diversity of views and opinions would alone be sufficient to tincture the exercise of the executive authority with a spirit of habitual feebleness and dilatoriness.

But one of the weightiest objections to a plurality in the Executive, and which lies as much against the last as the first plan, is, that it tends to conceal faults and destroy responsibility. Responsibility is of two kinds—to censure and to punishment. The first is the more important of the two, especially in an elective office. Man, in public trust, will much oftener act in such a manner as to render him unworthy of being any longer trusted, than in such a manner as to make him obnoxious to legal punishment. But the multiplication of the Executive adds to the difficulty of detection in either case. It often becomes impossible, amidst mutual accusations, to determine on whom the blame or the punishment of a pernicious measure, or series of pernicious measures ought really to fall. It is shifted from one to another with so much dexterity, and under such plausible appearances, that the public opinion is left in suspense about the real author. The circumstances which may have led to any national miscarriage or misfortune are sometimes so complicated that, where there are a number of actors who may have had different degrees and kinds of agency, though we may clearly see upon the whole that there has been mismanagement, yet it may be impracticable to pronounce to whose account the evil which may have been incurred is truly chargeable.

"I was overruled by my council. The council were so divided in their opinions that it was impossible to obtain any better resolution on the point." These and similar pretexts are constantly at hand, whether true or false. And who is there that will either take the trouble or incur the odium, of a strict scrutiny into the secret springs of the transaction? Should there be found a citizen zealous enough to undertake the unpromising task, if there happen to be collusion between the parties concerned, how easy it is to clothe the circumstances with so much ambiguity, as to render it uncertain what was the precise conduct of any of those parties?

In the single instance in which the governor of this State is coupled with a council—that is, in the appointment to offices, we have seen the mischiefs of it in the view now under consideration. Scandalous appointments to important offices have been made. Some cases, indeed, have been so flagrant that ALL PARTIES have agreed in the impropriety of the thing. When inquiry has been made, the blame has been laid by the governor on the members of the council, who, on their part, have charged it upon his nomination; while the people remain altogether at a loss to determine, by whose influence their interests have been committed to hands so unqualified and so manifestly improper. In tenderness to individuals, I forbear to descend to particulars.

It is evident from these considerations, that the plurality of the Executive tends to deprive the people of the two greatest securities they can have for the faithful exercise of any delegated power, *first,* the restrains of public opinion, which lose their efficacy, as well on account of the division of the censure attendant on bad measures among a number, as on account of the uncertainty on whom it ought to fall; and, *secondly,* the opportunity of discovering with facility and clearness the misconduct of the persons they trust, in order either to their removal from office, or to their actual punishment in cases which admit of it.

In England, the king is a perpetual magistrate; and it is a maxim which has obtained for the sake of the public peace, that he is unaccountable for his administration, and his person sacred. Nothing, therefore, can be wiser in that kingdom, than to annex to the king a constitutional council, who may be responsible to the nation for the advice they give. Without this, there would be no responsibility whatever in the executive department—an idea inadmissible in a free government. But even there the king is not bound by the resolutions of his council, though they are answerable for the advice they give. He is the absolute master of his own conduct in the exercise of his office, and may observe or disregard the counsel given to him at his sole discretion.

But in a republic, where every magistrate ought to be personally responsible for his behavior in office the reason which in the British Constitution dictates the propriety of a council, not only ceases to apply, but turns against the institution. In the monarchy of Great Britain, it furnishes a substitute for the prohibited responsibility of the chief magistrate, which serves in some degree as a hostage to the national justice for his good behavior. In the American republic, it would serve to destroy, or would greatly diminish, the intended and necessary responsibility of the Chief Magistrate himself.

The idea of a council to the Executive, which has so generally obtained in the State constitutions, has been derived from that maxim of republican jealousy which considers power as safer in the hands of a number of men than of a single man. If the maxim should be admitted to be applicable to the case, I should contend that the advantage on that side would not counterbalance the numerous disadvantages on the opposite side. But I do not think the rule at all applicable to the executive power. I clearly concur in opinion, in this particular, with a writer whom the celebrated Junius pronounces to be "deep, solid, and ingenious," that "the executive power is more easily confined when it is ONE";* that it is far more safe there should be a single object for the jealousy and watchfulness of the people; and, in a word, that all multiplication of the Executive is rather dangerous than friendly to liberty.

A little consideration will satisfy us, that the species of security sought for in the multiplication of the Executive, is unattainable. Numbers must be so great as to render combination difficult, or they are rather a source of danger than of security. The united credit and influence of several individuals must be more formidable to liberty, than the credit and influence of either of them separately. When power, therefore, is placed in the hands of so small a number of men, as to admit of their interests and views being easily combined in a common enterprise, by an artful leader, it becomes more liable to abuse, and more dangerous when abused, than if it be lodged in the hands of one man; who, from the very circumstance of his being alone, will be more narrowly watched and more readily suspected, and who cannot unite so great a mass of influence as when he is associated with others. The Decemvirs of Rome, whose name denotes their number,** were more to be dreaded in their usurpation than any ONE of them would have been. No person would think of proposing an Executive much more numerous than that body; from six to a dozen have been suggested for the number of the council. The extreme of these numbers, is not too great for an easy combination; and from such a combination America would have more to fear, than from the ambition of any single individual. A council to a magistrate, who is himself responsible for what he does, are generally nothing better than a clog upon his good intentions, are often the instruments and accomplices of his bad, and are almost always a cloak to his faults.

I forbear to dwell upon the subject of expense; though it be evident that if the council should be numerous enough to answer the principal end aimed at by the institution, the salaries of the members, who must be drawn from their homes to reside at the seat of government, would form an item in the catalogue of public expenditures too serious to be incurred for an object of equivocal utility. I will only add that, prior to the appearance of the Constitution, I rarely met with an intelligent man from any of the States, who did not admit, as the result of experience, that the UNITY of the executive of this State was one of the best of the distinguishing features of our constitution.

PUBLIUS.

---

*De Lolme.

**Ten.

The Federalist, *No. 72*

MARCH 19, 1788

To the People of the State of New York:

The administration of government, in its largest sense, comprehends all the operations of the body politic, whether legislative, executive, or judiciary; but in its most usual and perhaps in its most precise signification, it is limited to executive details, and falls peculiarly within the province of the executive department. The actual conduct of foreign negotiations, the preparatory plans of finance, the application and disbursement of the public moneys in conformity to the general appropriations of the legislature, the arrangement of the army and navy, the direction of the operations of war,—these, and other matters of a like nature, constitute what seems to be most properly understood by the administration of government. The persons, therefore, to whose immediate management these different matters are committed, ought to be considered as the assistants or deputies of the chief magistrate, and on this account, they ought to derive their offices from his appointment, at least from his nomination, and ought to be subject to his superintendence. This view of the subject will at once suggest to us the intimate connection between the duration of the executive magistrate in office and the stability of the system of administration. To reverse and undo what has been done by a predecessor, is very often considered by a successor as the best proof he can give of his own capacity and desert; and in addition to this propensity, where the alteration has been the result of public choice, the person substituted is warranted in supposing that the dismission of his predecessor has proceeded from a dislike to his measures; and that the less he resembles him, the more he will recommend himself to the favor of his constituents. These considerations, and the influence of personal confidences and attachments, would be likely to induce every new President to promote a change of men to fill the subordinate stations; and these causes together could not fail to occasion a disgraceful and ruinous mutability in the administration of the government.

With a positive duration of considerable extent, I connect the circumstance of reëligibility. The first is necessary to give to the officer himself the inclination and the resolution to act his part well, and to the community time and leisure to observe the tendency of his measures, and thence to form an experimental estimate of their merits. The last is necessary to enable the people, when they see reason to approve of his conduct, to continue him in his station, in order to prolong the utility of his talents and virtues, and to secure to the government the advantage of permanency in a wise system of administration.

Nothing appears more plausible at first sight, nor more ill-founded upon close inspection, than a scheme which in relation to the present point has had some respectable advocates,—I mean that of continuing the chief magistrate in office for a certain time, and then excluding him from it either for a limited period or forever after. This exclusion, whether temporary or perpetual, would have nearly the same effects, and these effects would be for the most part rather pernicious than salutary.

One ill effect of the exclusion would be a diminution of the inducements to good behavior. There are few men who would not feel much less zeal in the discharge of a duty, when they were conscious that the advantages of the station with which it was connected must be relinquished at a determinate period, than when they were permitted to entertain a hope of *obtaining,* by *meriting,* a continuance of them. This position will not be disputed so long as it is admitted that the desire of reward is one of the strongest incentives of human conduct; or that the best security for the fidelity of mankind is to make their interest coincide with their duty. Even the love of fame, the ruling passion of the noblest minds, which would prompt a man to plan and undertake extensive and arduous enterprises for the public benefit, requiring considerable time to mature and perfect them, if he could flatter himself with the prospect of being allowed to finish what he had begun, would, on the contrary, deter him from the undertaking, when he foresaw that he must quit the scene before he could accomplish the work, and must commit that, together with his own reputation, to hands which might be unequal or unfriendly to the task. The most to be expected from the generality of men, in such a situation, is the negative merit of not doing harm, instead of the positive merit of doing good.

Another ill effect of the exclusion would be the temptation to sordid views, to peculation, and, in some instances, to usurpation. An avaricious man, who might happen to fill the office, looking forward to a time when he must at all events yield up the emoluments he enjoyed, would feel a propensity, not easy to be resisted by such a man, to make the best use of the opportunity he enjoyed while it lasted, and might not scruple to have recourse to the most corrupt expedients to make the harvest as abundant as it was transitory; though the same man, probably, with a different prospect before him, might content himself with the regular perquisites of his situation, and might even be unwilling to risk the consequences of an abuse of his opportunities. His avarice might be a guard upon his avarice. Add to this that the same man might be vain or ambitious, as well as avaricious. And if he could expect to prolong his honors by his good conduct, he might hesitate to sacrifice his appetite for them to his appetite for gain. But with the prospect before him of approaching an inevitable annihilation, his avarice would be likely to get the victory over his caution, his vanity, or his ambition.

An ambitious man, too, when he found himself seated on the summit of his country's honors, when he looked forward to the time at which he must descend from the exalted eminence for ever, and reflected that no exertion of merit on his part could save him from the unwelcome reverse; such a man, in such a situation, would be much more violently tempted to embrace a favorable conjuncture for attempting the prolongation of his power, at every personal hazard, than if he had the probability of answering the same end by doing his duty.

Would it promote the peace of the community, or the stability of the government to have half a dozen men who had had credit enough to be raised to the seat of the supreme magistracy, wandering among the people like discontented ghosts, and sighing for a place which they were destined never more to possess?

A third ill effect of the exclusion would be, the depriving the community of the advantage of the experience gained by the chief magistrate in the exercise of his office. That experience is the parent of wisdom, is an adage the truth of which is recognized by the wisest as well as the simplest of mankind. What more desirable or more essential than this quality in the governors of nations? Where more desirable or more essential than in the first magistrate of a nation? Can it be wise to put this desirable and essential quality under the ban of the Constitution, and to declare that the moment it is acquired, its possessor shall be compelled to abandon the station in which it was acquired, and to which it is adapted? This, nevertheless, is the precise import of all those regulations which exclude men from serving their country, by the choice of their fellow-citizens, after they have by a course of service fitted themselves for doing it with a greater degree of utility.

A fourth ill effect of the exclusion would be the banishing men from stations in which, in certain emergencies of the state, their presence might be of the greatest moment to the public interest or safety. There is no nation which has not, at one period or another, experienced an absolute necessity of the services of particular men in particular situations; perhaps it would not be too strong to say, to the preservation of its political existence. How unwise, therefore, must be every such self-denying ordinance as serves to prohibit a nation from making use of its own citizens in the manner best suited to its exigencies and circumstances! Without supposing the personal essentiality of the man, it is evident that a change of the chief magistrate, at the breaking out of a war, or at any similar crisis, for another, even of equal merit, would at all times be detrimental to the community, inasmuch as it would substitute inexperience to experience, and would tend to unhinge and set afloat the already settled train of the administration.

A fifth ill effect of the exclusion would be, that it would operate as a constitutional interdiction of stability in the administration. By *necessitating* a change of men, in the first office of the nation, it would necessitate a mutability of measures. It is not generally to be expected, that men will vary and measures remain uniform. The contrary is the usual course of things. And we need not be apprehensive that there will be too much stability, while there is even the option of changing; nor need we desire to prohibit the people from continuing their confidence where they think it may be safely placed, and where, by constancy on their part, they may obviate the fatal inconveniences of fluctuating councils and a variable policy.

These are some of the disadvantages which would flow from the principle of exclusion. They apply most forcibly to the scheme of a perpetual exclusion; but when we consider that even a partial exclusion would always render the readmission of the person a remote and precarious object, the observations which have been made will apply nearly as fully to one case as to the other.

What are the advantages promised to counterbalance these disadvantages? They are represented to be: 1st, greater independence in the magistrate; 2d, greater security to the people. Unless the exclusion be perpetual, there will be no pretence to infer the first advantage. But even in that case, may he have no object beyond his present station, to which he may sacrifice his independence? May he have no connections, no friends, for whom he may sacrifice it? May he not be less willing, by a firm conduct, to make personal enemies, when he acts under the impression that a time is fast approaching, on the arrival of which he not only MAY, but MUST, be exposed to their resentments, upon an equal, perhaps upon an inferior, footing? It is not an easy point to determine whether his independence would be most promoted or impaired by such an arrangement.

As to the second supposed advantage, there is still greater reason to entertain doubts concerning it. If the exclusion were to be perpetual, a man of irregular ambition, of whom alone there could be reason in any case to entertain apprehension, would, with infinite reluctance, yield to the necessity of taking his leave forever of a post in which his passion for power and preëminence had acquired the force of habit. And if he had been fortunate or adroit enough to conciliate the good-will of the people, he might induce them to consider as a very odious and unjustifiable restraint upon themselves, a provision which was calculated to debar them of the right of giving a fresh proof of their attachment to a favorite. There may be conceived circumstances in which this disgust of the people, seconding the thwarted ambition of such a favorite, might occasion greater danger to liberty, than could ever reasonably be dreaded from the possibility of a perpetuation in office, by the voluntary suffrages of the community, exercising a constitutional privilege.

There is an excess of refinement in the idea of disabling the people to continue in office men who had entitled themselves, in their opinion, to approbation and confidence; the advantages of which are at best speculative and equivocal, and are overbalanced by disadvantages far more certain and decisive.

PUBLIUS.

The Federalist, *No. 78*

MAY 28, 1788

To the People of the State of New York:

We proceed now to an examination of the judiciary department of the proposed government.

In unfolding the defects of the existing Confederation, the utility and necessity of a federal judicature have been clearly pointed out. It is the less necessary to recapitulate the considerations there urged, as the propriety of the institution in the abstract is not disputed; the only questions which have been raised being relative to the manner of constituting it, and to its extent. To these points, therefore, our observations shall be confined.

The manner of constituting it seems to embrace these several objects: 1st. The mode of appointing the judges. 2d. The tenure by which they are to hold their places. 3d. The partition of the judiciary authority between different courts, and their relations to each other.

First. As to the mode of appointing the judges; this is the same with that of appointing the officers of the Union in general, and has been so fully discussed in the two last numbers, that nothing can be said here which would not be useless repetition.

Second. As to the tenure by which the judges are to hold their places: this chiefly concerns their duration in office; the provisions for their support; the precautions for their responsibility.

According to the plan of the convention, all judges who may be appointed by the United States are to hold their offices *during good behavior;* which is conformable to the most approved of the State constitutions, and among the rest, to that of this State. Its propriety having been drawn into question by the adversaries of that plan, is no light symptom of the rage for objection, which disorders their imaginations and judgments. The standard of good behavior for the continuance in office of the judicial magistracy, is certainly one of the most valuable of the modern improvements in the practice of government. In a monarchy it is an excellent barrier to the despotism of the prince; in a republic it is a no less excellent barrier to the encroachments and oppressions of the representative body. And it is the best expedient which can be devised in any government, to secure a steady, upright, and impartial administration of the laws.

Whoever attentively considers the different departments of power must perceive, that, in a government in which they are separated from each other, the judiciary, from the nature of its functions, will always be the least dangerous to the political rights of the Constitution; because it will be least in a capacity to annoy or injure them. The Executive not only dispenses the honors, but holds the sword of the community. The legislature not only commands the purse, but prescribes the rules by which the duties and rights of every citizen are to be regulated. The judiciary, on the contrary, has no influence over either the sword or the purse; no direction either of the strength or of the wealth of the society; and can take no active resolution whatever. It may truly be said to have neither FORCE nor WILL, but merely judgment; and must ultimately depend upon the aid of the executive arm even for the efficacy of its judgments.

This simple view of the matter suggests several important consequences. It proves incontestably, that the judiciary is beyond comparison the weakest of the three departments of power;* that it can never attack with success either of the other two; and that all possible care is requisite to enable it to defend itself against their attacks. It equally proves, that though individual oppression may now and then proceed from the courts of justice, the general liberty of the people can never be endangered from that quarter; I mean so long as the judiciary remains truly distinct from both the legisla-

*The celebrated Montesquieu, speaking of them, says: "Of the three powers above mentioned, the judiciary is next to nothing."—*Spirit of Laws,* vol. I, page 186.

ture and the Executive. For I agree, that "there is no liberty, if the power of judging be not separated from the legislative and executive powers."* And it proves, in the last place, that as liberty can have nothing to fear from the judiciary alone, but would have every thing to fear from its union with either of the other departments; that as all the effects of such a union must ensue from a dependence of the former on the latter, notwithstanding a nominal and apparent separation; that as, from the natural feebleness of the judiciary, it is in continual jeopardy of being overpowered, awed, or influenced by its co-ordinate branches; and that as nothing can contribute so much to its firmness and independence as permanency in office, this quality may therefore be justly regarded as an indispensable ingredient in its constitution, and, in a great measure, as the citadel of the public justice and the public security.

The complete independence of the courts of justice is peculiarly essential in a limited Constitution. By a limited Constitution, I understand one which contains certain specified exceptions to the legislative authority; such, for instance, as that it shall pass no bills of attainder, no *ex-post-facto* laws, and the like. Limitations of this kind can be preserved in practice no other way than through the medium of courts of justice, whose duty it must be to declare all acts contrary to the manifest tenor of the Constitution void. Without this, all the reservations of particular rights or privileges would amount to nothing.

Some perplexity respecting the rights of the courts to pronounce legislative acts void, because contrary to the Constitution, has arisen from an imagination that the doctrine would imply a superiority of the judiciary to the legislative power. It is urged that the authority which can declare the acts of another void, must necessarily be superior to the one whose acts may be declared void. As this doctrine is of great importance in all the American constitutions, a brief discussion of the ground on which it rests cannot be unacceptable.

There is no position which depends on clearer principles, than that every act of a delegated authority, contrary to the tenor of the commission under which it is exercised, is void. No legislative act, therefore, contrary to the Constitution, can be valid. To deny this, would be to affirm, that the deputy is greater than his principal; that the servant is above his master; that the representatives of the people are superior to the people themselves; that men acting by virtue of powers, may do not only what their powers do not authorize, but what they forbid.

**Idem*, page 181.

If it be said that the legislative body are themselves the constitutional judges of their own powers, and that the construction they put upon them is conclusive upon the other departments, it may be answered, that this cannot be the natural presumption, where it is not to be collected from any particular provisions in the Constitution. It is not otherwise to be supposed, that the Constitution could intend to enable the representatives of the people to substitute their *will* to that of their constituents. It is far more rational to suppose, that the courts were designed to be an intermediate body between the people and the legislature, in order, among other things, to keep the latter within the limits assigned to their authority. The interpretation of the laws is the proper and peculiar province of the courts. A constitution is, in fact, and must be regarded by the judges, as a fundamental law. It therefore belongs to them to ascertain its meaning, as well as the meaning of any particular act proceeding from the legislative body. If there should happen to be an irreconcilable variance between the two, that which has the superior obligation and validity ought, of course, to be preferred; or, in other words, the Constitution ought to be preferred to the statute, the intention of the people to the intention of their agents.

Nor does this conclusion by any means suppose a superiority of the judicial to the legislative power. It only supposes that the power of the people is superior to both; and that where the will of the legislature, declared in its statutes, stands in opposition to that of the people, declared in the Constitution, the judges ought to be governed by the latter rather than the former. They ought to regulate their decisions by the fundamental laws, rather than by those which are not fundamental.

This exercise of judicial discretion, in determining between two contradictory laws, is exemplified in a familiar instance. It not uncommonly happens, that there are two statutes existing at one time, clashing in whole or in part with each other, and neither of them containing any repealing clause or expression. In such a case, it is the province of the courts to liquidate and fix their meaning and operation. So far as they can, by any fair construction, be reconciled to each other, reason and law conspire to dictate that this should be done; where this is impracticable, it becomes a matter of necessity to give effect to one, in exclusion of the other. The rule which has obtained in the courts for determining their relative validity is, that the last in order of time shall be preferred to the first. But this is a mere rule of construction, not derived from any positive law, but from the nature and reason of the thing. It is a rule not enjoined upon the courts by legislative provision, but adopted by themselves, as consonant to truth and propriety, for the direction of their conduct as interpreters of the law. They thought it reasonable, that between the interfering acts of an *equal* authority, that which was the last indication of its will should have the preference.

But in regard to the interfering acts of a superior and subordinate authority, of an original and derivative power, the nature and reason of the thing indicate the converse of that rule as proper to be followed. They teach us that the prior act of a superior ought to be preferred to the subsequent act of an inferior and subordinate authority; and that accordingly, whenever a particular statute contravenes the Constitution, it will be the duty of the judicial tribunals to adhere to the latter and disregard the former.

It can be of no weight to say that the courts, on the pretence of a repugnancy, may substitute their own pleasure to the constitutional intentions of the legislature. This might as well happen in the case of two contradictory statutes; or it might as well happen in every adjudication upon any single statute. The courts must declare the sense of the law; and if they should be disposed to exercise WILL instead of JUDGMENT, the consequence would equally be the substitution of their pleasure to that of the legislative body. The observation, if it prove any thing, would prove that there ought to be no judges distinct from that body.

If, then, the courts of justice are to be considered as the bulwarks of a limited Constitution against legislative encroachments, this consideration will afford a strong argument for the permanent tenure of judicial offices, since nothing will contribute so much as this to that independent spirit in the judges which must be essential to the faithful performance of so arduous a duty.

This independence of the judges is equally requisite to guard the Constitution and the rights of individuals from the effects of those ill humors, which the arts of designing men, or the influence of particular conjunctures, sometimes disseminate among the people themselves, and which, though they speedily give place to better information, and more deliberate reflection, have a tendency, in the meantime, to occasion dangerous innovations in the government, and serious oppressions of the minor party in the community. Though I trust the friends of the proposed Constitution will never concur with its enemies,* in questioning that fundamental principle of republican government, which admits the right of the people to alter or abolish the established Constitution, whenever they find it inconsistent with their happiness, yet it is not to be inferred from this principle, that the representatives of the people, whenever a momentary inclination

***Vide,* "Protest of the Minority of the Convention of Pennsylvania," Martin's Speech, etc.

happens to lay hold of a majority of their constituents, incompatible with the provisions in the existing Constitution, would, on that account, be justifiable in a violation of those provisions; or that the courts would be under a greater obligation to connive at infractions in this shape, than when they had proceeded wholly from the cabals of the representative body. Until the people have, by some solemn and authoritative act, annulled or changed the established form, it is binding upon themselves collectively, as well as individually; and no presumption, or even knowledge, of their sentiments, can warrant their representatives in a departure from it, prior to such an act. But it is easy to see, that it would require an uncommon portion of fortitude in the judges to do their duty as faithful guardians of the Constitution, where legislative invasions of it had been instigated by the major voice of the community.

But it is not with a view to infractions of the Constitution only, that the independence of the judges may be an essential safeguard against the effects of occasional ill humors in the society. These sometimes extend no farther than to the injury of the private rights of particular classes of citizens, by unjust and partial laws. Here also the firmness of the judicial magistracy is of vast importance in mitigating the severity and confining the operation of such laws. It not only serves to moderate the immediate mischiefs of those which may have been passed, but it operates as a check upon the legislative body in passing them; who, perceiving that obstacles to the success of iniquitous intention are to be expected from the scruples of the courts, are in a manner compelled, by the very motives of the injustice they meditate, to qualify their attempts. This is a circumstance calculated to have more influence upon the character of our governments, than but few may be aware of. The benefits of the integrity and moderation of the judiciary have already been felt in more States than one; and though they may have displeased those whose sinister expectations they may have disappointed, they must have commanded the esteem and applause of all the virtuous and disinterested. Considerate men, of every description, ought to prize whatever will tend to beget or fortify that temper in the courts; as no man can be sure that he may not be to-morrow the victim of a spirit of injustice, by which he may be a gainer to-day. And every man must now feel, that the inevitable tendency of such a spirit is to sap the foundations of public and private confidence, and to introduce in its stead universal distrust and distress.

That inflexible and uniform adherence to the rights of the Constitution, and of individuals, which we perceive to be indispensable in the courts of justice, can certainly not be expected from judges who hold their offices by a temporary commission. Periodical appointments, however regulated, or by whomsoever made, would, in some way or other, be fatal to their necessary independence. If the power of making them was committed either to the Executive or legislature, there would be danger of an improper complaisance to the branch which possessed it; if to both, there would be an unwillingness to hazard the displeasure of either; if to the people, or to persons chosen by them for the special purpose, there would be too great a disposition to consult popularity to justify a reliance that nothing would be consulted but the Constitution and the laws.

There is yet a further and a weightier reason for the permanency of the judicial offices, which is deducible from the nature of the qualifications they require. It has been frequently remarked, with great propriety, that a voluminous code of laws is one of the inconveniences necessarily connected with the advantages of a free government. To avoid an arbitrary discretion in the courts, it is indispensable that they should be bound down by strict rules and precedents, which serve to define and point out their duty in every particular case that comes before them; and it will readily be conceived from the variety of controversies which grow out of the folly and wickedness of mankind, that the records of those precedents must unavoidably swell to a very considerable bulk, and must demand long and laborious study to acquire a competent knowledge of them. Hence it is, that there can be but few men in the society who will have sufficient skill in the laws to qualify them for the stations of judges. And making the proper deductions for the ordinary depravity of human nature, the number must be still smaller of those who unite the requisite integrity with the requisite knowledge. These considerations apprise us, that the government can have no great option between fit character; and that a temporary duration in office, which would naturally discourage such characters from quitting a lucrative line of practice to accept a seat on the bench, would have a tendency to throw the administration of justice into hands less able, and less well qualified, to conduct it with utility and dignity. In the present circumstances of this country, and in those in which it is likely to be for a long time to come, the disadvantages on this score would be greater than they may at first sight appear; but it must be confessed, that they are far inferior to those which present themselves under the other aspects of the subject.

Upon the whole, there can be no room to doubt that the convention acted wisely in copying from the models of those constitutions which have established *good behavior* as the tenure of their judicial offices, in point of duration; and that so far from being blamable on this account, their plan would have been inexcusably defective, if it had wanted this important feature of good government. The experience of Great Britain affords an illustrious comment on the excellence of the institution.

PUBLIUS.

To George Washington

NEW YORK, AUGUST 13, 1788.

Sir:

[. . .] I have delivered to Mr. Madison, to be forwarded to you, a set of the papers under the signature of Publius, neatly enough bound to be honored with a place in your library. I presume you have understood that the writers of these papers are chiefly Mr. Madison and myself, with some aid from Mr. Jay.

I take it for granted, sir, you have concluded to comply with what will no doubt be the general call of your country in relation to the new government. You will permit me to say that it is indispensable you should lend yourself to its first operations. It is of little purpose to have *introduced* a system, if the weightiest influence is not given to its firm *establishment* in the outset.

To Lafayette

NEW YORK, OCTOBER 6TH. 1789.

My Dear Marquis:

I have seen with a mixture of pleasure and apprehension the progress of the events which have lately taken place in your country. As a friend to mankind and to liberty, I rejoice in the efforts which you are making to establish it, while I fear much for the final success of the attempts, for the fate of those I esteem who are engaged in it, and for the danger, in case of success, of innovations greater than will consist with the real felicity of your nation. If your affairs still go well when this reaches you, you will ask why this foreboding of ill, when all the appearances have been so much in your favor. I will tell you. I dread disagreements among those who are now united (which will be likely to be improved by the adverse party) about the nature of your constitution; I dread the vehement character of your people, whom I fear you may find it more easy to bring on, than to keep within proper bounds after you have put them in motion; I dread the interested refractoriness of your nobles, who cannot be gratified, and who may be unwilling to submit to the requisite sacrifices. And I dread the reveries of your philosophic politicians, who appear in the moment to have great influence, and who, being mere speculatists, may aim at more refinement than suits either with human nature or the composition of your nation.

These, my dear Marquis, are my apprehensions. My wishes for your personal success and that of the cause of liberty are incessant. Be virtuous amidst the seductions of ambition, and you can hardly in any event be unhappy. You are combined with a great and good man; you will anticipate the name of Neckar. I trust you and he will never cease to harmonize.

You will, I presume, have heard before this gets to hand, that I have been appointed to the head of the finances of this country. This event, I am sure, will give you pleasure. In undertaking the task I hazard much, but I thought it an occasion that called upon me to hazard. I have no doubt that the reasonable expectation of the public may be satisfied, if I am properly supported by the Legislature, and in this respect I stand at present on the most encouraging footing.

The debt due to France will be among the first objects of my attention. Hitherto it has been from necessity neglected. The session of Congress is now over. It has been exhausted in the organization of the government and in a few laws of immediate urgency respecting navigation and commercial imposts. The subject of the debt, foreign and domestic, has been referred to the next session, which will commence the first Monday in January, with an instruction to me to prepare and report a plan comprehending an adequate provision for the support of the public credit. There were many good reasons for a temporary adjournment.

From this sketch you will perceive that I am not in a situation to address any thing officially to your administration; but I venture to say to you, as my friend, that if the installments of the principal of the debt could be suspended for a few years, it would be a valuable accommodation to the United States. In this suggestion, I contemplate a speedy payment of the *arrears* of *interest* now due, and effectual provision for the punctual payment of future interest as it arises. Could an arrangement of this sort meet the approbation of your government, it would be best on every account that the offer should come unsolicited as a fresh mark of good-will.

I wrote you last by Mr. De Warville. I presume you received my letter. As it touched upon some delicate topics I should be glad to know its fate.

Yours with unalterable esteem and affection

P.S.—The latest accounts from France have abated some of my apprehensions. The abdications of privileges patronized by your nobility in the States-General are truly noble, and bespeak a patriotic and magnanimous policy which promises good both to them and their country.

Memorandum by George Beckwith on a Conversation with Alexander Hamilton

OCTOBER 1789

I have requested to see you on this occasion from a Wish to Explain Certain points, relative to our situation, and from a desire to suggest a measure, which I conceive to be both for the interest of Great Britain, and of this Country to adopt. We have lately Established a Government upon principles, that in my opinion render it safe for any Nation to Enter into Treaties with us, Either Commercial or Political, which has not hitherto been the Case; I have always preferred a Connexion with you, to that of any other Country, *We think in English,* and have a similarity of prejudices, and of predilections; I have been in the habits of considering this subject, We are a young and a growing Empire, with much Enterprize and vigour, but undoubtedly are, and must be for years, rather an Agricultural, than a manufacturing people; yet our policy has had a tendency to suggest the Necessity of introducing manufactures, which Accordingly have made some progress in Connecticut, where Cloth has been manufactured to some Extent, leaving already a clear profit of between six and seven per cent to the proprietors, and Pensylvania has gone further in her Exertions in different branches. These and similar Efforts are to no Comparative Extent, but doubtless their Encrease will be proportioned to your Conduct.

I am free to say, that Although France has been indulgent to us, in certain points, yet, what she can furnish, is by no means so Essential or so suited to us as Your productions, nor do our raw Materials suit her so well as they do you.

The Government of a Country Cannot altogether change Either the taste or the disposition of a people, but its influence may check or cherish it.

We wish to form a Commercial treaty with you to Every Extent, to which you may think it for Your interest to go. [. . .]

Report on Public Credit

JANUARY 9, 1790

[. . .] While the observance of that good faith, which is the basis of public credit, is recommended by the strongest inducements of political expediency, it is enforced by considerations of still greater authority. There are arguments for it which rest on the immutable principles of moral obligation. And in proportion as the mind is disposed to contemplate, in the order of Providence, an intimate connection between public virtue and public happiness, will be its repugnancy to a violation of those principles.

This reflection derives additional strength from the nature of the debt of the United States. It was the price of liberty. The faith of America has been repeatedly pledged for it, and with solemnities that give peculiar force to the obligation. There is, indeed, reason to regret that it has not hitherto been kept; that the necessities of the war, conspiring with inexperience in the subjects of finance, produced direct infractions; and that the subsequent period has been a continued scene of negative violation or non-compliance. But a diminution of this regret arises from the reflection, that the last seven years have exhibited an earnest and uniform effort, on the part of the Government of the Union, to retrieve the national credit, by doing justice to the creditors of the nation; and that the embarrassments of a defective Constitution, which defeated this laudable effort, have ceased. [. . .]

The Secretary [. . .] entertains a full conviction that an assumption of the debts of the particular States by the Union, and a like provision for them as for those of the Union, will be a measure of sound policy and substantial justice.

It would, in the opinion of the Secretary, contribute, in an eminent degree, to an orderly, stable, and satisfactory arrangement of the national finances. Admitting, as ought to be the case, that a provision must be made, in some way or other, for the entire debt, it will follow that no greater revenues will be required whether that provision be made wholly by the United States, or partly by them and partly by the States separately. [. . .]

Persuaded, as the Secretary is, that the proper funding of the present debt will render it a national blessing, yet he is so far from acceding to the position, in the latitude in which it is sometimes laid down, that "public debts are public benefits"—a position inviting to prodigality and liable to dangerous abuse—that he ardently wishes to see it incorporated as a fundamental maxim in the system of public credit of the United States, that the creation of debt should always be accompanied with the means of extinguishment. This he regards as the true secret for rendering public credit immortal. And he presumes that it is difficult to conceive a situation in which there may not be an adherence to the maxim. At least, he feels an unfeigned solicitude that this may be attempted by the United States, and that they may commence their measures for the establishment of credit with the observance of it. [. . .]

Report on a National Bank

DECEMBER 13, 1790

[. . .] Considerations of public advantage suggest a further wish, which is—that the Bank could be established upon principles that would cause the profits of it to redound to the immediate benefit of the State. This is contemplated by many who speak of a National Bank, but the idea seems liable to insuperable objections. To attach full confidence to an institution of this nature, it appears to be an essential ingredient in its structure, that it shall be under a *private* not a *public* direction—under the guidance of *individual interest,* not of *public policy;* which would be supposed to be, and, in certain emergencies, under a feeble or too sanguine administration, would really be, liable to being too much influenced by *public necessity.* The suspicion of this would, most probably, be a canker that would continually corrode the vitals of the credit of the Bank, and would be most likely to prove fatal in those situations in which the public good would require that they should be most sound and vigorous. It would, indeed, be little less than a miracle, should the credit of the Bank be at the disposal of the government, if, in a long series of time, there was not experienced a calamitous abuse of it. It is true, that it would be the real interest of the government not to abuse it; its genuine policy to husband and cherish it with the most guarded circumspection, as an inestimable treasure. But what government ever uniformly consulted its true interests in opposition to the temptations of momentary exigencies? What nation was ever blessed with a constant succession of upright and wise administrators?

The keen, steady, and, as it were, magnetic sense of their own interest as proprietors, in the Directors of a Bank, pointing invariably to its true pole—the prosperity of the institution,—is the only security that can always be relied upon for a careful and prudent administration. It is, therefore, the only basis on which an enlightened, unqualified, and permanent confidence can be expected to be erected and maintained. [. . .]

Report on Manufactures

DECEMBER 5, 1791

The Secretary of the Treasury, in obedience to the order of the House of Representatives, of the 15th day of January, 1790, has applied his attention, at as early a period as his other duties would permit, to the subject of Manufactures, and particularly to the means of promoting such as will tend to render the United States independent on foreign nations for military and other essential supplies; and he thereupon respectfully submits the following report:

The expediency of encouraging manufactures in the United States, which was not long since deemed very questionable, appears at this time to be pretty generally admitted. The embarrassments which have obstructed the progress of our external trade, have led to serious reflections on the necessity of enlarging the sphere of our domestic commerce. The restrictive regulations, which, in foreign markets, abridge the vent of the increasing surplus of our agricultural produce, serve to beget an earnest desire that a more extensive demand for that surplus may be created at home; and the complete success which has rewarded manufacturing enterprise in some valuable branches, conspiring with the promising symptoms which attend some less mature essays in others, justify a hope that the obstacles to the growth of this species of industry are less formidable than they were apprehended to be, and that it is not difficult to find, in its further extension, a full indemnification for any external disadvantages, which are or may be experienced, as well as an accession of resources, favorable to national independence and safety. [. . .]

It ought readily be conceded that the cultivation of the earth, as the primary and most certain source of national supply, as the immediate and chief source of subsistence to a man, as the principal source of those materials which constitute the nutriment of other kinds of labor, as including a state most favorable to the freedom and independence of the human mind—one, perhaps, most conducive to the multiplication of the human species, has intrinsically a strong claim to pre-eminence over every other kind of industry.

But, that it has a title to any thing like an exclusive predilection, in any country, ought to be admitted with great caution; that it is even more productive than every other branch of industry, requires more evidence than has yet been given in support of the position. That its real interests, precious and important as, without the help of exaggeration, they truly are, will be advanced, rather than injured, by the due encouragement of manufactures, may, it is believed, be satisfactorily demonstrated. And it is also believed that the expediency of such encouragement, in a general view, may be shown to be recommended by the most cogent and persuasive motives of national policy. [. . .]

1. As to the division of labor

It has justly been observed, that there is scarcely any thing of greater moment in the economy of a nation than the proper division of labor. The separation of occupations causes each to be carried to a much greater perfection than it could possibly acquire if they were blended. This arises principally from three circumstances:

1st. The greater skill and dexterity naturally resulting from a constant and undivided application to a single object. [. . .]

2d. The economy of time, by avoiding the loss of it, incident to a frequent transition from one operation to another of a different nature. [. . .]

3d. An extension of the use of machinery. A man occupied on a single object will have it more in his power, and will be more naturally led to exert his imagination, in devising methods to facilitate and abridge labor, than if he were perplexed by a variety of independent and dissimilar operations. Besides this the fabrication of machines, in numerous instances, becoming itself a distinct trade, the artist who follows it has all the advantages which have been enumerated, for improvement in his particular art; and, in both ways, the invention and application of machinery are extended.

And from these causes united, the mere separation of the occupation of the cultivator from that of the artificer, has the effect of augmenting the productive powers of labor, and with them, the total mass of the produce or revenue of a country. In this single view of the subject, therefore, the utility of artificers or manufacturers, towards producing an increase of productive industry, is apparent.

2. As to an extension of the use of machinery, a point which, though partly anticipated, requires to be placed in one or two additional lights

The employment of machinery forms an item of great importance in the general mass of national industry. It is an artificial force brought in aid of the natural force of man; and, to all the purposes of labor, is an increase of hands, an accession of strength, unencumbered too by the expense of maintaining the laborer. May it not, therefore, be fairly inferred, that those occupations which give greatest scope to the use of this auxiliary, contribute most to the general stock of industrious effort, and, in consequence, to the general product of industry?

It shall be taken for granted, and the truth of the position referred to observation, that manufacturing pursuits are susceptible, in a greater degree, of the application of machinery, than those of agriculture. If so, all the difference is lost to a community which, instead of manufacturing for itself, procures the fabrics requisite to its supply from other countries. The substitution of foreign for domestic manufactures is a transfer to foreign nations of the advantages accruing from the employment of machinery, in the modes in which it is capable of being employed with most utility and to the greatest extent.

The cotton-mill, invented in England, within the last twenty years, is a signal illustration of the general proposition which has been just advanced. In consequence of it, all the different processes for spinning cotton are performed by means of machines, which are put in motion by water, and attended chiefly by women and children—and by a smaller number of persons, in the whole, than are requisite in the ordinary mode of spinning. And it is an advantage of great moment, that the operations of this mill continue with convenience during the night as well as through the day. The prodigious effect of such a machine is easily conceived. To this invention is to be attributed, essentially, the immense progress which has been so suddenly made in Great Britain, in the various fabrics of cotton.

3. As to the additional employment of classes of the community not originally engaged in the particular business

This is not among the least valuable of the means by which manufacturing institutions contribute to augment the general stock of industry and production. In places where those institutions prevail, besides the persons regularly engaged in them, they afford occasional and extra employment to industrious individuals and families, who are willing to devote the leisure resulting from the intermissions of their ordinary pursuits to collateral labors, as a resource for multiplying their acquisitions or their enjoyments. The husbandman himself experiences a new source of profit and support from the increased industry of his wife and daughters, invited and stimulated by the demands of the neighboring manufactories.

Besides this advantage of occasional employment to classes having different occupations, there is another, of a nature allied to it, and of a similar tendency. This is the employment of persons who would otherwise be idle, and in many cases a burthen on the community, either from the bias of temper, habit, infirmity of body, or some other cause, indisposing or disqualifying them for the toils of the country. It is worthy of particular remark that, in general, women and children are rendered more useful, and the latter more early useful, by manufacturing establishments, than they would otherwise be. Of the number of persons employed in the cotton manufactories of Great Britain, it is computed that four sevenths, nearly, are women and children, of whom the greatest proportion are children, and many of them of a tender age.

And thus it appears to be one of the attributes of manufactures, and one of no small consequence, to give occasion to the exertion of a greater quantity of industry, even by the same number of persons, where they happen to prevail, than would exist if there were no such establishments.

4. As to the promoting of emigration from foreign countries

Men reluctantly quit one course of occupation and livelihood for another, unless invited to it by very apparent and proximate advantages. Many who would go from one country to another, if they had a prospect of continuing with more benefit the callings to which they have been educated, will often not be tempted to change their situation by the hope of doing better in some other way. Manufacturers who, listening to the powerful invitations of a better price for their fabrics or their labor, of greater cheapness of provisions and raw materials, of an exemption from the chief part of the taxes, burthens, and restraints which they endure in the Old World, of greater personal independence and consequence, under the operation of a more equal government, and of what is far more precious than mere religious toleration, a perfect equality of religious privileges, would probably flock from Europe to the United States, to pursue their own trades or professions, if they were once made sensible of the advantages they would enjoy, and were inspired with an assurance of encouragement and employment, will, with difficulty, be induced to transplant themselves, with a view to becoming cultivators of land.

If it be true, then, that it is the interest of the United States to open every possible avenue to emigration from abroad, it affords a weighty argument for the encouragement of manufactures; which, for the reasons just assigned, will have the strongest tendency to multiply the inducements to it.

Here is perceived an important resource, not only for extending the population, and with it the useful and productive labor of the country, but likewise for the prosecution of manufactures, without deducting from the number of hands which might otherwise be drawn to tillage, and even for the indemnification of agriculture for such as might happen to be diverted from it. Many, whom manufacturing views would induce to emigrate, would, afterwards, yield to the temptations which the particular situation of this country holds out to agricultural pursuits. And while agriculture would, in other respects, derive many signal and unmingled advantages from the growth of manufactures, it is a problem whether it would gain or lose, as to the article of the number of persons employed in carrying it on.

5. *As to the furnishing greater scope for the diversity of talents and dispositions, which discriminate men from each other*

This is a much more powerful means of augmenting the fund of national industry, than may at first sight appear. It is a just observation, that minds of the strongest and most active powers for their proper objects, fall below mediocrity, and labor without effect, if confined to uncongenial pursuits. And it is thence to be inferred, that the results of human exertion may be immensely increased by diversifying its objects. When all the different kinds of industry obtain in a community, each individual can find his proper element, and can call into activity the whole vigor of his nature. And the community is benefited by the services of its respective members, in the manner in which each can serve it with most effect.

If there be any thing in a remark often to be met with, namely, that there is, in the genius of the people of this country, a peculiar aptitude for mechanic improvements, it would operate as a forcible reason for giving opportunities to the exercise of that species of talent, by the propagation of manufactures.

6. *As to the affording a more ample and various field for enterprise*

This also is of greater consequence in the general scale of national exertion than might, perhaps, on a superficial view be supposed, and has effects not altogether dissimilar from those of the circumstance last noticed. To cherish and stimulate the activity of the human mind, by multiplying the objects of enterprise, is not among the least considerable of the expedients by which the wealth of a nation may be promoted. Even things in themselves not positively advantageous sometimes become so, by their tendency to provoke exertion. Every new scene which is opened to the busy nature of man to rouse and exert itself, is the addition of a new energy to the general stock of effort.

The spirit of enterprise, useful and prolific as it is, must necessarily be contracted or expanded, in proportion to the simplicity or variety of the occupations and productions which are to be found in a society. It must be less in a nation of mere cultivators, than in a nation of cultivators and merchants; less in a nation of cultivators and merchants, than in a nation of cultivators, artificers, and merchants.

7. As to the creating, in some instances, a new, and securing, in all, a more certain and steady demand for the surplus produce of the soil

[. . .] It is evident that the exertions of the husbandman will be steady or fluctuating, vigorous or feeble, in proportion to the steadiness or fluctuation, adequateness or inadequateness, of the markets on which he must depend for the vent of the surplus which may be produced by his labor; and that such surplus, in the ordinary course of things, will be greater or less in the same proportion.

For the purpose of this vent, a domestic market is greatly to be preferred to a foreign one; because it is, in the nature of things, far more to be relied upon. [. . .]

To secure such a market there is no other expedient than to promote manufacturing establishments. Manufacturers, who constitute the most numerous class, after the cultivators of land, are for that reason the principal consumers of the surplus of their labor.

This idea of an extensive domestic market for the surplus produce of the soil, is of the first consequence. It is, of all things, that which most effectually conduces to a flourishing state of agriculture. If the effect of manufactories should be to detach a portion of the hands which would otherwise be engaged in tillage, it might possibly cause a smaller quantity of lands to be under cultivation; but, by their tendency to procure a more certain demand for the surplus produce of the soil, they would, at the same time, cause the lands which were in cultivation to be better improved and more productive. And while, by their influence, the condition of each individual farmer would be meliorated, the total mass of agricultural production would probably be increased. For this must evidently depend as much upon the degree of improvement, if not more, than upon the number of acres under culture.

It merits particular observation, that the multiplication of manufactories not only furnishes a market for those articles which have been accustomed to be produced in abundance in a country, but it likewise creates a demand for such as were either unknown or produced in inconsiderable quantities. The bowels as well as the surface of the earth are ransacked for articles which were before neglected. Animals, plants, and minerals acquire a utility and a value which were before unexplored. [. . .]

[. . .] Industry, if left to itself, will naturally find its way to the most useful and profitable employment. Whence it is inferred that manufactures, without the aid of government, will grow up as soon and as fast as the natural state of things and the interest of the community may require. [. . .]

Experience teaches, that men are often so much governed by what they are accustomed to see and practise, that the simplest and most obvious improvements, in the most ordinary occupations, are adopted with hesitation, reluctance, and by slow gradations. The spontaneous transition to new pursuits, in a community long habituated to different ones, may be expected to be attended with proportionably greater difficulty. When former occupations ceased to yield a profit adequate to the subsistence of their followers, or when there was an absolute deficiency of employment in them, owing to the superabundance of hands, changes would ensue; but these changes would be likely to be more tardy than might consist with the interest either of individuals or of the society. In many cases they would not happen, while a bare support could be insured by an adherence to ancient courses, though a resort to a more profitable employment might be practicable. To produce the desirable changes as early as may be expedient may therefore require the incitement and patronage of government.

The apprehension of failing in new attempts is, perhaps, a more serious impediment. There are dispositions apt to be attracted by the mere novelty of an undertaking; but these are not always the best calculated to give it success. To this it is of importance that the confidence of cautious, sagacious capitalists, both citizens and foreigners, should be excited. And to inspire this description of persons with confidence, it is essential that they should be made to see in any project which is new—and for that reason alone, if for no other, precarious—the prospect of such a degree of countenance and support from government, as may be capable of overcoming the obstacles inseparable from first experiments. [. . .]

There is, at the present juncture, a certain fermentation of mind, a certain activity of speculation and enterprise which, if properly directed, may be made subservient to useful purposes; but which, if left entirely to itself, may be attended with pernicious effects.

The disturbed state of Europe inclining its citizens to emigration, the requisite workmen will be more easily acquired than at another time; and the effect of multiplying the opportunities of employment to those who emigrate, may be an increase of the number and extent of valuable acquisitions to the population, arts, and industry of the country.

To find pleasure in the calamities of other nations would be criminal; but to benefit ourselves, by opening an asylum to those who suffer in consequence of them, is as justifiable as it is politic. [. . .]

Except the simple and ordinary kinds of household manufacture or those for which there are very commanding local advantages, pecuniary bounties are, in most cases, indispensable to the introduction of a new branch. A stimulus and a support, not less powerful and direct, is, generally speaking, essential to the overcoming of the obstacles which arise from the competitions of superior skill and maturity elsewhere. Bounties are especially essential in regard to articles upon which those foreigners, who have been accustomed to supply a country, are in the practice of granting them.

The continuance of bounties on manufactures long established must almost always be of questionable policy; because a presumption would arise, in every such case, that there were natural and inherent impediments to success. But, in new undertakings, they are as justifiable as they are oftentimes necessary.

There is a degree of prejudice against bounties, from an appearance of giving away the public money without an immediate consideration, and from a supposition that they serve to enrich particular classes at the expense of the community.

But neither of these sources of dislike will bear a serious examination. There is no purpose to which public money can be more beneficially applied than to the acquisition of a new and useful branch of industry; no consideration more valuable than a permanent addition to the general stock of productive labor. [. . .]

A question has been made concerning the constitutional right of the Government of the United States to apply this species of encouragement, but there is certainly no good foundation for such a question. The National Legislature has express authority "to lay and collect taxes, duties, imposts, and excises, to pay the debts, and provide for the common defence and general welfare," with no other qualifications than that "all duties, imposts, and excises shall be uniform throughout the United States; and that no capitation or other direct tax shall be laid, unless in proportion to numbers ascertained by a census or enumeration, taken on the principles prescribed in the Constitution," and that "no tax or duty shall be laid on articles exported from any State."

These three qualifications excepted, the power to raise money is plenary and indefinite, and the objects to which it may be appropriated are no less comprehensive than the payment of the public debts, and the providing for the common defence and general welfare. The terms "general welfare" were doubtless intended to signify more than was expressed or imported in those which preceded; otherwise, numerous exigencies incident to the affairs of a nation would have been left without a provision. The phrase is as comprehensive as any that could have been used, because it was not fit that the constitutional authority of the Union to appropriate its revenues should have been restricted within narrower limits than the "general welfare," and because this necessarily embraces a vast variety of particulars, which are susceptible neither of specification nor of definition.

It is, therefore, of necessity, left to the discretion of the National Legislature to pronounce upon the objects which concern the general welfare, and for which, under that description, an appropriation of money is requisite and proper. And there seems to be no room for a doubt that whatever concerns the general interests of learning, of agriculture, of manufactures, and of commerce, are within the sphere of the national councils, as far as regards an application of money.

The only qualification of the generality of the phrase in question, which seems to be admissible, is this: That the object to which an appropriation of money is to be made be general, and not local; its operation extending in fact or by possibility throughout the Union, and not being confined to a particular spot. [. . .]

To Edward Carrington

PHILADELPHIA, MAY 26TH, 1792

My Dear Sir:

Believing that I possess a share of your personal friendship and confidence, and yielding to that which I feel towards you; persuaded also, that our political creed is the same on two essential points—first, the necessity of Union to the respectability and happiness of this country, and second, the necessity of an efficient general government to maintain the Union, I have concluded to unbosom myself to you, on the present state of political parties and views. [. . .]

When I accepted the office I now hold, it was under full persuasion, that from similarity of thinking, conspiring with personal good-will, I should have the firm support of Mr. Madison, in the general course of my administration. Aware of the intrinsic difficulties of the situation, and of the powers of Mr. Madison, I do not believe I should have accepted under a different supposition.

I have mentioned the similarity of thinking between that gentleman and myself. This was relative, not merely to the general principles of national policy and government, but to the leading points, which were likely to constitute questions in the administration of the finances. I mean, first, the expediency of funding the debt; second, the inexpediency of discrimination between original and present holders; third, the expediency of assuming the State debts.

As to the first point, the evidence of Mr. Madison's sentiments, at one period, is to be found in the address of Congress, of April twenty-sixth, seventeen hundred and eighty-three, which was planned by him, in conformity to his own ideas, and without any previous suggestions from the committee, and with his hearty co-operation in every part of the business. His conversations upon various occasions since have been expressive of a continuance in the same sentiment; nor, indeed, has he yet contradicted it, by any part of his official conduct. How far there is reason to apprehend a change in this particular, will be stated hereafter.

As to the second part, the same address is an evidence of Mr. Madison's sentiments at the same period. And I had been informed that at a later period he had been, in the Legislature of Virginia, a strenuous and successful opponent of the principle of discrimination. Add to this, that a variety of conversations had taken place between him and myself, respecting the public debt, down to the commencement of the new government, in none of which had he glanced at the idea of a change of opinion. I wrote him a letter after my appointment, in the recess of Congress, to obtain his sentiments on the subject of the finances. In his answer, there is not a lisp of his new system.

As to the third point, the question of an assumption of the State debts by the United States was in discussion when the convention that framed the present government was sitting at Philadelphia, and in a long conversation which I had with Mr. Madison in an afternoon's walk, I well remember that we were perfectly agreed in the expediency and propriety of such a measure; though we were both of opinion that it would be more advisable to make it a measure of administration than an article of

Constitution, from the impolicy of multiplying obstacles to its reception on collateral details.

Under these circumstances you will naturally imagine that it must have been matter of surprise to me when I was apprised that it was Mr. Madison's intention to oppose my plan on both the last-mentioned points. Before the debate commenced, I had a conversation with him on my report; in the course of which I alluded to the calculation I had made of his sentiments, and the grounds of that calculation. He did not deny them; but alleged in his justification that the very considerable alienation of the debt, subsequent to the periods at which he had opposed a discrimination, had essentially changed the state of the question; and that as to the assumption, he had contemplated it to take place as matters stood at the peace. [. . .]

At this time and afterwards repeated intimations were given to me that Mr. Madison, from a spirit of rivalship, or some other cause, had become personally unfriendly to me; and one gentleman in particular, whose honor I have no reason to doubt, assured me that Mr. Madison, in a conversation with him, had made a pretty direct attempt to insinuate unfavorable impressions of me. Still I suspended my opinion on the subject. I knew the malevolent officiousness of mankind too well to yield a very ready acquiescence to the suggestions which were made, and resolved to wait till time and more experience should afford a solution. It was not till the last session that I became unequivocally convinced of the following truth: "that Mr. Madison, co-operating with Mr. Jefferson, is at the head of a faction decidedly hostile to me and my administration; and actuated by views, in my judgment, subversive of the principles of good government and dangerous to the Union, peace, and happiness of the country."

These are strong expressions, they may pain your friendship for one or both of the gentlemen whom I have named. I have not lightly resolved to hazard them. They are the result of a serious alarm in my mind for the public welfare, and of a full conviction that what I have alleged is a truth, and a truth which ought to be told, and well attended to by all the friends of the Union and efficient national government. The suggestion will, I hope, at least, awaken attention free from the bias of former prepossessions.

This conviction, in my mind, is the result of a long train of circumstances, many of them minute. To attempt to detail them all would fill a volume. I shall therefore confine myself to the mention of a few.

First—As to the point of opposition to me and my administration.

Mr. Jefferson, with very little reserve, manifests his dislike of the funding system generally, calling in question the expediency of funding a debt at all. [. . .] In the question concerning the bank he not only delivered an opinion in writing against its constitutionality and expediency, but he did it in a style and manner which I felt as partaking of asperity and ill humor toward me. [. . .]

With regard to Mr. Madison, [. . .] in his public conduct there has been a more uniform and persevering opposition than I have been able to resolve into a sincere difference of opinion. I cannot persuade myself that Mr. Madison and I, whose politics had formerly so much the same point of departure, should now diverge so widely in our opinions of the measures which are proper to be pursued. The opinion I once entertained of the candor and simplicity and fairness of Mr. Madison's character, has, I acknowledge, given way to a decided opinion that it is one of a peculiarly artificial and complicated kind. [. . .] When the Department of the Treasury was established, Mr. Madison was an unequivocal advocate of the principles which prevailed in it, and of the powers and duties which were assigned by it to the head of the department. This appeared, both from his private and public discourse, and I will add, that I have personal evidence that Mr. Madison is as well convinced as any man in the United States of the necessity of the arrangement which characterizes that establishment, to the orderly conducting of the business of the finances. Mr. Madison nevertheless opposed a reference to me to report ways and means for the Western expedition, and combated, on principle, the propriety of such references.

He well knew that if he had prevailed a certain consequence was my resignation; that I would not be fool enough to make pecuniary sacrifices and endure a life of extreme drudgery without opportunity either to do material good or to acquire reputation. [. . .]

Mr. Jefferson, it is known, did not in the first instance cordially acquiesce in the new Constitution for the United States; he had many doubts and reserves. He left this country before we had experienced the imbecilities of the former.

In France, he saw government only on the side of its abuses. He drank freely of the French philosophy, in religion, in science, in politics. He came from France in the moment of a fermentation, which he had a share in exciting, and in the passions and feelings of which he shared both from temperament and situation. He came here probably with a too partial idea of his own powers; and with the expectation of a greater share in the direction of our councils than he has in reality enjoyed. I am not sure that he had not peculiarly marked out for himself the department of the finances.

He came, electrified with attachment to France, and with the project of knitting together the two countries in the closest political bands.

Mr. Madison had always entertained an exalted opinion of the talents, knowledge, and virtues of Mr. Jefferson. The sentiment was probably reciprocal. A close correspondence subsisted between them during the time of Mr. Jefferson's absence from the country. A close intimacy arose upon his return. [. . .]

Another circumstance has contributed to widening the breach. 'Tis evident, beyond a question, from every movement, that Mr. Jefferson aims with ardent desire at the Presidential chair. This, too, is an important object of the party-politics. It is supposed, from the nature of my former personal and political connections, that I may favor some other candidate more than Mr. Jefferson, when the question shall occur by the retreat of the present gentleman. My influence, therefore, with the community becomes a thing, on ambitious and personal grounds, to be resisted and destroyed. [. . .]

A word on another point. I am told that serious apprehensions are disseminated in your State as to the existence of a monarchical party meditating the destruction of State and republican government. If it is possible that so absurd an idea can gain ground, it is necessary that it should be combated. I assure you, on my private faith and honor as a man, that there is not, in my judgment, a shadow of foundation for it. A very small number of men indeed may entertain theories less republican than Mr. Jefferson and Mr. Madison, but I am persuaded there is not a man among them who would not regard as both criminal and visionary any attempt to subvert the republican system of the country. Most of these men rather fear that it may not justify itself by its fruits, than feel a predilection for a different form; and their fears are not diminished by the factious and fanatical politics which they find prevailing among a certain set of gentlemen and threatening to disturb the tranquillity and order of the government.

As to the destruction of State governments, the great and real anxiety is to be able to preserve the national from the too potent and counteracting influence of those governments. As to my own political creed, I give it to you with the utmost sincerity. I am affectionately attached to the republican theory. I desire above all things to see the equality of political rights, exclusive of all hereditary distinction, firmly established by a practical demonstration of its being consistent with the order and happiness of society. As to State governments, the prevailing bias of my judgment is that if they can be circumscribed within bounds, consistent with the preservation of the national government, they will prove useful and salutary. [. . .]

To George Washington

PHILADELPHIA, JULY 30TH, 1792

Sir:

I received the most sincere pleasure at finding in our late conversation, that there was some relaxation in the disposition you had before discovered to decline a re-election. Since your departure, I have left no opportunity of sounding the opinions of persons, whose opinions were worth knowing on these two points. 1st. The effect of your declining, upon the public affairs, and upon your own reputation. 2dly. The effect of your continuing, in reference to the declarations you have made of your disinclination to public life; and I can truly say that I have not found the least difference of sentiment on either point. The impression is uniform, that your declining would be to be deplored as the greatest evil, that could befall the country at the present juncture, and as critically hazardous to your own reputation; that your continuance will be justified in the mind of every friend to his country, by the evident necessity for it. 'Tis clear, says every one with whom I have conversed, that the affairs of the national government are not yet firmly established—that its enemies, generally speaking, are as inveterate as ever—that their enmity has been sharpened by its success, and by all the resentments which flow from disappointed predictions and mortified vanity—that a general and strenuous effort is making in every State to place the administration of it in the hands of its enemies, as if they were its safest guardians—that the period of the next House of Representatives is likely to prove the crisis of its permanent character—that if you continue in office nothing materially mischievous is to be apprehended, if you quit, much is to be dreaded—that the same motives which induced you to accept originally ought to decide you to continue till matters have assumed a more determinate aspect—that indeed it would have been better, as it regards your own character, that you had never consented to come forward, than now to leave the business unfinished and in danger of being undone—that in the event of storms arising, there would be an imputation either of want of foresight or want of firmness—and, in fine, that on public and personal accounts, on patriotic and prudential considerations, the clear path to be pursued by you will be, again to obey the voice of your country, which, it is not doubted, will be as earnest and as unanimous as ever. [. . .]

I trust, sir, and I pray God, that you will determine to make a further sacrifice of your tranquillity and happiness to the public good. I trust that it need not continue above a year or two more; and I think that it will be more eligible to retire from office before the expiration of a term of election, than to decline a re-election. [. . .]

To George Washington

PHILADELPHIA, SEPTEMBER 9 1792

Sir

I have the pleasure of your private letter of the 26th of August.

The feelings and views which are manifested in that letter are such as I expected would exist. And I most sincerely regret the causes of the uneasy sensations you experience. It is my most anxious wish, as far as may depend upon me, to smooth the path of your administration, and to render it prosperous and happy. And if any prospect shall open of healing or terminating the differences which exist, I shall most chearfully embrace it; though I consider myself as the deeply injured party. The recommendation of such a spirit is worthy of the moderation and wisdom which dictated it; and if your endeavours should prove unsuccessful, I do not hesitate to say that in my opinion the period is not remote when the public good will require *substitutes* for the *differing members* of your administration. The continuance of a division there must destroy the energy of Government, which will be little enough with the strictest Union. On my part there will be a most chearful acquiescence in such a result.

I trust, Sir, that the greatest frankness has always marked and will always mark every step of my conduct towards you. In this disposition, I cannot conceal from you that I have had some instrumentality of late in the retaliations which have fallen upon certain public characters and that I find myself placed in a situation not to be able to recede *for the present*.

I considered myself as compelled to this conduct by reasons public as well as personal of the most cogent nature. I *know* that I have been an object of uniform opposition from Mr. Jefferson, from the first moment of his coming to the City of New York to enter upon his present office. I *know*, from the most authentic sources, that I have been the frequent subject of the most unkind whispers and insinuating from the same quarter. I have long seen a formed party in the Legislature, under his auspices, bent upon my subversion. I cannot doubt, from the evidence I possess, that the National Gazette was instituted by him for political purposes and that one leading object of it has been to render me and all the measures connected with my department as odious as possible.

Nevertheless I can truly say, that, except explanations to confidential friends, I never directly or indirectly retaliated or countenanced retaliation till very lately. I can even assure you, that I was instrumental in preventing a very severe and systematic attack upon Mr. Jefferson, by an association of two or three individuals, in consequence of the persecution, which he brought upon the Vice President, by his indiscreet and light letter to the Printer, transmitting *Paine's* pamphlet.

As long as I saw no danger to the Government, from the machinations which were going on, I resolved to be a silent sufferer of the injuries which were done me. I determined to avoid giving occasion to any thing which could manifest to the world dissentions among the principal characters of the government; a thing which can never happen without weakening its hands, and in some degree throwing a stigma upon it.

But when I no longer doubted, that there was a formed party deliberately bent upon the subversion of measures, which in its consequences would subvert the Government—when I saw, that the undoing of the funding system in particular (which, whatever may be the original merits of that system, would prostrate the credit and the honor of the Nation, and bring the Government into contempt with that description of Men, who are in every society the only firm supporters of government) was an avowed object of the party; and that all possible pains were taking to produce that effect by rendering it odious to the body of the people—I considered it as a duty, to endeavour to resist the torrent, and as an essential mean to this end, to draw aside the veil from the principal Actors. To this strong impulse, to this decided conviction, I have yielded. And I think events will prove that I have judged rightly.

Nevertheless I pledge my honor to you Sir, that if you shall hereafter form a plan to reunite the members of your administration, upon some steady principle of cooperation, I will faithfully concur in executing it during my continuance in office. And I will not directly or indirectly say or do a thing, that shall endanger a feud.

I have had it very much at heart to make an excursion to Mount Vernon, by way of the Fœderal City in the course of this Month—and have been more than once on the point of asking your permission for it. But I now despair of being able to effect it. I am nevertheless equally obliged by your kind invitation.

The subject mentioned in the Postscript of your letter shall with great pleasure be carefully attended to. With the most faithful and affectionate attachment I have the honor to remain

Sir Your most Obed & humble servant

P.S I had written you two letters on public business, one of which will go with this; but the other will be witheld, in consequence of a slight indisposition of the Attorney General, to be sent by express sometime in the course of tomorrow.

Cabinet Report to George Washington on France

MAY 2, 1793

[. . .] The Convention [in France] on the 19th of November, passed a decree in these words:

"The National Convention declare, in the name of the French nation, that they will grant FRATERNITY and ASSISTANCE TO EVERY PEOPLE who wish to recover their liberty; and they charge the executive power to send the necessary orders to the generals to give assistance to such people, and to *defend* those citizens *who may have been or who may be vexed for the cause of liberty.*" Which decree was ordered to be printed IN ALL LANGUAGES.

This decree ought justly to be regarded in an exceptionable light by the government of every country. For though it be lawful and meritorious to assist a people in a virtuous and rational struggle for liberty, *when the particular case happens,* yet it is not justifiable in any government or nation to hold out to the world a *general invitation* and *encouragement* to *revolution* and insurrection, under a promise of *fraternity* and *assistance.*

Such a step is of a nature to disturb the repose of mankind, to excite fermentation in every country, to endanger government everywhere. Nor can there be a doubt that wheresoever a spirit of this kind appears, it is lawful to repress and repel it. [. . .]

The pretext of propagating liberty can make no difference. Every nation has a right to carve out its own happiness in its own way, and it is the height of presumption in another to attempt to fashion its political creed. [. . .]

Americanus, I

THE AMERICAN DAILY ADVERTISER, FEBRUARY 1, 1794.

[. . .] There was a time when all men in this country entertained the same favorable view of the French Revolution. At the present time, they all still unite in the wish that the troubles of France may terminate in the establishment of a free and good government; and dispassionate, well-informed men must equally unite in the doubt whether this be likely to take place under the auspices of those who now govern the affairs of that country. But, agreeing in these two points, there is a great and serious diversity of opinion as to the real merits and probable issue of the French Revolution.

None can deny that the cause of France has been stained by excesses and extravagances, for which it is not easy, if possible, to find a parallel in the history of human affairs, and from which reason and humanity recoil. Yet many find apologies and extenuations with which they satisfy themselves; they still see in the cause of France the cause of liberty; they are still sanguine in the hope that it will be crowned with success; that the French nation will establish for themselves not only a free but a republican government, capable of promoting solidly their happiness. Others, on the contrary, discern no adequate apology for the horrid and disgusting scenes which have been, and continue to be, acted. They conceive that the excesses which have been committed, transcend greatly the measure of those which, with every due allowance for circumstances, were reasonably to have been expected. They perceive in them proofs of atrocious depravity in the most influential leaders of the revolution. They observe that among these, a MARAT and a ROBESPIERRE, assassins still reeking with the blood of their fellow-citizens, monsters who outdo the fabled enormities of a *Busiris* and a *Procrustes,* are predominant in influence as well as iniquity. They find everywhere marks of an unexampled dissolution of all the social and moral ties. They see nowhere any thing but principles and opinions so wild, so extreme, passions so turbulent, so tempestuous, as almost to forbid the hope of agreement in any rational or well-organized system of government. They conclude that a state of things like this is calculated to extend disgust and disaffection throughout the nation, to nourish more and more a spirit of insurrection and mutiny, facilitating the progress of the invading armies, and exciting in the bowels of France commotions, of which it is impossible to compute the mischief, the duration, or the end; that if by the energy of the national character, and the intrinsic difficulty of the enterprise, the enemies of France shall be compelled to leave her to herself, this era may only prove the commencement of greater misfortunes; that after wading through seas of blood, in a furious and sanguinary civil war, France may find herself at length the slave of some victorious Sylla, or Marius, or Cæsar: and they draw this afflicting inference from the whole view of the subject, that there is more reason to fear that the CAUSE OF TRUE LIBERTY has received a deep wound in the mismanagements of it, by those who, unfortunately for the French nation, have for a considerable time past maintained an ascendant in its affairs, than to regard the revolution of France in the form it has lately worn, as entitled to the honors due to that sacred and all-important cause, or as a safe bark in which to freight the fortunes, the liberties, and the reputation of this now respectable and happy land. [. . .]

The Defence, No. 2

JULY 25, 1795

[. . .] Few nations can have stronger inducements than the United States to cultivate peace. Their infant state in general, their want of a marine in particular, to protect their commerce, would render war, in an extreme degree, a calamity. It would not only arrest our present rapid progress to strength and prosperity, but would probably throw us back into a state of debility and impoverishment, from which it would require years to emerge. [. . .]

A very powerful state may frequently hazard a high and haughty tone with good policy; but a weak state can scarcely ever do it without imprudence. The last is yet our character; though we are the embryo of a great empire. It is, therefore, better suited to our situation to measure each step with the utmost caution; to hazard as little as possible, in the cases in which we are injured; to blend moderation with firmness; and to brandish the weapons of hostility only when it is apparent that the use of them is unavoidable.

It is not to be inferred from this, that we are to crouch to any power on earth, or tamely to suffer our rights to be violated. A nation which is capable of this meanness will quickly have no rights to protect, or honor to defend.

But the true inference is, that we ought not lightly to seek or provoke a resort to arms; that, in the differences between us and other nations, we ought carefully to avoid measures which tend to widen the breach; and that we should scrupulously abstain from whatever may be construed into reprisals, till after the employment of all amicable means has reduced it to a certainty that there is no alternative.

If we can avoid a war for ten or twelve years more, we shall then have acquired a maturity, which will make it no more than a common calamity, and will authorize us, in our national discussions, to take a higher and more imposing tone.

This is a consideration of the greatest weight to determine us to exert all our prudence and address to keep out of war as long as it shall be possible; to defer, to a state of manhood, a struggle to which infancy is ill adapted. This is the most effectual way to disappoint the enemies of our welfare; to pursue a contrary conduct may be to play into their hands, and to gratify their wishes. If there be a foreign power which sees with envy or ill-will our growing prosperity, that power must discern that our infancy is the time for clipping our wings. We ought to be wise enough to see that this is not a time for trying our strength. [. . .]

To George Washington

NEW YORK, MAY 19. 1798.

My Dear Sir:

At the present dangerous crisis of public affairs, I make no apology for troubling you with a political letter. Your impressions of our situation, I am persuaded, are not different from mine. There is certainly great probability that we may have to enter into a very serious struggle with France; and it is more and more evident that the powerful faction which has for years opposed the government, is determined to go every length with France. I am sincere in declaring my full conviction, as the result of a long course of observation, that they are ready to *new-model* our Constitution under the *influence* or *coercion* of France, to form with her a perpetual alliance, *offensive* and *defensive*, and to give her a monopoly of our trade by *peculiar* and *exclusive* privileges. This would be in substance, whatever it might be in name, to make this country a province of France. Neither do I doubt that her standard, displayed in this country, would be directly or indirectly seconded by them, in pursuance of the project I have mentioned.

It is painful and alarming to remark, that the opposition faction assumes so much a geographical complexion. As yet, from the south of Maryland nothing has been heard but accounts of disapprobation of our government, and approbation of or apology for France. This is a most portentous symptom, and demands every human effort to change it.

In such a state of public affairs, it is impossible not to look up to you, and to wish that your influence could in some proper mode be brought into direct action. Among the ideas which have passed through my mind for this purpose, I have asked myself whether it might not be expedient for you to make a circuit through Virginia and North Carolina, under some pretence of health, etc. This would call forth addresses, public dinners, etc., which would give you an opportunity of expressing sentiments in answers, toasts, etc., which would throw the weight of your character into the scale of the government, and revive an enthusiasm for your person, that may be turned into the right channel.

I am aware that the step is delicate, and ought to be well considered before it is taken. I have even not settled my own opinion as to its propriety, but I have concluded to bring the general idea under your view, confident that your judgment will make a right choice; and that you will take no step which is not well calculated. The conjuncture, however, is extraordinary, and now, or very soon, will demand extraordinary measures.

You ought also to be aware, my dear sir, that in the event of an open rupture with France, the public voice will again call you to command the armies of your country; and, though all who are attached to you will, from attachment, as well as from public considerations, deplore an occasion which should once more tear you from that repose to which you have so good a right, yet it is the opinion of all those with whom I converse, that you will be compelled to make the sacrifice. All your past labor may demand to give it efficacy this further, this very great sacrifice. Adieu, my Dear Sir Respectfully & Affecly Yr very obed servt

To James McHenry [Private]

NEW YORK, MARCH 18. 1799

Beware, my Dear Sir, of magnifying a riot into an insurrection, by employing, in the first instance, an inadequate force. 'Tis better far to err on the other side.

Whenever the government appears in arms, it ought to appear like a *Hercules,* and inspire respect by the display of strength. The consideration of expence is of no moment compared with the advantages of energy. 'Tis true this is always a relative question, but 'tis always important to make no mistake. I only offer a *principle* and a *caution.*

A large corps of auxiliary cavalry may be had in Jersey, New York, Delaware, Maryland, without interfering with farming pursuits.

Will it be inexpedient to put under marching orders a large force provisionally, as an eventual support of the corps to be employed, to awe the disaffected?

Let all be well considered.

Yrs. truly

To Tobias Lear

NEW YORK, JAN. 2, 1800.

Dear Sir:

Your letter of the 15th of December last was delayed in getting to hand by the circumstance of its having gone to New York while I was at Philadelphia, and of its having arrived at Philadelphia after I had set out on my return to New York.

The very painful event which it announces had, previous to the receipt of it, filled my heart with bitterness. Perhaps no man in this community has equal cause with myself to deplore the loss. I have been much indebted to the kindness of the General, and he was an *Ægis very essential to me.* But regrets are unavailing. For great misfortunes it is the business of reason to seek consolation. The friends of General Washington have very noble ones. If virtue can secure happiness in another world, he is happy. In this the seal is now put upon *his* glory. It is no longer in jeopardy from the fickleness of fortune.

P.S.—In whose hands are his papers gone? Our very confidential situation will not permit this to be a point of indifference to me.

To John Jay

NEW YORK, MAY 7. 1800.

Dear Sir

You have been informed of the loss of our Election in this City. It is also known that we have been unfortunate throughout Long Island & in West Chester. According to the Returns hitherto, it is too probable that we lose our Senators for this District.

The moral certainty therefore is that there will be an Antifœderal Majority in the Ensuing Legislature, and this very high probability is that this will bring *Jefferson* into the Chief Magistracy; unless it be prevented by the measure which I shall now submit to your consideration, namely the immediate calling together of the existing Legislature.

I am aware that there are weighty objections to the measure; but the reasons for it appear to me to outweigh the objections. And in times like these in which we live, it will not do to be overscrupulous. It is easy to sacrifice the substantial interests of society by a strict adherence to ordinary rules.

In observing this, I shall not be supposed to mean that any thing ought to be done which integrity will forbid—but merely that the scruples of delicacy and propriety, as relative to a common course of things, ought to yield to the extraordinary nature of the crisis. They ought not to hinder the taking of a *legal* and *constitutional* step, to prevent an *Atheist* in Religion and a *Fanatic* in politics from getting possession of the helm of the State.

You Sir know in a great degree the Antifœderal party, but I fear that you do not know them as well as I do. Tis a composition indeed of very incongruous materials but all tending to mischief—some of them to the overthrow of the Government by stripping it of its due energies others of them to a Revolution after the manner of Buonaparte. I speak from indubitable facts, not from conjectures & inferences.

In proportion as the true character of this party is understood is the force of the considerations which urge to every effort to disappoint it. And it seems to me that there is a very solemn obligation to employ the means in our power.

The calling of the Legislature will have for object the choosing of Electors by the people in Districts. This (as Pennsylvania will do nothing) will insure a Majority of votes in the U States for Fœderal Candidates.

The measure will not fail to be approved by all the Fœderal Party; while it will no doubt be condemned by the opposite. As to its intrinsic nature it is justified by unequivocal reasons for *public safety*.

The reasonable part of the world will I believe approve it. They will see it as a proceeding out of the common course but warranted by the particular nature of the Crisis and the great cause of social order.

If done the motive ought to be frankly avowed. In your communication to the Legislature they ought to be told that Temporary circumstances had rendered it probable that without their interposition the executive authority of the General Government would be transfered to hands hostile to the system heretofore pursued with so much success and dangerous to the peace happiness and order of the Country—that under this impression from facts convincing to your own mind you had thought it your duty to give the existing Legislature an opportunity of deliberating whether it would not be proper to interpose and endeavour to prevent so great an evil by referring the choice of Electors to the People distributed into Districts.

In weighing this suggestion you will doubtless bear in mind that Popular Governments must certainly be overturned & while they endure prove engines of mischief—if one party will call to its aid all the resources which *Vice* can give and if the other, however pressing the emergency, confines itself within all the ordinary forms of delicacy and decorum.

The legislature can be brought together in three weeks. So that there will be full time for the object; but none ought to be lost.

Think well my Dear Sir of this proposition. Appreciate the extreme danger of the Crisis; and I am unusually mistaken in my view of the matter, if you do not see it right and expedient to adopt the measure.

Respectfully & Affecty Yrs.

To Theodore Sedgwick

NEW YORK, MAY 10. 1800.

Dear Sir:

I am very sorry for the information contained in your letter of the 7th. But I am not intimate enough with Dexter to put myself upon paper to him.

If on his return I can catch him at New York I shall have a particular conversation with him.

He is, I am persuaded, much mistaken as to the opinion entertained of Mr. Adams by the federal party. Were I to determine from my own observation, I should say *most* of the most *influential men* of that party consider him as a very *unfit* and *incapable* character.

For my individual part my mind is made up. I will never more be responsible for him by my direct support, even though the consequence should be the election of *Jefferson.*

If we must have an *enemy* at the head of the government, let it be one whom we can oppose, and for whom we are not responsible, who will not involve our party in the disgrace of his foolish and bad measures. Under *Adams,* as under *Jefferson,* the government will sink. The party in the hands of whose chief it shall sink will sink with it, and the advantage will all be on the side of his adversaries.

'Tis a notable expedient for keeping the federal party together, to have at the head of it a man who hates and is despised by those men of it who, in time past, have been its most efficient supporters. If the cause is to be sacrificed to a weak and perverse man, I withdraw from the party and act upon my own ground—never certainly against my principles, but in pursuance of them in my own way. I am mistaken if others do not do the same.

The only way to prevent a fatal schism in the Federal party is to support General Pinckney in good earnest.

If I can be perfectly satisfied that Adams and Pinckney will be upheld in the East with entire good faith, on the ground of conformity, I will, wherever my influence may extend, pursue the same plan. If not, I will pursue Mr. Pinckney as my single object.

Adieu Yrs. truly

To Gouverneur Morris

NEW YORK, 26 DECR. 1800.

Dear Sir

The post of yesterday gave me the pleasure of a letter from you. I thank you for the communication. I trust that a letter which I wrote you the day before the receipt of yours will have duly reached you, as it contains some very free and confidential observations ending in two results.

1st. That the convention with France ought to be ratified as the least of two evils.

2d. That *on the same ground Jefferson* ought to be preferred to *Burr*.

I trust the Federalists will not finally be so mad as to vote for the *latter*. I speak with an intimate and accurate knowledge of character. His elevation can only promote the purposes of the desperate and profligate.

If there be a man in the world I ought to hate, it is Jefferson. With *Burr* I have always been personally well. But the public good must be paramount to every private consideration.

My opinion may be freely used with such reserves as you shall think discreet.

Yrs. very truly

To Gouverneur Morris

NEW YORK, FEBY 29, 1802.

My Dear Sir:

[. . .] Mine is an odd destiny. Perhaps no man in the United States has sacrificed or done more for the present Constitution than myself; and contrary to all my anticipations of its fate, as you know from the very beginning, I am still laboring to prop the frail and worthless fabric. Yet I have the murmurs of its friends no less than the curses of its foes for my reward. What can I do better than withdraw from the Scene? Every day proves to me more and more, that this American world was not made for me. [. . .]

CORRESPONDENCE RELATING TO THE DUEL WITH BURR

Aaron Burr to Alexander Hamilton

NEW YORK, 18 JUNE 1804.

Sir:

I send you for your perusal a letter signed Charles D. Cooper, which, though apparently published some time ago, has but very recently come to my knowledge. Mr. Van Ness, who does me the honor to deliver this, will point out to you that clause of the letter to which I particularly request your attention.

You must perceive, sir, the necessity of a prompt and unqualified acknowledgment or denial of the use of any expressions which would warrant the assertions of Dr. Cooper.

I have the honor to be Your obt svt

A. Burr

Hamilton to Burr

NEW YORK, JUNE 20. 1804.

Sir

I have maturely reflected on the subject of your letter of the eighteenth instant, and the more I have reflected, the more I have become convinced that I could not, without manifest impropriety, make the avowal or disavowal which you seem to think necessary. The clause pointed out by Mr. Van Ness is in these terms: "I could detail to you a still more despicable opinion which General Hamilton has expressed of Mr. Burr." To endeavor to discover the meaning of this declaration, I was obliged to seek in the antecedent part of this letter for the opinion to which it referred, as having been already disclosed. I found it in these words: "General Hamilton and Judge Kent have declared in substance that they looked upon Mr. Burr to be a dangerous man, and one who ought not to be trusted with the reins of government."

The language of Dr. Cooper plainly implies that he considered this opinion of you, which he attributes to me, as a despicable one; but he affirms that I have expressed some other, more despicable, without, however, mentioning to whom, when, or where. 'T is evident that the phrase "still more despicable" admits of infinite shades, from very light to very dark. How am I to judge of the degree intended, or how shall I annex any precise idea to language so indefinite?

Between gentlemen, despicable and more despicable are not worth the pains of distinction; when, therefore, you do not interrogate me as to the opinion which is specifically ascribed to me, I must conclude that you view it as within the limits to which the animadversions of political opponents upon each other may justifiably extend, and consequently as not warranting the idea of it which Dr. Cooper appears to entertain. If so, what precise inference could you draw as a guide for your conduct, were I to acknowledge that I had expressed an opinion of you still more despicable than the one which is particularized? How could you be sure that even this opinion had exceeded the bounds which you yourself deem admissible between political opponents?

But I forbear further comment on the embarrassment to which the requisition you have made naturally leads. The occasion forbids a more ample illustration, though nothing could be more easy than to pursue it.

Repeating, that I cannot reconcile it with propriety to make the acknowledgment you desire, I will add that I deem it inadmissible, on principle, to consent to be interrogated as to the justness of the inferences which may be drawn by others from what I may have said of a political opponent in the course of fifteen years' competition. If there were no other objection to it, this is sufficient, that it would tend to expose my sincerity and delicacy to injurious imputation from every person who may at any time have conceived the import of my expressions differently from what I may then have intended or may afterwards recollect.

I stand ready to avow or disavow, promptly and explicitly, any precise or definite opinion which I may be, charged with having declared of any gentleman. More than this cannot fitly be expected from me, and especially it cannot be reasonably expected that I shall enter into an explanation upon a basis so vague as that which you have adopted. I trust, on mature reflection, you will see the matter in the same light with me. If not, I can only regret the circumstance, and must abide the consequences.

The publication of Dr. Cooper was never seen by me until after the receipt of your letter.

I have the honor to be Sir Your obed. servt

A. Hamilton

Burr to Hamilton

NEW YORK, 21 JUNE 1804.

Sir:

Your letter of the 20th inst. has been this day received. Having considered it attentively, I regret to find in it nothing of that sincerity and delicacy which you profess to value.

Political opposition can never absolve gentlemen from the necessity of a rigid adherence to the laws of honor and the rules of decorum. I neither claim such privilege nor indulge it in others.

The Common sense of Mankind affixes to the epithet adopted by Dr. Cooper, the idea of dishonor. It has been publicly applied to me under the sanction of your name. The question is not whether he has understood the meaning of the word, or has used it according to syntax and with grammatical accuracy, but whether you have authorized this application, either directly or by uttering expressions or opinions derogatory to my honor. The time "when" is in your own knowledge, but no way material to me, as the calumny has now first been disclosed, so as to become the subject of my notice, and as the effect is present and palpable.

Your letter has furnished me with new reasons for requiring a definite reply.

I have the honor to be Sir your obt st

A. Burr

Hamilton to Burr

NEW YORK, JUNE 22D. 1804

Sir:

Your first letter, in a style too peremptory, made a demand, in my opinion, unprecedented and unwarrantable. My answer, pointing out the embarrassment, gave you an opportunity of taking a less exceptionable course. You have not chosen to do it; but by your last letter, received this day, containing expressions indecorous and improper, you have increased the difficulties to explanation intrinsically incident to the nature of your application.

If by a "definite reply," you mean the direct avowal or disavowal required in your first letter; I have no other answer to give, than that which has already been given. If you mean any thing different, admitting of greater latitude, it is requisite you should explain.

I have the honor to be Sir Your obed servt.

A. Hamilton

To Elizabeth Hamilton

JULY 4. 1804.

This letter, my dear Eliza, will not be delivered to you, unless I shall first have terminated my earthly career, to begin, as I humbly hope, from redeeming grace and divine mercy, a happy immortality. If it had been possible for me to have avoided the interview, my love for you and my precious children would have been alone a decisive motive. But it was not possible, without sacrifices which would have rendered me unworthy of your esteem. I need not tell you of the pangs I feel from the idea of quitting you, and exposing you to the anguish I know you would feel. Nor could I dwell on the topic, lest it should unman me. The consolations of religion, my beloved, can alone support you; and these you have a right to enjoy. Fly to the bosom of your God, and be comforted. With my last idea I shall cherish the sweet hope of meeting you in a better world. Adieu, best of wives—best of women. Embrace all my darling children for me.

Ever yours

Statement by Hamilton as to His Motives in Meeting Burr

C. JULY 10, 1804

On my expected interview with Col. Burr, I think it proper to make some remarks explanatory of my conduct, motives, and views. I was certainly desirous of avoiding this interview for the most cogent reasons:

1 My religious and moral principles are strongly opposed to the practice of duelling, and it would ever give me pain to be obliged to shed the blood of a fellow-creature in a private combat forbidden by the laws.

2 My wife and children are extremely dear to me, and my life is of the utmost importance to them in various views.

3 I feel a sense of obligation towards my creditors; who, in case of accident to me by the forced sale of my property, may be in some degree suf-

ferers. I did not think myself at liberty as a man of probity lightly to expose them to this hazard.

4 I am conscious of no *ill-will* to Col. Burr, distinct from political opposition, which, as I trust, has proceeded from pure and upright motives.

Lastly, I shall hazard much and can possibly gain nothing by the issue of the interview.

But it was, as I conceive, impossible for me to avoid it. There were *intrinsic* difficulties in the thing and *artificial* embarrassments, from the manner of proceeding on the part of Col. Burr.

Intrinsic, because it is not to be denied that my animadversions on the political principles, character, and views of Col. Burr have been extremely severe; and on different occasions I, in common with many others, have made very unfavorable criticisms on particular instances of the private conduct of this gentleman.

In proportion as these impressions were entertained with sincerity and uttered with motives and for purposes which might appear to me commendable, would be the difficulty (until they could be removed by evidence of their being erroneous) of explanation or apology. The disavowal required of me by Col. Burr in a general and indefinite form was out of my power, if it had really been proper for me to submit to be questioned, but I was sincerely of opinion that this could not be, and in this opinion I was confirmed by that of a very moderate and judicious friend whom I consulted. Besides that, Col. Burr appeared to me to assume, in the first instance, a tone unnecessarily peremptory and menacing, and, in the second, positively offensive. Yet I wished, as far as might be practicable, to leave a door open to accommodation. This, I think, will be inferred from the written communication made by me and by my directions, and would be confirmed by the conversations between Mr. Van Ness and myself which arose out of the subject.

I am not sure, whether under all the circumstances I did not go further in the attempt to accommodate than a punctilious delicacy will justify. If so, I hope the motives I have stated will excuse me.

It is not my design, by what I have said, to affix any odium on the conduct of Col. Burr in this case. He doubtless has heard of animadversions of mine which bore very hard upon him, and it is probable that as usual they were accompanied with some falsehoods. He may have supposed himself under a necessity of acting as he has done. I hope the grounds of his proceeding have been such as ought to satisfy his own conscience.

I trust, at the same time, that the world will do me the justice to believe that I have not censured him on light grounds nor from unworthy inducements. I certainly have had strong reasons for what I have said, though it is possible that in some particulars I may have been influenced by misconstruction or misinformation. It is also my ardent wish that I may have been more mistaken than I think I have been; and that he, by his future conduct, may show himself worthy of all confidence and esteem and prove an ornament and a blessing to the Country.

As well, because it is possible that I may have injured Col. Burr, however convinced myself that my opinions and declarations have been well-founded, as from my general principles and temper in relation to similar affairs, I have resolved, if our interview is conducted in the usual manner, and it pleases God to give me the opportunity, to reserve and throw away my first fire, and I have thoughts even of reserving my second fire, and thus giving a double opportunity to Col. Burr to pause and reflect.

It is not, however, my intention to enter into any explanations on the ground. Apology from principle, I hope, rather than pride, is out of the question.

To those who, with me, abhorring the practice of duelling, may think that I ought on no account to have added to the number of bad examples, I answer that my relative situation, as well in public as private, enforcing all the considerations which constitute what men of the world denominate honor, imposed on me (as I thought) a peculiar necessity not to decline the call. The ability to be in future useful, whether in resisting mischief or in effecting good, in those crises of our public affairs which seem likely to happen, would probably be inseparable from a conformity with public prejudice in this particular.

To Theodore Sedgwick

NEW YORK, JULY 10, 1804

My Dear Sir

I have received two letters from you since we last saw each other—that of the latest date being the 24 of May. I have had in hand for some time a long letter to you, explaining my view of the course and tendency of our Politics, and my intentions as to my own future conduct. But my plan embraced so large a range that owing to much avocation, some indifferent health, and a growing distaste for Politics, the letter is still considerably short of being finished. I write this now to satisfy you, that want of regard for you has not been the cause of my silence.

I will here express but one sentiment, which is, that Dismembrement of our Empire will be a clear sacrifice of great positive advantages, without any counterballancing good; administering no relief to our real Disease; which is DEMOCRACY, the poison of which by a subdivision will only be the more concentered in each part, and consequently the more virulent.

King is on his way for Boston where you may chance to see him, and hear from himself his sentiments.

God bless you

William P. Van Ness's Amendments to the Joint Statement Made by Nathaniel Pendleton and Him on the Duel Between Alexander Hamilton and Aaron Burr

[NEW YORK, JULY 21, 1804]

The second of G H having considered it proper to subjoin an explanatory note to the statement mutually furnished, it becomes proper for the gentleman who attended Col Burr to state also his impressions with respect to those points on which their exists a variance of opinion. In doing this he pointedly disclaims any idea disrespectful to the memory of G H, or an intention to ascribe any conduct to him that is not in his opinion perfectly honorable & correct.

The parties met as has been above related & took their respective stations as directed: the pistols were then handed to them by the seconds. Gen Hamilton elevated his, as if to try the light, & lowering it said I beg pardon for delaying you but the direction of the light renders it necessary, at the same time feeling his pockets with his left hand, & drawing forth his spectacles put them on. The second then asked if they were prepared which was replied to in the affirmative. The word *present* was then given, on which both parties took aim. The pistol of General Hamilton was first discharged, and Col Burr fired immediately after, only five or six seconds of time intervening. On this point the second of Col Burr has full & perfect reccollection. He noticed particularly the discharge of G H's pistol, & looked to his principal to ascertain whether he was hurt, he then clearly saw Col Bs pistol discharged. At this moment of looking at Col B on the discharge of G H's pistol he perceived a slight motion in his person, which induced the idea of his being struck. On this point he conversed with his principal on their return, who ascribed that circumstance to a small stone under his foot, & observed that the smoke of G Hs pistol obscured him for a moment in the interval of their firing.

When G H fell Col B advanced toward him as stated & was checked by his second who urged the importance of his immediately repairing to the barge, conceiving that G H was mortally wounded, & being desirous to secure his principal from the sight of the surgeon & bargemen who might be called in evidence. Col B complied with his request.

He shortly followed him to the boat, and Col B again expressed a wish to return, saying with an expression of much concern, I must go & speak to him. I again urged the obvious impropriety stating that the G was surrounded by the Surgeon & Bargemen by whom he must not be seen & insisted on immediate departure.

JOHN ADAMS
1735–1826

Introduction

"The sentiment, that you have attributed to me," an irked Adams wrote to Jefferson in 1813, "I totally disclaim."[1] Jefferson had charged him with looking backwards, to the writings of the ancient philosophers, instead of to his own revolutionary generation, for wisdom about government and politics. Jefferson divided political thinkers into two camps: In one were intrepid men like himself who were eager to chart a bold, adventurous course for the nation's future; in the other, fearful individuals who clung to the lessons of their forefathers, convinced that the human mind could not advance beyond them.[2]

Was it true that Adams felt at home in the past, satisfied to mine antiquity for knowledge and insight? Though Adams hotly denied the accusation, Jefferson had located the smoking gun, a speech Adams had given in 1798 to the young men of Philadelphia. "You . . . will find no principles, institutions, or systems of education more fit, in general, to be transmitted to your posterity," Adams had said, "than those you have received from your ancestors."[3]

John Adams—the man who had played a starring role in mobilizing the patriot movement in Boston, in opposing the Stamp Act, in attacking the sovereignty of Parliament, in challenging the royal governor of Massachusetts, Thomas Hutchinson—seduced by the past, indifferent to the political innovations being made around him? It was Adams who had exulted in the boldness of the Boston Tea Party, who had recommended in 1776 that the thirteen colonial assemblies draft constitutions and establish new governments, and who had responded to John Dickinson's forceful argument against separation from Great Britain with a compelling speech that moved the delegates at the Continental Congress to vote for independence.

It was Adams who, in 1776, had hailed his own epoch for permitting unparalleled political creativity and the creation of "the wisest and happiest government that human wisdom can contrive."[4] But it was also he who, that same year, sounded a different note, writing "I dread the Spirit of Innovation."[5]

For Adams, a successful revolution involved more than political reform: There would have to be a revolution in people's hearts and souls, too. The new government, he wrote to Abigail in 1776, would "require a purification from our vices, and an augmentation of our virtues, or they will be no blessings."[6] Doubtless, he set too unrealistic a standard for the triumph of the revolutionary project, for he would soon become utterly disenchanted with revolutionary idealism and with the notion of the perfectibility of man. By the 1780s, he realized that Americans did not possess "very exalted Virtue"; indeed, "their nature is the same with that of others."[7] Where were the "Perfection and perfectibility of human Nature?" a disgusted Adams later demanded of Jefferson. "Where is now, the progress of the human Mind? Where is the Amelioration of Society?"[8]

For his part, James Madison had never counted on a virtuous people or even on "enlightened statesmen" at the helm.[9] "If men were angels," he wrote in *Federalist* No. 51, "no government would be necessary." Nor had Madison expected a transformation of human nature. Quite the contrary. Checks and balances, along with indirect and staggered elections, were needed, he believed, to protect people and politicians from each other and themselves.

But the disabused Adams would come to demand more than mild checks and balances; his revolutionary hopes for an egalitarian, democratic republic dashed, he developed a darker vision of government than Madison's. Convinced that every society possessed an ambitious aristocracy as well as a voracious people, he decided that each "order" of society had to be contained within its own branch of government.

Adams thus proposed a traditional "mixed" government: an aristocratical senate limited to people of birth, wealth, education, and talent; a legislative chamber representing the people, unruly and uneducated; and a "monarchical" executive appointed for life to defend the people against the aristocracy, their historic enemy. It was a form of government that had served European nations for centuries—and that was the problem. It held no appeal for his generation of Americans, who were not about to recreate in the New World the dreary class-bound societies of Europe.

Adams's revolutionary zeal had evaporated. Whereas Madison considered the people "the only legitimate fountain of power,"[10] Adams came to believe that they were entitled only to a "share"[11] in the sovereignty of the nation. Whereas Jefferson called for frequent elections, Adams feared them. "Elections, my dear sir," he wrote to Jefferson in 1790, "I look at with terror."[12] Whereas Washington, in his First Inaugural Address, praised the "invisible hand" that seemed to have guided Americans in their steady advance toward independence and freedom, Adams, that same spring, sullenly predicted that Americans would eventually have to turn to hereditary institutions "as an Asylum against Discord, Seditions and Civil War, and that at no very distant period of time."[13] For the men of his generation, his political thought was unwelcome—worse, irrelevant.[14]

A blunt, forthright man of great integrity, possessing vast knowledge of history and political theory, afflicted with poignant insecurities and a prickly temperament, Adams, in the end, went his own way, charting his own course. Neither a Hamiltonian statist nor a Jeffersonian democrat, he was a conservative—in the Roman sense: a man deeply disappointed that his nation had not lived up to the classical Roman notion of virtue, statesmanship, and glory.

THE WRITINGS OF JOHN ADAMS

Diary Entries

JANUARY 16, 1756

We have the most moderate winter that ever was known in this country. For a long time together we have had serene and temperate weather, and all the roads perfectly settled and smooth like summer.

The Church of Rome has made it an article of faith that no man can be saved out of their church, and all other religious sects approach to this dreadful opinion in proportion to their ignorance, and the influence of ignorant or wicked priests.

Still reading the Independent Whig.

Oh! that I could wear out of my mind every mean and base affectation; conquer my natural pride and self-conceit; expect no more deference from my fellows than I deserve; acquire that meekness and humility which are the sure mark and characters of a great and generous soul; subdue every unworthy passion, and treat all men as I wish to be treated by all. How happy should I then be in the favor and good will of all honest men and the sure prospect of a happy immortality!

JANUARY 19, 1756

No man is entirely free from weakness and imperfection in this life. Men of the most exalted genius and active minds are generally most perfect slaves to the love of fame. They sometimes descend to as mean tricks and artifices in pursuit of honor or reputation as the miser descends to in pursuit of gold. The greatest men have been the most envious, malicious, and revengeful. The miser toils by night and day, fasts and watches, till he emaciates his body to fatten his purse and increase his coffers. The ambitious man rolls and tumbles in his bed, a stranger to refreshing sleep and repose, through anxiety about a preferment he has in view. The philosopher sweats and labors at his book, and ruminates in his closet, till his bearded and grim countenance exhibits the effigies of pale want and care and death, in quest of hard words, solemn nonsense, and ridiculous grimace. The gay gentleman rambles over half the globe, buys one thing and steals another, murders one man and disables another, and gets his own limbs and head broke for a few transitory flashes of happiness. Is this perfection, or downright madness and distraction?

JANUARY 21, 1756

Snow about ankle deep. I find, by repeated experiment and observation in my school, that human nature is more easily wrought upon and governed by promises, and encouragement, and praise, than by punishment, and threatening, and blame. But we must be cautious and sparing of our praise, lest it become too familiar and cheap, and so, contemptible; corporal as well as disgraceful punishments depress the spirits, but commendation enlivens and stimulates them to a noble ardor and emulation.

Dissertation on the Canon and Feudal Law

FEBRUARY 1765

[. . .] The fact is certain, we have been excessively cautious of giving offence by complaining of grievances. And it is as certain, that American governors, and their friends, and all the crown officers, have availed themselves of this disposition in the people. They have prevailed on us to consent to many things which were grossly injurious to us, and to surrender many others, with voluntary tameness, to which we had the clearest right. Have we not been treated, formerly, with abominable insolence, by officers of the navy? I mean no insinuation against any gentleman now on this station, having heard no complaint of any one of them to his dishonor. Have not some generals from England treated us like servants, nay, more like slaves than like Britons? Have we not been under the most ignominious contribution, the most abject submission, the most supercilious insults, of some custom-house officers? Have we not been trifled with, brow-beaten, and trampled on, by former governors, in a manner which no king of England since James the Second has dared to indulge towards his subjects? Have we not raised up one family, in them placed an unlimited confidence, and been soothed and flattered and intimidated by their influence, into a great part of this infamous tameness and submission? "These are serious and alarming questions, and deserve a dispassionate consideration."

This disposition has been the great wheel and the mainspring in the American machine of court politics. We have been told that "the word *rights* is an offensive expression;" "that the king, his ministry, and parliament, will not endure to hear Americans talk of their *rights;*" "that Britain is the mother and we the children, that a filial duty and submission is due from us to her," and that "we ought to doubt our own judgment, and presume that she is right, even when she seems to us to shake the foundation of government;" that "Britain is immensely rich and great and powerful, has fleets and armies at her command which have been the dread and terror of the universe, and that she will force her own judgment into execution, right or wrong." But let me entreat you, sir, to pause. Do you consider yourself as a missionary of loyalty or of rebellion? Are you not representing your king, his ministry, and parliament, as tyrants,—imperious, unrelenting tyrants,—by such reasoning as this? Is not this representing your most gracious sovereign as endeavoring to destroy the foundations of his own throne? Are you not representing every member of parliament as renouncing the transactions at Runing Mede, (the meadow, near Windsor, where Magna Charta was signed;) and as repealing in effect the bill of rights, when the Lords and Commons asserted and vindicated the rights of the people and their own rights, and insisted on the king's assent to that assertion and vindication? Do you not represent them as forgetting that the prince of Orange was created King William, by the people, on purpose that their rights might be eternal and inviolable? Is there not something extremely fallacious in the common-place images of mother country and children colonies? Are we the children of Great Britain any more than the cities of London, Exeter, and Bath? Are we not brethren and fellow subjects with those in Britain, only under a somewhat different method of legislation, and a totally different method of taxation? But admitting we are children, have not children a right to complain when their parents are attempting to break their limbs, to administer poison, or to sell them to enemies for slaves? [. . .]

[. . .] Let us dare to read, think, speak, and write. Let every order and degree among the people rouse their attention and animate their resolution. Let them all become attentive to the grounds and principles of government, ecclesiastical and civil. Let us study the law of nature; search into the spirit of the British constitution; read the histories of ancient ages; contemplate the great examples of Greece and Rome; set before us the conduct of our own British ancestors, who have defended for us the inherent rights of mankind against foreign and domestic tyrants and usurpers, against arbitrary kings and cruel priests, in short, against the gates of earth and hell. Let us read and recollect and impress upon our souls the views and ends of our own more immediate forefathers, in exchanging their native country for a dreary, inhospitable wilderness. Let us examine into the nature of that power, and the cruelty of that oppression, which drove them from their homes. Recollect their amazing fortitude, their bitter sufferings,—the hunger, the nakedness, the cold, which they patiently endured,—the severe labors of clearing their grounds, building their houses, raising their provisions, amidst dangers from wild beasts and savage men, before they had time or money or materials for commerce. Recollect the civil and religious principles and hopes and expectations which constantly supported and carried them through all hardships with patience and resignation. Let us recollect it was liberty, the hope of liberty for themselves and us and ours, which conquered all discouragements, dangers, and trials. In such researches as these, let us all in our several departments cheerfully engage,—but especially the proper patrons and supporters of law, learning, and religion!

Let the pulpit resound with the doctrines and sentiments of religious liberty. Let us hear the danger of thraldom to our consciences from ignorance, extreme poverty, and dependence, in short, from civil and political slavery. Let us see delineated before us the true map of man. Let us hear the dignity of his nature, and the noble rank he holds among the works of God,—that consenting to slavery is a sacrilegious breach of trust, as offensive in the sight of God as it is derogatory from our own honor or interest or happiness,—and that God Almighty has promulgated from heaven, liberty, peace, and good-will to man!

Let the bar proclaim, "the laws, the rights, the generous plan of power" delivered down from remote antiquity,—inform the world of the mighty struggles and numberless sacrifices made by our ancestors in defence of freedom. Let it be known, that British liberties are not the grants of princes or parliaments, but original rights, conditions of original contracts, coequal with prerogative, and coeval with government; that many of our rights are inherent and essential, agreed on as maxims, and established as preliminaries, even before a parliament existed. Let them search for the foundations of British laws and government in the frame of human nature, in the constitution of the intellectual and moral world. There let us see that truth, liberty, justice, and benevolence, are its everlasting basis; and if these could be removed, the superstructure is overthrown of course.

Let the colleges join their harmony in the same delightful concert. Let every declamation turn upon the beauty of liberty and virtue, and the deformity, turpitude, and malignity, of slavery and vice. Let the public disputations become researches into the grounds and nature and ends of government, and the means of preserving the good and demolishing the evil. Let the dialogues, and all the exercises, become the instruments of impressing on the tender mind, and of spreading and distributing far and wide, the ideas of right and the sensations of freedom.

In a word, let every sluice of knowledge be opened and set a-flowing. The encroachments upon liberty in the reigns of the first James and the first Charles, by turning the general attention of learned men to government, are said to have produced the greatest number of consummate statesmen which has ever been seen in any age or nation. The Brookes, Hampdens, Vanes, Seldens, Miltons, Nedhams, Harringtons, Nevilles, Sidneys, Lockes, are all said to have owed their eminence in political knowledge to the tyrannies of those reigns. The prospect now before us in

America, ought in the same manner to engage the attention of every man of learning, to matters of power and of right, that we may be neither led nor driven blindfolded to irretrievable destruction. Nothing less than this seems to have been meditated for us, by somebody or other in Great Britain. There seems to be a direct and formal design on foot, to enslave all America. This, however, must be done by degrees. The first step that is intended, seems to be an entire subversion of the whole system of our fathers, by the introduction of the canon and feudal law into America. The canon and feudal systems, though greatly mutilated in England, are not yet destroyed. Like the temples and palaces in which the great contrivers of them once worshipped and inhabited, they exist in ruins; and much of the domineering spirit of them still remains. The designs and labors of a certain society, to introduce the former of them into America, have been well exposed to the public by a writer of great abilities; and the further attempts to the same purpose, that may be made by that society, or by the ministry or parliament, I leave to the conjectures of the thoughtful. But it seems very manifest from the Stamp Act itself, that a design is formed to strip us in a great measure of the means of knowledge, by loading the press, the colleges, and even an almanack and a newspaper, with restraints and duties; and to introduce the inequalities and dependencies of the feudal system, by taking from the poorer sort of people all their little subsistence, and conferring it on a set of stamp officers, distributors, and their deputies. But I must proceed no further at present. The sequel, whenever I shall find health and leisure to pursue it, will be a "disquisition of the policy of the stamp act." In the mean time, however, let me add,—These are not the vapors of a melancholy mind, nor the effusions of envy, disappointed ambition, nor of a spirit of opposition to government, but the emanations of a heart that burns for its country's welfare. No one of any feeling, born and educated in this once happy country, can consider the numerous distresses, the gross indignities, the barbarous ignorance, the haughty usurpations, that we have reason to fear are meditating for ourselves, our children, our neighbors, in short, for all our countrymen and all their posterity, without the utmost agonies of heart and many tears.

Diary Entry

BRAINTREE, DECEMBER 18, 1765

How great is my loss in neglecting to keep a regular journal through the last Spring, Summer, and Fall! In the course of my business, as a surveyor of highways, as one of the committee for dividing, planning, and selling the North Commons, in the course of my two great journeys to Pownalborough and Martha's Vineyard, and in several smaller journeys to Plymouth, Taunton, and Boston, I had many fine opportunities and materials for speculation. The year 1765 has been the most remarkable year of my life. That enormous engine, fabricated by the British Parliament, for battering down all the rights and liberties of America, I mean the Stamp Act, has raised and spread through the whole continent a spirit that will be recorded to our honor with all future generations. In every colony, from Georgia to New Hampshire inclusively, the stamp distributers and inspectors have been compelled by the unconquerable rage of the people to renounce their offices. Such and so universal has been the resentment of the people, that every man who has dared to speak in favor of the stamps, or to soften the detestation in which they are held, how great soever his abilities and virtues had been esteemed before, or whatever his fortune, connections, and influence had been, has been seen to sink into universal contempt and ignominy.

The people, even to the lowest ranks, have become more attentive to their liberties, more inquisitive about them, and more determined to defend them, than they were ever before known or had occasion to be; innumerable have been the monuments of wit, humor, sense, learning, spirit, patriotism, and heroism, erected in the several colonies and provinces in the course of this year. Our presses have groaned, our pulpits have thundered, our legislatures have resolved, our towns have voted; the crown officers have everywhere trembled, and all their little tools and creatures been afraid to speak and ashamed to be seen.

This spirit, however, has not yet been sufficient to banish from persons in authority that timidity which they have discovered from the beginning. The executive courts have not yet dared to adjudge the Stamp Act void, nor to proceed with business as usual, though it should seem that necessity alone would be sufficient to justify business at present, though the act should be allowed to be obligatory. The stamps are in the castle. Mr. Oliver has no commission. The Governor has no authority to distribute or even to unpack the bales; the Act has never been proclaimed nor read in the Province; yet the probate office is shut, the custom-house is shut, the courts of justice are shut, and all business seems at a stand. Yesterday and the day before, the two last days of service for January Term, only one man asked me for a writ, and he was soon determined to waive his request. I have not drawn a writ since the first of November.

How long we are to remain in this languid condition, this passive obedience to the Stamp Act, is not certain. But such a pause cannot be lasting.

Debtors grow insolent; creditors grow angry; and it is to be expected that the public offices will very soon be forced open, unless such favorable accounts should be received from England as to draw away the fears of the great, or unless a greater dread of the multitude should drive away the fear of censure from Great Britain.

It is my opinion that by this inactivity we discover cowardice, and too much respect to the Act. This rest appears to be, by implication at least, an acknowledgment of the authority of Parliament to tax us. And if this authority is once acknowledged and established, the ruin of America will become inevitable. This long interval of indolence and idleness will make a large chasm in my affairs, if it should not reduce me to distress, and incapacitate me to answer the demands upon me. But I must endeavor, in some degree, to compensate the disadvantage, by posting my books, reducing my accounts into better order, and by diminishing my expenses,—but, above all, by improving the leisure of this winter in a diligent application to my studies.

I find that idleness lies between business and study; that is, the transition from the hurry of a multiplicity of business to the tranquillity that is necessary for intense study, is not easy. There must be a vacation, an interval between them, for the mind to recollect itself.

The bar seem to me to behave like a flock of shot pigeons; they seem to be stopped; the net seems to be thrown over them, and they have scarcely courage left to flounce and to flutter. So sudden an interruption in my career is very unfortunate for me. I was but just getting into my gears, just getting under sail, and an embargo is laid upon the ship. Thirty years of my life are passed in preparation for business; I have had poverty to struggle with, envy and jealousy and malice of enemies to encounter, no friends, or but few, to assist me; so that I have groped in dark obscurity, till of late, and had but just become known and gained a small degree of reputation, when this execrable project was set on foot for my ruin as well as that of America in general, and of Great Britain.

Diary Entry

MAY 24, 1773.

To-morrow is our general election. The plots, plans, schemes, and machinations of this evening and night will be very numerous. By the number of ministerial, governmental people returned, and by the secrecy of the friends of liberty relating to the grand discovery of the complete evidence of the whole mystery of iniquity, I much fear the elections will go unhappily. For myself, I own, I tremble at the thought of an election. What will be expected of me? What will be required of me? What duties and obligations will result to me from an election? What duties to my God, my king, my country, my family, my friends, myself? What perplexities, and intricacies, and difficulties shall I be exposed to? What snares and temptations will be thrown in my way? What self-denials and mortifications shall I be obliged to bear?

If I should be called in the course of providence to take a part in public life, I shall act a fearless, intrepid, undaunted part at all hazards, though it shall be my endeavor likewise, to act a prudent, cautious, and considerate part. But if I should be excused by a non-election, or by the exertions of prerogative from engaging in public business, I shall enjoy a sweet tranquillity in the pursuit of my private business, in the education of my children, and in a constant attention to the preservation of my health. This last is the most selfish and pleasant system, the first, the more generous, though arduous and disagreeable. But I was not sent into this world to spend my days in sports, diversions, and pleasures; I was born for business, for both activity and study. I have little appetite or relish for any thing else. I must double and redouble my diligence. I must be more constant to my office and my pen; constancy accomplishes more than rapidity; continual attention will do great things; frugality of time is the greatest art, as well as virtue. This economy will produce knowledge as well as wealth. [. . .]

Diary Entry

DECEMBER 17, 1773

Last night, three cargoes of Bohea tea were emptied into the sea. This morning a man-of-war sails. This is the most magnificent movement of all. There is a dignity, a majesty, a sublimity, in this last effort of the patriots, that I greatly admire. The people should never rise without doing something to be remembered, something notable and striking. This destruction of the tea is so bold, so daring, so firm, intrepid and inflexible, and it must have so important consequences, and so lasting, that I cannot but consider it as an epocha in history. This, however, is but an attack upon property. Another similar exertion of popular power may produce the destruction of lives. Many persons wish that as many dead carcasses were floating in the harbor, as there are chests of tea. A much less number of lives, however, would remove the causes of all our calamities. The malicious pleasure with which Hutchinson the Governor, the consignees of the tea, and the officers of the customs, have stood and looked upon the distresses of the people and their struggles to get the tea back to London, and at last the destruction of it, is amazing. 'T is hard to believe persons so hardened and abandoned.

What measures will the Ministry take in consequence of this? Will they resent it? Will they dare to resent it? Will they punish us? How? By quartering troops upon us? by annulling our charter? by laying on more duties? by restraining our trade? by sacrifice of individuals? or how?

The question is, Whether the destruction of this tea was necessary? I apprehend it was absolutely and indispensably so. They could not send it back. The Governor, Admiral, and Collector and Comptroller would not suffer it. It was in their power to have saved it, but in no other. It could not get by the castle, the men-of-war, &c. Then there was no other alternative but to destroy it or let it be landed. To let it be landed, would be giving up the principle of taxation by parliamentary authority, against which the continent has struggled for ten years. It was losing all our labor for ten years, and subjecting ourselves and our posterity forever to Egyptian task-masters; to burthens, indignities; to ignominy, reproach and contempt; to desolation and oppression; to poverty and servitude. But it will be said, it might have been left in the care of a committee of the town, or in Castle William. To this many objections may be made. [. . .]

Novanglus, No. 8

[1774–1775]

[. . .] How [. . .] do we New Englandmen derive our laws? I say, not from parliament, not from common law, but from the law of nature, and the compact made with the king in our charters. Our ancestors were entitled to the common law of England when they emigrated, that is, to just so much of it as they pleased to adopt, and no more. They were not bound or obliged to submit to it, unless they chose it. By a positive principle of the common law they were bound, let them be in what part of the world they would, to do nothing against the allegiance of the king. But no kind of provision was ever made by common law for punishing or trying any man, even for treason committed out of the realm. [. . .]

So that our ancestors, when they emigrated, having obtained permission of the king to come here, and being never commanded to return into the realm, had a clear right to have erected in this wilderness a British constitution, or a perfect democracy, or any other form of government they saw fit. They, indeed, while they lived, could not have taken arms against the

King of England, without violating their allegiance; but their children would not have been born within the king's allegiance, would not have been natural subjects, and consequently not entitled to protection, or bound to the king. [. . .]

[. . .] Our patriots have never determined or desired to be independent states, if a voluntary cession of a right to regulate their trade can make them dependent even on parliament; though they are clear in theory that, by the common law and the English constitution, parliament has no authority over them. None of the patriots of this province, of the present age, have ever denied that parliament has a right, from our voluntary cession, to make laws which shall bind the colonies, so far as their commerce extends.

"There is no possible medium between absolute independence and subjection to the authority of parliament." If this is true, it may be depended upon, that all North America are as fully convinced of their independence, their absolute independence, as they are of their own existence; and as fully determined to defend it at all hazards, as Great Britain is to defend her independence against foreign nations. But it is not true. An absolute independence on parliament, in all internal concerns and cases of taxation, is very compatible with an absolute dependence on it, in all cases of external commerce.

"He must be blind indeed, that cannot see our dearest interest in the latter, (that is, in an absolute subjection to the authority of parliament,) notwithstanding many pant after the former," (that is, absolute independence.) The man who is capable of writing, in cool blood, that our interest lies in an absolute subjection to parliament, is capable of writing or saying any thing for the sake of his pension. A legislature that has so often discovered a want of information concerning us and our country; a legislature interested to lay burdens upon us; a legislature, two branches of which, I mean the lords and commons, neither love nor fear us! Every American of fortune and common sense, must look upon his property to be sunk downright one half of its value, the moment such an absolute subjection to parliament is established.

That there are any who pant after "independence," (meaning by this word a new plan of government over all America, unconnected with the crown of England, or meaning by it an exemption from the power of parliament to regulate trade,) is as great a slander upon the province as ever was committed to writing. The patriots of this province desire nothing new; they wish only to keep their old privileges. They were, for one hundred and fifty years, allowed to tax themselves, and govern their internal concerns as they thought best. Parliament governed their trade as they thought fit. This plan they wish may continue forever. But it is honestly confessed, rather than become subject to the absolute authority of parliament in all cases of taxation and internal polity, they will be driven to throw off that of regulating trade. [. . .]

To Mercy Warren

BRAINTREE, JANY. 8, 1776

Dear Madam,—Your Friend insists upon my Writing to you and altho I am conscious it is my Duty being deeply in Debt for a number of very agreeable Favours in the Epistolary Way, yet I doubt whether a sense of this Duty would have overcome my Inclination to Indolence and Relaxation with which my own Fire Side always inspires me, if it had not been Stimulated and quickened by her.

I was charmed with three Characters drawn by a most masterly Pen, which I recd at the southward. Copley's Pencil could not have touched off with more exquisite Finishings the Faces of those Gentlemen. Whether I ever answered that Letter I know not. But I hope Posterity will see it, if they do I am sure they will admire it. I think I will make a Bargain with you, to draw the Character of every new Personage I have an opportunity of knowing, on Condition you will do the same. My View will be to learn the Art of penetrating into Men's Bosoms, and then the more difficult Art of painting what I shall see there. You Ladies are the most infallible judges of Characters, I think.

Pray Madam, are you for an American Monarchy or Republic? Monarchy is the genteelest and most fashionable Government, and I dont know why the Ladies ought not to consult Elegance and the Fashion as well in Government as Gowns, Bureaus or Chariots.

For my own part I am so tasteless as to prefer a Republic, if We must erect an independent Government in America, which you know is utterly against my Inclination. But a Republic, altho it will infallibly beggar me and my Children, will produce Strength, Hardiness Activity, Courage, Fortitude and Enterprise; the manly noble and Sublime Qualities in human Nature, in Abundance. A Monarchy would probably, somehow or other make me rich, but it would produce so much Taste and Politeness so much Elegance in Dress, Furniture, Equipage, so much Musick and Dancing, so much Fencing and Skaiting, so much Cards and Backgammon; so much Horse Racing and Cockfighting, so many Balls and Assemblies, so many Plays and Concerts that the very Imagination of them makes me feel vain, light, frivolous and insignificant.

It is the Form of Government which gives the decisive Colour to the Manners of the People, more than any other Thing. Under a well regulated Commonwealth, the People must be wise virtuous and cannot be otherwise. Under a Monarchy they may be as vicious and foolish as they please, nay, they cannot but be vicious and foolish. As Politicks therefore is the Science of human Happiness and human Happiness is clearly best promoted by Virtue, what thorough Politician can hesitate who has a new Government to build whether to prefer a Commonwealth or a Monarchy?

But, Madam, there is one Difficulty which I know not how to get over.

Virtue and Simplicity of Manners are indispensably necessary in a Republic among all orders and Degrees of Men. But there is so much Rascallity, so much Venality and Corruption, so much Avarice and Ambition such a Rage for Profit and Commerce among all Ranks and Degrees of Men even in America, that I sometimes doubt whether there is public Virtue enough to Support a Republic. There are two Vices most detestably predominant in every Part of America that I have yet seen which are as incompatible with the Spirit of a Commonwealth, as Light is with Darkness; I mean Servility and Flattery. A genuine Republican can no more fawn and cringe than he can domineer. Shew me the American who cannot do all. I know two or Three, I think, and very few more. However, it is the Part of a great Politician to make the Character of his People, to extinguish among them the Follies and Vices that he sees, and to create in them the Virtues and Abilities which he sees wanting. I wish I was sure that America has one such Politician but I fear she has not.

A Letter begun in Levity is likely to have [. . .] [conc]lusion, while I was writing the last Word [. . .] Paragraph my attention was called off [. . .] it and most melodious sounds my Ears [. . .] more Mortars and Musquettry.

A very hot Fire, both of Artillery and Small Arms, has continued for half an Hour, and has been succeeded by a luminous Phenomenon over Braintree North Common, occasioned by Burning Buildings I suppose.

Whether our People have attacked or defended, been victorious or vanquished is to me totally uncertain. But in Either Case I rejoice, for a Defeat appears to me preferable to total Inaction.

May the Supreme Ruler of Events overrule in our Favour. But if the Event of this Evening is unfortunate I think We ought at all Hazards and at any Loss to retrieve it tomorrow. I hope the Militia will be ready and our Honour be retrieved by making Boston our own.

I shall be in suspense this Night but very willing to take my Place with my Neighbours tomorrow and crush the Power of the Enemies or suffer under it.

I hope Coll Warren sleeps at Cushing's this night and that I shall see him in the Morning. Mean Time I think I shall sleep as soundly as ever.

I am Madam your most humble servant and sincere Friend.

Mrs. Adams desires to be remembered to Mrs. Warren.

Abigail Adams to John Adams

BRAINTREE, MARCH 31, 1776

I wish you would ever write me a Letter half as long as I write you; and tell me if you may where your Fleet are gone? What sort of Defence Virginia can make against our common Enemy? Whether it is so situated as to make an able Defence? Are not the Gentery Lords and the common people vassals, are they not like the uncivilized Natives Brittain represents us to be? I hope their Riffel Men who have shewen themselves very savage and even Blood thirsty; are not a specimen of the Generality of the people.

I am willing to allow the Colony great merrit for having produced a Washington but they have been shamefully duped by a Dunmore.

I have sometimes been ready to think that the passion for Liberty cannot be Eaquelly Strong in the Breasts of those who have been accustomed to deprive their fellow Creatures of theirs. Of this I am certain that it is not founded upon that generous and christian principal of doing to others as we would that others should do unto us.

Do not you want to see Boston; I am fearfull of the small pox, or I should have been in before this time. I got Mr. Crane to go to our House and see what state it was in. I find it has been occupied by one of the Doctors of a Regiment, very dirty, but no other damage has been done to it. The few things which were left in it are all gone. Cranch has the key which he never deliverd up. I have wrote to him for it and am determined to get it cleand as soon as possible and shut it up. I look upon it a new acquisition of property, a property which one month ago I did not value at a single Shilling, and could with pleasure have seen it in flames.

The Town in General is left in a better state than we expected, more oweing to a percipitate flight than any Regard to the inhabitants, tho some individuals discoverd a sense of honour and justice and have left the rent of the Houses in which they were, for the owners and the furniture unhurt, or if damaged sufficent to make it good.

Others have committed abominable Ravages. The Mansion House of your President is safe and the furniture unhurt whilst both the House and Furniture of the Solisiter General have fallen a prey to their own merciless party. Surely the very Fiends feel a Reverential awe for Virtue and patriotism, whilst they Detest the paricide and traitor.

I feel very differently at the approach of spring to what I did a month ago. We knew not then whether we could plant or sow with safety, whether when we had toild we could reap the fruits of our own industery, whether we could rest in our own Cottages, or whether we should not be driven from the sea coasts to seek shelter in the wilderness, but now we feel as if we might sit under our own vine and eat the good of the land.

I feel a gaieti de Coar to which before I was a stranger. I think the Sun looks brighter, the Birds sing more melodiously, and Nature puts on a more chearfull countanance. We feel a temporary peace, and the poor fugitives are returning to their deserted habitations.

Tho we felicitate ourselves, we sympathize with those who are trembling least the Lot of Boston should be theirs. But they cannot be in similar circumstances unless pusilanimity and cowardise should take possession of them. They have time and warning given them to see the Evil and shun it.—I long to hear that you have declared an independancy—and by the way in the new Code of Laws which I suppose it will be necessary for you to make I desire you would Remember the Ladies, and be more generous and favourable to them than your ancestors. Do not put such unlimited power into the hands of the Husbands. Remember all Men would be tyrants if they could. If perticuliar care and attention is not paid to the Laidies we are determined to foment a Rebelion, and will not hold ourselves bound by any Laws in which we have no voice, or Representation.

That your Sex are Naturally Tyrannical is a Truth so thoroughly established as to admit of no dispute, but such of you as wish to be happy willingly give up the harsh title of Master for the more tender and endearing one of Friend. Why then, not put it out of the power of the vicious and the Lawless to use us with cruelty and indignity with impunity. Men of Sense in all Ages abhor those customs which treat us only as the vassals of your Sex. Regard us then as Beings placed by providence under your protection and in immitation of the Supreem Being make use of that power only for our happiness. [. . .]

To James Sullivan

PHILADELPHIA, 26 MAY, 1776.

Your favors of May 9th and 17th are now before me; and I consider them as the commencement of a correspondence which will not only give me pleasure, but may be of service to the public, as in my present station I stand in need of the best intelligence, and the advice of every gentleman of abilities and public principles in the colony which has seen fit to place me here. [. . .]

It is certain, in theory, that the only moral foundation of government is, the consent of the people. But to what an extent shall we carry this principle? Shall we say that every individual of the community, old and young, male and female, as well as rich and poor, must consent, expressly, to every act of legislation? No, you will say, this is impossible. How, then, does the right arise in the majority to govern the minority, against their will? Whence arises the right of the men to govern the women, without their consent? Whence the right of the old to bind the young, without theirs?

But let us first suppose that the whole community, of every age, rank, sex, and condition, has a right to vote. This community is assembled. A motion is made, and carried by a majority of one voice. The minority will not agree to this. Whence arises the right of the majority to govern, and the obligation of the minority to obey?

From necessity, you will say, because there can be no other rule.

But why exclude women?

You will say, because their delicacy renders them unfit for practice and experience in the great businesses of life, and the hardy enterprises of war, as well as the arduous cares of state. Besides, their attention is so much engaged with the necessary nurture of their children, that nature has made them fittest for domestic cares. And children have not judgment or will of their own. True. But will not these reasons apply to others? Is it not equally true, that men in general, in every society, who are wholly destitute of property, are also too little acquainted with public affairs to form a right judgment, and too dependent upon other men to have a will of their own? If this is a fact, if you give to every man who has no property, a vote, will you not make a fine encouraging provision for corruption, by your fundamental law? Such is the frailty of the human heart, that very few men who have no property, have any judgment of their own. They talk and vote as they are directed by some man of property, who has attached their minds to his interest.

Upon my word, Sir, I have long thought an army a piece of clock-work, and to be governed only by principles and maxims, as fixed as any in mechanics; and, by all that I have read in the history of mankind, and in authors who have speculated upon society and government, I am much inclined to think a government must manage a society in the same manner; and that this is machinery too.

Harrington has shown that power always follows property. This I believe to be as infallible a maxim in politics, as that action and reaction are equal, is in mechanics. Nay, I believe we may advance one step farther, and affirm that the balance of power in a society, accompanies the balance of property in land. The only possible way, then, of preserving the balance of power on the side of equal liberty and public virtue, is to make the acquisition of land easy to every member of society; to make a division of the land into small quantities, so that the multitude may be possessed of landed estates. If the multitude is possessed of the balance of real estate, the multitude will have the balance of power, and in that case the multitude will take care of the liberty, virtue, and interest of the multitude, in all acts of government.

I believe these principles have been felt, if not understood, in the Massachusetts Bay, from the beginning; and therefore I should think that wisdom and policy would dictate in these times to be very cautious of making alterations. Our people have never been very rigid in scrutinizing into the qualifications of voters, and I presume they will not now begin to be so. But I would not advise them to make any alteration in the laws, at present, respecting the qualifications of voters.

Your idea that those laws which affect the lives and personal liberty of all, or which inflict corporal punishment, affect those who are not qualified to vote, as well as those who are, is just. But so they do women, as well as men; children, as well as adults. What reason should there be for excluding a man of twenty years eleven months and twenty-seven days old, from a vote, when you admit one who is twenty-one? The reason is, you must fix upon some period in life, when the understanding and will of men in general, is fit to be trusted by the public. Will not the same reason justify the state in fixing upon some certain quantity of property, as a qualification?

The same reasoning which will induce you to admit all men who have no property, to vote, with those who have, for those laws which affect the person, will prove that you ought to admit women and children; for, generally speaking, women and children have as good judgments, and as independent minds, as those men who are wholly destitute of property; these last being to all intents and purposes as much dependent upon others, who will please to feed, clothe, and employ them, as women are upon their husbands, or children on their parents.

As to your idea of proportioning the votes of men, in money matters, to the property they hold, it is utterly impracticable. There is no possible way of ascertaining, at any one time, how much every man in a community is worth; and if there was, so fluctuating is trade and property, that this state of it would change in half an hour. The property of the whole community is shifting every hour, and no record can be kept of the changes.

Society can be governed only by general rules. Government cannot accommodate itself to every particular case as it happens, nor to the circumstances of particular persons. It must establish general comprehensive regulations for cases and persons. The only question is, which general rule will accommodate most cases and most persons.

Depend upon it, Sir, it is dangerous to open so fruitful a source of controversy and altercation as would be opened by attempting to alter the qualifications of voters; there will be no end of it. New claims will arise; women will demand a vote; lads from twelve to twenty-one will think their rights not enough attended to; and every man who has not a farthing, will demand an equal voice with any other, in all acts of state. It tends to confound and destroy all distinctions, and prostrate all ranks to one common level.

To Abigail Adams

JULY 3, 1776

[. . .] Yesterday, the greatest question was decided, which ever was debated in America, and a greater, perhaps, never was nor will be decided among men. A resolution was passed, without one dissenting colony, "that these United Colonies are, and of right ought to be, free and independent States, and as such they have, and of right ought to have, full power to make war, conclude peace, establish commerce, and to do all other acts and things which other States may rightfully do." You will see in a few days a Declaration setting forth the causes which have impelled us to this mighty revolution, and the reasons which will justify it in the sight of God and man. A plan of confederation will be taken up in a few days.

When I look back to the year 1761, and recollect the argument concerning writs of assistance in the superior court, which I have hitherto considered as the commencement of this controversy between Great Britain and America, and run through the whole period, from that time to this, and recollect the series of political events, the chain of causes and effects, I am surprised at the suddenness as well as greatness of this revolution. Britain has been filled with folly, and America with wisdom. At least, this is my judgment. Time must determine. It is the will of Heaven that the two countries should be sundered forever. It may be the will of Heaven that America shall suffer calamities still more wasting, and distresses yet more dreadful. If this is to be the case, it will have this good effect at least. It will inspire us with many virtues which we have not, and correct many errors, follies, and vices, which threaten to disturb, dishonor, and destroy us. The furnace of affliction produces refinement in States as well as individuals. And the new governments we are assuming, in every part, will require a purification from our vices, and an augmentation of our virtues, or they will be no blessings. The people will have unbounded power, and the people are extremely addicted to corruption and venality, as well as the great. But I must submit all my hopes and fears to an overruling Providence, in which, unfashionable as the faith may be, I firmly believe.

Had a Declaration of Independency been made seven months ago, it would have been attended with many great and glorious effects. We might before this hour have formed alliances with foreign states. We should have mastered Quebec, and been in possession of Canada. You will, perhaps, wonder how such a declaration would have influenced our affairs in Canada; but if I could write with freedom, I could easily convince you that it would, and explain to you the manner how. Many gentlemen in high stations and of great influence have been duped by the ministerial bubble of commissioners to treat. And in real, sincere expectation of this event, which they so fondly wished, they have been slow and languid in promoting measures for the reduction of that province. Others there are in the colonies, who really wished that our enterprise in Canada would be defeated, that the colonies might be brought into danger and distress between two fires, and be thus induced to submit. Others really wished to defeat the expedition to Canada, lest the conquest of it should elevate the minds of the people too much to hearken to those terms of reconciliation, which they believed would be offered us. These jarring views, wishes, and designs occasioned an opposition to many salutary measures, which were proposed for the support of that expedition, and caused obstructions, embarrassments, and studied delays, which have finally lost us the province.

All these causes, however, in conjunction, would not have disappointed us, if it had not been for a misfortune which could not be foreseen, and, perhaps, could not have been prevented—I mean the prevalence of the smallpox among our troops. This fatal pestilence completed our destruction. It is a frown of providence upon us, which we ought to lay to heart.

But, on the other hand, the delay of this declaration to this time has many great advantages attending it. The hopes of reconciliation, which were fondly entertained by multitudes of honest and well-meaning, though weak and mistaken people, have been gradually, and, at last, totally extinguished. Time has been given for the whole people maturely to consider the great question of independence, and to ripen their judgment, dissipate their fears, and allure their hopes, by discussing it in newspapers and pamphlets, by debating it in assemblies, conventions, committees of safety and inspection, in town and county meetings, as well as in private conversations, so that the whole people, in every colony of the thirteen, have now adopted it as their own act. This will cement the union, and avoid those heats, and perhaps convulsions, which might have been occasioned by such a declaration six months ago.

But the day is past. The second day of July, 1776, will be the most memorable epocha in the history of America. I am apt to believe that it will be celebrated by succeeding generations as the great anniversary festival. It ought to be commemorated as the day of deliverance, by solemn acts of devotion to God Almighty. It ought to be solemnized with pomp and parade, with shows, games, sports, guns, bells, bonfires, and illuminations, from one end of this continent to the other, from this time forward, forevermore.

You will think me transported with enthusiasm, but I am not. I am well aware of the toil, and blood, and treasure that it will cost us to maintain this declaration, and support and defend these States. Yet, through all the gloom, I can see the rays of ravishing light and glory. I can see that the end is more than worth all the means, and that posterity will triumph in that day's transaction, even although we should rue it, which I trust in God we shall not.

To George Wythe: "Thoughts on Government"

1776

My Dear Sir,—If I was equal to the task of forming a plan for the government of a colony, I should be flattered with your request, and very happy to comply with it; because, as the divine science of politics is the science of social happiness, and the blessings of society depend entirely on the constitutions of government, which are generally institutions that last for many generations, there can be no employment more agreeable to a benevolent mind than a research after the best.

Pope flattered tyrants too much when he said,

"For forms of government let fools contest,
That which is best administered is best."

Nothing can be more fallacious than this. But poets read history to collect flowers, not fruits; they attend to fanciful images, not the effects of social institutions. Nothing is more certain, from the history of nations and nature of man, than that some forms of government are better fitted for being well administered than others.

We ought to consider what is the end of government, before we determine which is the best form. Upon this point all speculative politicians will agree, that the happiness of society is the end of government, as all divines and moral philosophers will agree that the happiness of the individual is the end of man. From this principle it will follow, that the form of government which communicates ease, comfort, security, or, in one word, happiness, to the greatest number of persons, and in the greatest degree, is the best.

All sober inquirers after truth, ancient and modern, pagan and Christian, have declared that the happiness of man, as well as his dignity, consists in virtue. Confucius, Zoroaster, Socrates, Mahomet, not to mention authorities really sacred, have agreed in this.

If there is a form of government, then, whose principle and foundation is virtue, will not every sober man acknowledge it better calculated to promote the general happiness than any other form?

Fear is the foundation of most governments; but it is so sordid and brutal a passion, and renders men in whose breasts it predominates so stupid and miserable, that Americans will not be likely to approve of any political institution which is founded on it.

Honor is truly sacred, but holds a lower rank in the scale of moral excellence than virtue. Indeed, the former is but a part of the latter, and consequently has not equal pretensions to support a frame of government productive of human happiness.

The foundation of every government is some principle or passion in the minds of the people. The noblest principles and most generous affections in our nature, then, have the fairest chance to support the noblest and most generous models of government. [. . .]

[. . .] [Reason] will convince any candid mind, that there is no good government but what is republican. That the only valuable part of the British constitution is so; because the very definition of a republic is "an empire of laws, and not of men." That, as a republic is the best of governments, so that particular arrangement of the powers of society, or, in other words, that form of government which is best contrived to secure an impartial and exact execution of the laws, is the best of republics.

Of republics there is an inexhaustible variety, because the possible combinations of the powers of society are capable of innumerable variations.

As good government is an empire of laws, how shall your laws be made? In a large society, inhabiting an extensive country, it is impossible that the whole should assemble to make laws. The first necessary step, then, is to depute power from the many to a few of the most wise and good. But by what rules shall you choose your representatives? Agree upon the number and qualifications of persons who shall have the benefit of choosing, or annex this privilege to the inhabitants of a certain extent of ground.

The principal difficulty lies, and the greatest care should be employed, in constituting this representative assembly. It should be in miniature an exact portrait of the people at large. It should think, feel, reason, and act like them. That it may be the interest of this assembly to do strict justice at all times, it should be an equal representation, or, in other words, equal interests among the people should have equal interests in it. Great care should be taken to effect this, and to prevent unfair, partial, and corrupt elections. Such regulations, however, may be better made in times of greater tranquillity than the present; and they will spring up themselves naturally, when all the powers of government come to be in the hands of the people's friends. At present, it will be safest to proceed in all established modes, to which the people have been familiarized by habit.

A representation of the people in one assembly being obtained, a question arises, whether all the powers of government, legislative, executive, and judicial, shall be left in this body? I think a people cannot be long free, nor ever happy, whose government is in one assembly. My reasons for this opinion are as follow:—

1. A single assembly is liable to all the vices, follies, and frailties of an individual; subject to fits of humor, starts of passion, flights of enthusiasm, partialities, or prejudice, and consequently productive of hasty results and absurd judgments. And all these errors ought to be corrected and defects supplied by some controlling power.

2. A single assembly is apt to be avaricious, and in time will not scruple to exempt itself from burdens, which it will lay, without compunction, on its constituents.

3. A single assembly is apt to grow ambitious, and after a time will not hesitate to vote itself perpetual. This was one fault of the Long Parliament; but more remarkably of Holland, whose assembly first voted themselves from annual to septennial, then for life, and after a course of years, that all vacancies happening by death or otherwise, should be filled by themselves, without any application to constituents at all.

4. A representative assembly, although extremely well qualified, and absolutely necessary, as a branch of the legislative, is unfit to exercise the executive power, for want of two essential properties, secrecy and despatch.

5. A representative assembly is still less qualified for the judicial power, because it is too numerous, too slow, and too little skilled in the laws.

6. Because a single assembly, possessed of all the powers of government, would make arbitrary laws for their own interest, execute all laws arbitrarily for their own interest, and adjudge all controversies in their own favor.

But shall the whole power of legislation rest in one assembly? Most of the foregoing reasons apply equally to prove that the legislative power ought to be more complex; to which we may add, that if the legislative power is wholly in one assembly, and the executive in another, or in a single person, these two powers will oppose and encroach upon each other, until the contest shall end in war, and the whole power, legislative and executive, be usurped by the strongest.

The judicial power, in such case, could not mediate, or hold the balance between the two contending powers, because the legislative would undermine it. And this shows the necessity, too, of giving the executive power a negative upon the legislative, otherwise this will be continually encroaching upon that.

To avoid these dangers, let a distinct assembly be constituted, as a mediator between the two extreme branches of the legislature, that which represents the people, and that which is vested with the executive power.

Let the representative assembly then elect by ballot, from among themselves or their constituents, or both, a distinct assembly, which, for the sake of perspicuity, we will call a council. It may consist of any number you please, say twenty or thirty, and should have a free and independent exercise of its judgment, and consequently a negative voice in the legislature.

These two bodies, thus constituted, and made integral parts of the legislature, let them unite, and by joint ballot choose a governor, who, after being stripped of most of those badges of domination, called prerogatives, should have a free and independent exercise of his judgment, and be made also an integral part of the legislature. This, I know, is liable to objections; and, if you please, you may make him only president of the council, as in Connecticut. But as the governor is to be invested with the executive power, with consent of council, I think he ought to have a negative upon the legislative. If he is annually elective, as he ought to be, he will always have so much reverence and affection for the people, their representatives and counsellors, that, although you give him an independent exercise of his judgment, he will seldom use it in opposition to the two houses, except in cases the public utility of which would be conspicuous; and some such cases would happen.

In the present exigency of American affairs, when, by an act of Parliament, we are put out of the royal protection, and consequently discharged from our allegiance, and it has become necessary to assume government for our immediate security, the governor, lieutenant-governor, secretary, treasurer, commissary, attorney-general, should be chosen by joint ballot of both houses. And these and all other elections, especially of representatives and counsellors, should be annual, there not being in the whole circle of the sciences a maxim more infallible than this, "where annual elections end, there slavery begins."

These great men, in this respect, should be, once a year,

> "Like bubbles on the sea of matter borne,
> They rise, they break, and to that sea return."

This will teach them the great political virtues of humility, patience, and moderation, without which every man in power becomes a ravenous beast of prey.

This mode of constituting the great offices of state will answer very well for the present; but if by experiment it should be found inconvenient, the legislature may, at its leisure, devise other methods of creating them, by elections of the people at large, as in Connecticut, or it may enlarge the term for which they shall be chosen to seven years, or three years, or for life, or make any other alterations which the society shall find productive of its ease, its safety, its freedom, or, in one word, its happiness.

A rotation of all offices, as well as of representatives and counsellors, has many advocates, and is contended for with many plausible arguments. It would be attended, no doubt, with many advantages; and if the society has a sufficient number of suitable characters to supply the great number of vacancies which would be made by such a rotation, I can see no objection to it. These persons may be allowed to serve for three years, and then be excluded three years, or for any longer or shorter term.

Any seven or nine of the legislative council may be made a quorum, for doing business as a privy council, to advise the governor in the exercise of the executive branch of power, and in all acts of state.

The governor should have the command of the militia and of all your armies. The power of pardons should be with the governor and council.

Judges, justices, and all other officers, civil and military, should be nominated and appointed by the governor, with the advice and consent of council, unless you choose to have a government more popular; if you do, all officers, civil and military, may be chosen by joint ballot of both houses; or, in order to preserve the independence and importance of each house, by ballot of one house, concurred in by the other. Sheriffs should be chosen by the freeholders of counties; so should registers of deeds and clerks of counties.

All officers should have commissions, under the hand of the governor and seal of the colony.

The dignity and stability of government in all its branches, the morals of the people, and every blessing of society depend so much upon an upright and skilful administration of justice, that the judicial power ought to be distinct from both the legislative and executive, and independent upon both, that so it may be a check upon both, as both should be checks upon that. The judges, therefore, should be always men of learning and experience in the laws, of exemplary morals, great patience, calmness, coolness, and attention. Their minds should not be distracted with jarring interests; they should not be dependent upon any man, or body of men. To these ends, they should hold estates for life in their offices; or, in other words, their commissions should be during good behavior, and their salaries ascertained and established by law. For misbehavior, the grand inquest of the colony, the house of representatives, should impeach them before the governor and council, where they should have time and opportunity to make their defence; but, if convicted, should be removed from their offices, and subjected to such other punishment as shall be thought proper.

A militia law, requiring all men, or with very few exceptions besides cases of conscience, to be provided with arms and ammunition, to be trained at certain seasons; and requiring counties, towns, or other small districts, to be provided with public stocks of ammunition and intrenching utensils, and with some settled plans for transporting provisions after the militia, when marched to defend their country against sudden invasions; and requiring certain districts to be provided with field-pieces, companies of matrosses, and perhaps some regiments of light-horse, is always a wise institution, and, in the present circumstances of our country, indispensable.

Laws for the liberal education of youth, especially of the lower class of people, are so extremely wise and useful, that, to a humane and generous mind, no expense for this purpose would be thought extravagant.

The very mention of sumptuary laws will excite a smile. Whether our countrymen have wisdom and virtue enough to submit to them, I know not; but the happiness of the people might be greatly promoted by them, and a revenue saved sufficient to carry on this war forever. Frugality is a great revenue, besides curing us of vanities, levities, and fopperies, which are real antidotes to all great, manly, and warlike virtues.

But must not all commissions run in the name of a king? No. Why may they not as well run thus, "The colony of _____ to A.B. greeting," and be tested by the governor?

Why may not writs, instead of running in the name of the king, run thus, "The colony of _____ to the sheriff," &c., and be tested by the chief justice?

Why may not indictments conclude, "against the peace of the colony of _____ and the dignity of the same?"

A constitution founded on these principles introduces knowledge among the people, and inspires them with a conscious dignity becoming freemen; a general emulation takes place, which causes good humor, sociability, good manners, and good morals to be general. That elevation of sentiment inspired by such a government, makes the common people brave and enterprising. That ambition which is inspired by it makes them sober, industrious, and frugal. You will find among them some elegance, perhaps, but more solidity; a little pleasure, but a great deal of business; some politeness, but more civility. If you compare such a country with the regions of domination, whether monarchical or aristocratical, you will fancy yourself in Arcadia or Elysium.

If the colonies should assume governments separately, they should be left entirely to their own choice of the forms; and if a continental constitution should be formed, it should be a congress, containing a fair and adequate representation of the colonies, and its authority should sacredly be confined to these cases, namely, war, trade, disputes between colony and colony, the post-office, and the unappropriated lands of the crown, as they used to be called.

These colonies, under such forms of government, and in such a union, would be unconquerable by all the monarchies of Europe.

You and I, my dear friend, have been sent into life at a time when the greatest lawgivers of antiquity would have wished to live. How few of the human race have ever enjoyed an opportunity of making an election of government, more than of air, soil, or climate, for themselves or their children! When, before the present epocha, had three millions of people full power and a fair opportunity to form and establish the wisest and happiest government that human wisdom can contrive? I hope you will avail yourself and your country of that extensive learning and indefatigable industry which you possess, to assist her in the formation of the happiest governments and the best character of a great people. For myself, I must beg you to keep my name out of sight; for this feeble attempt, if it should be known to be mine, would oblige me to apply to myself those lines of the immortal John Milton, in one of his sonnets:—

> "I did but prompt the age to quit their clogs
> By the known rules of ancient liberty,
> When straight a barbarous noise environs me
> Of owls and cuckoos, asses, apes, and dogs."

Diary Entry

FEBRUARY 11, 1779

When I arrived in France, the French nation had a great many questions to settle. The first was, Whether I was the famous Adams? Le fameux Adams? Ah, le fameux Adams. In order to speculate a little upon this subject, the pamphlet entitled "Common Sense," had been printed in the "Affaires de l'Angleterre et de l'Amérique," and expressly ascribed to Mr. Adams, the celebrated member of Congress—le célèbre membre du Congrès. It must be further known, that although the pamphlet, Common Sense, was received in France and in all Europe with rapture, yet there were certain parts of it that they did not choose to publish in France. The reasons of this any man may guess. Common Sense undertakes to prove that monarchy is unlawful by the Old Testament. They therefore gave the substance of it, as they said; and, paying many compliments to Mr. Adams, his sense and rich imagination, they were obliged to ascribe some parts to republican zeal. When I arrived at Bordeaux, all that I could say or do would not convince anybody but that I was the fameux Adams. "C'est un homme célèbre. Votre nom est bien connu ici." My answer was, It is another gentleman, whose name of Adams you have heard; it is Mr. Samuel Adams, who was excepted from pardon by General Gage's proclamation. "Oh non, Monsieur, c'est votre modestie."

But when I arrived at Paris, I found a very different style. I found great pains taken, much more than the question was worth, to settle the point that I was not the famous Adams. There was a dread of a sensation; sensations at Paris are important things. I soon found, too, that it was effectually settled in the English newspapers that I was not the famous Adams. Nobody went so far in France or England as to say that I was the infamous Adams. I make no scruple to say that I believe both parties, for parties there were, joined in declaring that I was not the famous Adams. I certainly joined both sides in this, in declaring that I was not the famous Adams, because this was the truth.

It being settled that he was not the famous Adams, the consequence was plain; he was some man that nobody had ever heard of before, and therefore a man of no consequence—a cipher. And I am inclined to think that all parties, both in France and England,—Whigs and Tories in England, the friends of Franklin, Deane, and Lee, in France,—differing in many other things, agreed in this, that I was not the famous Adams.

Seeing all this, and saying nothing,—for what could a man say?—seeing also that there were two parties formed among the Americans, as fixed in their aversion to each other as both were to Great Britain, if I had affected the character of a fool, in order to find out the truth and to do good by-and-by, I should have had the example of a Brutus for my justification; but I did not affect this character. I behaved with as much prudence and civility and industry as I could; but still it was a settled point at Paris and in the English newspapers that I was not the famous Adams; and therefore the consequence was settled, absolutely and unalterably, that I was a man of whom nobody had ever heard before,—a perfect cipher; a man who did not understand a word of French; awkward in his figure, awkward in his dress; no abilities; a perfect bigot and fanatic.

It is my indispensable duty to tell the Count de Vergennes that I think one great cause of this horrid address of Mr. Deane, is Mr. Franklin's certificate in his favor that he is an able and faithful negotiator, and that Mr. Franklin was deceived in this; that Mr. Franklin's knowledge actually in America, for a great many years, has not been long; that he was upright in this, but deceived; that there are such certain and infallible proofs of vanity, presumption, ambition, avarice, and folly, in Mr. Deane, as render him very unworthy of confidence, and therefore that Dr. Franklin has been deceived.

To Thomas Jefferson

LONDON, 6 DECEMBER, 1787.

Dear Sir,

The project of a new Constitution has objections against it, to which I find it difficult to reconcile myself; but I am so unfortunate as to differ somewhat from you in the articles, according to your last kind letter.

You are afraid of the one—I, of the few. We agree perfectly that the many should have a full, fair, and perfect representation. You are apprehensive of monarchy, I, of aristocracy. I would, therefore, have given more power to the president, and less to the senate. The nomination and appointment to all offices, I would have given to the president, assisted only by a privy council of his own creation; but not a vote or voice would I have given to the senate or any senator unless he were of the privy council. Faction and distraction are the sure and certain consequence of giving to a senate, a vote in the distribution of offices.

You are apprehensive that the president, when once chosen, will be chosen again and again as long as he lives. So much the better, as it appears to me.—You are apprehensive of foreign interference, intrigue, influence. So am I.—But as often as elections happen, the danger of foreign influence renews. The less frequently they happen, the less danger; and if the same man may be chosen again, it is possible he will be, and the danger of foreign influence will be less. Foreigners, seeing little prospect, will have less courage for enterprise.

Elections, my dear sir, elections to offices which are great objects of ambition, I look at with terror. Experiments of this kind have been so often tried, and so universally found productive of horrors, that there is great reason to dread them.

Mr. Littlepage, who will have the honor to deliver this, will tell you all the news.

I am, &c. &c.

To Thomas Brand-Hollis, esq.

FOUNTAIN INN, PORTSMOUTH, APRIL 5, 1788.

My Dear Sir,

If ever there was any philosophic solitude, your two friends have found it in this place, where we have been wind bound, a whole week, without a creature to speak to. Our whole business, pleasure and amusement has been reading Necker's Religious opinions, Hayley's Old Maids, and Cumberland's fourth Observer. Our whole stock is now exhausted, and if the ship should not arrive with a fresh supply of books, we shall be obliged to write romances to preserve us from melancholy.

I know not whether atheism has made much progress in England: and perhaps it would do more hurt than good to publish any thing upon the subject, otherwise Necker's book appears to me to deserve the best translation and edition that can be made of it. Mr. Mortimer perhaps might find his account in it. Necker's subject is so much more interesting to human nature, that I am almost disgusted with my own. Yet my countrymen have so much more need of arguments against errors in government, than in religion, that I am again comforted and encouraged. At this moment there is a greater fermentation throughout all Europe upon the subject of government, than was perhaps ever known, at any former period. France, Holland, and Flanders are alive to it. Is government a science or not? Are there any principles on which it is founded? What are its ends? If indeed there is no rule; no standard: all must be accident and chance. If there is a standard, what is it?—It is easier to make a people discontented with a bad government, than to teach them how to establish and maintain a good one. Liberty can never be created and preserved without a people: and by a people, I mean a common people, in contradistinction from the gentlemen; and a people can never be created and preserved without an executive authority in one hand, separated entirely from the body of the gentlemen. The two ladies Aristocratia and Democratia will eternally pull caps, till one or other is mistress. If the first is the conqueress she never fails to depress and debase her rival into the most deplorable servitude. If the last conquers, she eternally surrenders herself into the arms of a ravisher. Kings, therefore, are the natural allies of the common people, and the prejudices against them are by no means favorable to liberty. Kings and the common people have both a common enemy in the gentlemen, and they must unite in some degree or other against them, or both will be destroyed; the one dethroned and the other enslaved. The common people too are unable to defend themselves against their own ally, the king, without another ally in the gentlemen. It is, therefore, indispensably necessary, that the gentlemen in a body, or by representatives, should be an independent and essential branch of the constitution. By a king, I mean a single person possessed of the whole executive power. You have often said to me, that it is difficult to preserve the balance. This is true. It is difficult to preserve liberty. But there can be no liberty without some balance; and it is certainly easier to preserve a balance of three branches than of two.—If the people cannot preserve a balance of three branches, how is it possible for them to preserve one of two only? If the people of England find it difficult to preserve their balance at present, how would they do, if they had the election of a king, and an house of lords to make, once a year, or once in seven years, as well as of an house of commons? It seems evident at first blush, that periodical elections of the king and peers in England, in addition to the commons, would produce agitations that must destroy all order and safety as well as liberty. The gentlemen too, can never defend themselves against a brave and united common people, but by an alliance with a king; nor against a king, without an alliance with the common people. It is the insatiability of human passions, that is the foundation of all government. Men are not only ambitious, but their ambition is unbounded: they are not only avaricious, but their avarice is insatiable. The desires of kings, gentlemen and common people,—all increase, instead of being satisfied by indulgence. This fact being allowed, it will follow that it is necessary to place checks upon them all.—Pray write me upon these subjects when I arrive in America.

I am, with sincere esteem, my dear sir, yours

A Defence of the Constitutions of Government of the United States
Preface

[1787–1788]

The arts and sciences, in general, during the three or four last centuries, have had a regular course of progressive improvement. The inventions in mechanic arts, the discoveries in natural philosophy, navigation, and commerce, and the advancement of civilization and humanity, have occasioned changes in the condition of the world, and the human character, which would have astonished the most refined nations of antiquity. A continuation of similar exertions is every day rendering Europe more and more like one community, or single family. Even in the theory and practice of government, in all the simple monarchies, considerable improvements have been made. The checks and balances of republican governments have been in some degree adopted at the courts of princes. By the erection of various tribunals, to register the laws, and exercise the judicial power—by indulging the petitions and remonstrances of subjects, until by habit they are regarded as rights—a control has been established over ministers of state, and the royal councils, which, in some degree, approaches the spirit of republics. Property is generally secure, and personal liberty seldom invaded. The press has great influence, even where it is not expressly tolerated; and the public opinion must be respected by a minister, or his place becomes insecure. Commerce begins to thrive; and if religious toleration were established, personal liberty a little more protected, by giving an absolute right to demand a public trial in a certain reasonable time, and the states were invested with a few more privileges, or rather restored to some that have been taken away, these governments would be brought to as great a degree of perfection, they would approach as near to the character of governments of laws and not of men, as their nature will probably admit of. In so general a refinement, or more properly a reformation of manners and improvement in science, is it not unaccountable that the knowledge of the principles and construction of free governments, in which the happiness of life, and even the further progress of improvement in education and society, in knowledge and virtue, are so deeply interested, should have remained at a full stand for two or three thousand years?

According to a story in Herodotus, the nature of monarchy, aristocracy, and democracy, and the advantages and inconveniences of each, were as well understood at the time of the neighing of the horse of Darius, as they are at this hour. A variety of mixtures of these simple species were conceived and attempted, with various success, by the Greeks and Romans. Representations, instead of collections, of the people; a total separation of the executive from the legislative power, and of the judicial from both; and a balance in the legislature, by three independent, equal branches, are perhaps the only three discoveries in the constitution of a free government, since the institution of Lycurgus. Even these have been so unfortunate, that they have never spread: the first has been given up by all the nations, excepting one, which had once adopted it; and the other two, reduced to practice, if not invented, by the English nation, have never been imitated by any other, except their own descendants in America.

While it would be rash to say, that nothing further can be done to bring a free government, in all its parts, still nearer to perfection, the representations of the people are most obviously susceptible of improvement. The end to be aimed at, in the formation of a representative assembly, seems to be the sense of the people, the public voice. The perfection of the portrait consists in its likeness. Numbers, or property, or both, should be the rule; and the proportions of electors and members an affair of calculation. The duration should not be so long that the deputy should have time to forget the opinions of his constituents. Corruption in elections is the great enemy of freedom. Among the provisions to prevent it, more frequent elections, and a more general privilege of voting, are not all that might be devised. Dividing the districts, diminishing the distance of travel, and confining the choice to residents, would be great advances towards the annihilation of corruption. The modern aristocracies of Holland, Venice, Bern, &c., have tempered themselves with innumerable checks, by which they have given a great degree of stability to that form of government; and though liberty and life can never be there enjoyed so well as in a free republic, none is perhaps more capable of profound sagacity. We shall learn to prize the checks and balances of a free government, and even those of the modern aristocracies, if we recollect the miseries of Greece, which arose from its ignorance of them. The only balance attempted against the ancient kings was a body of nobles; and the consequences were perpetual alternations of rebellion and tyranny, and the butchery of thousands upon every revolution from one to the other. When kings were abolished, aristocracies tyrannized; and then no balance was attempted but between aristocracy and democracy. This, in the nature of things, could be no balance at all, and therefore the pendulum was forever on the swing.

It is impossible to read in Thucydides, his account of the factions and confusions throughout all Greece, which were introduced by this want of an equilibrium, without horror. "During the few days that Eurymedon, with his troops, continued at Corcyra, the people of that city extended the massacre to all whom they judged their enemies. The crime alleged was, their attempt to overturn the democracy. Some perished merely through private enmity; some, by the hands of the borrower, on account of the money they had lent. Every kind of death, every dreadful act, was perpetrated. Fathers slew their children; some were dragged from altars, some were butchered at them; numbers, immured in temples, were starved. The contagion spread through the whole extent of Greece; factions raged in every city; the licentious many contending for the Athenians, and the aspiring few for the Lacedæmonians. The consequence was, seditions in cities, with all their numerous and tragical incidents."

"Such things ever will be," says Thucydides, "so long as human nature continues the same." But if this nervous historian had known a balance of three powers, he would not have pronounced the distemper so incurable, but would have added—*so long as parties in cities remain unbalanced.* He adds,—"Words lost their signification; brutal rashness was fortitude; prudence, cowardice; modesty, effeminacy; and being wise in every thing, to be good for nothing: the hot temper was manly valor; calm deliberation, plausible knavery; he who boiled with indignation, was trustworthy; and he who presumed to contradict, was ever suspected. Connection of blood was less regarded than transient acquaintance; associations were not formed for mutual advantage, consistent with law, but for rapine against all law; trust was only communication of guilt; revenge was more valued, than never to have suffered an injury; perjuries were master-pieces of cunning; the dupes only blushed, the villains most impudently triumphed."

"The source of all these evils was a thirst of power, from rapacious and ambitious passions. The men of large influence, some contending for the just equality of the democratical, and others for the fair decorum of aristocratical government, by artful sounds, embarrassed those communities, for their own private lucre, by the keenest spirit, the most daring projects, and most dreadful machinations. Revenge, not limited by justice or the public welfare, was measured only by such retaliation as was judged the sweetest;

by capital condemnations, by iniquitous sentences, and by glutting the present rancor of their hearts with their own hands. The pious and upright conduct was on both sides disregarded; the moderate citizens fell victims to both. Seditions introduced every species of outrageous wickedness into the Grecian manners. Sincerity was laughed out of countenance; the whole order of human life was confounded; the human temper, too apt to transgress in spite of laws, now having gained the ascendant over law, seemed to glory that it was too strong for justice, and an enemy to all superiority."

Mr. Hume has collected, from Diodorus Siculus alone, a few massacres which happened in only sixty of the most polished years of Greece:—"From Sybaris, 500 nobles banished; of Chians, 600 citizens; at Ephesus, 340 killed, 1000 banished; of Cyrenians, 500 nobles killed, all the rest banished; the Corinthians killed 120, banished 500; Phæbidas banished 300 Bœotians. Upon the fall of the Lacedæmonians, democracies were restored in many cities, and severe vengeance taken of the nobles; the banished nobles returning, butchered their adversaries at Phialæ, in Corinth, in Megara, in Phliasia, where they killed 300 of the people; but these again revolting, killed above 600 of the nobles, and banished the rest. In Arcadia, 1400 banished, besides many killed; the banished retired to Sparta and Pallantium; the latter were delivered up to their countrymen, and all killed. Of the banished from Argos and Thebes, there were 500 in the Spartan army. The people, before the usurpation of Agathocles, had banished 600 nobles; afterwards that tyrant, in concurrence with the people, killed 4000 nobles, and banished 6000; and killed 4000 people at Gela; his brother banished 8000 from Syracuse. The inhabitants of Ægesta, to the number of 40,000, were killed, man, woman, and child, for the sake of their money; all the relations of the Libyan army, fathers, brothers, children, killed; 7000 exiles killed after capitulation. These numbers, compared with the population of those cities, are prodigious; yet Agathocles was a man of character, and not to be suspected of wanton cruelty, contrary to the maxims of his age."

Such were the fashionable outrages of unbalanced parties. In the name of human and divine benevolence, is such a system as this to be recommended to Americans, in this age of the world? Human nature is as incapable now of going through revolutions with temper and sobriety, with patience and prudence, or without fury and madness, as it was among the Greeks so long ago. The latest revolution that we read of was conducted, at least on one side, in the Grecian style, with laconic energy; and with a little Attic salt, at least, without too much patience, foresight, and prudence, on the other. Without three orders, and an effectual balance between them, in every American constitution, it must be destined to frequent unavoidable revolutions;

though they are delayed a few years, they must come in time. The United States are large and populous nations, in comparison with the Grecian commonwealths, or even the Swiss cantons; and they are growing every day more disproportionate, and therefore less capable of being held together by simple governments. Countries that increase in population so rapidly as the States of America did, even during such an impoverishing and destructive war as the last was, are not to be long bound with silken threads; lions, young or old, will not be bound by cobwebs. It would be better for America, it is nevertheless agreed, to ring all the changes with the whole set of bells, and go through all the revolutions of the Grecian States, rather than establish an absolute monarchy among them, notwithstanding all the great and real improvements which have been made in that kind of government.

The objection to it is not because it is supported by nobles, and a subordination of ranks; for all governments, even the most democratical, are supported by a subordination of offices, and of ranks too. None ever existed without it but in a state of anarchy and outrage, in a contempt of law and justice, no better than no government. But the nobles, in the European monarchies, support them more by opposing than promoting their ordinary views. The kings are supported by their armies; the nobles support the crown, as it is in full possession of the gift of all employments; but they support it still more by checking its ministers, and preventing them from running into abuses of power and wanton despotism; otherwise the people would be pushed to extremities and insurrections. It is thus that the nobles reconcile the monarchical authority to the obedience of the subjects; but take away the standing armies, and leave the nobles to themselves, and in a few years, they would overturn every monarchy in Europe, and erect aristocracies.

It is become a kind of fashion among writers, to admit, as a maxim, that if you could be always sure of a wise, active, and virtuous prince, monarchy would be the best of governments. But this is so far from being admissible, that it will forever remain true, that a free government has a great advantage over a simple monarchy. The best and wisest prince, by means of a freer communication with his people, and the greater opportunities to collect the best advice from the best of his subjects, would have an immense advantage in a free state over a monarchy. A senate consisting of all that is most noble, wealthy, and able in the nation, with a right to counsel the crown at all times, is a check to ministers, and a security against abuses, such as a body of nobles who never meet, and have no such right, can never supply. Another assembly, composed of representatives chosen by the people in all parts, gives free access to the whole nation, and communicates all its wants, knowledge, projects, and wishes to government; it excites emulation among all classes, removes complaints, redresses grievances, affords opportunities of exertion to genius, though in obscurity, and gives full scope to all the faculties of man; it opens a passage for every speculation to the legislature, to administration, and to the public; it gives a universal energy to the human character, in every part of the state, such as never can be obtained in a monarchy.

There is a third particular which deserves attention both from governments and people. In a simple monarchy, the ministers of state can never know their friends from their enemies; secret cabals undermine their influence, and blast their reputation. This occasions a jealousy ever anxious and irritated, which never thinks the government safe without an encouragement of informers and spies, throughout every part of the state, who interrupt the tranquillity of private life, destroy the confidence of families in their own domestics and in one another, and poison freedom in its sweetest retirements. In a free government, on the contrary, the ministers can have no enemies of consequence but among the members of the great or little council, where every man is obliged to take his side, and declare his opinion, upon every question. This circumstance alone, to every manly mind, would be sufficient to decide the preference in favor of a free government. Even secrecy, where the executive is entire in one hand, is as easily and surely preserved in a free government, as in a simple monarchy; and as to despatch, all the simple monarchies of the whole universe may be defied to produce greater or more numerous examples of it than are to be found in English history. An Alexander, or a Frederic, possessed of the prerogatives only of a king of England, and leading his own armies, would never find himself embarrassed or delayed in any honest enterprise. He might be restrained, indeed, from running mad, and from making conquests to the ruin of his nation, merely for his own glory; but this is no argument against a free government.

There can be no free government without a democratical branch in the constitution. Monarchies and aristocracies are in possession of the voice and influence of every university and academy in Europe. Democracy, simple democracy, never had a patron among men of letters. Democratical mixtures in government have lost almost all the advocates they ever had out of England and America. Men of letters must have a great deal of praise, and some of the necessaries, conveniences, and ornaments of life. Monarchies and aristocracies pay well and applaud liberally. The people have almost always expected to be served gratis, and to be paid for the honor of serving them; and their applauses and adorations are bestowed too often on artifices and tricks, on hypocrisy and superstition, on flattery, bribes, and largesses. It is no wonder then that democracies and democratical mixtures are annihilated all over Europe, except on a barren rock, a paltry fen, an inaccessible mountain, or an impenetrable forest. The people of England, to their immortal honor, are hitherto an exception; but, to the humiliation of human nature, they show very often that they are like other men. The people in America have now the best opportunity and the greatest trust in their hands, that Providence ever committed to so small a number, since the transgression of the first pair; if they betray their trust, their guilt will merit even greater punishment than other nations have suffered, and the indignation of Heaven. If there is one certain truth to be collected from the history of all ages, it is this; that the people's rights and liberties, and the democratical mixture in a constitution, can never be preserved without a strong executive, or, in other words, without separating the executive from the legislative power. If the executive power, or any considerable part of it, is left in the hands either of an aristocratical or a democratical assembly, it will corrupt the legislature as necessarily as rust corrupts iron, or as arsenic poisons the human body; and when the legislature is corrupted, the people are undone.

The rich, the well-born, and the able, acquire an influence among the people that will soon be too much for simple honesty and plain sense, in a house of representatives. The most illustrious of them must, therefore, be separated from the mass, and placed by themselves in a senate; this is, to all honest and useful intents, an ostracism. A member of a senate, of immense wealth, the most respected birth, and transcendent abilities, has no influence in the nation, in comparison of what he would have in a single representative assembly. When a senate exists, the most powerful man in the state may be safely admitted into the house of representatives, because the people have it in their power to remove him into the senate as soon as his influence becomes dangerous. The senate becomes the great object of ambition; and the richest and the most sagacious wish to merit an advancement to it by services to the public in the house. When he has obtained the object of his wishes, you may still hope for the benefits of his exertions, without dreading his passions; for the executive power being in other hands, he has lost much of his influence with the people, and can govern very few votes more than his own among the senators.

It was the general opinion of ancient nations, that the Divinity alone was adequate to the important office of giving laws to men. The Greeks entertained this prejudice throughout all their dispersions; the Romans cultivated the same popular delusion; and modern nations, in the consecration of kings, and in several superstitious chimeras of divine right in princes and nobles, are nearly unanimous in preserving remnants of it. Even the venerable magistrates of Amersfort devoutly believe themselves God's vicegerents. Is it that obedience to the laws can be obtained from mankind in no other manner? Are the jealousy of power, and the envy of superiority, so strong in all men, that no considerations of public or private utility are sufficient to engage their submission to rules for their own happiness? Or is the disposition to imposture so prevalent in men of experience, that their private views of ambition and avarice can be accomplished only by artifice? It was a tradition in antiquity that the laws of Crete were dictated to Minos by the inspiration of Jupiter. This legislator and his brother Rhadamanthus were both his sons; once in nine years they went to converse with their father, to propose questions concerning the wants of the people; and his answers were recorded as laws for their government. The laws of Lacedæmon were communicated by Apollo to Lycurgus; and, lest the meaning of the deity should not have been perfectly comprehended, or correctly expressed, they were afterwards confirmed by his oracle at Delphos. Among the Romans, Numa was indebted for those laws which procured the prosperity of his country to his conversations with Egeria. The Greeks imported these mysteries from Egypt and the East, whose despotisms, from the remotest antiquity to this day, have been founded in the same solemn empiricism; their emperors and nobles being all descended from their gods. Woden and Thor were divinities too; and their posterity ruled a thousand years in the north by the strength of a like credulity. Manco Capac was the child of the sun, the visible deity of the Peruvians; and transmitted his divinity, as well as his earthly dignity and authority, through a line of incas. And the rudest tribes of savages in North America have certain families from which their leaders are always chosen, under the immediate protection of the god War. There is nothing in which mankind have been more unanimous; yet nothing can be inferred from it more than this, that the multitude have always been credulous, and the few are always artful.

The United States of America have exhibited, perhaps, the first example of governments erected on the simple principles of nature; and if men are now sufficiently enlightened to disabuse themselves of artifice, imposture, hypocrisy, and superstition, they will consider this event as an era in their history. Although the detail of the formation of the American governments is at present little known or regarded either in Europe or in America, it may hereafter become an object of curiosity. [. . .] Unembarrassed by attachments to noble families, hereditary lines and successions, or any considerations of royal blood, even the pious mystery of holy oil had no more influence than that other one of holy water. The people were universally too enlightened to be imposed on by artifice; and their leaders, or more properly followers, were men of too much honor to attempt it. Thirteen governments thus founded on the natural authority of the people alone, without a pretence of miracle or mystery, and which are destined to spread over the northern part of that whole quarter of the globe, are a great point gained in favor of the rights of mankind. The experiment is made, and has completely succeeded; it can no longer be called in question, whether authority in magistrates and obedience of citizens can be grounded on reason, morality, and the Christian religion, without the monkery of priests, or the knavery of politicians. As the writer was personally acquainted with most of the gentlemen in each of the states, who had the principal share in the first draughts, the following work was really written to lay before the public a specimen of that kind of reading and reasoning which produced the American constitutions. [. . .]

[. . .] After all the turbulence, wars, and revolutions, which compose the history of Europe for so many ages, we find simple monarchies established everywhere. Whether the system will now become stationary, and last forever, by means of a few further improvements in monarchical government, we know not; or whether still further revolutions are to come. The most probable, or rather the only probable change, is the introduction of democratical branches into those governments. If the people should ever aim at more, they will defeat themselves; as they will, indeed, if they aim at this by any other than gentle means and by gradual advances, by improvements in general education, and by informing the public mind.

The systems of legislators are experiments made on human life and manners, society and government. Zoroaster, Confucius, Mithras, Odin, Thor, Mahomet, Lycurgus, Solon, Romulus, and a thousand others, may be compared to philosophers making experiments on the elements. Unhappily, political experiments cannot be made in a laboratory, nor determined in a few hours. The operation once begun, runs over whole quarters of the globe, and is not finished in many thousands of years. The experiment of Lycurgus lasted seven hundred years, but never spread beyond the limits of Laconia. The process of Solon expired in one century; that of Romulus lasted but two centuries and a half; but the Teutonic institutions, described by Cæsar and Tacitus, are the most memorable experiment, merely political, ever yet made in human affairs. They have spread all over Europe, and have lasted eighteen hundred years. They afford the strongest argument that can be imagined in support of the position assumed in these volumes. Nothing ought to have more weight with America, to determine her judgment against mixing the authority of the one, the few, and the many, confusedly in one assembly, than the widespread miseries and final slavery of almost all mankind, in consequence of such an ignorant policy in the ancient Germans. What is the ingredient which in England has preserved the democratical authority? The balance, and that only. The English have, in reality, blended together the feudal institutions with those of the Greeks and Romans, and out of all have made that noble composition, which avoids the inconveniences, and retains the advantages of both.

The institutions now made in America will not wholly wear out for thousands of years. It is of the last importance, then, that they should begin right. If they set out wrong, they will never be able to return, unless it be by accident, to the right path. After having known the history of Europe, and of England in particular, it would be the height of folly to go back to the institutions of Woden and of Thor, as the Americans are advised to do. If they had been counselled to adopt a single monarchy at once, it would have been less mysterious.

Robertson, Hume, and Gibbon have given such admirable accounts of the feudal institutions and their consequences, that it would have been, perhaps, more discreet to have referred to them, without saying any thing more upon the subject. To collect together the legislation of the Indians would take up much room, but would be well worth the pains. The sovereignty is in the nation, it is true, but the three powers are strong in every tribe; and their royal and aristocratical dignities are much more generally hereditary, from the popular partiality to particular families, and the superstitious opinion that such are favorites of the God of War, than late writers upon this subject have allowed.

To Benjamin Rush

NEW YORK, JUNE 19, 1789.

Dear Sir,—Your single Principle in your Letter of the 15th must fail you. You say "that Republican Systems have never had a fair Tryal." What do you mean by a "fair Tryal"? and what by Republican systems? Every Government that has more than one Man in its sovereignty is a republican system. Tryals innumerable have been made—as many as there have existed Nations. There is not and never was, I believe, on earth, a Nation, which has not been, at some Period of its duration, under a Republican Government: *i.e.* under a Government of more than one. All the various combinations and modifications which the subtle Brains of Men could invent have been attempted, to no other purpose but to shew that Discord, Anarchy and Uncertainty of Life, Liberty and Property, can be avoided only by a perfect equilibrium in the Constitution. You seem determined not to allow a limited monarchy to be a republican system, which it certainly is, and the best that has ever been tryed.

There is no Proposition, of the Truth of which I am more clearly convinced than this, that the "Influence of general Science," instead of curing any defects in an unballanced Republick, would only increase and inflame them and make them more intollerable: for this obvious and unanswerable Reason, that Parties would have in them, a greater number of able and ambitious Men, who would only understand the better, how to worry one another with greater Art and dexterity. Religion itself by no means cures this inveterate evil, for parties are always founded on some Principle, and the more conscientious Men are, the more determined they will be in pursuit of their Principle, System and Party.

I should as soon think of closing all my window shutters, to enable me to see, as of banishing the Classicks, to improve Republican Ideas. How can you say that Factions have been few in America? Have they not rendered Property insecure? have they not trampled Justice under foot? have not Majorities voted property out of the pocketts of others into their own, with the most decided Tyranny?

Have not our Parties behaved like all Republican Parties? is not the History of Hancock and Bowdoin, the History of the Medici and Albizi—that of Clinton and Yates, the same with that of the Cancellieri and the Panchiatichi? and so on through the Continent. And we shall find that without a Ballance the Progress will soon be, from Libels to Riots, from Riots to Seditions and from Seditions to Civil Wars.

Every Project to enlighten our Fellow Citizens has my most hearty good wishes: because it tends to bring them into a right way of thinking respecting the means of their Happiness, civil, political, social and religious.

I wish with all my heart, that the Constitution had expressed as much Homage to the Supreme Ruler of the Universe as the President has done in his first speech. The *Petit Maitres* who call themselves Legislators and attempt to found a Government on any other than an eternal Basis of Morals and Religion, have as much of my Pitty as can consist with Contempt.

I am my dear sir yours

To Roger Sherman

JULY 18, 1789

Dear Sir,—In my letter of yesterday I think it was demonstrated that the English government is a republic, and that the regal negative upon the laws is essential to that republic. Because, without it, that government would not be what it is, a monarchical republic; and, consequently, could not preserve the balance of power between the executive and legislative powers, nor that other balance which is in the legislature,—between the one, the few, and the many; in which two balances the excellence of that form of government must consist.

Let us now inquire, whether the new constitution of the United States is or is not a monarchical republic, like that of Great Britain. The monarchical and the aristocratical power in our constitution, it is true, are not hereditary; but this makes no difference in the nature of the power, in the nature of the balance, or in the name of the species of government. It would make no difference in the power of a judge or justice, or general or admiral, whether his commission were for life or years. His authority during the time it lasted, would be the same whether it were for one year or twenty, or for life, or descendible to his eldest son. The people, the nation, in whom all power resides originally, may delegate their power for one year or for ten years; for years, or for life; or may delegate it in fee simple or fee tail, if I may so express myself; or during good behavior, or at will, or till further orders.

A nation might unanimously create a dictator or a despot, for one year or more, or for life, or for perpetuity with hereditary descent. In such a case, the dictator for one year would as really be a dictator for the time his power lasted, as the other would be whose power was perpetual and descendible. A nation in the same manner might create a simple monarchy for years, life, or perpetuity, and in either case the creature would be equally a simple monarch during the continuance of his power. So the people of England might create king, lords, and commons, for a year, or for several years, or for life, and in any of these cases, their government would be a monarchical republic, or, if you will, a limited monarchy, during its continuance, as much as it is now, when the king and nobles are hereditary. They might make their house of commons hereditary too. What the consequence of this would be it is easy to foresee; but it would not in the first moment make any change in the legal power, nor in the name of the government.

Let us now consider what our constitution is, and see whether any other name can with propriety be given it, than that of a monarchical republic, or if you will, a limited monarchy. The duration of our president is neither perpetual nor for life; it is only for four years; but his power during those four years is much greater than that of an avoyer, a consul, a podestà, a doge, a stadtholder; nay, than a king of Poland; nay, than a king of Sparta. I know of no first magistrate in any republican government, excepting England and Neuchatel, who possesses a constitutional dignity, authority, and power comparable to his. The power of sending and receiving ambassadors, of raising and commanding armies and navies, of nominating and appointing and commissioning all officers, of managing the treasures, the internal and external affairs of the nation; nay, the whole executive power, coextensive with the legislative power, is vested in him, and he has the right, and his is the duty, to take care that the laws be faithfully executed. These rights and duties, these prerogatives and dignities, are so transcendent that they must naturally and necessarily excite in the nation all the jealousy, envy, fears, apprehensions, and opposition, that are so constantly observed in England against the crown.

That these powers are necessary, I readily admit. That the laws cannot be executed without them; that the lives, liberties, properties and characters of the citizens cannot be secure without their protection, is most clear. But it is equally certain, I think, that they ought to have been still greater, or much less. The limitations upon them in the cases of war, treaties, and appointments to office, and especially the limitation on the president's independence as a branch of the legislative, will be the destruction of this constitution, and involve us in anarchy, if not amended. I shall pass over all particulars for the present, except the last; because that is now the point in dispute between you and me. Longitude, and the philosopher's stone, have not been sought with more earnestness by philosophers than a guardian of the laws has been studied by legislators from Plato to Montesquieu; but every project has been found to be no better than committing the lamb to the custody of the wolf, except that one which is called a *balance of power.* A simple sovereignty in one, a few, or many, has no balance, and therefore no laws. A divided sovereignty without a balance, or in other words, where the division is unequal, is always at war, and consequently has no laws. In our constitution the sovereignty,—that is, the legislative power,—is divided into three branches. The house and senate are equal, but the third branch, though essential, is not equal. The president must pass judgment upon every law; but in some cases his judgment may be overruled. These cases will be such as attack his constitutional power; it is, therefore, certain he has not equal power to defend himself, or the constitution, or the judicial power, as the senate and house have.

Power naturally grows. Why? Because human passions are insatiable. But that power alone can grow which already is too great; that which is unchecked; that which has no equal power to control it. The legislative power, in our constitution, is greater than the executive; it will, therefore, encroach, because both aristocratical and democratical passions are insatiable. The legislative power will increase, the executive will diminish. In the legislature, the monarchical power is not equal either to the aristocratical or democratical; it will, therefore, decrease, while the other will increase. Indeed, I think the aristocratical power is greater than either the monarchical or democratical. That will, therefore, swallow up the other two.

In my letter of yesterday, I think it was proved, that a republic might make the supreme executive an integral part of the legislature. In this, it is equally demonstrated, as I think, that our constitution ought to be amended by a decisive adoption of that expedient. If you do not forbid me, I shall write to you again.

To Benjamin Rush

NEW YORK, 18 APRIL, 1790.

Your letter of April 13th soars above the visible, diurnal sphere. I own to you that avarice, ambition, the love of fame, &c., are all mysterious passions. They are the greatest absurdities, delusions, and follies that can be imagined, if in this life only we had hope. In the boat, on our return from Point-no-Point, the principal topic of conversation was independence. My sentiments on this head were no secret in Congress from May, 1775. An intercepted letter early in 1775 had informed the world that I was for independence. But I was left too much alone. The company in the boat appeared to me then and ever since to have invited me to be of their party that they might all assure me in that confidential manner that they were of my mind and would ultimately support me. There was not one of the company, I believe, who in the course of the passage did not repeatedly assure me that in his opinion we must be independent. That evening's conversation was a great comfort to me ever after.

How many follies and indiscreet speeches do your minutes in your note-book bring to my recollection, which I had forgotten forever! Alas! I fear I am not yet much more prudent. Your character of Mr. Paine is very well and very just. To the accusation against me which you have recorded in your note-book of the 17th of March last, I plead not guilty. I deny an attachment to monarchy, and I deny that I have changed my principles since 1776. No letter of mine to Mr. Hooper was ever printed that I know of. Indeed, I have but a very confused recollection of having ever written him any letter. If any letter has been printed in my name, I desire to see it. You know that a letter of mine to Mr. Wythe was printed by Dunlap, in January, 1776, under the title of "Thoughts on Government, in a letter from a gentleman to his friend." In that pamphlet I recommended a legislature in three independent branches, and to such a legislature I am still attached. But I own that at that time I understood very little of the subject, and, if I had changed my opinions, should have no scruple to avow it. I own that awful experience has concurred with reading and reflection, to convince me that Americans are more rapidly disposed to corruption in elections that I thought they were fourteen years ago.

My friend Dr. Rush will excuse me, if I caution him against a fraudulent use of the words *monarchy* and *republic.* I am a mortal and irreconcilable enemy to monarchy. I am no friend to *hereditary limited* monarchy in America. This I know can never be admitted without an hereditary Senate to control it, and a hereditary nobility or Senate in America I know to be unattainable and impracticable. I should scarcely be for it, if it were. Do not, therefore, my friend, misunderstand me and misrepresent me to posterity. I am for a balance between the legislative and executive powers, and I am for enabling the executive to be at all times capable of maintaining the balance between the Senate and House, or in other words, between the aristocratical and democratical interests. Yet I am for having all three branches elected at stated periods, and these elections, I hope, will continue until the people shall be convinced that fortune, providence, or chance, call it which you will, is better than election. If the time should come when corruption shall be added to intrigue and manœuvre in elections, and produce civil war, then, in my opinion, chance will be better than choice for all but the House of Representatives.

Accept my thanks for your polite and obliging invitation to Philadelphia. Nothing would give me more pleasure than such a visit; but I must deny myself that satisfaction. I know I have friends in Pennsylvania, and such as I esteem very much as friends of virtue, liberty, and good government. What you mean by "more than British degrees of corruption" at New York, and by "sophisticated government," I know not. The continent is a kind of whispering gallery, and acts and speeches are reverberated round from New York in all directions. The report is very loud at a distance, when the whisper is very gentle in the centre. But if you see such corruption in your countrymen, on what do you found your hopes? I lament the deplorable condition of my country, which seems to be under such a fatality that the people can agree upon nothing. When they seem to agree, they are so unsteady that it is but for a moment. That changes may be made for the better, is probable. I know of no change that would occasion much danger, but that of President. I wish very heartily that a change of Vice-President could be made to-morrow. I have been too ill-used in the office to be fond of it;—if I had not been introduced into it in a manner that made it a disgrace. I will never serve in it again upon such terms. Though I have acted in public with immense multitudes, I have had few friends, and those certainly not interested ones. These I shall love in public or private. Adieu.

To Richard Price

NEW YORK, 19 APRIL, 1790.

My Dear Friend,—Accept of my best thanks for your favor of February 1st, and the excellent discourse that came with it. I love the zeal and the spirit which dictated this discourse, and admire the general sentiments of it. From the year 1760 to this hour, the whole scope of my life has been to support such principles and propagate such sentiments. No sacrifices of myself or my family, no dangers, no labors, have been too much for me in this great cause. The revolution in France could not therefore be indifferent to me; but I have learned by awful experience to rejoice with trembling. I know that encyclopedists and economists, Diderot and D'Alembert, Voltaire and Rousseau, have contributed to this great event more than Sidney, Locke, or Hoadley, perhaps more than the American revolution; and I own to you, I know not what to make of a republic of thirty million atheists. The Constitution is but an experiment, and must and will be altered. I know it to be impossible that France should be long governed by it. If the sovereignty is to reside in one assembly, the king, princes of the blood, and principal quality, will govern it at their pleasure as long as they can agree; when they differ, they will go to war, and act over again all the tragedies of Valois, Bourbons, Lorraines, Guises, and Colignis, two hundred years ago. The Greeks sung the praises of Harmodius and Aristogiton for restoring equal laws. Too many Frenchmen, after the example of too many Americans, pant for equality of persons and property. The impracticability of this, God Almighty has decreed, and the advocates for liberty, who attempt it, will surely suffer for it.

I thank you, Sir, for your kind compliment. As it has been the great aim of my life to be useful, if I had any reason to think I was so, as you seem to suppose, it would make me happy. For "eminence" I care nothing; for though I pretend not to be exempt from ambition, or any other human passion, I have been convinced from my infancy and have been confirmed every year and day of my life, that the mechanic and peasant are happier than any nobleman, or magistrate, or king, and that the higher a man rises, if he has any sense of duty, the more anxious he must be. Our new government is an attempt to divide a sovereignty; a fresh essay at imperium in imperio. It cannot, therefore, be expected to be very stable or very firm. It will prevent us for a time from drawing our swords upon each other, and when it will do that no longer, we must call a new Convention to reform it. The difficulty of bringing millions to agree in any measures, to act by any rule, can never be conceived by him who has not tried it. It is incredible how small is the number, in any nation, of those who comprehend any system of constitution or administration, and those few it is wholly impossible to unite. I am a sincere inquirer after truth, but I find very few who discover the same truths. The king of Prussia has found one which has also fallen in my way. "That it is the peculiar quality of the human understanding, that example should correct no man. The blunders of the father are lost to his children, and every generation must commit its own." I have never sacrificed my judgment to kings, ministers, nor people, and I never will. When either shall see as I do, I shall rejoice in their protection, aid, and honor; but I see no prospect that either will ever think as I do, and therefore I shall never be a favorite with either. I do not desire to be; but I sincerely wish and devoutly pray, that a hundred years of civil wars may not be the portion of all Europe for want of a little attention to the true elements of the science of government. With sentiments, moral sentiments, which are and must be eternal, I am your friend, &c.

To Samuel Adams

NEW YORK, 18 OCTOBER, 1790.

Dear Sir,—I am thankful to our common friend, as well as to you, for your favor of the fourth, which I received last night. My fears are in unison with yours, that hay, wood, and stubble, will be the materials of the new political buildings in Europe, till men shall be more enlightened and friendly to each other.

You agree, that there are undoubtedly principles of political architecture. But, instead of particularizing any of them, you seem to place all your hopes in the universal, or at least more general, prevalence of knowledge and benevolence. I think with you, that knowledge and benevolence ought to be promoted as much as possible; but, despairing of ever seeing them sufficiently general for the security of society, I am for seeking institutions which may supply in some degree the defect. If there were no ignorance, error, or vice, there would be neither principles nor systems of civil or political government.

I am not often satisfied with the opinions of Hume; but in this he seems well founded, that all projects of government, founded in the supposition or expectation of extraordinary degrees of virtue, are evidently chimerical. Nor do I believe it possible, humanly speaking, that men should ever be greatly improved in knowledge or benevolence, without assistance from the principles and system of government.

I am very willing to agree with you in fancying, that in the greatest improvements of society, government will be in the republican form. It is a fixed principle with me, that all good government is and must be republican. But, at the same time, your candor will agree with me, that there is not in lexicography a more fraudulent word. Whenever I use the word *republic* with approbation, I mean a government in which the people have collectively, or by representation, an essential share in the sovereignty. The republican forms of Poland and Venice are much worse, and those of Holland and Bern very little better, than the monarchical form in France before the late revolution. By the republican form, I know you do not mean the plan of Milton, Nedham, or Turgot. For, after a fair trial of its miseries, the simple monarchical form will ever be, as it has ever been, preferred to it by mankind. Are we not, my friend, in danger of rendering the word *republican* unpopular in this country by an indiscreet, indeterminate, and equivocal use of it? The people of England have been obliged to wean themselves from the use of it, by making it unpopular and unfashionable, because they found it was artfully used by some, and simply understood by others, to mean the government of their interregnum parliament. They found they could not wean themselves from that destructive form of government so entirely, as that a mischievous party would not still remain in favor of it, by any other means than by making the words *republic* and *republican* unpopular. They have succeeded to such a degree, that, with a vast majority of that nation, a republican is as unamiable as a witch, a blasphemer, a rebel, or a tyrant. If, in this country, the word *republic* should be generally understood, as it is by some, to mean a form of government inconsistent with a mixture of three powers, forming a mutual balance, we may depend upon it that such mischievous effects will be produced by the use of it as will compel the people of America to renounce, detest, and execrate it as the English do. With these explanations, restrictions, and limitations, I agree with you in your love of republican governments, but in no other sense.

With you, I have also the honor most perfectly to harmonize in your sentiments of the humanity and wisdom of promoting education in knowledge, virtue, and benevolence. But I think that these will confirm mankind in the opinion of the necessity of preserving and strengthening the dikes against the ocean, its tides and storms. Human appetites, passions, prejudices, and self-love will never be conquered by benevolence and knowledge alone, introduced by human means. The millennium itself neither supposes nor implies it. All civil government is then to cease, and the Messiah is to reign. That happy and holy state is therefore wholly out of this question. You and I agree in the utility of universal education; but will nations agree in it as fully and extensively as we do, and be at the expense of it? We know, with as much certainty as attends any human knowledge, that they will not. We cannot, therefore, advise the people to depend for their safety, liberty, and security, upon hopes and blessings which we know will not fall to their lot. If we do our duty then to the people, we shall not deceive them, but advise them to depend upon what is in their power and will relieve them.

Philosophers, ancient and modern, do not appear to me to have studied nature, the whole of nature, and nothing but nature. Lycurgus's principle was war and family pride; Solon's was what the people would bear, &c. The best writings of antiquity upon government, those, I mean, of Aristotle, Zeno, and Cicero, are lost. We have human nature, society, and universal history to observe and study, and from these we may draw all the real principles which ought to be regarded. Disciples will follow their masters, and interested partisans their chieftains; let us like it or not, we cannot help it. But if the true principles can be discovered, and fairly, fully, and impartially laid before the people, the more light increases, the more the reason of them will be seen, and the more disciples they will have. Prejudice, passion, and private interest, which will always mingle in human inquiries, one would think might be enlisted on the side of truth, at least in the greatest number; for certainly the majority are interested in the truth, if they could see to the end of all its consequences. "Kings have been deposed by aspiring nobles." True, and never by any other. "These" (the nobles, I suppose,) "have waged everlasting war against the common rights of men." True, when they have been possessed of the *summa imperii* in one body, without a check. So have the plebeians; so have the people; so have kings; so has human nature, in every shape and combination, and so it ever will. But, on the other hand, the nobles have been essential parties in the preservation of liberty, whenever and wherever it has existed. In Europe, they alone have preserved it against kings and people, wherever it has been preserved; or, at least, with very little assistance from the people. One hideous despotism, as horrid as that of Turkey, would have been the lot of every nation of Europe, if the nobles had not made stands. By nobles, I mean not peculiarly an hereditary nobility, or any particular modification, but the natural and actual aristocracy among mankind. The existence of this you will not deny. You and I have seen four noble families rise up in Boston,—the

CRAFTS, GORES, DAWES, and AUSTINS. These are as really a nobility in our town, as the Howards, Somersets, Berties, &c., in England. Blind, undistinguishing reproaches against the aristocratical part of mankind, a division which nature has made, and we cannot abolish, are neither pious nor benevolent. They are as pernicious as they are false. They serve only to foment prejudice, jealousy, envy, animosity, and malevolence. They serve no ends but those of sophistry, fraud, and the spirit of party. It would not be true, but it would not be more egregiously false, to say that the people have waged everlasting war against the rights of men.

"The love of liberty," you say, "is interwoven in the soul of man." So it is, according to La Fontaine, in that of a wolf; and I doubt whether it be much more rational, generous, or social, in one than in the other, until in man it is enlightened by experience, reflection, education, and civil and political institutions, which are at first produced, and constantly supported and improved by a few; that is, by the nobility. The wolf, in the fable, who preferred running in the forest, lean and hungry, to the sleek, plump, and round sides of the dog, because he found the latter was sometimes restrained, had more love of liberty than most men. The numbers of men in all ages have preferred ease, slumber, and good cheer to liberty, when they have been in competition. We must not then depend alone upon the love of liberty in the soul of man for its preservation. Some political institutions must be prepared, to assist this love against its enemies. Without these, the struggle will ever end only in a change of impostors. When the people, who have no property, feel the power in their own hands to determine all questions by a majority, they ever attack those who have property, till the injured men of property lose all patience, and recur to finesse, trick, and stratagem, to outwit those who have too much strength, because they have too many hands to be resisted any other way. Let us be impartial, then, and speak the whole truth. Till we do, we shall never discover all the true principles that are necessary. The multitude, therefore, as well as the nobles, must have a check. This is one principle.

"Were the people of England free, after they had obliged King John to concede to them their ancient rights?" The people never did this. There was no people who pretended to any thing. It was the nobles alone. The people pretended to nothing but to be villains, vassals, and retainers to the king or the nobles. The nobles, I agree, were not free, because all was determined by a majority of their votes, or by arms, not by law. Their feuds deposed their "Henrys, Edwards, and Richards," to gratify lordly ambition, patrician rivalry, and "family pride." But, if they had not been deposed, those kings would have become despots, because the people would not and could not join the nobles in any regular and constitutional opposition to them. They would have become despots, I repeat it, and that by means of the villains, vassals, and retainers aforesaid. It is not family pride, my friend, but family popularity, that does the great mischief, as well as the great good. Pride, in the heart of man, is an evil fruit and concomitant of every advantage; of riches, of knowledge, of genius, of talents, of beauty, of strength, of virtue, and even of piety. It is sometimes ridiculous, and often pernicious. But it is even sometimes, and in some degree, useful. But the pride of families would be always and only ridiculous, if it had not family popularity to work with. The attachment and devotion of the people to some families inspires them with pride. As long as gratitude or interest, ambition or avarice, love, hope, or fear, shall be human motives of action, so long will numbers attach themselves to particular families. When the people will, in spite of all that can be said or done, cry a man or a family up to the skies, exaggerate all his talents and virtues, not hear a word of his weakness or faults, follow implicitly his advice, detest every man he hates, adore every man he loves, and knock down all who will not swim down the stream with them, where is your remedy? When a man or family are thus popular, how can you prevent them from being proud? You and I know of instances in which popularity has been a wind, a tide, a whirlwind. The history of all ages and nations is full of such examples.

Popularity, that has great fortune to dazzle; splendid largesses, to excite warm gratitude; sublime, beautiful, and uncommon genius or talents, to produce deep admiration; or any thing to support high hopes and strong fears, will be proud; and its power will be employed to mortify enemies, gratify friends, procure votes, emoluments, and power. Such family popularity ever did, and ever will govern in every nation, in every climate, hot and cold, wet and dry, among civilized and savage people, Christians and Mahometans, Jews and Heathens. Declamation against family pride is a pretty, juvenile exercise, but unworthy of statesmen. They know the evil and danger is too serious to be sported with. The only way, God knows, is to put these families into a hole by themselves, and set two watches upon them; a superior to them all on one side, and the people on the other.

There are a few popular men in the Massachusetts, my friend, who have, I fear, less honor, sincerity, and virtue, than they ought to have. These, if they are not guarded against, may do another mischief. They may excite a party spirit and a mobbish spirit, instead of the spirit of liberty, and produce another Wat Tyler's rebellion. They can do no more. But I really think their party language ought not to be countenanced, nor their shibboleths pronounced. The miserable stuff that they utter about the *well-born* is as despicable as themselves. The ευγενειζ– of the Greeks, the *bien nées* of the French, the *welgebohren* of the Germans and Dutch, the *beloved families* of the Creeks, are but a few samples of national expressions of the same thing, for which every nation on earth has a similar expression. One would think that our scribblers were all the sons of redemptioners or transported convicts. They think with Tarquin, "*In novo populo, ubi omnis repentina atque ex virtute nobilitas fit, futurum locum forti ac strenuo viro.*"

Let us be impartial. There is not more of family pride on one side, than of vulgar malignity and popular envy on the other. Popularity in one family raises envy in others. But the popularity of the least deserving will triumph over envy and malignity; while that which is acquired by real merit, will very often be overborne and oppressed by it.

Let us do justice to the people and to the nobles; for nobles there are, as I have before proved, in Boston as well as in Madrid. But to do justice to both, you must establish an arbitrator between them. This is another principle.

It is time that you and I should have some sweet communion together. I do not believe, that we, who have preserved for more than thirty years an uninterrupted friendship, and have so long thought and acted harmoniously together in the worst of times, are now so far asunder in sentiment as some people pretend; in full confidence of which, I have used this freedom, being ever your warm friend.

Inaugural Speech to Both Houses of Congress

MARCH 4, 1797.

When it was first perceived, in early times, that no middle course for America remained between unlimited submission to a foreign legislature and a total independence of its claims, men of reflection were less apprehensive of danger from the formidable power of fleets and armies they must determine to resist, than from those contests and dissensions, which would certainly arise, concerning the forms of government to be instituted, over the whole, and over the parts of this extensive country. Relying, however, on the purity of their intentions, the justice of their cause, and the integrity and intelligence of the people, under an overruling Providence, which had so signally protected this country from the first, the representatives of this nation, then consisting of little more than half its present numbers, not only broke to pieces the chains which were forging, and the rod of iron that was lifted up, but frankly cut asunder the ties which had bound them, and launched into an ocean of uncertainty.

The zeal and ardor of the people during the revolutionary war, supplying the place of government, commanded a degree of order, sufficient at least for the temporary preservation of society. The confederation, which was early felt to be necessary, was prepared from the models of the Batavian and Helvetic confederacies, the only examples which remain, with any detail and precision, in history, and certainly the only ones which the people at large had ever considered. But, reflecting on the striking difference in so many particulars between this country and those where a courier may go from the seat of government to the frontier in a single day, it was then certainly foreseen by some, who assisted in Congress at the formation of it, that it could not be durable.

Negligence of its regulations, inattention to its recommendations, if not disobedience to its authority, not only in individuals but in States, soon appeared, with their melancholy consequences; universal languor, jealousies, rivalries of States; decline of navigation and commerce; discouragement of necessary manufactures; universal fall in the value of lands and their produce; contempt of public and private faith; loss of consideration and credit with foreign nations; and, at length, in discontents, animosities, combinations, partial conventions, and insurrection; threatening some great national calamity.

In this dangerous crisis the people of America were not abandoned by their usual good sense, presence of mind, resolution, or integrity. Measures were pursued to concert a plan to form a more perfect union, establish justice, ensure domestic tranquillity, provide for the common defence, promote the general welfare, and secure the blessings of liberty. The public disquisitions, discussions, and deliberations, issued in the present happy constitution of government.

Employed in the service of my country abroad, during the whole course of these transactions, I first saw the Constitution of the United States in a foreign country. Irritated by no literary altercation, animated by no public debate, heated by no party animosity, I read it with great satisfaction, as a result of good heads, prompted by good hearts; as an experiment better adapted to the genius, character, situation, and relations of this nation and country, than any which had ever been proposed or suggested. In its general principles and great outlines, it was conformable to such a system of government as I had ever most esteemed, and in some States, my own native State in particular, had contributed to establish. Claiming a right of suffrage in common with my fellow-citizens, in the adoption or rejection of a constitution, which was to rule me and my posterity as well as them and theirs, I did not hesitate to express my approbation of it on all occasions, in public and in private. It was not then nor has been since any objection to it, in my mind, that the Executive and Senate were not more permanent. Nor have I entertained a thought of promoting any alteration in it, but such as the people themselves, in the course of their experience, should see and feel to be necessary or expedient, and by their representatives in Congress and the State legislatures, according to the Constitution itself, adopt and ordain.

Returning to the bosom of my country, after a painful separation from it for ten years, I had the honor to be elected to a station under the new order of things, and I have repeatedly laid myself under the most serious obligations to support the Constitution. The operation of it has equalled the most sanguine expectations of its friends; and, from an habitual attention to it, satisfaction in its administration, and delight in its effect upon the peace, order, prosperity, and happiness of the nation, I have acquired an habitual attachment to it, and veneration for it.

What other form of government, indeed, can so well deserve our esteem and love?

There may be little solidity in an ancient idea, that congregations of men into cities and nations, are the most pleasing objects in the sight of superior intelligences; but this is very certain, that, to a benevolent human mind, there can be no spectacle presented by any nation, more pleasing, more noble, majestic, or august, than an assembly like that which has so often been seen in this and the other chamber of Congress; of a government, in which the executive authority, as well as that of all the branches of the legislature, are exercised by citizens selected at regular periods by their neighbors, to make and execute laws for the general good. Can any thing essential, any thing more than mere ornament and decoration, be added to this by robes or diamonds? Can authority be more amiable or respectable, when it descends from accidents or institutions established in remote antiquity, than when it springs fresh from the hearts and judgments of an honest and enlightened people? For it is the people only that are represented; it is their power and majesty that is reflected, and only for their good, in every legitimate government, under whatever form it may appear. The existence of such a government as ours, for any length of time, is a full proof of a general dissemination of knowledge and virtue throughout the whole body of the people. And what object of consideration, more pleasing than this, can be presented to the human mind? If national pride is ever justifiable or excusable, it is when it springs, not from power or riches, grandeur or glory, but from conviction of national innocence, information, and benevolence.

In the midst of these pleasing ideas, we should be unfaithful to ourselves, if we should ever lose sight of the danger to our liberties, if any thing partial or extraneous should infect the purity of our free, fair, virtuous, and independent elections. If an election is to be determined by a majority of a single vote, and that can be procured by a party, through artifice or corruption, the government may be the choice of a party, for its own ends, not of the nation, for the national good. If that solitary suffrage can be obtained by foreign nations, by flattery or menaces; by fraud or violence; by terror, intrigue, or venality; the government may not be the choice of the American people, but of foreign nations. It may be foreign nations who govern us, and not we, the people, who govern ourselves. And candid men will acknowledge, that, in such cases, choice would have little advantage to boast of over lot or chance.

Such is the amiable and interesting system of government (and such are some of the abuses to which it may be exposed), which the people of America have exhibited, to the admiration and anxiety of the wise and virtuous of all nations, for eight years; under the administration of a citizen, who, by a long course of great actions regulated by prudence, justice, temperance, and fortitude, conducting a people, inspired with the same virtues, and animated with the same ardent patriotism and love of liberty, to independence and peace, to increasing wealth and unexampled prosperity, has merited the gratitude of his fellow-citizens, commanded the highest praises of foreign nations, and secured immortal glory with posterity.

In that retirement which is his voluntary choice, may he long live to enjoy the delicious recollection of his services, the gratitude of mankind, the happy fruits of them to himself and the world, which are daily increasing, and that splendid prospect of the future fortunes of his country, which is opening from year to year! His name may be still a rampart, and the knowledge that he lives, a bulwark against all open or secret enemies of his country's peace.

This example has been recommended to the imitation of his successors, by both Houses of Congress, and by the voice of the legislatures and the people throughout the nation.

On this subject it might become me better to be silent, or to speak with diffidence; but, as something may be expected, the occasion, I hope, will be admitted as an apology, if I venture to say, that, if a preference upon principle of a free republican government, formed upon long and serious reflection, after a diligent and impartial inquiry after truth; if an attachment to the Constitution of the United States, and a conscientious determination to support it, until it shall be altered by the judgments and the wishes of the people, expressed in the mode prescribed in it; if a respectful attention to the constitutions of the individual States, and a constant caution and delicacy towards the State governments; if an equal and impartial regard to the rights, interests, honor, and happiness of all the States in the Union, without preference or regard to a northern or southern, eastern or western position, their various political opinions on essential points, or their personal attachments; if a love of virtuous men of all parties and denominations; if a love of science and letters, and a wish to patronize every rational effort to encourage schools, colleges, universities, academies, and every institution for propagating knowledge, virtue, and religion among all classes of the people, not only for their benign influence on the happiness of life in all its stages and classes and of society in all its forms, but as the only means of preserving our constitution from its natural enemies, the spirit of sophistry, the spirit of party, the spirit of intrigue, profligacy, and corruption, and the pestilence of foreign influence, which is the angel of destruction to elective governments; if a love of equal laws, of justice and humanity, in the interior administration; if an inclination to improve agriculture, commerce, and manufactures for necessity, convenience, and defence; if a spirit of equity and humanity towards the aboriginal nations of America, and a disposition to meliorate their condition by inclining them to be more friendly to us, and our citizens to be more friendly to them; if an inflexible determination to maintain peace and inviolable faith with all nations, and that system of neutrality and impartiality among the belligerent powers of Europe, which has been adopted by the government, and so solemnly sanctioned by both Houses of Congress, and applauded by the legislatures of the States and the public opinion, until it shall be otherwise ordained by Congress; if a personal esteem for the French nation, formed in a residence of seven years chiefly among them, and a sincere desire to preserve the friendship which has been so much for the honor and interest of both nations; if, while the conscious honor and integrity of the people of America, and the internal sentiment of their own power and energies must be preserved, an earnest endeavor to investigate every just cause, and remove every colorable pretence of complaint; if an intention to pursue, by amicable negotiation, a reparation for the injuries that have been committed on the commerce of our fellow-citizens by whatever nation, and (if success cannot be obtained) to lay the facts before the legislature, that they may consider what further measures the honor and interest of the government and its constituents demand; if a resolution to do justice, as far as may depend upon me, at all times, and to all nations, and maintain peace, friendship, and benevolence with all the world; if an unshaken confidence in the honor, spirit, and resources of the American people, on which I have so often hazarded my all, and never been deceived; if elevated ideas of the high destinies of this country, and of my own duties towards it, founded on a knowledge of the moral principles and intellectual improvements of the people, deeply engraven on my mind in early life, and not obscured, but exalted by experience and age; and with humble reverence I feel it my duty to add, if a veneration for the religion of a people, who profess and call themselves Christians, and a fixed resolution to consider a decent respect for Christianity among the best recommendations for the public service;—can enable me in any degree to comply with your wishes, it shall be my strenuous endeavor that this sagacious injunction of the two Houses shall not be without effect.

With this great example before me, with the sense and spirit, the faith and honor, the duty and interest of the same American people, pledged to support the Constitution of the United States, I entertain no doubt of its continuance in all its energy; and my mind is prepared without hesitation, to lay myself under the most solemn obligations to support it to the utmost of my power.

And may that Being, who is supreme over all, the patron of order, the fountain of justice, and the protector, in all ages of the world, of virtuous liberty, continue his blessing upon this nation and its government, and give it all possible success and duration, consistent with the ends of his providence!

To the Young Men of the City of Philadelphia, the District of Southwark, and the Northern Liberties, Pennsylvania

MAY 7, 1798

Gentlemen,

Nothing of the kind could be more welcome to me than this address from the ingenuous youth of Philadelphia, in their virtuous anxiety to preserve the honor and independence of their country.

For a long course of years, my amiable young friends, before the birth of the oldest of you, I was called to act with your fathers in concerting measures the most disagreeable and dangerous, not from a desire of innovation, not from discontent with the government under which we were born and bred, but to preserve the honor of our country, and vindicate the immemorial liberties of our ancestors. In pursuit of these measures, it became, not an object of predilection and choice, but of indispensable necessity to assert our independence, which, with many difficulties and much suffering, was at length secured. I have long flattered myself that I might be gathered to the ashes of my fathers, leaving unimpaired and unassailed the liberties so dearly purchased; and that I should never be summoned a second time to act in such scenes of anxiety, perplexity, and danger, as war of any kind always exhibits. If my good fortune should not correspond with my earnest wishes, and I should be obliged to act with you, as with your ancestors, in defence of the honor and independence of our country, I sincerely wish that none of you may ever have your constancy of mind and strength of body put to so severe a trial, as to be compelled again in your advanced age to the contemplation and near prospect of any war of offence or defence.

It would neither be consistent with my character, nor yours, on this occasion, to read lessons to gentlemen of your education, conduct, and character; if, however, I might be indulged the privilege of a father, I should with the tenderest affection recommend to your serious and constant consideration, that science and morals are the great pillars on which this country has been raised to its present population, opulence, and prosperity, and that these alone can advance, support, and preserve it.

Without wishing to damp the ardor of curiosity, or influence the freedom of inquiry, I will hazard a prediction, that, after the most industrious and impartial researches, the longest liver of you all will find no principles, institutions, or systems of education more fit, in general, to be transmitted to your posterity, than those you have received from your ancestors.

No prospect or spectacle could excite a stronger sensibility in my bosom than this, which now presents itself before me. I wish you all the pure joys, the sanguine hopes, and bright prospects, which are decent at your age, and that your lives may be long, honorable, and prosperous, in the constant practice of benevolence to men and reverence to the Divinity, in a country persevering in liberty, and increasing in virtue, power, and glory.

The sentiments of this address, everywhere expressed in language as chaste and modest as it is elegant and masterly, which would do honor to the youth of any country, have raised a monument to your fame more durable than brass and marble. The youth of all America must exult in this early sample, at the seat of government, of their talents, genius, and virtues.

America and the world will look to our youth as one of our firmest bulwarks. The generous claim which you now present, of sharing in the difficulty, danger, and glory of our defence, is to me and to your country a sure and pleasing pledge, that your birth-rights will never be ignobly bartered or surrendered; but that you will in your turn transmit to future generations the fair inheritance obtained by the unconquerable spirit of your fathers.

To Benjamin Rush

QUINCY, 12 APRIL, 1809.

Thank you for your favor of the 1st. I might have quoted Job as well as St. Paul as a precedent, but as I mix religion with politics as little as possible, I chose to confine myself to Cicero. You advise me to write my own life. I have made several attempts, but it is so dull an employment that I cannot endure it. I look so much like a small boy in my own eyes that with all my vanity I cannot endure the sight of the picture. I am glad you have resolved to do yourself justice. I am determined to vindicate myself in some points while I live. Inclosed is a whimsical specimen. In future I shall not be so *goguenard.*

The dialogue between Diodati and me is literal truth, that is, it is a literal translation from the French, in which language the conversation was held, and which I reduced to writing. You may ask what reason I had for foreseeing such consequences. I will give you a few hints among a thousand.

1. When I went home to my family in May, 1770, from the town meeting in Boston, which was the first I had ever attended, and where I had been chosen in my absence, without any solicitation, one of their representatives, I said to my wife, "I have accepted a seat in the House of Representatives, and thereby have consented to my own ruin, to your ruin, and the ruin of our children. I give you this warning, that you may prepare your mind for your fate." She burst into tears, but instantly cried out in a transport of magnanimity, "Well, I am willing in this cause to run all risks with you, and to be ruined with you, if you are ruined." These were times, my friend, in Boston, which tried women's souls as well as men's.

2. I saw the awful prospect before me and my country in all its horrors, and, notwithstanding all my vanity, was conscious of a thousand defects in my own character as well as health, which made me despair of going through and weathering the storms in which I must be tossed.

3. In the same year, 1770, my sense of equity and humanity impelled me, against a torrent of unpopularity, and the inclination of all my friends, to engage in defence of Captain Preston and the soldiers. My successful exertions in that cause, though the result was perfectly conformable to law and justice, brought upon me a load of indignation and unpopularity, which I knew would never be forgotten, nor entirely forgiven. The Boston newspapers to this day show that my apprehensions were well founded.

4. You can testify for me that in 1774 my conduct in Congress drew upon me the jealousy and aversion, not only of the tories in Congress, who were neither few nor feeble, but of the whole body of Quakers and proprietary gentlemen in Pennsylvania. I have seen and felt the consequences of these prejudices to this day.

5. I call you to witness that I was the first member of Congress who ventured to come out in public, as I did in January, 1776, in my "Thoughts on Government, in a letter from a gentleman to his friend," that is, Mr. Wythe, in favor of a government in three branches, with an independent judiciary. This pamphlet, you know, was very unpopular. No man appeared in public to support it, but yourself. You attempted in the public papers to give it some countenance, but without much success. Franklin leaned against it. Dr. Young, Mr. Timothy Matlack, and Mr. James Cannon, and I suppose Mr. George Bryan were alarmed and displeased at it. Mr. Thomas Paine was so highly offended with it, that he came to visit me at my chamber at Mrs. Yard's to remonstrate and even scold at me for it, which he did in very ungenteel terms. In return, I only laughed heartily at him, and rallied him upon his grave arguments from the Old Testament to prove that monarchy was unlawful in the sight of God. "Do you seriously believe, Paine," said I, "in that pious doctrine of yours?" This put him in good humor and he laughed out. "The Old Testament!" said he, "I do not believe in the Old Testament. I have had thoughts of publishing my sentiments of it, but upon deliberation I have concluded to put that off till the latter part of life." Paine's wrath was excited because my plan of government was essentially different from the silly projects that he had published in his *Common Sense.* By this means I became suspected and unpopular with the leading demagogues and the whole Constitutional Party in Pennsylvania.

6. Upon my return from France in 1779, I found myself elected by my native town of Braintree a member of the Convention for forming a Constitution for the State of Massachusetts. I attended that convention of near four hundred members. Here I found such a chaos of absurd sentiments concerning government that I was obliged daily, before that great assembly, and afterwards in the Grand Committee, to propose plans and advocate doctrines, which were extremely unpopular with the greater number. Lieutenant-Governor Cushing was avowedly for a single assembly like Pennsylvania. Samuel Adams was of the same mind. Mr. Hancock kept aloof in order to be governor. In short, I had at first no support but from the Essex Junto, who had adopted my ideas in the "Letter to Mr. Wythe." They supported me timorously and at last would not go with me to so high a mark as I aimed at, which was a complete negative in the governor upon

all laws. They made me, however, draw up the Constitution, and it was finally adopted with some amendments very much for the worse. The bold, decided, and determined part I took in this assembly in favor of a good government acquired me the reputation of a man of high principles and strong notions in government, scarcely compatible with republicanism. A foundation was here laid of much jealousy and unpopularity among the democratical people in this State.

7. In Holland I had driven the English party and the statholders party before me, like clouds before the wind, and had brought that power to unite cordially with America, France, and Spain against England. If I had not before alienated the whole English nation from me, this would have been enough to produce an eternal jealousy of me; and I fully believe that whenever a free intercourse should take place between Britain and America, I might depend upon their perpetual ill will to me, and that their influence would be used to destroy mine.

8. In all my negotiations in France and Holland in 1778, 1779, 1780, 1781, 1782, 1783, and 1784, I had so uniformly resisted all the arts and intrigues of the Count de Vergennes and M. de Sartine and all their satellites, and that with such perfect success that I well knew, although they treated me with great external respect, yet in their hearts they had conceived an ineradicable jealousy and aversion to me. I well knew, therefore, that French influence in America would do all in its power to trip me up.

9. Dr. Franklin's behavior had been so excessively complaisant to the French ministry, and in my opinion had so endangered the essential interests of our country, that I had been frequently obliged to differ from him, and sometimes to withstand him to his face; so that I knew he had conceived an irreconcilable hatred of me, and that he had propagated and would continue to propagate prejudices, if nothing worse, against me in America from one end of it to the other. Look into Benjamin Franklin Bache's Aurora and Duane's Aurora for twenty years, and see whether my expectations have not been verified.

With all these reflections fresh in my mind, you may judge whether my anticipations in the good-humored conversation with Diodati were rash, peevish, or ill-grounded.

In short, I have every reason to acknowledge the protecting providence of God, from my birth, and especially through my public life. I have gone through life with much more safety and felicity than I ever expected. With devout gratitude I acknowledge the divine favor in many instances, and among others for giving me a friend in you, who, though you would never follow me as a disciple, have always been my friend.

To Benjamin Rush

QUINCY, 25 DECEMBER, 1811.

I never was so much at a loss how to answer a letter as yours of the 16th. Shall I assume a sober face and write a grave essay on religion, philosophy, laws, or government? Shall I laugh, like Bacchus among his grapes, wine vats, and bottles? Shall I assume the man of the world, the fine gentleman, the courtier, and bow and scrape, with a smooth, smiling face, soft words, many compliments and apologies; think myself highly honored, bound in gratitude, &c., &c.?

I perceive plainly enough, Rush, that you have been teasing Jefferson to write to me, as you did me some time ago to write to him. You gravely advise me "to receive the olive branch," as if there had been war; but there has never been any hostility on my part, nor that I know, on his. When there has been no war, there can be no room for negotiations of peace.

Mr. Jefferson speaks of my political opinions; but I know of no difference between him and myself relative to the Constitution or to forms of government in general. In measures of administration, we have differed in opinion. I have never approved the repeal of the judicial law, the repeal of the taxes, the neglect of the navy; and I have always believed that his system of gunboats for a national defence was defective. To make it complete, he ought to have taken a hint from Molière's *Femmes précieuses,* or his learned ladies, and appointed three or four brigades of horse, with a Major-General and three or four brigadiers, to serve on board his galleys of Malta. I have never approved his nonembargo, or any nonintercourse, or nonimportation laws.

But I have raised no clamors nor made any opposition to any of these measures. The nation approved them; and what is my judgment against that of the nation? On the contrary, he disapproved of the alien law and sedition law, which I believe to have been constitutional and salutary, if not necessary.

He disapproved of the eight per cent loan, and with good reason. For I hated it as much as any man, and the army, too, which occasioned it. He disapproved, perhaps, of the partial war with France, which I believed, as far as it proceeded, to be a holy war. He disapproved of taxes, and perhaps the whole scheme of my administration, &c., and so perhaps did the nation. But his administration and mine are passed away into the dark backwards, and are now of no more importance than the administration of the old Congress in 1774 and 1775.

We differed in opinion about the French Revolution. He thought it wise and good, and that it would end in the establishment of a free republic. I saw through it, to the end of it, before it broke out, and was sure it could end only in a restoration of the Bourbons, or a military despotism, after deluging France and Europe in blood. In this opinion I differed from you as much as from Jefferson; but all this made me no more of an enemy to you than to him, nor to him than to you. I believe you both to mean well to mankind and your country. I might suspect you both to sacrifice a little to the infernal gods, and perhaps unconsciously to suffer your judgments to be a little swayed by a love of popularity and possibly by a little spice of ambition.

In point of republicanism, all the differences I ever knew or could discover between you and me, or between Jefferson and me, consisted:

1. In the difference between speeches and messages. I was a monarchist because I thought a speech more manly, more respectful to Congress and the nation. Jefferson and Rush preferred messages.

2. I held levees once a week, that all my time might not be wasted by idle visits. Jefferson's whole eight years was a levee.

3. I dined a large company once or twice a week. Jefferson dined a dozen every day.

4. Jefferson and Rush were for liberty and straight hair. I thought curled hair was as republican as straight.

In these, and a few other points of equal importance, all miserable frivolities, that Jefferson and Rush ought to blush that they ever laid any stress upon them, I might differ; but I never knew any points of more consequence, on which there was any variation between us.

You exhort me to "forgiveness and love of enemies," as if I considered or had ever considered Jefferson as my enemy. This is not so; I have always loved him as a friend. If I ever received or suspected any injury from him, I have forgiven it long and long ago, and have no more resentment against him than against you.

You enforce your exhortations by the most solemn considerations that can enter the human mind. After mature reflection upon them, and laying them properly to heart, I could not help feeling that they were so unnecessary, that you must excuse me if I had some inclination to be ludicrous.

You often put me in mind that I am soon to die; I know it and shall not forget it. Stepping into my kitchen one day, I found two of my poor neighbors, as good sort of men as two drunkards could be. One had sotted himself into a consumption. His cough and his paleness and weakness showed him near the last stage. Tom, who was not so far gone as yet, though he soon followed, said to John, "You have not long for this world." John answered very quick: "I know it, Tom, as well as you do; but why do you tell me of it? I had rather you should strike me." This was one of those touches of nature which Shakspere or Cervantes would have noted in his ivory book.

But why do you make so much ado about nothing? Of what use can it be for Jefferson and me to exchange letters? I have nothing to say to him, but to wish him an easy journey to heaven, when he goes, which I wish may be delayed, as long as life shall be agreeable to him. And he can have nothing to say to me, but to bid me make haste and be ready. Time and chance, however, or possibly design, may produce ere long a letter between us.

To Thomas Jefferson

QUINCY, 9 JULY, 1813.

Lord! Lord! what can I do with so much Greek? When I was of your age, young man, that is, seven or eight years ago, I felt a kind of pang of affection for one of the flames of my youth, and again paid my addresses to Isocrates and Dionissius Hallicarnassensis, &c., &c., &c. I collected all my lexicons and grammars, and sat down to περὶ συνθεσεωζ ονοματων. In this way I amused myself for some time, but I found that if I looked a word to-day, in less than a week I had to look it again. It was to little better purpose than writing letters on a pail of water.

Whenever I sett down to write to you, I am precisely in the situation of the wood-cutter on Mount Ida. I cannot see wood for trees. So many subjects crowd upon me, that I know not with which to begin. But I will begin at random with Belsham, who is, as I have no doubt, a man of merit. He had no malice against you, nor any thought of doing mischief; nor has he done any, though he has been imprudent. The truth is, the dissenters of all denominations in England, and, especially, the Unitarians, are cowed, as we used to say at college. They are ridiculed, insulted, persecuted. They can scarcely hold their heads above water. They catch at straws and shadows to avoid drowning. Priestley sent your letter to Lindsay, and Belsham printed it from the same motive, i.e. to derive some countenance from the name of Jefferson. Nor has it done harm here. Priestley says to Lindsay, "You see he is almost one of us, and he hopes will soon be altogether such as we are." Even in our New England I have heard a high federal divine say, your letters had increased his respect for you.

"The same political parties, which now agitate the United States, have existed through all time." Precisely; and this is precisely the complaint in the preface to the first volume of my Defence. While all other sciences have advanced, that of government is at a stand; little better understood, little better practised now than three or four thousand years ago. What is the reason? I say, parties and factions will not suffer or permit improvements to be made. As soon as one man hints at an improvement, his rival opposes it. No sooner has one party discovered or invented an amelioration of the condition of man, or the order of society than the opposite party belies it, misconstrues it, misrepresents it, ridicules it, insults it, and persecutes it. Records are destroyed. Histories are annihilated or interpolated or prohibited; sometimes by Popes, sometimes by Emperors, sometimes by aristocratical, and sometimes by democratical assemblies, and sometimes by mobs.

Aristotle wrote the history and description of eighteen hundred republics which existed before his time. Cicero wrote two volumes of discourses on government, which, perhaps, were worth all the rest of his works. The works of Livy and Tacitus, &c., that are lost, would be more interesting than all that remain. Fifty Gospells have been destroyed, and where are St. Lukes world of books that had been written? If you ask my opinion, who has committed all the havoc? I will answer you candidly. Ecclesiastical and imperial despotisms has done it to conceal their frauds.

Why are the histories of all nations, more ancient than the Christian era, lost? Who destroyed the Alexandrian library? I believe that Christian priests, Jewish rabbis, Grecian sages, and Roman emperors, had as great a hand in it as Turks and Mahometans.

Democrats, rebels, and Jacobins, when they possessed a momentary power, have shown a disposition both to destroy and to forge records, as Vandalical as priests and despots. Such has been and such is the world we live in.

I recollect, near thirty years ago, to have said carelessly to you, that I wished I could find time and means to write something upon aristocracy. You seized upon the idea, and encouraged me to do it with all that friendly warmth that is natural and habitual to you. I soon began, and have been writing upon that subject ever since. I have been so unfortunate as never to be able to make myself understood. Your αριστοι are the most difficult animals to manage of any thing in the whole theory and practice of government. They will not suffer themselves to be governed. They not only exert all their own subtilty, industry, and courage, but they employ the commonalty to knock to pieces every plan and model that the most honest architects in legislation can invent to keep them within bounds. Both patricians and plebeians are as furious as the workmen in England to demolish labor-saving machinery.

But who are these αριστοι? Who shall judge? Who shall select these choice spirits from the rest of the congregation? Themselves? We must find out and determine who themselves are. Shall the congregation choose? Ask Xenophon. Perhaps, hereafter I may quote you Greek; too much in a hurry at present; English must suffice. Xenophon says, that the ecclesia always chooses the worst men they can find, because none others will do their dirty work. This wicked motive is worse than birth or wealth. Here I want to quote Greek again. But the day before I received your letter of June 27, I gave the book to George Washington Adams, going to the Academy at Hingham. The title is, ΗΘΙΚΗ ΠΟΙΗΣΙΣ, a collection of moral sentences from all the most ancient Greek poets. In one of the oldest of them I read, in Greek that I cannot repeat, a couplet, the sense of which was

"Nobility in men is worth as much as it is in horses, asses, or rams; but the meanest-blooded puppy in the world, if he gets a little money, is as good a man as the best of them." Yet birth and wealth together have prevailed over virtue and talents in all ages. The many will acknowledge no other υριστοι. Your experience of this truth will not much differ from that of your old friend.

To Thomas Jefferson

QUINCY, 13 JULY, 1813.

Let me allude to one circumstance more, in one of your letters to me, before I touch upon the subject of religion in your letters to Priestley. The first time that you and I differed in opinion on any material question was after your arrival from Europe; and that point was the French revolution.

You was well persuaded in your own mind that the nation would succeed in establishing a free republican government. I was as well persuaded in mine, that a project of such a government, over five-and-twenty millions people, when four-and-twenty millions and five hundred thousands of them could neither write nor read, was as unnatural, irrational, and impracticable as it would be over the elephants, lions, tigers, panthers, wolves, and bears, in the Royal Menagerie at Versailles. Napoleon has lately invented a word, which perfectly expresses my opinion at that time and ever since. He calls the project Ideology. And John Randolph, though he was, fourteen years ago, as wild an enthusiast for equality and fraternity as any of them, appears to be now a regenerated proselyte to Napoleon's opinion and mine, that it was all madness.

The Greeks, in their allegorical style, said that the two ladies, Αριστοκρατια ["Aristocracy"] and δημοκρατια ["democracy"], always in a quarrel, disturbed every neighborhood with their brawls. It is a fine observation of yours that "Whig and Tory belong to natural history." Inequalities of mind and body are so established by God Almighty in his constitution of human nature, that no art or policy can ever plain them down to a level. I have never read reasoning more absurd, sophistry more gross, in proof of the Athanasian creed, or transubstantiation, than the subtle labors of Helvetius and Rousseau to demonstrate the natural equality of mankind. *Jus cuique,* the golden rule, do as you would be done by, is all the equality that can be supported or defended by reason, or reconciled to common sense.

It is very true, as you justly observe, I can say nothing new on this or any other subject of government. But when La Fayette harrangued you and me, and John Quincy Adams, through a whole evening, in your hotel in the Cul de Sac, at Paris, and develloped the plans then in operation to reform France, though I was as silent as you was, I then thought I could say something new to him. In plain truth, I was astonished at the grossness of his ignorance of government and history, as I had been for years before, at that of Turgot, Rochefoucauld, Condorcet, and Franklin. This gross ideology of them all first suggested to me the thought and the inclination, which I afterwards hinted to you in London, of writing something upon aristocracy. I was restrained for years by many fearful considerations. Who and what was I? A man of no name or consideration in Europe. The manual exercise of writing was painful and distressing to me, almost like a blow on the elbow or the knee; my style was habitually negligent, unstudied, unpolished; I should make enemies of all the French patriots, the Dutch patriots, the English republicans, dissenters, reformers, call them what you will; and, what came nearer home to my bosom than all the rest, I knew I should give offence to many, if not all, of my best friends in America, and, very probably, destroy all the little popularity I ever had in a country where popularity had more omnipotence than the British parliament assumed. Where should I get the necessary books? What printer or bookseller would undertake to print such hazardous writings?

But, when the French Assembly of Notables met, and I saw that Turgot's "government in one centre, and that centre the nation," a sentence as mysterious or as contradictory as the Athanasian creed, was about to take place; and when I saw that Shays's Rebellion was breaking out in Massachusetts; and when I saw that even my obscure name was often quoted in France as an advocate for simple democracy; when I saw that the sympathies in America had caught the French flame, I was determined to wash my own hands as clean as I could of all this foulness. I had then strong forebodings that I was sacrificing all the honours and emoluments of this life; and so it has happened, but not in so great a degree as I apprehended.

In truth, my "Defence of the Constitutions" and "Discourses on Davila," laid the foundation of that immense unpopularity which fell like the tower of Siloam upon me. Your steady defence of democratical principles, and your invariable favorable opinion of the French Revolution, laid the foundation of your unbounded popularity.

Sic transit gloria mundi.

Now, I will forfeit my life, if you can find one sentence in my Defence of the Constitutions, or the Discourses on Davila, which, by a fair construction, can favor the introduction of hereditary monarchy or aristocracy into America.

They were all written to support and strengthen the Constitutions of the United States.

The wood-cutter on Ida, though he was puzzled to find a tree to chop at first, I presume knew how to leave off when he was weary. But I never know when to cease when I begin to write to you.

To John Taylor

APRIL 1814

[. . .] I believe that none but Helvetius will affirm, that all children are born with equal genius.

None will pretend, that all are born of dispositions exactly alike,—of equal weight; equal strength; equal length; equal delicacy of nerves; equal elasticity of muscles; equal complexions; equal figure, grace, or beauty.

I have seen, in the Hospital of Foundlings, the "*Enfans Trouvés,*" at Paris, fifty babes in one room;—all under four days old; all in cradles alike; all nursed and attended alike; all dressed alike; all equally neat. I went from one end to the other of the whole row, and attentively observed all their countenances. And I never saw a greater variety, or more striking inequalities, in the streets of Paris or London. Some had every sign of grief, sorrow, and despair; others had joy and gayety in their faces. Some were sinking in the arms of death; others looked as if they might live to fourscore. Some were as ugly and others as beautiful, as children or adults ever are; these were stupid; those sensible. These were all born to equal rights, but to very different fortunes; to very different success and influence in life.

The world would not contain the books, if one should produce all the examples that reading and experience would furnish. One or two permit me to hint.

Will any man say, would Helvetius say, that all men are born equal in strength? Was Hercules no stronger than his neighbors? How many nations, for how many ages, have been governed by his strength, and by the reputation and renown of it by his posterity? If you have lately read Hume, Robertson or the Scottish Chiefs, let me ask you, if Sir William Wallace was no more than equal in strength to the average of Scotchmen? and whether Wallace could have done what he did without that extraordinary strength?

Will Helvetius or Rousseau say that all men and women are born equal in beauty? Will any philosopher say, that beauty has no influence in human society? If he does, let him read the histories of Eve, Judith, Helen, the fair Gabrielle, Diana of Poitiers, Pompadour, Du Barry, Susanna, Abigail, Lady Hamilton, Mrs. Clark, and a million others. Are not despots, monarchs, aristocrats, and democrats, equally liable to be seduced by beauty to confer favors and influence suffrages?

Socrates calls beauty a short-lived tyranny; Plato, *the privilege of nature;* Theophrastus, a mute eloquence; Diogenes, the best letter of recommendation; Carneades, a queen without soldiers; Theocritus, a serpent covered with flowers; Bion, a good that does not belong to the possessor, because it is impossible to give ourselves beauty, or to preserve it. Madame du Barry expressed the philosophy of Carneades in more laconic language, when she said, "*La véritable royauté, c'est la beauté,*"—the genuine royalty is beauty. And she might have said with equal truth, that it is genuine aristocracy; for it has as much influence in one form of government as in any other; and produces aristocracy in the deepest democracy that ever was known or imagined, as infallibly as in any other form of government. What shall we say to all these philosophers, male and female? Is not beauty a privilege granted by nature, according to Plato and to truth, often more influential in society, and even upon laws and government, than stars, garters, crosses, eagles, golden fleeces, or any hereditary titles or other distinctions? The grave elders were not proof against the charms of Susanna. The Grecian sages wondered not at the Trojan war when they saw Helen. Holofernes's guards, when they saw Judith, said, "one such woman let go would deceive the whole earth."

Can you believe, Mr. Taylor, that the brother of such a sister, the father of such a daughter, the husband of such a wife, or even the gallant of such a mistress, would have but one vote in your moral republic? Ingenious,—

but not historical, philosophical, or political—learned, classical, poetical Barlow! I mourn over thy life and thy death. Had truth, instead of popularity and party, been thy object, your pamphlet on privileged orders would have been a very different thing!

That all men are born to equal rights is true. Every being has a right to his own, as clear, as moral, as sacred, as any other being has. This is as indubitable as a moral government in the universe. But to teach that all men are born with equal powers and faculties, to equal influence in society, to equal property and advantages through life, is as gross a fraud, as glaring an imposition on the credulity of the people, as ever was practised by monks, by Druids, by Brahmins, by priests of the immortal Lama, or by the self-styled philosophers of the French revolution. For honor's sake, Mr. Taylor, for truth and virtue's sake, let American philosophers and politicians despise it.

Mr. Adams leaves to Homer and Virgil, to Tacitus and Quintilian, to Mahomet and Calvin, to Edwards and Priestley, or, if you will, to Milton's angels reasoning high in pandemonium, all their acute speculations about fate, destiny, foreknowledge absolute, necessity, and predestination. He thinks it problematical, whether there is, or ever will be, more than one Being capable of understanding this vast subject. In his principles of legislation, he has nothing to do with these interminable controversies. He considers men as free, moral, and accountable agents; and he takes men as God has made them. And will Mr. Taylor deny, that God has made some men deaf and some blind, or will he affirm that these will infallibly have as much influence in society, and be able to procure as many votes as any who can see and hear?

Honor the day, and believe me no enemy. [. . .]

To Thomas Jefferson

QUINCY, 8 DECEMBER, 1818.

Dear Sir.—Your letter of November 13th gave me great delight, not only by the divine consolation it afforded me under my great affliction, but as it gave me full proof of your restoration to health.

While you live, I seem to have a bank at Monticello, on which I can draw for a letter of friendship and entertainment, when I please.

I know not how to prove, physically, that we shall meet and know each other in a future state; nor does revelation, as I can find, give us any positive assurance of such a felicity. My reasons for believing it, as I do most undoubtingly, are all moral and divine.

I believe in God and in his wisdom and benevolence: and I cannot conceive that such a being could make such a species as the human, merely to live and die on this earth. If I did not believe a future state, I should believe in no God. This universe, this all, this το παν, would appear, with all its swelling pomp, a boyish fire-work.

And, if there be a future state, why should the Almighty dissolve forever all the tender ties which unite us so delightfully in this world, and forbid us to see each other in the next?

Trumbull, with a band of associates, drew me, by the cords of old friendship, to see his picture, on Saturday, where I got a great cold. The air of Faneuil Hall is changed. I have not been used to catch cold there.

Sick or well, the friendship is the same of your old acquaintance.

To Robert J. Evans

QUINCY, 8 JUNE, 1819.

I respect the sentiments and motives, which have prompted you to engage in your present occupation, so much, that I feel an esteem and affection for your person, as I do a veneration for your assumed signature of Benjamin Rush. The turpitude, the inhumanity, the cruelty, and the infamy of the African commerce in slaves, have been so impressively represented to the public by the highest powers of eloquence, that nothing that I can say would increase the just odium in which it is and ought to be held. Every measure of prudence, therefore, ought to be assumed for the eventual total extirpation of slavery from the United States. If, however, humanity dictates the duty of adopting the most prudent measures for accomplishing so excellent a purpose, the same humanity requires, that we should not inflict severer calamities on the objects of our commiseration than those which they at present endure, by reducing them to despair, or the necessity of robbery, plunder, assassination, and massacre, to preserve their lives, some provision for furnishing them employment, or some means of supplying them with the necessary comforts of life. The same humanity requires that we should not by any rash or violent measures expose the lives and property of those of our fellow-citizens, who are so unfortunate as to be surrounded with these fellow-creatures, by hereditary descent, or by any other means without their own fault. I have, through my whole life, held the practice of slavery in such abhorrence, that I have never owned a negro or any other slave, though I have lived for many years in times, when the practice was not disgraceful, when the best men in my vicinity thought it not inconsistent with their character, and when it has cost me thousands of dollars for the labor and subsistence of free men, which I might have saved by the purchase of negroes at times when they were very cheap.

If any thing should occur to me, which I think may assist you, I will endeavor to communicate it to you; but at an age, when

> "From Marlborough's eyes the streams of dotage flow,
> And Swift expires a driveller and a show,"

very little can be expected from, Sir, your most obedient and most humble servant.

To John Quincy Adams

QUINCY, 18 FEBRUARY, 1825.

My Dear Son,—I have received your letter of the 9th. Never did I feel so much solemnity as upon this occasion. The multitude of my thoughts, and the intensity of my feelings are too much for a mind like mine, in its ninetieth year. May the blessing of God Almighty continue to protect you to the end of your life, as it has heretofore protected you in so remarkable a manner from your cradle! I offer the same prayer for your lady and your family, and am your affectionate father.

THOMAS JEFFERSON 1743–1826

Introduction

Too many Virginia boys, Jefferson complained in 1821, were going to Harvard, Yale, and Princeton for their education, "imbibing opinions and principles in discord with those of their own country." "The signs of the times," he sternly concluded, "admonish us to call them home."[1]

Jefferson could not forgive the northerners who had recently voted for the Missouri Compromise. He, too, wanted to eliminate slavery, but without the impetus and authority of the ever-expanding national government. It was no longer seasonable to furnish northern schools with Virginia "recruits," he wrote, or to "trust to *those who are against us* in position and principle, to fashion to their own form the minds & affections of our youth."[2]

And so, during the final years of his life, Jefferson poured his heart and energy into founding a first-class university for Virginia. He and Madison conceived the new school as a "nursery of *republican* patriots as well as genuine scholars"[3]—but the word "republican" translated as southern and states' rights. "If we are true and vigilant in our trust," Jefferson hopefully wrote to Madison, "within a dozen or twenty years a majority of our own legislature will be from one school, and many disciples will have carried its *doctrines* home with them to their several states."[4]

Virginia "doctrines" replaced the critical spirit Jefferson had long embraced. In his Act for Establishing Religious Freedom in 1779, he had written that "Almighty God hath created the mind free." And in 1813 he wrote that "ideas should freely spread from one to another over the globe."[5] But the final chapter of his life marked a retreat. The sophisticated, cosmopolitan former minister to France, the daring intellectual in love with radical ideas, the farsighted former president of the republic who doubled the size of the nation became, in the last years of his life, simply and militantly, a *Virginian.*

Only Virginia, Jefferson would stress in 1823, "has never swerved a hair's breadth from the line of republicanism & Americanism."[6] Dismayed that it seemed impossible to halt the corrupt, commercializing trends that were overrunning the North, he offered a radical remedy. States that were for "unlimited commerce and war" should withdraw from the union, and a new confederation should be formed of states that were for "peace and agriculture." "I have no hesitation in saying," Jefferson blithely wrote, "'let us separate.'"[7]

And yet, Jefferson's commitment to the American republic and to a democratic, participatory political community had stemmed from his efforts at reform in Virginia and his idealized notion of the Old Dominion as the land of "yeoman farmers"—independent, self-sufficient, literate, and engaged citizens. In order to open opportunities for land ownership and virtuous citizenship to more people, Jefferson had sought to abolish primogeniture and entails, to grant 50 acres to every Virginian, and to establish a statewide system of public education. Through his work in drafting Virginia's Statute for Religious Freedom, Jefferson had sought to ensure that the most precious kind of freedom—freedom of conscience—would flourish in Virginia.

Freedom in its myriad forms always ignited Jefferson's imagination. "I like a little rebellion now and then," he wrote to Abigail Adams in 1787, upon hearing about Shays's rebellion in western Massachusetts.[8] Abigail's husband did not share his friend's enthusiasm. "Mobs will never do to govern States," John Adams wrote that same winter. In 1793, Jefferson extolled the French Revolution, despite its ominous descent into violence, with his own apologia for violence. "Rather than [that the French Revolution] should have failed," he wrote, "I would have seen half the earth desolated. Were there but an Adam & an Eve left in every country, & left free, it would be better than as it now is."[9] The project of creating a republic for 25 million French people, when 24,500,000 of them could neither read nor write, sneered the disabused Adams, "was as unnatural irrational and impracticable as it would be [for] the Elephants Lions Tigers Panthers Wolves and Bears in the Royal Menagerie at Versailles."[10]

Perhaps John Adams displayed sounder judgment in his apprehension of Shays's mob and his scorn for revolutionary violence in France. And yet it was not Adams's sober reflections on the folly of men that would carry the young nation into the nineteenth century. It was, rather, Jefferson's forward-looking spirit, his buoyant optimism, his dream of liberation from tradition, and his radiant love of fresh ideas that—despite his blind spots about slavery and Virginia localism—would carry America into the future. "It is a good world on the whole," he wrote in 1816 to Adams. "I steer my bark with Hope in the head, leaving Fear astern. My hopes indeed sometimes fail; but not oftener than the forebodings of the gloomy."[11] Inspired by his deep faith in the ideals of the American Revolution, Jefferson bequeathed to his nation a triumphant vision of a freer, more democratic society.

To John Randolph

MONTICELLO, AUGUST 25, 1775.

Dear Sir, [. . .] I am sorry the situation of our country should render it not eligible to you to remain longer in it. I hope the returning wisdom of Great Britain will, ere long, put an end to this unnatural contest. There may be people to whose tempers and dispositions contention is pleasing, and who, therefore, wish a continuance of confusion, but to me it is of all states but one, the most horrid. My first wish is a restoration of our just rights; my second, a return of the happy period, when, consistently with duty, I may withdraw myself totally from the public stage, and pass the rest of my days in domestic ease and tranquillity, banishing every desire of ever hearing what passes in the world. Perhaps (for the latter adds considerably to the warmth of the former wish), looking with fondness towards a reconciliation with Great Britain, I cannot help hoping you may be able to contribute towards expediting this good work. I think it must be evident to yourself, that the Ministry have been deceived by their officers on this side of the water, who (for what purpose I cannot tell) have constantly represented the American opposition as that of a small faction, in which the body of the people took little part. This, you can inform them, of your own knowledge, is untrue. They have taken it into their heads, too, that we are cowards, and shall surrender at discretion to an armed force. The past and future operations of the war must confirm or undeceive them on that head. I wish they were thoroughly and minutely acquainted with every circumstance relative to America, as it exists in truth. I am persuaded, this would go far towards disposing them to reconciliation. Even those in Parliament who are called friends to America, seem to know nothing of our real determinations. I observe, they pronounced in the last Parliament, that the Congress of 1774 did not mean to insist rigorously on the terms they held out, but kept something in reserve, to give up; and, in fact, that they would give up everything but the article of taxation. Now, the truth is far from this, as I can affirm, and put my honor to the assertion. Their continuance in this error may, perhaps, produce very ill consequences. The Congress stated the lowest terms they thought possible to be accepted, in order to convince the world they were not unreasonable. They gave up the monopoly and regulation of trade, and all acts of Parliament prior to 1764, leaving to British generosity to render these, at some future time, as easy to America as the interest of Britain would admit. But this was before blood was spilt. I cannot affirm, but have reason to think, these terms would not now be accepted. I wish no false sense of honor, no ignorance of our real intentions, no vain hope that partial concessions of right will be accepted, may induce the Ministry to trifle with accommodation, till it shall be out of their power ever to accommodate. If, indeed, Great Britain, disjointed from her colonies, be a match for the most potent nations of Europe, with the colonies thrown into their scale, they may go on securely. But if they are not assured of this, it would be certainly unwise, by trying the event of another campaign, to risk our accepting a foreign aid, which, perhaps, may not be attainable, but on condition of everlasting avulsion from Great Britain. This would be thought a hard condition, to those who still wish for re-union with their parent country. I am sincerely one of those, and would rather be in dependence on Great Britain, properly limited, than on any other nation on earth, or than on no nation. But I am one of those, too, who, rather than submit to the rights of legislating for us, assumed by the British Parliament, and which late experience has shown they will so cruelly exercise, would lend my hand to sink the whole Island in the ocean.

If undeceiving the Minister, as to matters of fact, may change his disposition, it will, perhaps, be in your power, by assisting to do this, to render service to the whole empire, at the most critical time, certainly, that it has ever seen. Whether Britain shall continue the head of the greatest empire on earth, or shall return to her original station in the political scale of Europe, depends, perhaps, on the resolutions of the succeeding winter. God send they may be wise and salutary for us all. I shall be glad to hear from you as often as you may be disposed to think of things here. You may be at liberty, I expect, to communicate some things, consistently with your honor, and the duties you will owe to a protecting nation. Such a communication among individuals, may be mutually beneficial to the contending parties. On this or any future occasion, if I affirm to you any facts, your knowledge of me will enable you to decide on their credibility; if I hazard opinions on the dispositions of men or other speculative points, you can only know they are my opinions. My best wishes for your felicity, attend you, wherever you go, and believe me to be assuredly, Your friend and servant.

The Declaration of Independence

JULY 4, 1776

When in the Course of human events, it becomes necessary for one people to dissolve the political bands which have connected them with another, and to assume among the Powers of the earth, the separate and equal station to which the Laws of Nature and of Nature's God entitle them, a decent respect to the opinions of mankind requires that they should declare the causes which impel them to the separation.

We hold these truths to be self-evident, that all men are created equal, that they are endowed by their Creator with certain unalienable Rights, that among these are Life, Liberty and the pursuit of Happiness. That to secure these rights, Governments are instituted among Men, deriving their just powers from the consent of the governed, That whenever any Form of Government becomes destructive of these ends, it is the Right of the People to alter or to abolish it, and to institute new Government, laying its foundation on such principles and organizing its powers in such form, as to them shall seem most likely to effect their Safety and Happiness. Prudence, indeed, will dictate that Governments long established should not be changed for light and transient causes; and accordingly all experience hath shewn, that mankind are more disposed to suffer, while evils are sufferable, than to right themselves by abolishing the forms to which they are accustomed. But when a long train of abuses and usurpations, pursuing invariably the same Object evinces a design to reduce them under absolute Despotism, it is their right, it is their duty, to throw off such Government, and to provide new Guards for their future security.—Such has been the patient sufferance of these colonies; and such is now the necessity which constrains them to alter their former Systems of Government. The history of the present King of Great Britain is a history of repeated injuries and usurpations, all having in direct object the establishment of an absolute Tyranny over these States. To prove this, let Facts be submitted to a candid world.

He has refused his Assent to Laws, the most wholesome and necessary for the public good.

He has forbidden his Governors to pass Laws of immediate and pressing importance, unless suspended in their operation till his Assent should be obtained; and when so suspended, he has utterly neglected to attend to them.

He has refused to pass other Laws for the accommodation of large districts of people, unless those people would relinquish the right of Representation in the Legislature, a right inestimable to them and formidable to tyrants only.

He has called together legislative bodies at places unusual, uncomfortable, and distant from the depository of their Public Records, for the sole purpose of fatiguing them into compliance with his measures.

He has dissolved Representative Houses repeatedly, for opposing with manly firmness his invasions on the rights of the people.

He has refused for a long time, after such dissolutions, to cause others to be elected; whereby the Legislative Powers, incapable of Annihilation, have returned to the People at large for their exercise; the State remaining in the mean time exposed to all the dangers of invasion from without, and convulsions within.

He has endeavoured to prevent the population of these States; for that purpose obstructing the Laws for Naturalization of Foreigners; refusing to pass others to encourage their migration hither, and raising the conditions of new Appropriations of Lands.

He has obstructed the Administration of Justice, by refusing his Assent to Laws for establishing Judiciary Powers.

He has made Judges dependent on his Will alone, for the tenure of their offices, and the amount and payment of their salaries.

He has erected a multitude of New Offices, and sent hither swarms of Officers to harrass our People, and eat out their substance.

He has kept among us, in times of peace, Standing Armies without the Consent of our Legislatures.

He has affected to render the Military independent of and superior to the Civil Power.

He has combined with others to subject us to a jurisdiction foreign to our constitution, and unacknowledged by our laws; giving his Assent to their Acts of pretended Legislation:

For quartering large bodies of armed troops among us:

For protecting them, by a mock Trial, from Punishment for any Murders which they should commit on the Inhabitants of these States:

For cutting off our Trade with all parts of the world:

For imposing Taxes on us without our Consent:

For depriving us in many cases, of the benefits of Trial by Jury:

For transporting us beyond Seas to be tried for pretended offences:

For abolishing the free System of English Laws in a neighbouring Province, establishing therein an Arbitrary government, and enlarging its Boundaries so as to render it at once an example and fit instrument for introducing the same absolute rule into these Colonies:

For taking away our Charters, abolishing our most valuable Laws, and altering fundamentally the Forms of our Governments:

For suspending our own Legislatures, and declaring themselves invested with Power to legislate for us in all cases whatsoever.

He has abdicated Government here, by declaring us out of his Protection and waging War against us.

He has plundered our seas, ravaged our Coasts, burnt our towns, and destroyed the Lives of our People.

He is at this time transporting large Armies of foreign Mercenaries to compleat the works of death, desolation and tyranny, already begun with circumstances of Cruelty & perfidy scarcely paralleled in the most barbarous ages, and totally unworthy the Head of a civilized nation.

He has constrained our fellow Citizens taken Captive on the high Seas to bear Arms against their Country, to become the executioners of their friends and Brethren, or to fall themselves by their Hands.

He has excited domestic insurrections amongst us, and has endeavoured to bring on the inhabitants of our frontiers, the merciless Indian Savages, whose known rule of warfare, is an undistinguished destruction of all ages, sexes and conditions.

In every stage of these Oppressions We have petitioned for Redress in the most humble terms: Our repeated Petitions have been answered only by repeated injury. A Prince, whose character is thus marked by every act which may define a Tyrant, is unfit to be the ruler of a free People.

Nor have We been wanting in attentions to our British brethren. We have warned them from time to time of attempts by their legislature to extend an unwarrantable jurisdiction over us. We have reminded them of the circumstances of our emigration and settlement here. We have appealed to their native justice and magnanimity, and we have conjured them by the ties of our common kindred to disavow these usurpations, which, would inevitably interrupt our connections and correspondence. They too have been deaf to the voice of justice and of consanguinity. We must, therefore, acquiesce in the necessity, which denounces our Separation, and hold them, as we hold the rest of mankind, Enemies in War, in Peace Friends.

We, therefore, the Representatives of the united States of America, in General Congress, Assembled, appealing to the Supreme Judge of the world for the rectitude of our intentions, do, in the Name, and by the Authority of the good People of these Colonies, solemnly publish and declare, That these United Colonies are, and of Right ought to be Free and Independent States; that they are Absolved from all Allegiance to the British Crown, and that all political connection between them and the State of Great Britain, is and ought to be totally dissolved; and that as Free and Independent States, they have full Power to levy War, conclude

Peace, contract Alliances, establish Commerce, and to do all other Acts and Things which Independent States may of right do. And for the support of this Declaration, with a firm reliance on the Protection of Divine Providence, we mutually pledge to each other our Lives, our Fortunes and our sacred Honor.

A Bill for Establishing Religious Freedom

[1779]

SECTION I. Well aware that the opinions and belief of men depend not on their own will, but follow involuntarily the evidence proposed to their minds; that Almighty God hath created the mind free, and manifested his supreme will that free it shall remain by making it altogether insusceptible of restraint; that all attempts to influence it by temporal punishments, or burthens, or by civil incapacitations, tend only to beget habits of hypocrisy and meanness, and are a departure from the plan of the holy author of our religion, who being lord both of body and mind, yet choose not to propagate it by coercions on either, as was in his Almighty power to do, but to exalt it by its influence on reason alone; that the impious presumption of legislature and ruler, civil as well as ecclesiastical, who, being themselves but fallible and uninspired men, have assumed dominion over the faith of others, setting up their own opinions and modes of thinking as the only true and infallible, and as such endeavoring to impose them on others, hath established and maintained false religions over the greatest part of the world and through all time: That to compel a man to furnish contributions of money for the propagation of opinions which he disbelieves and abhors, is sinful and tyrannical; that even the forcing him to support this or that teacher of his own religious persuasion, is depriving him of the comfortable liberty of giving his contributions to the particular pastor whose morals he would make his pattern, and whose powers he feels most persuasive to righteousness; and is withdrawing from the ministry those temporary rewards, which proceeding from an approbation of their personal conduct, are an additional incitement to earnest and unremitting labours for the instruction of mankind; that our civil rights have no dependance on our religious opinions, any more than our opinions in physics or geometry; and therefore the proscribing any citizen as unworthy the public confidence by laying upon him an incapacity of being called to offices of trust or emolument, unless he profess or renounce this or that religious opinion, is depriving him injudiciously of those privileges and advantages to which, in common with his fellow-citizens, he has a natural right; that it tends also to corrupt the principles of that very religion it is meant to encourage, by bribing with a monopoly of worldly honours and emoluments, those who will externally profess and conform to it; that though indeed these are criminals who do not withstand such temptation, yet neither are those innocent who lay the bait in their way; that the opinions of men are not the object of civil government, nor under its jurisdiction; that to suffer the civil magistrate to intrude his powers into the field of opinion and to restrain the profession or propagation of principles on supposition of their ill tendency is a dangerous falacy, which at once destroys all religious liberty, because he being of course judge of that tendency will make his opinions the rule of judgment, and approve or condemn the sentiments of others only as they shall square with or suffer from his own; that it is time enough for the rightful purposes of civil government for its officers to interfere when principles break out into overt acts against peace and good order; and finally, that truth is great and will prevail if left to herself; that she is the proper and sufficient antagonist to error, and has nothing to fear from the conflict unless by human interposition disarmed of her natural weapons, free argument and debate; errors ceasing to be dangerous when it is permitted freely to contradict them.

SECT. II. WE the General Assembly of Virginia do enact that no man shall be compelled to frequent or support any religious worship, place, or ministry whatsoever, nor shall be enforced, restrained, molested, or burthened in his body or goods, nor shall otherwise suffer, on account of his religious opinions or belief; but that all men shall be free to profess, and by argument to maintain, their opinions in matters of religion, and that the same shall in no wise diminish, enlarge, or affect their civil capacities.

SECT. III. AND though we well know that this Assembly, elected by the people for their ordinary purposes of legislation only, have no power to restrain the acts of succeeding Assemblies, constituted with powers equal to our own, and that therefore to declare this act to be irrevocable would be of no effect in law; yet we are free to declare, and do declare, that the rights hereby asserted are of the natural rights of mankind, and that if any act shall be hereafter passed to repeal the present or to narrow its operations, such act will be an infringement of natural right.

To James Monroe

MONTICELLO, MAY 20, 1782.

Dear Sir,—I have been gratified with the receipt of your two favours of the 6th & 11th inst. It gives me pleasure that your county has been wise enough to enlist your talents into their service. I am much obliged by the kind wishes you express of seeing me also in Richmond, and am always mortified when anything is expected from me which I cannot fulfill, & more especially if it relate to the public service. Before I ventured to declare to my countrymen my determination to retire from public employment, I examined well my heart to know whether it were thoroughly cured of every principle of political ambition, whether no lurking particle remained which might leave me uneasy when reduced within the limits of mere private life. I became satisfied that every fibre of that passion was thoroughly eradicated. I examined also in other views my right to withdraw. I considered that I had been thirteen years engaged in public service, that during that time I had so totally abandoned all attention to my private affairs as to permit them to run into great disorder and ruin, that I had now a family advanced to years which require my attention & instruction, that to these were added the hopeful offspring of a deceased friend whose memory must be forever dear to me who have no other reliance for being rendered useful to themselves & their country, that by a constant sacrifice of time, labour, loss, parental & family duties, I had been so far from gaining the affection of my countrymen, which was the only reward I ever asked or could have felt, that I had even lost the small estimation I before possessed. That however I might have comforted myself under the disapprobation of the well-meaning but uninformed people yet that of their representatives was a shock on which I had not calculated: that this indeed had been followed by an exculpatory declaration. But in the meantime I had been suspected & suspended in the eyes of the world without the least hint then or afterwards made public which might restrain them from supposing that I stood arraigned for treason of the heart and not merely weakness of the head; and I felt that these injuries, for such they have been since acknowledged had inflicted a wound on my spirit which will only be cured by the all-healing grave. If reason & inclination unite in justifying my retirement, the laws of my country are equally in favor of it. Whether the state may command the political services of all it's members to an indefinite extent, or if these be among the rights never wholly ceded to the public power, is a question which I do not find expressly decided in England.

Obiter dictums on the subject I have indeed met with, but the complexion of the times in which these have dropped would generally answer them, besides that this species of authority is not acknowledged in our profession. In this country however since the present government has been established the point has been settled by uniform, pointed & multiplied precedents. Offices of every kind, and given by every power, have been daily & hourly declined & resigned from the declaration of independance to this moment. The genl assembly has accepted these without discrimination of office, and without ever questioning them in point of right. If a difference between the office of a delegate & any other could ever have been supposed, yet in the case of Mr. Thompson Mason who declined the office of delegate & was permitted so to do by the house that supposition has been proved to be groundless. But indeed no such distinction of offices can be admitted. Reason and the opinions of the lawyers putting all on a footing as to this question and so giving to the delegate the aid of all the precedents of the refusal of other offices. The law then does not warrant the assumption of such a power by the state over it's members. For if it does where is that law? nor yet does reason, for tho' I will admit that this does subject every individual if called on to an equal tour of political duty yet it can never go so far as to submit to it his whole existence. If we are made in some degree for others, yet in a greater are we made for ourselves. It were contrary to feeling & indeed ridiculous to suppose that a man had less right in himself than one of his neighbors or indeed all of them put together. This would be slavery & not that liberty which the bill of rights has made inviolable and for the preservation of which our government has been charged. Nothing could so completely divest us of that liberty as the establishment of the opinion that the state has a *perpetual* right to the services of all it's members. This to men of certain ways of thinking would be to annihilate the blessing of existence; to contradict the giver of life who gave it for happiness & not for wretchedness; and certainly to such it were better that they had never been born. However with these I may think public service & private misery inseparably linked together, I have not the vanity to count myself among those whom the state would think worth oppressing with perpetual service. I have received a sufficient memento to the contrary. I am persuaded that having hitherto dedicated to them the whole of the active & useful part of my life I shall be permitted to pass the rest in mental quiet. I hope too that I did not mistake the modes any more than the matter of right when I preferred a simple act of renunciation to the taking sanctuary under those disqualifications provided by the law for other purposes indeed, but which affording asylum also for rest to the wearied. I dare say you did not expect by the few words you dropped on the right of renunciation to expose yourself to the fatigue of so long a letter, but I wished you to see that if I had done wrong I had been betrayed by a semblance of right at least.

I take the liberty of inclosing to you a letter for Genl Chattelux for which you will readily find means of conveyance. But I meant to give you more trouble with the one to Pelham who lives in the neighborhood of Manchester & to ask the favor of you to send it by your servant express which I am in hopes may be done without absenting him from your person but during those hours in which you will be engaged in the house. I am anxious that it should be received immediately. Mrs Jefferson has added another daughter to our family. She has been ever since & still continues very dangerously ill. It will give me great pleasure to see you here whenever you can favor us with your company. You will find me still busy but in lighter occupations. But in these & all others you will find me to retain a due sense of your friendship & to be with sincere esteem, Dr Sir

Your mo ob & mo hble servt.

Notes on the State of Virginia

[1785]

QUERY XVIII, Manners

The particular *customs and manners that may happen to be received in that state?*

It is difficult to determine on the standard by which the manners of a nation may be tried, whether *catholic* or *particular.* It is more difficult for a native to bring to that standard the manners of his own nation, familiarized to him by habit. There must doubtless be an unhappy influence on the manners of our people produced by the existence of slavery among us. The whole commerce between master and slave is a perpetual exercise of the most boisterous passions, the most unremitting despotism on the one part, and degrading submission on the other. Our children see this, and learn to imitate it; for man is an imitative animal. This quality is the germ of all education in him. From his cradle to his grave he is learning to do what he sees others do. If a parent could find no motive either in his philanthropy or his self-love, for restraining the intemperance of passion towards his slave, it should always be a sufficient one that his child is present. But generally it is not sufficient. The parent storms, the child looks on, catches the lineaments of wrath, puts on the same airs in the circle of smaller slaves, gives a loose to the worst of passions, and thus nursed, educated, and daily exercised in tyranny, cannot but be stamped by it with odious peculiarities. The man must be a prodigy who can retain his manners and morals undepraved by such circumstances. And with what execration should the statesman be loaded, who, permitting one half the citizens thus to trample on the rights of the other, transforms those into despots, and these into enemies, destroys the morals of the one part, and the amor patriæ of the other. For if a slave can have a country in this world, it must be any other in preference to that in which he is born to live and labor for another; in which he must lock up the faculties of his nature, contribute as far as depends on his individual endeavors to the evanishment of the human race, or entail his own miserable condition on the endless generations proceeding from him. With the morals of the people, their industry also is destroyed. For in a warm climate, no man will labor for himself who can make another labor for him. This is so true, that of the proprietors of slaves a very small proportion indeed are ever seen to labor. And can the liberties of a nation be thought secure when we have removed their only firm basis, a conviction in the minds of the people that these liberties are of the gift of God? That they are not to be violated but with His wrath? Indeed I tremble for my country when I reflect that God is just; that his justice cannot sleep for ever; that considering numbers, nature and natural means only, a revolution of the wheel of fortune, an exchange of situation is among possible events; that it may become probable by supernatural interference! The Almighty has no attribute which can take side with us in such a contest. But it is impossible to be temperate and to pursue this subject through the various considerations of policy, of morals, of history natural and civil. We must be contented to hope they will force their way into every one's mind. I think a change already perceptible, since the origin of the present revolution. The spirit of the master is abating, that of the slave rising from the dust, his condition mollifying, the way I hope preparing, under the auspices of heaven, for a total emancipation, and that this is disposed, in the order of events, to be with the consent of the masters, rather than by their extirpation.

QUERY XIX: Manufactures

The present state of manufactures, commerce, interior and exterior trade?

We never had an interior trade of any importance. Our exterior commerce has suffered very much from the beginning of the present contest.

During this time we have manufactured within our families the most necessary articles of cloathing. Those of cotton will bear some comparison with the same kinds of manufacture in Europe; but those of wool, flax and hemp are very coarse, unsightly, and unpleasant: and such is our attachment to agriculture, and such our preference for foreign manufactures, that be it wise or unwise, our people will certainly return as soon as they can, to the raising raw materials, and exchanging them for finer manufactures than they are able to execute themselves.

The political œconomists of Europe have established it as a principle that every state should endeavour to manufacture for itself: and this principle, like many others, we transfer to America, without calculating the difference of circumstance which should often produce a difference of result. In Europe the lands are either cultivated, or locked up against the cultivator. Manufacture must therefore be resorted to of necessity not of choice, to support the surplus of their people. But we have an immensity of land courting the industry of the husbandman. Is it best then that all our citizens should be employed in its improvement, or that one half should be called off from that to exercise manufactures and handicraft arts for the other? Those who labour in the earth are the chosen people of God, if ever he had a chosen people, whose breasts he has made his peculiar deposit for substantial and genuine virtue. It is the focus in which he keeps alive that sacred fire, which otherwise might escape from the face of the earth. Corruption of morals in the mass of cultivators is a phænomenon of which no age nor nation has furnished an example. It is the mark set on those, who not looking up to heaven, to their own soil and industry, as does the husbandman, for their subsistance, depend for it on the casualties and caprice of customers. Dependance begets subservience and venality, suffocates the germ of virtue, and prepares fit tools for the designs of ambition. This, the natural progress and consequence of the arts, has sometimes perhaps been retarded by accidental circumstances: but, generally speaking, the proportion which the aggregate of the other classes of citizens bears in any state to that of its husbandmen, is the proportion of its unsound to its healthy parts, and is a good-enough barometer whereby to measure its degree of corruption. While we have land to labour then, let us never wish to see our citizens occupied at a work-bench, or twirling a distaff. Carpenters, masons, smiths, are wanting in husbandry: but, for the general operations of manufacture, let our work-shops remain in Europe. It is better to carry provisions and materials to workmen there, than bring them to the provisions and materials, and with them their manners and principles. The loss by the transportation of commodities across the Atlantic will be made up in happiness and permanence of government. The mobs of great cities add just so much to the support of pure government, as sores do to the strength of the human body. It is the manners and spirit of a people which preserve a republic in vigour. A degeneracy in these is a canker which soon eats to the heart of its laws and constitution.

To Maria Cosway

PARIS, OCTOBER 12, 1786

My Dear Madam,—Having performed the last sad office of landing you into your carriage at the pavillon de St. Denis, and seen the wheels get actually into motion, I turned on my heel & walked, more dead than alive, to the opposite door, where my own was awaiting me. Mr. Danquerville was missing. He was sought for, found, & dragged down stairs. We were crammed into the carriage, like recruits for the Bastille, & not having soul enough to give orders to the coachman, he presumed Paris our destination, & drove off. After a considerable interval, silence was broke with a "*Je suis vraiment affligе du depart de ces bons gens.*" This was a signal for a mutual confession of distress. We began immediately to talk of Mr. & Mrs. Cosway, of their goodness, their talents, their amiability; & tho we spoke of nothing else, we seemed hardly to have entered into matter when the coachman announced the rue St. Denis, & that we were opposite Mr. Danquerville's. He insisted on descending there & traversing a short passage to his lodgings. I was carried home. Seated by my fireside, solitary & sad, the following dialogue took place between my Head & my Heart:

Head. Well, friend, you seem to be in a pretty trim.

Heart. I am indeed the most wretched of all earthly beings. Overwhelmed with grief, every fibre of my frame distended beyond its natural powers to bear, I would willingly meet whatever catastrophe should leave me no more to feel or to fear.

Head. These are the eternal consequences of your warmth & precipitation. This is one of the scrapes into which you are ever leading us. You confess your follies indeed; but still you hug & cherish them; & no reformation can be hoped, where there is no repentance.

Heart. Oh, my friend! this is no moment to upbraid my foibles. I am rent into fragments by the force of my grief! If you have any balm, pour it into my wounds; if none, do not harrow them by new torments. Spare me in this awful moment! At any other I will attend with patience to your admonitions. [. . .]

Head. [. . .] This is not a world to live at random in as you do. To avoid those eternal distresses, to which you are forever exposing us, you must learn to look forward before you take a step which may interest our peace. Everything in this world is a matter of calculation. Advance then with caution, the balance in your hand. Put into one scale the pleasures which any object may offer; but put fairly into the other the pains which are to follow, & see which preponderates. The making an acquaintance is not a matter of indifference. When a new one is proposed to you, view it all round. Consider what advantages it presents, & to what inconveniences it may expose you. Do not bite at the bait of pleasure till you know there is no hook beneath it. The art of life is the art of avoiding pain: & he is the best pilot who steers clearest of the rocks & shoals with which he is beset. Pleasure is always before us; but misfortune is at our side: while running after that, this arrests us. The most effectual means of being secure against pain is to retire within ourselves, & to suffice for our own happiness. [. . .]

Heart. [. . .] In a life where we are perpetually exposed to want & accident, yours is a wonderful proposition to insulate ourselves, to retire from all aid, & to wrap ourselves in the mantle of self-sufficiency! For assuredly nobody will care for him who cares for nobody. [. . .] Let the gloomy monk, sequestered from the world, seek unsocial pleasures in the bottom of his cell! [. . .]

To Abigail Adams

PARIS FEB. 22. 1787.

Dear Madam,—I am to acknowlege the honor of your letter of Jan. 29. and of the papers you were so good as to send me. They were the latest I had seen or have yet seen. They left off too in a critical moment; just at the point where the Malcontents make their submission on condition of pardon, & before the answer of government was known. I hope they pardoned them. The spirit of resistance to government is so valuable on certain occasions, that I wish it to be always kept alive. It will often be exercised when wrong but better so than not to be exercised at all. I like a little rebellion now & then. It is like a storm in the Atmosphere. It is wonderful that no letter or paper tells us who is president of Congress, tho' there are letters in Paris to the beginning of January. I suppose I shall hear when I come back from my journey, which will be eight months after he will have been chosen, and yet they complain of us for not giving them intelligence. Our Notables assembled to-day, and I hope before the departure of Mr. Cairnes I shall have heard something of their proceedings worth communicating to Mr. Adams. The most remarkable effect of this convention as yet is the number of puns & bon mots it has generated. I think were they all collected it would make a more voluminous work than the Encyclopedie. This occasion, more than any thing I have seen, convinces me that this nation is incapable of any serious effort but under the word of command. The people at large view every object only as it may furnish puns and bon mots; and I pronounce that a good punster would disarm the whole nation were they ever so seriously disposed to revolt. Indeed, Madam, they are gone. When a measure so capable of doing good as the calling the Notables is treated with so much ridicule, we may conclude the nation desperate, & in charity pray that heaven may send them good kings.—The bridge at the place Louis XV is begun, the hotel dieu is to be abandoned & new ones to be built. The old houses on the bridges are in a course of demolition. This is all I know of Paris. We are about to lose the Count d'Arande, who has desired & obtained his recall. Fernand Nunnez, before destined for London, is to come here. The Abbés Arnoux & Chalut are well. The Dutchess Danville somewhat recovered from the loss of her daughter. Mrs. Barrett very homesick and fancying herself otherwise sick. They will probably remove to Honfleur. This is all our news. I have only to add then that Mr. Cairnes has taken charge of 15 aunes of black lace for you at 9 livres the aune, purchased by Petit & therefore I hope better purchased than some things have been for you; and that I am with sincere esteem dear Madam, your affectionate humble servant.

To James Madison

PARIS, DEC. 20, 1787.

Dear Sir,— [. . .] I will [add] a few words on the Constitution proposed by our Convention. I like much the general idea of framing a government which should go on of itself peaceably, without needing continual recurrence to the state legislatures. I like the organization of the government into Legislative, Judiciary & Executive. I like the power given the Legislature to levy taxes, and for that reason solely approve of the greater house being chosen by the people directly. For tho' I think a house chosen by them will be very illy qualified to legislate for the Union, for foreign nations

&c. yet this evil does not weigh against the good of preserving inviolate the fundamental principle that the people are not to be taxed but by representatives chosen immediately by themselves. I am captivated by the compromise of the opposite claims of the great & little states, of the latter to equal, and the former to proportional influence. I am much pleased too with the substitution of the method of voting by persons, instead of that of voting by states: and I like the negative given to the Executive with a third of either house, though I should have liked it better had the Judiciary been associated for that purpose, or invested with a similar and separate power. There are other good things of less moment. I will now add what I do not like. First the omission of a bill of rights providing clearly & without the aid of sophisms for freedom of religion, freedom of the press, protection against standing armies, restriction against monopolies, the eternal & unremitting force of the habeas corpus laws, and trials by jury in all matters of fact triable by the laws of the land & not by the law of nations. To say, as Mr. Wilson does that a bill of rights was not necessary because all is reserved in the case of the general government which is not given, while in the particular ones all is given which is not reserved, might do for the audience to whom it was addressed, but is surely a gratis dictum, opposed by strong inferences from the body of the instrument, as well as from the omission of the clause of our present confederation which had declared that in express terms. It was a hard conclusion to say because there has been no uniformity among the states as to the cases triable by jury, because some have been so incautious as to abandon this mode of trial, therefore the more prudent states shall be reduced to the same level of calamity. It would have been much more just & wise to have concluded the other way that as most of the states had judiciously preserved this palladium, those who had wandered should be brought back to it, and to have established general right instead of general wrong. Let me add that a bill of rights is what the people are entitled to against every government on earth, general or particular, & what no just government should refuse, or rest on inferences. The second feature I dislike, and greatly dislike, is the abandonment in every instance of the necessity of rotation in office, and most particularly in the case of the President. Experience concurs with reason in concluding that the first magistrate will always be re-elected if the Constitution permits it. He is then an officer for life. This once observed, it becomes of so much consequence to certain nations to have a friend or a foe at the head of our affairs that they will interfere with money & with arms. A Galloman or an Angloman will be supported by the nation he befriends. If once elected, and at a second or third election out voted by one or two votes, he will pretend false votes, foul play, hold possession of the reins of government, be supported by the States voting for him, especially if they are the central ones lying in a compact body themselves & separating their opponents: and they will be aided by one nation of Europe, while the majority are aided by another. The election of a President of America some years hence will be much more interesting to certain nations of Europe than ever the election of a king of Poland was. Reflect on all the instances in history antient & modern, of elective monarchies, and say if they do not give foundation for my fears. The Roman emperors, the popes, while they were of any importance, the German emperors till they became hereditary in practice, the kings of Poland, the Deys of the Ottoman dependancies. It may be said that if elections are to be attended with these disorders, the seldomer they are renewed the better. But experience shews that the only way to prevent disorder is to render them uninteresting by frequent changes. An incapacity to be elected a second time would have been the only effectual preventative. The power of removing him every fourth year by the vote of the people is a power which will not be exercised. The king of Poland is removeable every day by the Diet, yet he is never removed.—Smaller objections are the Appeal in fact as well as law, and the binding all persons Legislative Executive & Judiciary by oath to maintain that constitution. I do not pretend to decide what would be the best method of procuring the establishment of the manifold good things in this constitution, and of getting rid of the bad. Whether by adopting it in hopes of future amendment, or, after it has been duly weighed & canvassed by the people, after seeing the parts they generally dislike, & those they generally approve, to say to them 'We see now what you wish. Send together your deputies again, let them frame a constitution for you omitting what you have condemned, & establishing the powers you approve. Even these will be a great addition to the energy of your government.'—At all events I hope you will not be discouraged from other trials, if the present one should fail of its full effect.—I have thus told you freely what I like & dislike: merely as a matter of curiosity, for I know your own judgment has been formed on all these points after having heard everything which could be urged on them. I own I am not a friend to a very energetic government. It is always oppressive. The late rebellion in Massachusetts has given more alarm than I think it should have done. Calculate that one rebellion in 13 states in the course of 11 years, is but one for each state in a century & a half. No country should be so long without one. Nor will any degree of power in the hands of government prevent insurrections. France, with all it's despotism, and two or three hundred thousand men always in arms has had three insurrections in the three years I have been here in every one of which greater numbers were engaged than in Massachusetts & a great deal more blood was spilt. In Turkey, which Montesquieu supposes more despotic, insurrections are the events of every day. In England, where the hand of power is lighter than here, but heavier than with us they happen every half dozen years. Compare again the ferocious depredations of their insurgents with the order, the moderation & the almost self extinguishment of ours.—After all, it is my principle that the will of the majority should always prevail. If they approve the proposed Convention in all it's parts, I shall concur in it cheerfully, in hopes that they will amend it whenever they shall find it work wrong. I think our governments will remain virtuous for many centuries; as long as they are chiefly agricultural; and this will be as long as there shall be vacant lands in any part of America. When they get piled upon one another in large cities, as in Europe, they will become corrupt as in Europe. Above all things I hope the education of the common people will be attended to; convinced that on their good sense we may rely with the most security for the preservation of a due degree of liberty. I have tired you by this time with my disquisitions & will therefore only add assurances of the sincerity of those sentiments of esteem & attachment with which I am Dear Sir your affectionate friend & servant

P.S. The instability of our laws is really an immense evil. I think it would be well to provide in our constitutions that there shall always be a twelvemonth between the ingrossing a bill & passing it: that it should then be offered to it's passage without changing a word: and that if circumstances should be thought to require a speedier passage, it should take two thirds of both houses instead of a bare majority.

To James Madison

PARIS, SEPTEMBER 6, 1789.

Dear Sir,—I sit down to write to you without knowing by what occasion I shall send my letter. I do it because a subject comes into my head which I would wish to develope a little more than is practicable in the hurry of the moment of making up general despatches.

The question Whether one generation of men has a right to bind another, seems never to have been started either on this or our side of the water. Yet it is a question of such consequences as not only to merit decision, but place also, among the fundamental principles of every government. The course of reflection in which we are immersed here on the elementary principles of society has presented this question to my mind; and that no such obligation can be transmitted I think very capable of proof. I set out on this ground which I suppose to be self evident, *"that the earth belongs in usufruct to the living;"* that the dead have neither powers nor rights over it. The portion occupied by an individual ceases to be his when himself ceases to be, and reverts to the society. If the society has formed no rules for the appropriation of its lands in severalty, it will be taken by the first occupants. These will generally be the wife and children of the decedent. If they have formed rules of appropriation, those rules may give it to the wife and children, or to some one of them, or to the legatee of the deceased. So they may give it to his creditor. But the child, the legatee or creditor takes it, not by any natural right, but by a law of the society of which they are members, and to which they are subject. Then no man can by *natural right* oblige the lands he occupied, or the persons who succeed him in that occupation, to the paiment of debts contracted by him. For if he could, he might during his own life, eat up the usufruct of the lands for several generations to come, and then the lands would belong to the dead, and not to the living, which would be reverse of our principle. What is true of every member of the society individually, is true of them all collectively, since the rights of the whole can be no more than the sum of the rights of individuals. To keep our ideas clear when applying them to a multitude, let us suppose a whole generation of men to be born on the same day, to attain mature age on the same day, and to die on the same day, leaving a succeeding generation in the moment of attaining their mature age all together. Let the ripe age be supposed of 21. years, and their period of life 34. years more, that being the average term given by the bills of mortality to persons who have already attained 21. years of age. Each successive generation would, in this way, come on and go off the stage at a fixed moment, as individuals do now. Then I say the earth belongs to each of these generations during it's course, fully, and in their own right. The 2d. generation receives it clear of the debts and incumbrances of the 1st., the 3d. of the 2d. and so on. For if the 1st. could charge it with a debt, then the earth would belong to the dead and not the living generation. Then no generation can contract debts greater than may be paid during the course of it's own existence. At 21. years of age they may bind themselves and their lands for 34. years to come: at 22. for 33: at 23 for 32. and at 54 for one year only; because these are the terms of life which remain to them at those respective epochs. But a material difference must be noted between the succession of an individual and that of a whole generation. Individuals are parts only of a society, subject to the laws of a whole. These laws may appropriate the portion of land occupied by a decedent to his creditor rather than to any other, or to his child, on condition he satisfies his creditor. But when a whole generation, that is, the whole society dies, as in the case we have supposed, and another generation or society succeeds, this forms a whole, and there is no superior who can give their territory to a third society, who may have lent money to their predecessors beyond their faculty of paying.

What is true of a generation all arriving to self-government on the same day, and dying all on the same day, is true of those on a constant course of decay and renewal, with this only difference. A generation coming in and going out entire, as in the first case, would have a right in the 1st year of their self dominion to contract a debt for 33. years, in the 10th. for 24. in the 20th. for 14. in the 30th. for 4. whereas generations changing daily, by daily deaths and births, have one constant term beginning at the date of their contract, and ending when a majority of those of full age at that date shall be dead. The length of that term may be estimated from the tables of mortality, corrected by the circumstances of climate, occupation &c. peculiar to the country of the contractors. Take, for instance, the table of M. de Buffon wherein he states that 23,994 deaths, and the ages at which they happened. Suppose a society in which 23,994 persons are born every year and live to the ages stated in this table. The conditions of that society will be as follows. 1st. it will consist constantly of 617,703 persons of all ages. 2dly. of those living at any one instant of time, one half will be dead in 24. years 8. months. 3dly. 10,675 will arrive every year at the age of 21. years complete. 4thly. it will constantly have 348,417 persons of all ages above 21. years. 5ly. and the half of those of 21. years and upwards living at any one instant of time will be dead in 18. years 8. months, or say 19. years as the nearest integral number. Then 19. years is the term beyond which neither the representatives of a nation, nor even the whole nation itself assembled, can validly extend a debt.

To render this conclusion palpable by example, suppose that Louis XIV. and XV. had contracted debts in the name of the French nation to the amount of 10,000 milliards of livres and that the whole had been contracted in Genoa. The interest of this sum would be 500 milliards, which is said to be the whole rent-roll, or nett proceeds of the territory of France. Must the present generation of men have retired from the territory in which nature produced them, and ceded it to the Genoese creditors? No. They have the same rights over the soil on which they were produced, as the preceding generations had. They derive these rights not from their predecessors, but from nature. They then and their soil are by nature clear of the debts of their predecessors. Again suppose Louis XV. and his contemporary generation had said to the money lenders of Genoa, give us money that we may eat, drink, and be merry in our day; and on condition you will demand no interest till the end of 19. years, you shall then forever after receive an annual interest of 12.5 per cent. The money is lent on these conditions, is divided among the living, eaten, drank, and squandered. Would the present generation be obliged to apply the produce of the earth and of their labour to replace their dissipations? Not at all.

I suppose that the received opinion, that the public debts of one generation devolve on the next, has been suggested by our seeing habitually in private life that he who succeeds to lands is required to pay the debts of his ancestor or testator, without considering that this requisition is municipal only, not moral, flowing from the will of the society which has found it convenient to appropriate the lands become vacant by the death of their occupant on the condition of a paiment of his debts; but that between society and society, or generation and generation there is no municipal obligation, no umpire but the law of nature. We seem not to have perceived that, by the law of nature, one generation is to another as one independant nation to another.

The interest of the national debt of France being in fact but a two thousandth part of it's rent-roll, the paiment of it is practicable enough; and so becomes a question merely of honor or expediency. But with respect to future debts; would it not be wise and just for that nation to declare in the constitution they are forming that neither the legislature, nor the nation itself can validly contract more debt, than they may pay within their own age, or within the term of 19. years? And that all future contracts shall be deemed void as to what shall remain unpaid at the end of 19. years from their date? This would put the lenders, and the borrowers also, on their guard. By reducing too the faculty of borrowing within its natural limits, it would bridle the spirit of war, to which too free a course has been procured by the inattention of money lenders to this law of nature, that succeeding generations are not responsible for the preceding.

On similar ground it may be proved that no society can make a perpetual constitution, or even a perpetual law. The earth belongs always to the living generation. They may manage it then, and what proceeds from it, as they please, during their usufruct. They are masters too of their own persons, and consequently may govern them as they please. But persons and property make the sum of the objects of government. The constitution and the laws of their predecessors extinguished them, in their natural course, with those whose will gave them being. This could preserve that being till it ceased to be itself, and no longer. Every constitution, then, and every law, naturally expires at the end of 19. years. If it be enforced longer, it is an act of force and not of right.

It may be said that the succeeding generation exercising in fact the power of repeal, this leaves them as free as if the constitution or law had been expressly limited to 19. years only. In the first place, this objection admits the right, in proposing an equivalent. But the power of repeal is not an equivalent. It might be indeed if every form of government were so perfectly contrived that the will of the majority could always be obtained fairly and without impediment. But this is true of no form. The people cannot assemble themselves; their representation is unequal and vicious. Various checks are opposed to every legislative proposition. Factions get possession of the public councils. Bribery corrupts them. Personal interests lead them astray from the general interests of their constituents; and other impediments arise so as to prove to every practical man that a law of limited duration is much more manageable than one which needs a repeal.

This principle that the earth belongs to the living and not to the dead is of very extensive application and consequences in every country, and most especially in France. It enters into the resolution of the questions Whether the nation may change the descent of lands holden in tail? Whether they may change the appropriation of lands given antiently to the church, to hospitals, colleges, orders of chivalry, and otherwise in perpetuity? whether they may abolish the charges and privileges attached on lands, including the whole catalogue ecclesiastical and feudal? it goes to hereditary offices, authorities and jurisdictions; to hereditary orders, distinctions and appellations; to perpetual monopolies in commerce, the arts or sciences; with a long train of *et ceteras:* and it renders the question of reimbursement a question of generosity and not of right. In all these cases the legislature of the day could authorize such appropriations and establishments for their own time, but no longer; and the present holders, even where they or their ancestors have purchased, are in the case of *bona fide* purchasers of what the seller had no right convey.

Turn this subject in your mind, my Dear Sir, and particularly as to the power of contracting debts, and develope it with that perspicuity and cogent logic which is so peculiarly yours. Your station in the councils of our country gives you an opportunity of producing it to public consideration, of forcing it into discussion. At first blush it may be rallied as a theoretical speculation; but examination will prove it to be solid and salutary. It would furnish matter for a fine preamble to our first law for appropriating the public revenue; and it will exclude, at the threshold of our new government the contagious and ruinous errors of this quarter of the globe, which have armed despots with means not sanctioned by nature for binding in chains their fellow-men. We have already given, in example one effectual check to the Dog of war, by transferring the power of letting him loose from the executive to the Legislative body, from those who are to spend to those who are to pay. I should be pleased to see this second obstacle held out by us also in the first instance. No nation can make a declaration against the validity of long-contracted debts so disinterestedly as we, since we do not owe a shilling which may not be paid with ease principal and interest, within the time of our own lives. Establish the principle also in the new law to be passed for protecting copy rights and new inventions, by securing the exclusive right for 19. instead of 14. years [*a line entirely faded*] an instance the more of our taking reason for our guide instead of English precedents, the habit of which fetters us, with all the political herecies of a nation, equally remarkable for it's encitement from some errors, as long slumbering under others. I write you no news, because when an occasion occurs I shall write a separate letter for that.

To the President of the United States [George Washington]

MONTICELLO, SEP. 9, 1792.

Dear Sir,—I received on the 2d inst the letter of Aug 23, which you did me the honor to write me; but the immediate return of our post, contrary to his custom, prevented my answer by that occasion. The proceedings of Spain mentioned in your letter are really of a complexion to excite uneasiness, & a suspicion that their friendly overtures about the Missisipi have been merely to lull us while they should be strengthening their holds on that river. [. . .]

I now take the liberty of proceeding to that part of your letter wherein you notice the internal dissentions which have taken place within our government, & their disagreeable effect on it's movements. That such dissentions have taken place is certain, & even among those who are nearest to you in the administration. To no one have they given deeper concern than myself: to no one equal mortification at being myself a part of them. Tho' I take to myself no more than my share of the general observations of your letter, yet I am so desirous ever that you should know the whole truth, & believe no more than the truth, that I am glad to seize every occasion of developing to you whatever I do or think relative to the government; & shall therefore ask permission to be more lengthy now than the occasion particularly calls for, or could otherwise perhaps justify.

When I embarked in the government, it was with a determination to intermeddle not at all with the legislature, & as little as possible with my co-departments. The first and only instance of variance from the former part of my resolution, I was duped into by the Secretary of the Treasury and made a tool for forwarding his schemes, not then sufficiently understood by me; and of all the errors of my political life, this has occasioned me the deepest regret. It has ever been my purpose to explain this to you, when, from being actors on the scene, we shall have become uninterested spectators only. The second part of my resolution has been religiously observed with the war department; & as to that of the Treasury, has never been farther swerved from than by the mere enunciation of my sentiments in conversation, and chiefly among those who, expressing the same sentiments, drew mine from me. If it has been supposed that I have ever intrigued among the members of the legislatures to defeat the plans of the Secretary of the Treasury, it is contrary to all truth. As I never had the desire to influence the members, so neither had I any other means than my friendships, which I valued too highly to risk by usurpations on their freedom of judgment, & the conscientious pursuit of their own sense of duty. That I have utterly, in my private conversations, disapproved of the system of the Secretary of the treasury, I acknolege & avow: and this was not merely a speculative difference. His system flowed from principles adverse to liberty, & was calculated to undermine and demolish the republic, by creating an influence of his department over the members of the legislature. I saw this influence actually produced, & it's first fruits to be the establishment of the great outlines of his project by the votes of the very persons who, having swallowed his bait were laying themselves out to profit by his plans: & that had these persons withdrawn, as those interested in a question ever should, the vote of the disinterested majority was clearly the reverse of what they made it. These were no longer the votes then of the representatives of the people, but of deserters from the rights & interests of the people: & it was impossible to consider their decisions, which had nothing in view but to enrich themselves, as the measures of the fair majority, which ought always to be respected.—If what was actually doing begat uneasiness in those who wished for virtuous government, what was further proposed was not less threatening to the friends of the Constitution. For, in a Report on the subject of manufactures (still to be acted on) it was expressly assumed that the general government has a right to exercise all powers which may be for the *general welfare,* that is to say, all the legitimate powers of government: since no government has a legitimate right to do what is not for the welfare of the governed. There was indeed a sham-limitation of the universality of this power *to cases where money is to be employed.* But about what is it that money cannot be employed? Thus the object of these plans taken together is to draw all the powers of government into the hands of the general legislature, to establish means for corrupting a sufficient corps in that legislature to divide the honest votes & preponderate, by their own, the scale which suited, & to have that corps under the command of the Secretary of the Treasury for the purpose of subverting step by step the principles of the constitution, which he has so often declared to be a thing of nothing which must be changed. Such views might have justified something more than mere expressions of dissent, beyond which, nevertheless, I never went.—Has abstinence from the department committed to me been equally observed by him? To say nothing of other interferences equally known, in the case of the two nations with which we have the most intimate connections, France & England, my system was to give some satisfactory distinctions to the former, of little cost to us, in return for the solid advantages yielded us by them; & to have met the English with some restrictions which might induce them to abate their severities against our commerce. I have always supposed this coincided with your sentiments. Yet the Secretary of the treasury, by his cabals with members of the legislature, & by high-toned declamation on other occasions, has forced down his own system, which was exactly the reverse. He undertook, of his own authority, the conferences with the ministers of those two nations, & was, on every consultation, provided with some report of a conversation with the one or the other of them, adapted to his views. These views, thus made to prevail, their execution fell of course to me; & I can safely appeal to you, who have seen all my letters & proceedings, whether I have not carried them into execution as sincerely as if they had been my own, tho' I ever considered them as inconsistent with the honor & interest of our country. That they have been inconsistent with our interest is but too fatally proved by the stab to our navigation given by the French.—So that if the question be By whose fault is it that Colo Hamilton & myself have not drawn together? the answer will depend on that to two other questions; whose principles of administration best justify, by their purity, conscientious adherence? and which of us has, notwithstanding, stepped farthest into the controul of the department of the other?

To this justification of opinions, expressed in the way of conversation, against the views of Colo Hamilton, I beg leave to add some notice of his late charges against me in Fenno's gazette; for neither the stile, matter, nor venom of the pieces alluded to can leave a doubt of their author. Spelling my name & character at full length to the public, while he conceals his own under the signature of "an American" he charges me [. . .] with having written letters from Europe to my friends to oppose the present constitution while depending. [. . .] You will there see that my objection to the constitution was that it wanted a bill of rights securing freedom of religion, freedom of the press, freedom from standing armies, trial by jury, & a constant Habeas corpus act. Colo Hamilton's was that it wanted a king and house of lords. The sense of America has approved my objection & added the bill of rights, not the king and lords. I also thought a longer term of service, insusceptible of renewal, would have made a President more independant. My country has thought otherwise, & I have acquiesced implicitly. He wishes the general government should have power to make laws binding the states in all cases whatsoever. Our country has thought otherwise: has he acquiesced? Notwithstanding my wish for a bill of rights, my letters strongly urged the adoption of the constitution, by nine states at least, to secure the good it contained. [. . .] —So much for the past. A word now of the future.

When I came into this office, it was with a resolution to retire from it as soon as I could with decency. [. . .] I look to that period with the longing of a wave-worn mariner, who has at length the land in view, & shall count the days & hours which still lie between me & it. [. . .] To a thorough disregard of the honors & emoluments of office I join as great a value for the esteem of my countrymen, & conscious of having merited it by an integrity which cannot be reproached, & by an enthusiastic devotion to their rights & liberty, I will not suffer my retirement to be clouded by the slanders of a man whose history, from the moment at which history can stoop to notice him, is a tissue of machinations against the liberty of the country. [. . .] In the meantime & ever am with great and sincere affection & respect, dear Sir, your most obedient and most humble servant.

To William Short

PHILADELPHIA, JAN 3. 1793.

Dear Sir,—My last private letter to you was of Oct. 16. since which I have received your No. 103, 107, 108, 109, 110, 112, 113 & 114 and yesterday your private one of Sep 15, came to hand. The tone of your letters had for some time given me pain, on account of the extreme warmth with which they censured the proceedings of the Jacobins of France. I considered that sect as the same with the Republican patriots, & the Feuillants as the Monarchical patriots, well known in the early part of the revolution, & but little distant in their views, both having in object the establishment of a free constitution, & differing only on the question whether their chief Executive should be hereditary or not. The Jacobins (as since called) yielded to the Feuillants & tried the experiment of retaining their hereditary Executive. The experiment failed completely, and would have brought on the reestablishment of despotism had it been pursued. The Jacobins saw this, and that the expunging that officer was of absolute necessity. And the Nation was with them in opinion, for however they might have been formerly for the constitution framed by the first assembly, they were come over from their hope in it, and were now generally Jacobins. In the struggle which was necessary, many guilty persons fell without the forms of trial, and with them some innocent. These I deplore as much as any body, & shall deplore some of them to the day of my death. But I deplore them as I should have done had they fallen in battle. It was necessary to use the arm of the people, a machine not quite so blind as balls and bombs, but blind to a certain degree. A few of their cordial friends met at their hands the fate of enemies. But time and truth will rescue & embalm their memories, while their posterity will be enjoying that very liberty for which they would never have hesitated to offer up their lives. The liberty of the whole earth was depending on the issue of the contest, and was ever such a prize won with so little innocent blood? My own affections have been deeply wounded by some of the martyrs to this cause, but rather than it should have failed, I would have seen half the earth desolated. Were there but an Adam & an Eve left in every country, & left free, it would be better than as it now is. I have expressed to you my sentiments, because they are really those of 99. in an hundred of our citizens. The universal feasts, and rejoicings which have lately been had on account of the successes of the French shewed the genuine effusions of their hearts. You have been wounded by the sufferings of your friends, and have by this circumstance been hurried into a temper of mind which would be extremely disrelished if known to your countrymen. The *reserve of the President of the United States* had never permitted me to discover the light in which he viewed it, and as I was more anxious that you should satisfy him than me, I had still avoided explanations with you on the subject. But your 113. induced him to break silence and to notice the extreme acrimony of your expressions. He added that he had been informed the sentiments you expressed *in your conversations* were equally offensive to our allies, & that you should consider yourself as the representative of your country and that what you say might be imputed to your constituents. He desired me therefore to write to you on this subject. He added that he considered *France as the sheet anchor of this country and its friendship as a first object.* There are in the U.S. some characters of opposite principles; some of them are high in office, others possessing great wealth, and all of them hostile to France and fondly looking to England as the staff of their hope. These I named to you on a former occasion. Their prospects have certainly not brightened. Excepting them, this country is entirely republican, friends to the constitution, anxious to preserve it and to have it administered according to it's own republican principles. The little party above mentioned have espoused it only as a stepping stone to monarchy, and have endeavored to approximate it to that in it's administration in order to render it's final transition more easy. The successes of republicanism in France have given the coup de grace to their prospects, and I hope to their projects.—I have developed to you faithfully the sentiments of your country, that you may govern yourself accordingly. I know your republicanism to be pure, and that it is no decay of that which has embittered you against it's votaries in France, but too great a sensibility at the partial evil which it's object has been accomplished there. I have written to you in the stile to which I have been always accustomed with you, and which perhaps it is time I should lay aside. But while old men are sensible enough of their own advance in years, they do not sufficiently recollect it in those whom they have seen young. In writing too the last private letter which will probably be written under present circumstances, in contemplating that your correspondence will shortly be turned over to I know not whom, but certainly to some one not in the habit of considering your interests with the same fostering anxieties I do, I have presented things without reserve, satisfied you will ascribe what I have said to it's true motive, use it for your own best interest, and in that fulfil completely what I had in view.

[. . .] I am with unalterable affection & wishes for your prosperity, my dear Sir, your sincere friend and servant.

To James Madison

JUNE 9, 1793.

I have to acknolege the receipt of your two favors of May 27 & 29, since the date of my last which was of the 2 inst. In that of the 27th you say 'you must not make your final exit from public life till it will be marked with justifying circumstances which all good citizens will respect, & to which your friends can appeal.'—To my fellow-citizens the debt of service has been fully & faithfully paid. I acknolege that such a debt exists, that a tour of duty, in whatever line he can be most useful to his country, is due from every individual.

It is not easy perhaps to say of what length exactly this tour should be, but we may safely say of what length it should not be. Not of our whole life, for instance, for that would be to be born a slave—not even of a very large portion of it. I have now been in the public service four & twenty years; one half of which has been spent in total occupation with their affairs, & absence from my own. I have served my tour then. No positive engagement, by word or deed, binds me to their further service. No commitment of their interests in any enterprise by me requires that I should see them through it.—I am pledged by no act which gives any tribunal a call upon me before I withdraw. Even my enemies do not pretend this. I stand clear then of public right on all points.—My friends I have not committed. No circumstances have attended my passage from office to office, which could lead them, & others through them, into deception as to the time I might remain; & particularly they & all have known with what reluctance I engaged & have continued in the present one, & of my uniform determination to retire from it at an early day.—If the public then has no claim on me, & my friends nothing to justify; the decision will rest on my own feelings alone. There has been a time when these were very different from what they are now: when perhaps the esteem of the world was of higher value in my eye than everything in it. But age, experience & reflection, preserving to that only it's due value, have set a higher on tranquility. The motion of my blood no longer keeps time with the tumult of the world. It leads me to seek for happiness in the lap and love of my family, in the society of my neighbors & my books, in the wholesome occupations of my farm & my affairs, in an interest or affection in every bud that opens, in every breath that blows around me, in an entire freedom of rest or motion, of thought or incogitancy, owing account to myself alone of my hours & actions. What must be the principle of that calculation which should balance against these the circumstances of my present existence! worn down with labours from morning to night, & day to day; knowing them as fruitless to others as they are vexatious to myself, committed singly in desperate & eternal contest against a host who are systematically undermining the public liberty & prosperity, even the rare hours of relaxation sacrificed to the society of persons in the same intentions, of whose hatred I am conscious even in those moments of conviviality when the heart wishes most to open itself to the effusions of friendship & confidence, cut off from my family & friends, my affairs abandoned to chaos & derangement, in short giving everything I love, in exchange for everything I hate, and all this without a single gratification in possession or prospect, in present enjoyment or future wish.—Indeed my dear friend, duty being out of the question, inclination cuts off all argument, & so never let there be more between you & me, on this subject.

I inclose you some papers which have passed on the subject of a new loan. You will see by them that the paper-Coryphæus is either undaunted, or desperate. I believe that the statement inclosed has secured a decision against his proposition.—I dined yesterday in a company where Morris & Bingham were, & happened to sit between them. In the course of a conversation after dinner Morris made one of his warm declarations that after the expiration of his present Senatorial term nothing on earth should ever engage him to serve again in any public capacity. He did this with such solemnity as renders it impossible he should not be in earnest.—The President is not well. Little lingering fevers have been hanging about him for a week or ten days, and have affected his looks most remarkably. He is also extremely affected by the attacks made & kept up on him in the public papers. I think he feels those things more than any person I ever yet met with. I am sincerely sorry to see them. I remember an observation of yours, made when I first went to New York, that the satellites & sycophants which surrounded him had wound up the ceremonials of the government to a pitch of stateliness which nothing but his personal character could have supported, & which no character after him could ever maintain. It appears now that even his will be insufficient to justify them in the appeal of the times to common sense as the arbiter of everything. Naked he would have been sanctimoniously reverenced, but inveloped in the rags of royalty, they can hardly be torn off without laceration. It is the more unfortunate that this attack is planted on popular ground, on the love of the people to France & it's cause, which is universal.—Genet mentions freely enough in conversation that France does not wish to involve us in the war by our guarantee. The information from St. Domingo & Martinique is that those two islands are disposed & able to resist any attack which Great Britain can make on them by land. A blockade would be dangerous, could it be maintained in that climate for any length of time. I delivered to Genet your letter to Roland. As the latter is out of office, he will direct it to the Minister of the Interior. I found every syllable of it strictly proper. Your ploughs shall be duly attended to. Have you ever taken notice of Tull's horse-houghing plough? I am persuaded that that, where you wish your work to be very exact, & our great plough where a less degree will suffice, leave us nothing to wish for from other countries as to ploughs, under our circumstances.—I have not yet received my threshing machine. I fear the late long & heavy rains must have extended to us, & affected our wheat. Adieu. Yours affectionately.

To James Madison, with Enclosure to John Adams

JAN. 1. 97.

Yours of Dec. 19. has come safely. The event of the election has never been a matter of doubt in my mind. I knew that the Eastern states were disciplined in the schools of their town meetings to sacrifice differences of opinion to the great object of operating in phalanx, & that the more free & moral agency practiced in the other states would always make up the supplement of their weight. Indeed the vote comes much nearer an equality than I had expected. I know the difficulty of obtaining belief to one's declarations of a disinclination to honors, & that it is greatest with those who still remain in the world. But no arguments were wanting to reconcile me to a relinquishment of the first office or acquiescence under the second. As to the first it was impossible that a more solid unwillingness settled on full calculation, could have existed in any man's mind, short of the degree of absolute refusal. The only view on which I would have gone into it for awhile was to put our vessel on her republican tack before she should be thrown too much to leeward of her true principles. As to the second, it is the only office in the world about which I am unable to decide in my own mind whether I had rather have it or not have it. Pride does not enter into the estimate; for I think with the Romans that the general of today should be a soldier tomorrow if necessary. I can particularly have no feelings which would revolt at a secondary position to mr. Adams. I am his junior in life, was his junior in Congress, his junior in the diplomatic line, his junior lately in the civil government. Before the receipt of your letter I had written the enclosed one to him. I had intended it some time, but had deferred it from time to time under the discouragement of a despair of making him believe I could be sincere in it. The papers by the last post not rendering it necessary to change anything in the letter I enclose it open for your perusal, not only that you may possess the actual state of dispositions between us, but that if anything should render the delivery of it ineligible in your opinion, you may return it to me. If mr. Adams can be induced to administer the government on it's true principles, & to relinquish his bias to an English constitution, it is to be considered whether it would not be on the whole for the public good to come to a good understanding with him as to his future elections. He is perhaps the only sure barrier against Hamilton's getting in. [. . .]

[Enclosure to John Adams]

MONTICELLO, DEC. 28, 1796.

Dear Sir,—The public & the papers have been much occupied lately in placing us in a point of opposition to each other. I trust with confidence that less of it has been felt by ourselves personally. In the retired canton where I am, I learn little of what is passing: pamphlets I see never: papers but a few; and the fewer the happier. Our latest intelligence from Philadelphia at present is of the 16th inst. but tho' at that date your election to the first magistracy seems not to have been known as a fact, yet with me it has never been doubted. I knew it impossible you should lose a vote north of the Delaware, and even if that of Pennsylvania should be against you in the mass, yet that you would get enough South of that to place your succession out of danger. I have never one single moment expected a different issue; & tho' I know I shall not be believed, yet it is not the less true that I have never wished it. My neighbors as my compurgators could aver that fact, because they see my occupations & my attachment to them. Indeed it is impossible that you may be cheated of your succession by a trick worthy the subtlety of your arch-friend of New York who has been able to make of your real friends tools to defeat their and your just wishes. Most probably he will be disappointed as to you; and my inclinations place me out of his reach. I leave to others the sublime delights of riding in the storm, better pleased with sound sleep and a warm birth below, with the society of neighbors, friends & fellow-laborers of the earth, than of spies & sycophants. No one then will congratulate you with purer disinterestedness than myself. The share indeed which I may have had in the late vote, I shall still value highly, as an evidence of the share I have in the esteem of my fellow citizens. But while in this point of view, a few votes less would be little sensible, the difference in the effect of a few more would be very sensible and oppressive to me. I have no ambition to govern men. It is a painful and thankless office. Since the day too on which you signed the treaty of Paris our horizon was never so overcast. I devoutly wish you may be able to shun for us this war by which our agriculture, commerce & credit will be destroyed. If you are, the glory will be all your own; and that your administration may be filled with glory, and happiness to yourself and advantage to us is the sincere wish of one who tho' in the course of our own voyage thro' life, various little incidents have happened or been contrived to separate us, retains still for you the solid esteem of the moments when we were working for our independence, and sentiments of respect & affectionate attachment.

To John Taylor

PHILADELPHIA, JUNE 4, 1798.

[. . .] In every free and deliberating society, there must, from the nature of man, be opposite parties, and violent dissensions and discords; and one of these, for the most part, must prevail over the other for a longer or shorter time. Perhaps this party division is necessary to induce each to watch and delate to the people the proceedings of the other. But if on a temporary superiority of the one party, the other is to resort to a scission of the Union, no federal government can ever exist. If to rid ourselves of the present rule of Massachusetts and Connecticut, we break the Union, will the evil stop there? Suppose the New England States alone cut off, will our nature be changed? Are we not men still to the south of that, and with all the passions of men? Immediately, we shall see a Pennsylvania and a Virginia party arise in the residuary confederacy, and the public mind will be distracted with the same party spirit. What a game too will the one party have in their hands, by eternally threatening the other that unless they do so and so, they will join their northern neighbors. If we reduce our Union to Virginia and North Carolina, immediately the conflict will be established between the representatives of these two States, and they will end by breaking into their simple units. Seeing, therefore, that an association of men who will not quarrel with one another is a thing which never yet existed, from the greatest confederacy of nations down to a town meeting or a vestry; seeing that we must have somebody to quarrel with, I had rather keep our New England associates for that purpose, than to see our bickerings transferred to others. They are circumscribed within such narrow limits, and their population so full, that their numbers will ever be the minority, and they are marked, like the Jews, with such a peculiarity of character, as to constitute, from that circumstance, the natural division of our parties. A little patience, and we shall see the reign of witches pass over, their spells dissolved, and the people recovering their true sight, restore their government to it's true principles. It is true, that in the meantime, we are suffering deeply in spirit, and incurring the horrors of a war, and long oppressions of enormous public debt. But who can say what would be the evils of a scission, and when and where they would end? Better keep together as we are, hawl off from Europe as soon as we can, and from all attachments to any portions of it. And if we feel their power just sufficiently to hoop us together, it will be the happiest situation in which we can exist. If the game runs sometimes against us at home, we must have patience till luck turns, and then we shall have an opportunity of winning back the *principles* we have lost, for this is a game where principles are the stake. Better luck, therefore, to us all; and health, happiness and friendly salutations to yourself. Adieu.

P.S. It is hardly necessary to caution you to let nothing of mine get before the public; a single sentence got hold of by the Porcupines, will suffice to abuse and persecute me in their papers for months.

Draft of the Kentucky Resolutions

OCTOBER 1798

1. *Resolved,* That the several States composing the United States of America, are not united on the principle of unlimited submission to their General Government; but that, by a compact under the style and title of a Constitution for the United States, and of amendments thereto, they constituted a General Government for special purposes,—delegated to that government certain definite powers, reserving, each State to itself, the residuary mass of right to their own self-government; and that whensoever the General Government assumes undelegated powers, its acts are unauthoritative, void, and of no force; [. . .] as in all other cases of compact among powers having no common judge, each party has an equal right to judge for itself, as well of infractions as of the mode and measure of redress. [. . .]

8th. *Resolved,* [. . .] This commonwealth is determined, as it doubts not its co-States are, to submit to undelegated, and consequently unlimited powers in no man, or body of men on earth: that in cases of an abuse of the delegated powers, the members of the General Government, being chosen by the people, a change by the people would be the constitutional remedy; but, where powers are assumed which have not been delegated, a nullification of the act is the rightful remedy: that every State has a natural right in cases not within the compact, (casus non fœderis,) to nullify of their own authority all assumptions of power by others within their limits: that without this right, they would be under the dominion, absolute and unlimited, of whosoever might exercise this right of judgment for them: [. . .] the barrier of the Constitution thus swept away from us all, no rampart now remains against the passions and the powers of a majority in Congress to protect from a like exportation, or other more grievous punishment, the minority of the same body: [. . .] the friendless alien has indeed been selected as the safest subject of a first experiment; but the citizen will soon follow, or rather, has already followed, for already has a sedition act marked him as its prey: that these and successive acts of the same character, unless arrested at the threshold, necessarily drive these States into revolution and blood, and will furnish new calumnies against republican government, and new pretexts for those who wish it to be believed that man cannot be governed but by a rod of iron. [. . .]

To Elbridge Gerry

PHILADELPHIA, JAN 26, 1799.

[. . .] I shall make to you a profession of my political faith; in confidence that you will consider every future imputation on me of a contrary complexion, as bearing on its front the mark of falsehood & calumny.

I do then, with sincere zeal, wish an inviolable preservation of our present federal constitution, according to the true sense in which it was adopted by the States, that in which it was advocated by it's friends, & not that which it's enemies apprehended, who therefore became it's enemies; and I am opposed to the monarchising it's features by the forms of it's administration, with a view to conciliate a first transition to a President & Senate for life, & from that to a hereditary tenure of these offices, & thus to worm out the elective principle. I am for preserving to the States the powers not yielded by them to the Union, & to the legislature of the Union it's constitutional share in the division of powers; and I am not for transferring all the powers of the States to the general government, & all those of that government to the Executive branch. I am for a government rigorously frugal & simple, applying all the possible savings of the public revenue to the discharge of the national debt; and not for a multiplication of officers & salaries merely to make partisans, & for increasing, by every device, the public debt, on the principle of it's being a public blessing. I am for relying, for internal defence, on our militia solely, till actual invasion, and for such a naval force only as may protect our coasts and harbors from such depredations as we have experienced; and not for a standing army in time of peace, which may overawe the public sentiment; nor for a navy, which, by it's own expenses and the eternal wars in which it will implicate us, will grind us with public burthens, & sink us under them. I am for free commerce with all nations; political connection with none; & little or no diplomatic establishment. And I am not for linking ourselves by new treaties with the quarrels of Europe; entering that field of slaughter to preserve their balance, or joining in the confederacy of kings to war against the principles of liberty. I am for freedom of religion, & against all maneuvres to bring about a legal ascendancy of one sect over another: for freedom of the press, & against all violations of the constitution to silence by force & not by reason the complaints or criticisms, just or unjust, of our citizens against the conduct of their agents. And I am for encouraging the progress of science in all it's branches; and not for raising a hue and cry against the sacred name of philosophy; for awing the human mind by stories of raw-head & bloody bones to a distrust of its own vision, & to repose implicitly on that of others; to go backwards instead of forwards to look for improvement; to believe that government, religion, morality, & every other science were in the highest perfection in ages of the darkest ignorance, and that nothing can ever be devised more perfect than what was established by our forefathers. To these I will add, that I was a sincere well-wisher to the success of the French revolution, and still wish it may end in the establishment of a free & well-ordered republic; but I have not been insensible under the atrocious depredations they have committed on our commerce. The first object of my heart is my own country. In that is embarked my family, my fortune, & my own existence. I have not one farthing of interest, nor one fibre of attachment out of it, nor a single motive of preference of any one nation to another, but in proportion as they are more or less friendly to us. But though deeply feeling the injuries of France, I did not think war the surest means of redressing them. I did believe, that a mission sincerely disposed to preserve peace, would obtain for us a peaceable & honorable settlement & retribution; and I appeal to you to say, whether this might not have been obtained, if either of your colleagues had been of the same sentiment with yourself.

These, my friend, are my principles; they are unquestionably the principles of the great body of our fellow citizens, and I know there is not one of them which is not yours also. [. . .]

First Inaugural Address

MARCH 4, 1801

Friends and Fellow-Citizens,

Called upon to undertake the duties of the first executive office of our country, I avail myself of the presence of that portion of my fellow-citizens which is here assembled to express my grateful thanks for the favor with which they have been pleased to look toward me, to declare a sincere consciousness that the task is above my talents, and that I approach it with those anxious and awful presentiments which the greatness of the charge and the weakness of my powers so justly inspire. A rising nation, spread over a wide and fruitful land, traversing all the seas with the rich productions of their industry, engaged in commerce with nations who feel power and forget right, advancing rapidly to destinies beyond the reach of mortal eye—when I contemplate these transcendent objects, and see the honor, the happiness, and the hopes of this beloved country committed to the issue and the auspices of this day, I shrink from the contemplation, and humble myself before the magnitude of the undertaking. Utterly, indeed, should I despair did not the presence of many whom I here see remind me that in the other high authorities provided by our Constitution I shall find resources of wisdom, of virtue, and of zeal on which to rely under all difficulties. To you, then, gentlemen, who are charged with the sovereign functions of legislation, and to those associated with you, I look with encouragement for that guidance and support which may enable us to steer with safety the vessel in which we are all embarked amidst the conflicting elements of a troubled world.

During the contest of opinion through which we have passed the animation of discussions and of exertions has sometimes worn an aspect which might impose on strangers unused to think freely and to speak and to write what they think; but this being now decided by the voice of the nation, announced according to the rules of the Constitution, all will, of course, arrange themselves under the will of the law, and unite in common efforts for the common good. All, too, will bear in mind this sacred principle, that though the will of the majority is in all cases to prevail, that will to be rightful must be reasonable; that the minority possess their equal rights, which equal law must protect, and to violate would be oppression. Let us, then, fellow-citizens, unite with one heart and one mind. Let us restore to social intercourse that harmony and affection without which liberty and even life itself are but dreary things. And let us reflect that, having banished from our land that religious intolerance under which mankind so long bled and suffered, we have yet gained little if we countenance a political intolerance as despotic, as wicked, and capable of as bitter and bloody persecutions. During the throes and convulsions of the ancient world, during the agonizing spasms of infuriated man, seeking through blood and slaughter his long-lost liberty, it was not wonderful that the agitation of the billows should reach even this distant and peaceful shore; that this should be more felt and feared by some and less by others, and should divide opinions as to measures of safety. But every difference of opinion is not a difference of principle. We have called by different names brethren of the same principle. We are all Republicans, we are all Federalists. If there be any among us who would wish to dissolve this Union or to change its republican form, let them stand undisturbed as monuments of the safety with which error of opinion may be tolerated where reason is left free to combat it. I know, indeed, that some honest men fear that a republican government can not be strong, that this Government is not strong enough; but would the honest patriot, in the full tide of successful experiment, abandon a government which has so far kept us free and firm on the theoretic and visionary fear that this Government, the world's best hope, may by possibility want energy to preserve itself? I trust not. I believe this, on the contrary, the strongest Government on earth. I believe it the only one where every man, at the call of the law, would fly to the standard of the law, and would meet invasions of the public order as his own personal concern. Sometimes it is said that man can not be trusted with the government of himself. Can he, then, be trusted with the government of others? Or have we found angels in the forms of kings to govern him? Let history answer this question.

Let us, then, with courage and confidence pursue our own Federal and Republican principles, our attachment to union and representative government. Kindly separated by nature and a wide ocean from the exterminating havoc of one quarter of the globe; too high-minded to endure the degradations of the others; possessing a chosen country, with room enough for our descendants to the thousandth and thousandth generation; entertaining a due sense of our equal right to the use of our own faculties, to the acquisitions of our own industry, to honor and confidence from our fellow-citizens, resulting not from birth, but from our actions and their sense of them; enlightened by a benign religion, professed, indeed, and practiced in various forms, yet all of them inculcating honesty, truth, temperance, gratitude, and the love of man; acknowledging and adoring an overruling Providence, which by all its dispensations proves that it delights in the happiness of man here and his greater happiness hereafter—with all these blessings, what more is necessary to make us a happy and a prosperous people? Still one thing more, fellow-citizens—a wise and frugal Government, which shall restrain men from injuring one another, shall leave them otherwise free to regulate their own pursuits of industry and improvement, and shall not take from the mouth of labor the bread it has earned. This is the sum of good government, and this is necessary to close the circle of our felicities.

About to enter, fellow-citizens, on the exercise of duties which comprehend everything dear and valuable to you, it is proper you should understand what I deem the essential principles of our Government, and consequently those which ought to shape its Administration. I will compress them within the narrowest compass they will bear, stating the general principle, but not all its limitations. Equal and exact justice to all men, of whatever state or persuasion, religious or political; peace, commerce, and honest friendship with all nations, entangling alliances with none; the support of the State governments in all their rights, as the most competent administrations for our domestic concerns and the surest bulwarks against antirepublican tendencies; the preservation of the General Government in its whole constitutional vigor, as the sheet anchor of our peace at home and safety abroad; a jealous care of the right of election by the people—a mild and safe corrective of abuses which are lopped by the sword of revolution where peaceable remedies are unprovided; absolute acquiescence in the decisions of the majority, the vital principle of republics, from which is no appeal but to force, the vital principle and immediate parent of despotism; a well-disciplined militia, our best reliance in peace and for the first moments of war till regulars may relieve them; the supremacy of the civil over the military authority; economy in the public expense, that labor may be lightly burthened; the honest payment of our debts and sacred preservation of the public faith; encouragement of agriculture, and of commerce as its handmaid; the diffusion of information and arraignment of all abuses at the bar of the public reason; freedom of religion; freedom of the press, and freedom of person under the protection of the habeas corpus, and trial by juries impartially selected. These principles form the bright constellation which has gone before us and guided our steps through an age of revolution and reformation. The wisdom of our sages and blood of our heroes have been devoted to their attainment. They should be the creed of our political faith, the text of civic instruction, the touchstone by which to try the services of those we trust; and should we wander from them in moments of error or of alarm, let us hasten to retrace our steps and to regain the road which alone leads to peace, liberty, and safety.

I repair, then, fellow-citizens, to the post you have assigned me. With experience enough in subordinate offices to have seen the difficulties of this the greatest of all, I have learnt to expect that it will rarely fall to the lot of imperfect man to retire from this station with the reputation and the favor which bring him into it. Without pretensions to that high confidence you reposed in our first and greatest revolutionary character, whose preeminent services had entitled him to the first place in his country's love and destined for him the fairest page in the volume of faithful history, I ask so much confidence only as may give firmness and effect to the legal administration of your affairs. I shall often go wrong through defect of judgment. When right, I shall often be thought wrong by those whose positions will not command a view of the whole ground. I ask your indulgence for my own errors, which will never be intentional, and your support against the errors of others, who may condemn what they would not if seen in all its parts. The approbation implied by your suffrage is a great consolation to me for the past, and my future solicitude will be to retain the good opinion of those who have bestowed it in advance, to conciliate that of others by doing them all the good in my power, and to be instrumental to the happiness and freedom of all.

Relying, then, on the patronage of your good will, I advance with obedience to the work, ready to retire from it whenever you become sensible how much better choice it is in your power to make. And may that Infinite Power which rules the destinies of the universe lead our councils to what is best, and give them a favorable issue for your peace and prosperity.

To John Dickinson

WASHINGTON, MAR. 6, 1801.

Dear Sir,—No pleasure can exceed that which I received from reading your letter of the 21st ult. It was like the joy we expect in the mansions of the blessed, when received with the embraces of our fathers, we shall be welcomed with their blessing as having done our part not unworthily of them. The storm through which we have passed, has been tremendous indeed. The tough sides of our Argosie have been thoroughly tried. Her strength has stood the waves into which she was steered, with a view to sink her. We shall put her on her republican tack, & she will now show by the beauty of her motion the skill of her builders. Figure apart, our fellow citizens have been led hood-winked from their principles, by a most extraordinary combination of circumstances. But the band is removed, and they now see for themselves. I hope to see shortly a perfect consolidation, to effect which, nothing shall be spared on my part, short of the abandonment of the principles of our revolution. A just and solid republican government maintained here, will be a standing monument & example for the aim & imitation of the people of other countries; and I join with you in the hope and belief that they will see, from our example, that a free government is of all others the most energetic; that the inquiry which has been excited among the mass of mankind by our revolution & it's consequences, will ameliorate the condition of man over a great portion of the globe. What a satisfaction have we in the contemplation of the benevolent effects of our efforts, compared with those of the leaders on the other side, who have discountenanced all advances in science as dangerous innovations, have endeavored to render philosophy and republicanism terms of reproach, to persuade us that man cannot be governed but by the rod, &c. I shall have the happiness of living & dying in the contrary hope. Accept assurances of my constant & sincere respect and attachment, and my affectionate salutations.

To the U.S. Minister to France (Robert R. Livingston)

WASHINGTON, APR. 18, 1802.

Dear Sir— [. . .] The cession of Louisiana and the Floridas by Spain to France works most sorely on the U.S. On this subject the Secretary of State has written to you fully. Yet I cannot forbear recurring to it personally, so deep is the impression it makes in my mind. It compleatly reverses all the political relations of the U.S. and will form a new epoch in our political course. Of all nations of any consideration France is the one which hitherto has offered the fewest points on which we could have any conflict of right, and the most points of a communion of interests. From these causes we have ever looked to her as our *natural friend,* as one with which we never could have an occasion of difference. Her growth therefore we viewed as our own, her misfortunes ours. There is on the globe one single spot, the possessor of which is our natural and habitual enemy. It is New Orleans, through which the produce of three-eighths of our territory must pass to market, and from its fertility it will ere long yield more than half of our whole produce and contain more than half our inhabitants. France placing herself in that door assumes to us the attitude of defiance. Spain might have retained it quietly for years. Her pacific dispositions, her feeble state, would induce her to increase our facilities there, so that her possession of the place would be hardly felt by us, and it would not perhaps be very long before some circumstance might arise which might make the cession of it to us the price of something of more worth to her. Not so can it ever be in the hands of France. The impetuosity of her temper, the energy and restlessness of her character, placed in a point of eternal friction with us, and our character, which though quiet, and loving peace and the pursuit of wealth, is high-minded, despising wealth in competition with insult or injury, enterprising and energetic as any nation on earth, these circumstances render it impossible that France and the U.S. can continue long friends when they meet in so irritable a position. They as well as we must be blind if they do not see this; and we must be very improvident if we do not begin to make arrangements on that hypothesis. The day that France takes possession of N. Orleans fixes the sentence which is to restrain her forever within her low water mark. It seals the union of two nations who in conjunction can maintain exclusive possession of the ocean. From that moment we must marry ourselves to the British fleet and nation. We must turn all our attentions to a maritime force, for which our resources place us on very high grounds: and having formed and cemented together a power which may render reinforcement of her settlements here impossible to France, make the first cannon, which shall be fired in Europe the signal for tearing up any settlement she may have made, and for holding the two continents of America in sequestration for the common purposes of the united British and American nations. This is not a state of things we seek or desire. It is one which this measure, if adopted by France, forces on us, as necessarily as any other cause, by the laws of nature, brings on its necessary effect. It is not from a fear of France that we deprecate this measure proposed by her. For however greater her force is than ours compared in the abstract, it is nothing in comparison of ours when to be exerted on our soil. But it is from a sincere love of peace, and a firm persuasion that bound to France by the interests and the strong sympathies still existing in the minds of our citizens, and holding relative positions which ensure their continuance we are secure of a long course of peace. Whereas the change of friends, which will be rendered necessary if France changes that position, embarks us necessarily as a belligerent power in the first war of Europe. In that case France will have held possession of New Orleans during the interval of a peace, long or short, at the end of which it will be wrested from her. Will this short-lived possession have been an equivalent to her for the transfer of such a weight into the scale of her enemy? Will not the amalgamation of a young, thriving, nation continue to that enemy the health and force which are at present so evidently on the decline? And will a few years possession of N. Orleans add equally to the strength of France? She may say she needs Louisiana for the supply of her West Indies. She does not need it in time of peace. And in war she could not depend on them because they would be so easily intercepted. I should suppose that all these considerations might in some proper form be brought into view of the government of France. Tho' stated by us, it ought not to give offence; because we do not bring them forward as a menace, but as consequences not controulable by us, but inevitable from the course of things. We mention them not as things which we desire by any means, but as things we deprecate; and we beseech a friend to look forward and to prevent them for our common interests.

If France considers Louisiana however as indispensable for her views she might perhaps be willing to look about for arrangements which might reconcile it to our interests. If anything could do this it would be the ceding to us the island of New Orleans and the Floridas. This would certainly in a great degree remove the causes of jarring and irritation between us, and perhaps for such a length of time as might produce other means of making the measure permanently conciliatory to our interests and friendships. It would at any rate relieve us from the necessity of taking immediate measures for countervailing such an operation by arrangements in another quarter. Still we should consider N. Orleans and the Floridas as equivalent for the risk of a quarrel with France produced by her vicinage. I have no doubt you have urged these considerations on every proper occasion with the government where you are. They are such as must have effect if you can find the means of producing thorough reflection on them by that government. The idea here is that the troops sent to St. Domingo, were to proceed to Louisiana after finishing their work in that island. If this were the arrangement, it will give you time to return again and again to the charge, for the conquest of St. Domingo will not be a short work. It will take considerable time to wear down a great number of souldiers. Every eye in the U.S. is now fixed on this affair of Louisiana. Perhaps nothing since the revolutionary war has produced more uneasy sensations through the body of the nation. Notwithstanding temporary bickerings have taken place with France, she has still a strong hold on the affections of our citizens generally. I have thought it not amiss, by way of supplement to the letters of the Secretary of State to write you this private one to impress you with the importance we affix to this transaction. I pray you to cherish Dupont. He has the best dispositions for the continuance of friendship between the two nations, and perhaps you may be able to make a good use of him. Accept assurances of my affectionate esteem and high consideration.

To Dr. Benjamin Rush, with a "Syllabus"

WASHINGTON, APR. 21, 1803.

Dear Sir,—In some of the delightful conversations with you, in the evenings of 1798–99, and which served as an anodyne to the afflictions of the crisis through which our country was then laboring, the Christian religion was sometimes our topic; and I then promised you, that one day or other, I would give you my views of it. They are the result of a life of inquiry & reflection, and very different from that anti-Christian system imputed to me by those who know nothing of my opinions. To the corruptions of Christianity I am indeed opposed; but not to the genuine precepts of Jesus himself. I am a Christian, in the only sense he wished any one to be; sincerely attached to his doctrines, in preference to all others; ascribing to himself every *human* excellence; & believing he never claimed any other. At the short intervals since these conversations, when I could justifiably abstract my mind from public affairs, the subject has been under my contemplation. But the more I considered it, the more it expanded beyond the measure of either my time or information. In the moment of my late departure from Monticello, I received from Doctr Priestley, his little treatise of "Socrates & Jesus compared." This being a section of the general view I had taken of the field, it became a subject of reflection while on the road, and unoccupied otherwise. The result was, to arrange in my mind a syllabus, or outline of such an estimate of the comparative merits of Christianity, as I wished to see executed by some one of more leisure and information for the task, than myself. This I now send you, as the only discharge of my promise I can probably ever execute. And in confiding it to you, I know it will not be exposed to the malignant perversions of those who make every word from me a text for new misrepresentations & calumnies. I am moreover averse to the communication of my religious tenets to the public; because it would countenance the presumption of those who have endeavored to draw them before that tribunal, and to seduce public opinion to erect itself into that inquisition over the rights of conscience, which the laws have so justly proscribed. It behoves every man who values liberty of conscience for himself, to resist invasions of it in the case of others; or their case may, by change of circumstances, become his own. It behoves him, too, in his own case, to give no example of concession, betraying the common right of independent opinion, by answering questions of faith, which the laws have left between God & himself. Accept my affectionate salutations.

Syllabus of an Estimate of the Merit of the Doctrines of Jesus, Compared with Those of Others

APRIL, 1803.

In a comparative view of the Ethics of the enlightened nations of antiquity, of the Jews and of Jesus, no notice should be taken of the corruptions of reason among the ancients, to wit, the idolatry & superstition of the vulgar, nor of the corruptions of Christianity by the learned among its professors.

Let a just view be taken of the moral principles inculcated by the most esteemed of the sects of ancient philosophy, or of their individuals; particularly Pythagoras, Socrates, Epicurus, Cicero, Epictetus, Seneca, Antoninus.

I. Philosophers. 1. Their precepts related chiefly to ourselves, and the government of those passions which, unrestrained, would disturb our tranquillity of mind. In this branch of philosophy they were really great.

2. In developing our duties to others, they were short and defective. They embraced, indeed, the circles of kindred & friends, and inculcated patriotism, or the love of our country in the aggregate, as a primary obligation: toward our neighbors & countrymen they taught justice, but scarcely viewed them as within the circle of benevolence. Still less have they inculcated peace, charity & love to our fellow men, or embraced with benevolence the whole family of mankind.

II. Jews. 1. Their system was Deism; that is, the belief of one only God. But their ideas of him & of his attributes were degrading & injurious.

2. Their Ethics were not only imperfect, but often irreconcilable with the sound dictates of reason & morality, as they respect intercourse with those around us; & repulsive & anti-social, as respecting other nations. They needed reformation, therefore, in an eminent degree.

III. Jesus. In this state of things among the Jews, Jesus appeared. His parentage was obscure; his condition poor; his education null; his natural endowments great; his life correct and innocent: he was meek, benevolent, patient, firm, disinterested, & of the sublimest eloquence.

The disadvantages under which his doctrines appear are remarkable.

1. Like Socrates & Epictetus, he wrote nothing himself.

2. But he had not, like them, a Xenophon or an Arrian to write for him. On the contrary, all the learned of his country, entrenched in its power and riches, were opposed to him, lest his labors should undermine their advantages; and the committing to writing his life & doctrines fell on the most unlettered & ignorant men; who wrote, too, from memory, & not till long after the transactions had passed.

3. According to the ordinary fate of those who attempt to enlighten and reform mankind, he fell an early victim to the jealousy & combination of the altar and the throne, at about 33. years of age, his reason having not yet attained the *maximum* of its energy nor the course of his preaching, which was but of 3. years at most, presented occasions for developing a complete system of morals.

4. Hence the doctrines which he really delivered were defective as a whole, and fragments only of what he did deliver have come to us mutilated, misstated, & often unintelligible.

5. They have been still more disfigured by the corruptions of schismatising followers, who have found an interest in sophisticating & perverting the simple doctrines he taught by engrafting on them the mysticisms of a Grecian sophist, frittering them into subtleties, & obscuring them with jargon, until they have caused good men to reject the whole in disgust, & to view Jesus himself as an impostor.

Notwithstanding these disadvantages, a system of morals is presented to us, which, if filled up in the true style and spirit of the rich fragments he left us, would be the most perfect and sublime that has ever been taught by man.

The question of his being a member of the Godhead, or in direct communication with it, claimed for him by some of his followers, and denied by others, is foreign to the present view, which is merely an estimate of the intrinsic merit of his doctrines.

1. He corrected the Deism of the Jews, confirming them in their belief of one only God, and giving them juster notions of his attributes and government.

2. His moral doctrines, relating to kindred & friends, were more pure & perfect than those of the most correct of the philosophers, and greatly more so than those of the Jews; and they went far beyond both in inculcating universal philanthropy, not only to kindred and friends, to neighbors and countrymen, but to all mankind, gathering all into one family, under the bonds of love, charity, peace, common wants and common aids. A development of this head will evince the peculiar superiority of the system of Jesus over all others.

3. The precepts of philosophy, & of the Hebrew code, laid hold of actions only. He pushed his scrutinies into the heart of man; erected his tribunal in the region of his thoughts, and purified the waters at the fountain head.

4. He taught, emphatically, the doctrines of a future state, which was either doubted, or disbelieved by the Jews; and wielded it with efficacy, as an important incentive, supplementary to the other motives to moral conduct.

To John C. Breckinridge

MONTICELLO, AUGUST 12, 1803.

Dear Sir,—The enclosed letter, tho' directed to you, was intended to me also, and was left open with a request, that when perused, I would forward it to you. It gives me occasion to write a word to you on the subject of

Louisiana, which being a new one, an interchange of sentiments may produce correct ideas before we are to act on them.

Our information as to the country is very incomplete; we have taken measures to obtain it full as to the settled part, which I hope to receive in time for Congress. The boundaries, which I deem not admitting question, are the high lands on the western side of the Mississippi enclosing all it's waters, the Missouri of course, and terminating in the line drawn from the northwestern point of the Lake of the Woods to the nearest source of the Mississippi, as lately settled between Great Britain and the United States. We have some claims, to extend on the seacoast westwardly to the Rio Norte or Bravo, and better, to go eastwardly to the Rio Perdido, between Mobile and Pensacola, the ancient boundary of Louisiana. These claims will be a subject of negotiation with Spain, and if, as soon as she is at war, we push them strongly with one hand, holding out a price in the other, we shall certainly obtain the Floridas, and all in good time. In the meanwhile, without waiting for permission, we shall enter into the exercise of the natural right we have always insisted on with Spain, to wit, that of a nation holding the upper part of streams, having a right of innocent passage through them to the ocean. We shall prepare her to see us practise on this, and she will not oppose it by force.

Objections are raising to the eastward against the vast extent of our boundaries, and propositions are made to exchange Louisiana, or a part of it, for the Floridas. But, as I have said, we shall get the Floridas without, and I would not give one inch of the waters of the Mississippi to any nation, because I see in a light very important to our peace the exclusive right to its navigation, and the admission of no nation into it, but as into the Potomac or Delaware, with our consent and under our police. These federalists see in this acquisition the formation of a new confederacy, embracing all the waters of the Mississippi, on both sides of it, and a separation of it's eastern waters from us. These combinations depend on so many circumstances which we cannot foresee, that I place little reliance on them. We have seldom seen neighborhood produce affection among nations. The reverse is almost the universal truth. Besides, if it should become the great interest of those nations to separate from this, if their happiness should depend on it so strongly as to induce them to go through that convulsion, why should the Atlantic States dread it? But especially why should we, their present inhabitants, take side in such a question? When I view the Atlantic States, procuring for those on the eastern waters of the Mississippi friendly instead of hostile neighbors on it's western waters, I do not view it as an

Englishman would be procuring future blessings for the French nation, with whom he has no relations of blood or affection. The future inhabitants of the Atlantic and Mississippi States will be our sons. We leave them in distinct but bordering establishments. We think we see their happiness in their union, and we wish it. Events may prove it otherwise; and if they see their interest in separation, why should we take side with our Atlantic rather than our Mississippi descendants? It is the elder and the younger son differing. God bless them both, and keep them in union, if it be for their good, but separate them, if it be better. The inhabited part of Louisiana, from Point Coupée to the sea, will of course be immediately a territorial government, and soon a State. But above that, the best use we can make of the country for some time, will be to give establishments in it to the Indians on the east side of the Mississippi, in exchange for their present country, and open land offices in the last, and thus make this acquisition the means of filling up the eastern side, instead of drawing off it's population. When we shall be full on this side, we may lay off a range of States on the western bank from the head to the mouth, and so, range after range, advancing compactly as we multiply.

This treaty must of course be laid before both Houses, because both have important functions to exercise respecting it. They, I presume, will see their duty to their country in ratifying and paying for it, so as to secure a good which would otherwise probably be never again in their power. But I suppose they must then appeal to *the nation* for an additional article to the Constitution, approving and confirming an act which the nation had not previously authorized. The Constitution has made no provision for our holding foreign territory, still less for incorporating foreign nations into our Union. The executive in seizing the fugitive occurrence which so much advances the good of their country, have done an act beyond the Constitution. The Legislature in casting behind them metaphysical subtleties, and risking themselves like faithful servants, must ratify and pay for it, and throw themselves on their country for doing for them unauthorized, what we know they would have done for themselves had they been in a situation to do it. It is the case of a guardian, investing the money of his ward in purchasing an important adjacent territory; and saying to him when of age, I did this for your good; I pretend to no right to bind you: you may disavow me, and I must get out of the scrape as I can: I thought it my duty to risk myself for you. But we shall not be disavowed by the nation, and their act of indemnity will confirm and not weaken the Constitution, by more strongly marking out its lines.

We have nothing later from Europe than the public papers give. I hope yourself and all the western members will make a sacred point of being at the first day of the meeting of Congress; for *vestra res agitur.*

Accept my affectionate salutations and assurances of esteem and respect.

A Memorandum on Rules of Etiquette

[C. NOVEMBER 1803.]

I. In order to bring the members of society together in the first instance, the custom of the country has established that residents shall pay the first visit to strangers, and, among strangers, first comers to later comers, foreign and domestic; the character of stranger ceasing after the first visits. To this rule there is a single exception. Foreign ministers, from the necessity of making themselves known, pay the first visit to the ministers of the nation, which is returned.

II. When brought together in society, all are perfectly equal, whether foreign or domestic, titled or untitled, in or out of office.

All other observances are but exemplifications of these two principles.

I. 1st. The families of foreign ministers, arriving at the seat of government, receive the first visit from those of the national ministers, as from all other residents.

2d. Members of the Legislature and of the Judiciary, independent of their offices, have a right as strangers to receive the first visit.

II. 1st. No title being admitted here, those of foreigners give no precedence.

2d. Differences of grade among diplomatic members, gives no precedence.

3d. At public ceremonies, to which the government invites the presence of foreign ministers and their families, a convenient seat or station will be provided for them, with any other strangers invited and the families of the national ministers, each taking place as they arrive, and without any precedence.

4th. To maintain the principle of equality, or of pêle mêle, and prevent the growth of precedence out of courtesy, the members of the Executive will practice at their own houses, and recommend an adherence to the ancient usage of the country, of gentlemen in mass giving precedence to the ladies in mass, in passing from one apartment where they are assembled into another.

Second Inaugural Address

MARCH 4, 1805.

Proceeding, fellow citizens, to that qualification which the constitution requires, before my entrance on the charge again conferred upon me, it is my duty to express the deep sense I entertain of this new proof of confidence from my fellow citizens at large, and the zeal with which it inspires me, so to conduct myself as may best satisfy their just expectations.

On taking this station on a former occasion, I declared the principles on which I believed it my duty to administer the affairs of our commonwealth. My conscience tells me that I have, on every occasion, acted up to that declaration, according to its obvious import, and to the understanding of every candid mind.

In the transaction of your foreign affairs, we have endeavored to cultivate the friendship of all nations, and especially of those with which we have the most important relations. We have done them justice on all occasions, favored where favor was lawful, and cherished mutual interests and intercourse on fair and equal terms. We are firmly convinced, and we act on that conviction, that with nations, as with individuals, our interests soundly calculated, will ever be found inseparable from our moral duties; and history bears witness to the fact, that a just nation is taken on its word, when recourse is had to armaments and wars to bridle others.

At home, fellow citizens, you best know whether we have done well or ill. The suppression of unnecessary offices, of useless establishments and expenses, enabled us to discontinue our internal taxes. These covering our land with officers, and opening our doors to their intrusions, had already begun that process of domiciliary vexation which, once entered, is scarcely to be restrained from reaching successively every article of produce and property. If among these taxes some minor ones fell which had not been inconvenient, it was because their amount would not have paid the officers who collected them, and because, if they had any merit, the state authorities might adopt them, instead of others less approved.

The remaining revenue on the consumption of foreign articles, is paid cheerfully by those who can afford to add foreign luxuries to domestic comforts, being collected on our seaboards and frontiers only, and incorporated with the transactions of our mercantile citizens, it may be the pleasure and pride of an American to ask, what farmer, what mechanic, what laborer, ever sees a tax-gatherer of the United States? These contributions enable us to support the current expenses of the government, to fulfil contracts with foreign nations, to extinguish the native right of soil within our limits, to extend those limits, and to apply such a surplus to our public debts, as places at a short day their final redemption, and that redemption once effected, the revenue thereby liberated may, by a just repartition among the states, and a corresponding amendment of the constitution, be applied, *in time of peace,* to rivers, canals, roads, arts, manufactures, education, and other great objects within each state. *In time of war,* if injustice, by ourselves or others, must sometimes produce war, increased as the same revenue will be increased by population and consumption, and aided by other resources reserved for that crisis, it may meet within the year all the expenses of the year, without encroaching on the rights of future generations, by burdening them with the debts of the past. War will then be but a suspension of useful works, and a return to a state of peace, a return to the progress of improvement.

I have said, fellow citizens, that the income reserved had enabled us to extend our limits; but that extension may possibly pay for itself before we are called on, and in the meantime, may keep down the accruing interest; in all events, it will repay the advances we have made. I know that the acquisition of Louisiana has been disapproved by some, from a candid apprehension that the enlargement of our territory would endanger its union. But who can limit the extent to which the federative principle may operate effectively? The larger our association, the less will it be shaken by local passions; and in any view, is it not better that the opposite bank of the Mississippi should be settled by our own brethren and children, than by strangers of another family? With which shall we be most likely to live in harmony and friendly intercourse?

In matters of religion, I have considered that its free exercise is placed by the constitution independent of the powers of the general government. I have therefore undertaken, on no occasion, to prescribe the religious exercises suited to it; but have left them, as the constitution found them, under the direction and discipline of state or church authorities acknowledged by the several religious societies.

The aboriginal inhabitants of these countries I have regarded with the commiseration their history inspires. Endowed with the faculties and the rights of men, breathing an ardent love of liberty and independence, and occupying a country which left them no desire but to be undisturbed, the stream of overflowing population from other regions directed itself on these shores; without power to divert, or habits to contend against, they have been overwhelmed by the current, or driven before it; now reduced within limits too narrow for the hunter's state, humanity enjoins us to teach them agriculture and the domestic arts; to encourage them to that industry which alone can enable them to maintain their place in existence, and to prepare them in time for that state of society, which to bodily comforts adds the improvement of the mind and morals. We have therefore liberally furnished them with the implements of husbandry and household use; we have placed among them instructors in the arts of first necessity; and they are covered with the ægis of the law against aggressors from among ourselves.

But the endeavors to enlighten them on the fate which awaits their present course of life, to induce them to exercise their reason, follow its dictates, and change their pursuits with the change of circumstances, have powerful obstacles to encounter; they are combated by the habits of their bodies, prejudice of their minds, ignorance, pride, and the influence of interested and crafty individuals among them, who feel themselves something in the present order of things, and fear to become nothing in any other. These persons inculcate a sanctimonious reverence for the customs of their ancestors; that whatsoever they did, must be done through all time; that reason is a false guide, and to advance under its counsel, in their physical, moral, or political condition, is perilous innovation; that their duty is to remain as their Creator made them, ignorance being safety, and knowledge full of danger; in short, my friends, among them is seen the action and counteraction of good sense and bigotry; they, too, have their anti-philosophers, who find an interest in keeping things in their present state, who dread reformation, and exert all their faculties to maintain the ascendency of habit over the duty of improving our reason, and obeying its mandates.

In giving these outlines, I do not mean, fellow citizens, to arrogate to myself the merit of the measures; that is due, in the first place, to the reflecting character of our citizens at large, who, by the weight of public opinion, influence and strengthen the public measures; it is due to the sound discretion with which they select from among themselves those to whom they confide the legislative duties; it is due to the zeal and wisdom of the characters thus selected, who lay the foundations of public happiness in wholesome laws, the execution of which alone remains for others; and it is due to the able and faithful auxiliaries, whose patriotism has associated with me in the executive functions.

During this course of administration, and in order to disturb it, the artillery of the press has been levelled against us, charged with whatsoever its licentiousness could devise or dare. These abuses of an institution so important to freedom and science, are deeply to be regretted, inasmuch as they tend to lessen its usefulness, and to sap its safety; they might, indeed, have been corrected by the wholesome punishments reserved and provided by the laws of the several States against falsehood and defamation; but public duties more urgent press on the time of public servants, and the offenders have therefore been left to find their punishment in the public indignation.

Nor was it uninteresting to the world, that an experiment should be fairly and fully made, whether freedom of discussion, unaided by power, is not sufficient for the propagation and protection of truth—whether a government, conducting itself in the true spirit of its constitution, with zeal and purity, and doing no act which it would be unwilling the whole world should witness, can be written down by falsehood and defamation. The experiment has been tried; you have witnessed the scene; our fellow citizens have looked on, cool and collected; they saw the latent source from which these outrages proceeded; they gathered around their public functionaries, and when the constitution called them to the decision by suffrage, they pronounced their verdict, honorable to those who had served them, and consolatory to the friend of man, who believes he may be intrusted with his own affairs.

No inference is here intended, that the laws, provided by the State against false and defamatory publications, should not be enforced; he who has time, renders a service to public morals and public tranquillity, in reforming these abuses by the salutary coercions of the law; but the experiment is noted, to prove that, since truth and reason have maintained their ground against false opinions in league with false facts, the press, confined to truth, needs no other legal restraint; the public judgment will correct false reasonings and opinions, on a full hearing of all parties; and no other definite line can be drawn between the inestimable liberty of the press and its demoralizing licentiousness. If there be still improprieties which this rule would not restrain, its supplement must be sought in the censorship of public opinion.

Contemplating the union of sentiment now manifested so generally, as auguring harmony and happiness to our future course, I offer to our country sincere congratulations. With those, too, not yet rallied to the same point, the disposition to do so is gaining strength; facts are piercing through the veil drawn over them; and our doubting brethren will at length see, that the mass of their fellow citizens, with whom they cannot yet resolve to act, as to principles and measures, think as they think, and desire what they desire; that our wish, as well as theirs, is, that the public efforts may be directed honestly to the public good, that peace be cultivated, civil and religious liberty unassailed, law and order preserved; equality of rights maintained, and that state of property, equal or unequal, which results to every man from his own industry, or that of his fathers. When satisfied of these views, it is not in human nature that they should not approve and support them; in the meantime, let us cherish them with patient affection; let us do them justice, and more than justice, in all competitions of interest; and we need not doubt that truth, reason, and their own interests, will at length prevail, will gather them into the fold of their country, and will complete their entire union of opinion, which gives to a nation the blessing of harmony, and the benefit of all its strength.

I shall now enter on the duties to which my fellow citizens have again called me, and shall proceed in the spirit of those principles which they have approved. I fear not that any motives of interest may lead me astray; I am sensible of no passion which could seduce me knowingly from the path of justice; but the weakness of human nature, and the limits of my own understanding, will produce errors of judgment sometimes injurious to your interests. I shall need, therefore, all the indulgence I have heretofore experienced—the want of it will certainly not lessen with increasing years. I shall need, too, the favor of that Being in whose hands we are, who led our forefathers, as Israel of old, from their native land, and planted them in a country flowing with all the necessaries and comforts of life; who has covered our infancy with his providence, and our riper years with his wisdom and power; and to whose goodness I ask you to join with me in supplications, that he will so enlighten the minds of your servants, guide their councils, and prosper their measures, that whatsoever they do, shall result in your good, and shall secure to you the peace, friendship, and approbation of all nations.

To Thomas Jefferson Randolph

WASHINGTON, NOV. 24TH, 1808.

My Dear Jefferson,—I have just received the enclosed letter under cover from Mr. Bankhead which I presume is from Anne, and will inform you she is well. Mr. Bankhead has consented to go & pursue his studies at Monticello, and live with us till his pursuits or circumstances may require a separate establishment. Your situation, thrown at such a distance from us, & alone, cannot but give us all great anxieties for you. As much has been secured for you, by your particular position and the acquaintance to which you have been recommended, as could be done towards shielding you from the dangers which surround you. But thrown on a wide world, among entire strangers, without a friend or guardian to advise, so young too and with so little experience of mankind, your dangers are great, & still your safety must rest on yourself. A determination never to do what is wrong, prudence and good humor, will go far towards securing to you the estimation of the world. When I recollect that at 14 years of age, the whole care & direction of myself was thrown on myself entirely, without a relation or friend qualified to advise or guide me, and recollect the various sorts of bad company with which I associated from time to time, I am astonished I did not turn off with some of them, & become as worthless to society as they were. I had the good fortune to become acquainted very early with some characters of very high standing, and to feel the incessant wish that I could ever become what they were. Under temptations & difficulties, I would ask myself what would Dr. Small, Mr. Wythe, Peyton Randolph do in this situation? What course in it will ensure me their approbation? I am certain that this mode of deciding on my conduct, tended more to it's correctness than any reasoning powers I possessed. Knowing the even & dignified line they pursued, I could never doubt for a moment which of two courses would be in character for them. Whereas, seeking the same object through a process of moral reasoning, & with the jaundiced eye of youth, I should often have erred. From the circumstances of my position, I was often thrown into the society of horseracers, cardplayers, foxhunters, scientific & professional men, and of dignified men; and many a time have I asked myself, in the enthusiastic moment of the death of a fox, the victory of a favorite horse, the issue of a question eloquently argued at the bar, or in the great council of the nation, well, which of these kinds of reputation should I prefer? That of a horse jockey? a foxhunter? an orator? or the honest advocate of my country's rights? Be assured, my dear Jefferson, that these little returns into ourselves, this self-catechising habit, is not trifling nor useless, but leads to the prudent selection & steady pursuits of what is right.

I have mentioned good humor as one of the preservatives of our peace & tranquillity. It is among the most effectual, and it's effect is so well imitated and aided, artificially, by politeness, that this also becomes an acquisition of first rate value. In truth, politeness is artificial good humor, it covers the natural want of it, & ends by rendering habitual a substitute nearly equivalent to the real virtue. It is the practice of sacrificing to those whom we meet in society, all the little conveniences & preferences which will gratify them, & deprive us of nothing worth a moment's consideration; it is the giving a pleasing & flattering turn to our expressions, which will conciliate others, and make them pleased with us as well as themselves. How cheap a price for the good will of another! When this is in return for a rude thing said by another, it brings him to his senses, it mortifies & corrects him in the most salutary way, and places him at the feet of your good nature, in the eyes of the company. But in stating prudential rules for our government in society, I must not omit the important one of never entering into dispute or argument with another. I never saw an instance of one of two disputants convincing the other by argument. I have seen many, on their getting warm, becoming rude, & shooting one another. Conviction is the effect of our own dispassionate reasoning, either in solitude, or weighing within ourselves, dispassionately, what we hear from others, standing uncommitted in argument ourselves. It was one of the rules which, above all others, made Doctr. Franklin the most amiable of men in society, "never to contradict anybody." If he was urged to announce an opinion, he did it rather by asking questions, as if for information, or by suggesting doubts. When I hear another express an opinion, which is not mine, I say to myself, He has a right to his opinion, as I to mine; why should I question it. His error does me no injury, and shall I become a Don Quixot to bring all men by force of argument, to one opinion? If a fact be misstated, it is probable he is gratified by a belief of it, & I have no right to deprive him of the gratification. If he wants information, he will ask it, & then I will give it in measured terms; but if he still believes his own story, & shows a desire to dispute the fact with me, I hear him & say nothing. It is his affair, not mine, if he prefers error. There are two classes of disputants most frequently to be met with among us. The first is of young students, just entered the threshold of science, with a first view of it's outlines, not yet filled up with the details & modifications which a further progress would bring to their knoledge. The other consists of the ill-tempered & rude men in society, who have taken up a passion for politics. (Good humor & politeness never introduce into mixed society a question on which they foresee there will be a difference of opinion.) From both of those classes of disputants, my dear Jefferson, keep aloof, as you would from the infected subjects of yellow fever or pestilence. Consider yourself, when with them, as among the patients of Bedlam, needing medical more than moral counsel. Be a listener only, keep within yourself, and endeavor to establish with yourself the habit of silence, especially on politics. In the fevered state of our country, no good can ever result from any attempt to set one of these fiery zealots to rights, either in fact or principle. They are determined as to the facts they will believe, and the opinions on which they will act. Get by them, therefore, as you would by an angry bull; it is not for a man of sense to dispute the road with such an animal. You will be more exposed than others to have these animals shaking their horns at you, because of the relation in which you stand with me & to hate me as a chief in the antagonist party, your presence will be to them what the vomit-grass is to the sick dog, a nostrum for producing ejaculation. Look upon them exactly with that eye, and pity them as objects to whom you can administer only occasional ease. My character is not within their power. It is in the hands of my fellow citizens at large, and will be consigned to honor or infamy by the verdict of the republican mass of our country, according to what themselves will have seen, not what their enemies and mine shall have said. Never, therefore, consider these puppies in politics as requiring any notice from you, & always show that you are not afraid to leave my character to the umpirage of public opinion. Look steadily to the pursuits which have carried you to Philadelphia, be very select in the society you attach yourself to; avoid taverns, drinkers, smokers, idlers, & dissipated persons generally; for it is with such that broils & contentions arise; and you will find your path more easy and tranquil. The limits of my paper warn me that it is time for me to close with my affectionate Adieux.

To John Tyler

MONTICELLO, MAY 26, 1810.

Dear Sir,—Your friendly letter of the 12th has been duly received. Although I have laid it down as a law to myself, never to embarrass the President with my solicitations, and have not till now broken through it, yet I have made a part of your letter the subject of one to him, and have done it with all my heart, and in the full belief that I serve him and the public in urging that appointment. We have long enough suffered under the base prostitution of law to party passions in one judge, and the imbecility of another. In the hands of one the law is nothing more than an ambiguous text, to be explained by his sophistry into any meaning which may subserve his personal malice. Nor can any milk-and-water associate maintain his own dependence, and by a firm pursuance of what the law really is, extend its protection to the citizens or the public. I believe you will do it, and where you cannot induce your colleague to do what is right, you will be firm enough to hinder him from doing what is wrong, and by opposing sense to sophistry, leave the juries free to follow their own judgment.

I have long lamented with you the depreciation of law science. The opinion seems to be that Blackstone is to us what the Alcoran is to the Mahometans, that everything which is necessary is in him, and what is not in him is not necessary. I still lend my counsel and books to such young students as will fix themselves in the neighborhood. Coke's institutes and reports are their first, and Blackstone their last book, after an intermediate course of two or three years. It is nothing more than an elegant digest of what they will then have acquired from the real fountains of the law. Now, men are born scholars, lawyers, doctors; in our day, this was confined to poets. You wish to see me again in the legislature, but this is impossible; my mind is now so dissolved in tranquillity, that it can never again encounter a contentious assembly; the habits of thinking and speaking off-hand, after a disuse of five and twenty years, have given place to the slower process of the pen. I have indeed two great measures at heart, without which no republic can maintain itself in strength. 1. That of general education, to enable every man to judge for himself what will secure or endanger his freedom. 2. To divide every county into hundreds, of such size that all the children of each will be within reach of a central school in it. But this division looks to many other fundamental provisions. Every hundred, besides a school, should have a justice of the peace, a constable and a captain of militia. These officers, or some others within the hundred, should be a corporation to manage all its concerns, to take care of its roads, its poor, and its police by patrols, etc., (as the select men of the eastern townships). Every hundred should elect one or two jurors to serve where requisite, and all other elections should be made in the hundreds separately, and the votes of all the hundreds be brought together. Our present Captaincies might be declared hundreds for the present, with a power to the courts to alter them occasionally. These little republics would be the main strength of the great one. We owe to them the vigor given to our revolution in its commencement in the Eastern States, and by them the Eastern States were enabled to repeal the embargo in opposition to the Middle, Southern and Western States, and their large and lubberly division into counties which can never be assembled. General orders are given out from a centre to the foreman of every hundred, as to the sergeants of an army, and the whole nation is thrown into energetic action, in the same direction in one instant and as one man, and becomes absolutely irresistible. Could I once see this I should consider it as the dawn of the salvation of the republic, and say with old Simeon, "nunc dimittis Domine." But our children will be as wise as we are, and will establish in the fullness of time those things not yet ripe for establishment. So be it, and to yourself health, happiness and long life.

To Dr. Benjamin Rush

MONTICELLO, JANUARY 16, 1811.

Dear Sir,—I had been considering for some days, whether it was not time by a letter, to bring myself to your recollection, when I received your welcome favor of the 2d instant. I had before heard of the heart-rending calamity you mention, and had sincerely sympathized with your afflictions. But I had not made it the subject of a letter, because I knew that condolences were but renewals of grief. Yet I thought, and still think, this is one of the cases wherein we should "not sorrow, even as others who have no hope." I have myself known so many cases of recovery from confirmed insanity, as to reckon it ever among the recoverable diseases. One of them was that of a near relative and namesake of mine, who, after many years of madness of the first degree, became entirely sane, and amused himself to a good old age in keeping school; was an excellent teacher and much valued citizen.

You ask if I have read Hartley? I have not. My present course of life admits less reading than I wish. From breakfast, or noon at latest, to dinner, I am mostly on horseback, attending to my farm or other concerns, which I find healthful to my body, mind and affairs; and the few hours I can pass in my cabinet, are devoured by correspondences; not those with my intimate friends, with whom I delight to interchange sentiments, but with others, who, writing to me on concerns of their own in which I have had an agency, or from motives of mere respect and approbation, are entitled to be answered with respect and a return of good will. My hope is that this obstacle to the delights of retirement, will wear away with the oblivion which follows that, and that I may at length be indulged in those studious pursuits, from which nothing but revolutionary duties would ever have called me.

I shall receive your proposed publication and read it with the pleasure which everything gives me from your pen. Although much of a sceptic in the practice of medicine, I read with pleasure its ingenious theories.

I receive with sensibility your observations on the discontinuance of friendly correspondence between Mr. Adams and myself, and the concern you take in its restoration. This discontinuance has not proceeded from me, nor from the want of sincere desire and of effort on my part, to renew our intercourse. You know the perfect coincidence of principle and of action, in the early part of the Revolution, which produced a high degree of mutual respect and esteem between Mr. Adams and myself. Certainly no man was ever truer than he was, in that day, to those principles of rational republicanism which, after the necessity of throwing off our monarchy, dictated all our efforts in the establishment of a new government. And although he swerved, afterwards, towards the principles of the English constitution, our friendship did not abate on that account. While he was Vice President, and I Secretary of State, I received a letter from President Washington, then at Mount Vernon, desiring me to call together the Heads of departments, and to invite Mr. Adams to join us (which, by-the-bye, was the only instance of that being done) in order to determine on some measure which required despatch; and he desired me to act on it, as decided, without again recurring to him. I invited them to dine with me, and after dinner, sitting at our wine, having settled our question, other conversation came on, in which a collision of opinion arose between Mr. Adams and Colonel Hamilton, on the merits of the British constitution, Mr. Adams giving it as his opinion, that, if some of its defects and abuses were corrected, it would be the most perfect constitution of government ever devised by man. Hamilton, on the contrary, asserted, that with its existing vices, it was the most perfect model of government that could be formed; and that the correction of its vices would render it an impracticable government. And this you may be assured was the real line of difference between the political principles of these two gentlemen. Another incident took place on the same occasion, which will further delineate Mr. Hamilton's political principles. The room being hung around with a collection of the portraits of remarkable men, among them were those of Bacon, Newton and Locke, Hamilton asked me who they were. I told him they were my trinity of the three greatest men the world had ever produced, naming them. He paused for some time: "the greatest man," said he, "that ever lived, was Julius Cæsar." Mr. Adams was honest as a politician, as well as a man; Hamilton honest as a man, but, as a politician, believing in the necessity of either force or corruption to govern men.

You remember the machinery which the federalists played off, about that time, to beat down the friends to the real principles of our constitution, to silence by terror every expression in their favor, to bring us into war with France and alliance with England, and finally to homologize our constitution with that of England. Mr. Adams, you know, was overwhelmed with feverish addresses, dictated by the fear, and often by the pen, of the *bloody buoy*, and was seduced by them into some open indications of his new principles of government, and in fact, was so elated as to mix with his kindness a little superciliousness towards me. Even Mrs. Adams, with all her good sense and prudence, was sensibly flushed. And you recollect the short suspension of our intercourse, and the circumstance which gave rise to it, which you were so good as to bring to an early explanation, and have set to rights, to the cordial satisfaction of us all. The nation at length passed condemnation on the political principles of the federalists, by refusing to continue Mr. Adams in the Presidency. On the day on which we learned in Philadelphia the vote of the city of New York, which it was well known would decide the vote of the State, and that, again, the vote of the Union, I called on Mr. Adams on some official business. He was very sensibly affected, and accosted me with these words: "Well, I understand that you are to beat me in this contest, and I will only say that I will be as faithful a subject as any you will have." "Mr. Adams," said I, "this is no personal contest between you and me. Two systems of principles on the subject of government divide our fellow citizens into two parties. With one of these you concur, and I with the other. As we have been longer on the public stage than most of those now living, our names happen to be more generally known. One of these parties, therefore, has put your name at its head, the other mine. Were we both to die to-day, to-morrow two other names would be in the place of ours, without any change in the motion of the machinery. Its motion is from its principle, not from you or myself." "I believe you are right," said he, "that we are but passive instruments, and should not suffer this matter to affect our personal dispositions." But he did not long retain this just view of the subject. I have always believed that the thousand calumnies which the federalists, in bitterness of heart, and mortification at their ejection, daily invented against me, were carried to him by their busy intriguers, and made some impression. When the election between Burr and myself was kept in suspense by the federalists, and they were mediating to place the President of the Senate at the head of the government, I called on Mr. Adams with a view to have this desperate measure prevented by his negative. He grew warm in an instant, and said with a vehemence he had not used towards me before, "Sir, the event of the election is within your own power. You have only to say you will do justice to the public creditors, maintain the navy, and not disturb those holding offices, and the government will instantly be put into your hands. We know it is the wish of the people it should be so." "Mr. Adams," said I, "I know not what part of my conduct, in either public or private life, can have authorized a doubt of my fidelity to the public engagements. I say, however, I will not come into the government by capitulation. I will not enter on it, but in perfect freedom to follow the dictates of my own judgment." I had before given the same answer to the same intimation from Gouverneur Morris. "Then," said he, "things must take their course." I turned the conversation to something else, and soon took my leave. It was the first time in our lives we had ever parted with anything like dissatisfaction. And then followed those scenes of midnight appointment, which have been condemned by all men. The last day of his political power, the last hours, and even beyond the midnight, were employed in filling all offices, and especially permanent ones, with the bitterest federalists, and providing for me the alternative, either to execute the government by my enemies, whose study it would be to thwart and defeat all my measures, or to incur the odium of such numerous removals from office, as might bear me down. A little time and reflection effaced in my mind this temporary dissatisfaction with Mr. Adams, and restored me to that just estimate of his virtues and passions, which a long acquaintance had enabled me to fix. And my first wish became that of making his retirement easy by any means in my power; for it was understood he was not rich. I suggested to some republican members of the delegation from his State, the giving him, either directly or indirectly, an office, the most lucrative in that State, and then offered to be resigned, if they thought he would not deem it affrontive. They were of opinion he would take great offence at the offer; and moreover, that the body of republicans would consider such a step in the outset as arguing very ill of the course I meant to pursue. I dropped the idea, therefore, but did not cease to wish for some opportunity of renewing our friendly understanding.

Two or three years after, having had the misfortune to lose a daughter, between whom and Mrs. Adams there had been a considerable attachment, she made it the occasion of writing me a letter, in which, with the tenderest expressions of concern at this event, she carefully avoided a single one of friendship towards myself, and even concluded it with the wishes "of her who *once* took pleasure in subscribing herself your friend, Abigail Adams." Unpromising as was the complexion of this letter, I determined to make an effort towards removing the cloud from between us. This brought on a correspondence which I now enclose for your perusal, after which be so good as to return it to me, as I have never communicated it to any mortal breathing, before. I send it to you, to convince you I have not been wanting either in the desire, or the endeavor to remove this misunderstanding. Indeed, I thought it highly disgraceful to us both, as indicating minds not sufficiently elevated to prevent a public competition from affecting our personal friendship. I soon found from the correspondence that conciliation was desperate, and yielding to an intimation in her last letter, I ceased from further explanation. I have the same good opinion of Mr. Adams which I ever had. I know him to be an honest man, an able one with his pen, and he was a powerful advocate on the floor of Congress. He has been alienated from me, by belief in the lying suggestions contrived for electioneering purposes, that I perhaps mixed in the activity and intrigues of the occasion. My most intimate friends can testify that I was perfectly passive. They would sometimes, indeed, tell me what was going on; but no man ever heard me take part in such conversations; and none ever misrepresented Mr. Adams in my presence, without my asserting his just character. With very confidential persons I have doubtless disapproved of the principles and practices of his administration. This was unavoidable. But never with those with whom it could do him any injury. Decency would have required this conduct from me, if disposition had not; and I am satisfied Mr. Adams' conduct was equally honorable towards me. But I think it part of his character to suspect foul play in those of whom he is jealous, and not easily to relinquish his suspicions.

I have gone, my dear friend, into these details, that you might know everything which had passed between us, might be fully possessed of the state of facts and dispositions, and judge for yourself whether they admit a revival of that friendly intercourse for which you are so kindly solicitous. I shall certainly not be wanting in anything on my part which may second your efforts, which will be the easier with me, inasmuch as I do not entertain a sentiment of Mr. Adams, the expression of which could give him reasonable offence. And I submit the whole to yourself, with the assurance, that whatever be the issue, my friendship and respect for yourself will remain unaltered and unalterable.

To Isaac McPherson

MONTICELLO, AUGUST 13, 1813.

Sir,— [. . .] It has been pretended by some, (and in England especially,) that inventors have a natural and exclusive right to their inventions, and not merely for their own lives, but inheritable to their heirs. But while it is a moot question whether the origin of any kind of property is derived from nature at all, it would be singular to admit a natural and even an hereditary right to inventors. It is agreed by those who have seriously considered the subject, that no individual has, of natural right, a separate property in an acre of land, for instance. By an universal law, indeed, whatever, whether fixed or movable, belongs to all men equally and in common, is the property for the moment of him who occupies it; but when he relinquishes the occupation, the property goes with it. Stable ownership is the gift of social law, and is given late in the progress of society. It would be curious then, if an idea, the fugitive fermentation of an individual brain, could, of natural right, be claimed in exclusive and stable property. If nature has made any one thing less susceptible than all others of exclusive property, it is the action of the thinking power called an idea, which an individual may exclusively possess as long as he keeps it to himself; but the moment it is divulged, it forces itself into the possession of every one, and the receiver cannot dispossess himself of it. Its peculiar character, too, is that no one possesses the less, because every other possesses the whole of it. He who receives an idea from me, receives instruction himself without lessening mine; as he who lights his taper at mine, receives light without darkening me. That ideas should freely spread from one to another over the globe, for the moral and mutual instruction of man, and improvement of his condition, seems to have been peculiarly and benevolently designed by nature, when she made them, like fire, expansible over all space, without lessening their density in any point, and like the air in which we breathe, move, and have our physical being, incapable of confinement or exclusive appropriation. Inventions then cannot, in nature, be a subject of property. Society may give an exclusive right to the profits arising from them, as an encouragement to men to pursue ideas which may produce utility, but this may or may not be done, according to the will and convenience of the society, without claim or complaint from anybody. [. . .]

To John Adams

MONTICELLO, OCT. 28, 1813

Dear Sir,— [. . .] I agree with you that there is a natural aristocracy among men. The grounds of this are virtue and talents. Formerly, bodily powers gave place among the aristoi. But since the invention of gunpowder has armed the weak as well as the strong with missile death, bodily strength, like beauty, good humor, politeness and other accomplishments, has become but an auxiliary ground for distinction. There is also an artificial aristocracy, founded on wealth and birth, without either virtue or talents; for with these it would belong to the first class. The natural aristocracy I consider as the most precious gift of nature, for the instruction, the trusts, and government of society. And indeed, it would have been inconsistent in creation to have formed man for the social state, and not to have provided virtue and wisdom enough to manage the concerns of the society. May we not even say, that that form of government is the best, which provides the most effectually for a pure selection of these natural aristoi into the offices of government? The artificial aristocracy is a mischievous ingredient in government, and provision should be made to prevent it's ascendency. On the question, What is the best provision, you and I differ; but we differ as rational friends, using the free exercise of our own reason, and mutually indulging it's errors. *You* think it best to put the Pseudo-aristoi into a separate chamber of legislation, where they may be hindered from doing mischief by their coordinate branches, and where, also, they may be a protection to wealth against the Agrarian and plundering enterprises of the majority of the people. I think that to give them power in order to prevent them from doing mischief, is arming them for it, and increasing instead of remedying the evil. For if the coordinate branches can arrest their action, so may they that of the coordinates. Mischief may be done negatively as well as positively. Of this, a cabal in the Senate of the United States has furnished many proofs. Nor do I believe them necessary to protect the wealthy; because enough of these will find their way into every branch of the legislation, to protect themselves. From fifteen to twenty legislatures of our own, in action for thirty years past, have proved that no fears of an equalisation of property are to be apprehended from them.

I think the best remedy is exactly that provided by all our constitutions, to leave to the citizens the free election and separation of the aristoi from the pseudo-aristoi, of the wheat from the chaff. In general they will elect the really good and wise. In some instances, wealth may corrupt, and birth blind them; but not in sufficient degree to endanger the society.

It is probable that our difference of opinion may, in some measure, be produced by a difference of character in those among whom we live. From what I have seen of Massachusetts and Connecticut myself, and still more from what I have heard, and the character given of the former by yourself, who know them so much better, there seems to be in those two States a traditionary reverence for certain families, which has rendered the offices of the government nearly hereditary in those families. I presume that from an early period of your history, members of those families happening to possess virtue and talents, have honestly exercised them for the good of the people, and by their services have endeared their names to them.

In coupling Connecticut with you, I mean it politically only, not morally. For having made the Bible the common law of their land, they seemed to have modeled their morality on the story of Jacob and Laban. But although this hereditary succession to office with you, may, in some degree, be founded in real family merit, yet in a much higher degree, it has proceeded from your strict alliance of Church and State. These families are canonised in the eyes of the people on the common principle, "you tickle me, and I will tickle you." In Virginia we have nothing of this. Our clergy, before the revolution, having been secured against rivalship by fixed salaries, did not give themselves the trouble of acquiring influence over the people. Of wealth, there were great accumulations in particular families, handed down from generation to generation, under the English law of entails. But the only object of ambition for the wealthy was a seat in the King's Council. All their court then was paid to the crown and its creatures; and they Philipised in all collisions between the King and the people. Hence they were unpopular; and that unpopularity continues attached to their names. A Randolph, a Carter, or a Burwell must have great personal superiority over a common competitor to be elected by the people even at this day.

At the first session of our legislature after the Declaration of Independence, we passed a law abolishing entails. And this was followed by one abolishing the privilege of Primogeniture, and dividing the lands of intestates equally among all their children, or other representatives. These laws, drawn by myself, laid the axe to the foot of pseudo-aristocracy. And had another which I prepared been adopted by the legislature, our work would have been complete. It was a Bill for the more general diffusion of learning. This proposed to divide every county into wards of five or six miles square, like your townships; to establish in each ward a free school for reading, writing and common arithmetic; to provide for the annual selection of the best subjects from these schools, who might receive, at the public expence, a higher degree of education at a district school; and from these district schools to select a certain number of the most promising subjects, to be completed at an University, where all the useful sciences should be taught. Worth and genius would thus have been sought out from every condition of life, and completely prepared by education for defeating the competition of wealth and birth for public trusts.

My proposition had, for a further object, to impart to these wards those portions of self-government for which they are best qualified, by confiding to them the care of their poor, their roads, police, elections, the nomination of jurors, administration of justice in small cases, elementary exercises of militia; in short, to have made them little republics, with a Warden at the head of each, for all those concerns which, being under their eye, they would better manage than the larger republics of the county or State. A general call of ward meetings by their Wardens on the same day through the State, would at any time produce the genuine sense of the people on any required point, and would enable the State to act in mass, as your people have so often done, and with so much effect by their town meetings. The law for religious freedom, which made a part of this system, having put down the aristocracy of the clergy, and restored to the citizen the freedom of the mind, and those of entails and descents nurturing an equality of condition among them, this on Education would have raised the mass of the people to the high ground of moral respectability necessary to their own safety, and to orderly government; and would have completed the great object of qualifying them to select the veritable aristoi, for the trusts of government, to the exclusion of the pseudalists. [. . .]

[. . .] Here every one may have land to labor for himself, if he chooses; or, preferring the exercise of any other industry, may exact for it such compensation as not only to afford a comfortable subsistence, but wherewith to provide for a cessation from labor in old age. Every one, by his property, or by his satisfactory situation, is interested in the support of law and order. And such men may safely and advantageously reserve to themselves a wholesome control over their public affairs, and a degree of freedom, which, in the hands of the *canaille* of the cities of Europe, would be instantly perverted to the demolition and destruction of every thing public and private. The history of the last twenty-five years of France, and of the last forty years in America, nay of it's last two hundred years, proves the truth of both parts of this observation. [. . .]

I have thus stated my opinion on a point on which we differ, not with a view to controversy, for we are both too old to change opinions which are the result of a long life of inquiry and reflection; but on the suggestions of a former letter of yours, that we ought not to die before we have explained ourselves to each other. We acted in perfect harmony, through a long and perilous contest for our liberty and independence. A constitution has been acquired, which, though neither of us think perfect, yet both consider as competent to render our fellow citizens the happiest and the securest on whom the sun has ever shone. If we do not think exactly alike as to it's imperfections, it matters little to our country, which, after devoting to it long lives of disinterested labor, we have delivered over to our successors in life, who will be able to take care of it and of themselves.

Of the pamphlet on aristocracy which has been sent to you, or who may be it's author, I have heard nothing but through your letter. If the person you suspect, it may be known from the quaint, mystical and hyperbolical ideas, involved in affected, new-fangled and pedantic terms which stamp his writings. Whatever it be, I hope your quiet is not to be affected at this day by the rudeness or intemperance of scribblers; but that you may continue in tranquillity to live and to rejoice in the prosperity of our country, until it shall be your own wish to take your seat among the Aristoi who have gone before you. Ever and affectionately yours.

To Dr. Walter Jones

MONTICELLO, JANUARY 2, 1814.

Dear Sir,—Your favor of November the 25th reached this place December the 21st, having been near a month on the way. How this could happen I know not, as we have two mails a week both from Fredericksburg and Richmond. It found me just returned from a long journey and absence, during which so much business had accumulated, commanding the first attentions, that another week has been added to the delay.

I deplore, with you, the putrid state into which our newspapers have passed, and the malignity, the vulgarity, and mendacious spirit of those who write for them; and I enclose you a recent sample, the production of a New England judge, as a proof of the abyss of degradation into which we are fallen. These ordures are rapidly depraving the public taste, and lessening its relish for sound food. As vehicles of information, and a curb on our functionaries, they have rendered themselves useless, by forfeiting all title to belief. That this has, in a great degree, been produced by the violence and malignity of party spirit, I agree with you; and I have read with great pleasure the paper you enclosed me on that subject, which I now return. It is at the same time a perfect model of the style of discussion which candor and decency should observe, of the tone which renders difference of opinion even amiable, and a succinct, correct, and dispassionate history of the origin and progress of party among us. It might be incorporated as it stands, and without changing a word, into the history of the present epoch, and would give to posterity a fairer view of the times than they will probably derive from other sources. In reading it with great satisfaction, there was but a single passage where I wished a little more development of a very sound and catholic idea; a single intercalation to rest it solidly on true bottom. It is near the end of the first page, where you make a statement of genuine republican maxims; saying, "that the people ought to possess as much political power as can possibly exist with the order and security of society." Instead of this, I would say, "that the people, being the only safe depository of power, should exercise in person every function which their qualifications enable them to exercise, consistently with the order and security of society; that we now find them equal to the election of those who shall be invested with their executive and legislative powers, and to act themselves in the judiciary, as judges in questions of fact; that the range of their powers ought to be enlarged," &c. This gives both the reason and exemplification of the maxim you express, "that they ought to possess as much political power," &c. I see nothing to correct either in your facts or principles.

You say that in taking General Washington on your shoulders, to bear him harmless through the federal coalition, you encounter a perilous topic. I do not think so. You have given the genuine history of the course of his mind through the trying scenes in which it was engaged, and of the seductions by which it was deceived, but not depraved. I think I knew General Washington intimately and thoroughly; and were I called on to delineate his character, it should be in terms like these.

His mind was great and powerful, without being of the very first order; his penetration strong, though not so acute as that of a Newton, Bacon, or Locke; and as far as he saw, no judgment was ever sounder. It was slow in operation, being little aided by invention or imagination, but sure in conclusion. Hence the common remark of his officers, of the advantage he derived from councils of war, where hearing all suggestions, he selected whatever was best; and certainly no General ever planned his battles more judiciously. But if deranged during the course of the action, if any member of his plan was dislocated by sudden circumstances, he was slow in readjustment. The consequence was, that he often failed in the field, and rarely against an enemy in station, as at Boston and York. He was incapable of fear, meeting personal dangers with the calmest unconcern. Perhaps the strongest feature in his character was prudence, never acting until every circumstance, every consideration, was maturely weighed; refraining if he saw a doubt, but, when once decided, going through with his purpose, whatever obstacles opposed. His integrity was most pure, his justice the most inflexible I have ever known, no motives of interest or consanguinity, of friendship or hatred, being able to bias his decision. He was, indeed, in every sense of the words, a wise, a good, and a great man. His temper was naturally high toned; but reflection and resolution had obtained a firm and habitual ascendency over it. If ever, however, it broke its bonds, he was most tremendous in his wrath. In his expenses he was honorable, but exact; liberal in contributions to whatever promised utility; but frowning and unyielding on all visionary projects and all unworthy calls on his charity. His heart was not warm in its affections; but he exactly calculated every man's value, and gave him a solid esteem proportioned to it. His person, you know, was fine, his stature exactly what one would wish, his deportment easy, erect and noble; the best horseman of his age, and the most graceful figure that could be seen on horseback. Although in the circle of his friends, where he might be unreserved with safety, he took a free share in conversation, his colloquial talents were not above mediocrity, possessing neither copiousness of ideas, nor fluency of words. In public, when called on for a sudden opinion, he was unready, short and embarrassed. Yet he wrote readily, rather diffusely, in an easy and correct style. This he had acquired by conversation with the world, for his education was merely reading, writing and common arithmetic, to which he added surveying at a later day. His time was employed in action chiefly, reading little, and that only in agriculture and English history. His correspondence became necessarily extensive, and, with journalizing his agricultural proceedings, occupied most of his leisure hours within doors. On the whole, his character was, in its mass, perfect, in nothing bad, in few points indifferent; and it may truly be said, that never did nature and fortune combine more perfectly to make a man great, and to place him in the same constellation with whatever worthies have merited from man an everlasting remembrance. For his was the singular destiny and merit, of leading the armies of his country successfully through an arduous war, for the establishment of its independence; of conducting its councils through the birth of a government, new in its forms and principles, until it had settled down into a quiet and orderly train; and of scrupulously obeying the laws through the whole of his career, civil and military, of which the history of the world furnishes no other example.

How, then, can it be perilous for you to take such a man on your shoulders? I am satisfied the great body of republicans think of him as I do. We were, indeed, dissatisfied with him on his ratification of the British treaty. But this was short lived. We knew his honesty, the wiles with which he was encompassed, and that age had already begun to relax the firmness of his purposes; and I am convinced he is more deeply seated in the love and gratitude of the republicans, than in the Pharisaical homage of the federal monarchists. For he was no monarchist from preference of his judgment. The soundness of that gave him correct views of the rights of man, and his severe justice devoted him to them. He has often declared to me that he considered our new constitution as an experiment on the practicability of republican government, and with what dose of liberty man could be trusted for his own good; that he was determined the experiment should have a fair trial, and would lose the last drop of his blood in support of it. And these declarations he repeated to me the oftener and more pointedly, because he knew my suspicions of Colonel Hamilton's views, and probably had heard from him the same declarations which I had, to wit, "that the British constitution, with its unequal representation, corruption and other existing abuses, was the most perfect government which had ever been established on earth, and that a reformation of those abuses would make it an impracticable government." I do believe that General Washington had not a firm confidence in the durability of our government. He was naturally distrustful of men, and inclined to gloomy apprehensions; and I was ever persuaded that a belief that we must at length end in something like a British constitution, had some weight in his adoption of the ceremonies of levees, birth-days, pompous meetings with Congress, and other forms of the same character, calculated to prepare us gradually for a change which he believed possible, and to let it come on with as little shock as might be to the public mind.

These are my opinions of General Washington, which I would vouch at the judgment seat of God, having been formed on an acquaintance of thirty years. I served with him in the Virginia legislature from 1769 to the Revolutionary war, and again, a short time in Congress, until he left us to take command of the army. During the war and after it we corresponded occasionally, and in the four years of my continuance in the office of Secretary of State, our intercourse was daily, confidential and cordial. After I retired from that office, great and malignant pains were taken by our federal monarchists, and not entirely without effect, to make him view me as a theorist, holding French principles of government, which would lead infallibly to licentiousness and anarchy. And to this he listened the more easily, from my known disapprobation of the British treaty. I never saw him afterwards, or these malignant insinuations should have been dissipated before his just judgment, as mists before the sun. I felt on his death, with my countrymen, that "verily a great man hath fallen this day in Israel."

More time and recollection would enable me to add many other traits of his character; but why add them to you who knew him well? And I cannot justify to myself a longer detention of your paper.

Vale, proprieque tuum, me esse tibi persuadeas.

To Edward Coles

MONTICELLO, AUGUST 25, 1814

Dear Sir,—Your favour of July 31, was duly received, and was read with peculiar pleasure. The sentiments breathed through the whole do honor to both the head and heart of the writer. Mine on the subject of slavery of negroes have long since been in possession of the public, and time has only served to give them stronger root. The love of justice and the love of country plead equally the cause of these people, and it is a moral reproach to us that they should have pleaded it so long in vain, and should have produced not a single effort, nay I fear not much serious willingness to relieve them & ourselves from our present condition of moral & political reprobation. From those of the former generation who were in the fulness of age when I came into public life, which was while our controversy with England was on paper only, I soon saw that nothing was to be hoped. Nursed and educated in the daily habit of seeing the degraded condition, both bodily and mental, of those unfortunate beings, not reflecting that that degradation was very much the work of themselves & their fathers, few minds have yet doubted but that they were as legitimate subjects of property as their horses and cattle. The quiet and monotonous course of colonial life has been disturbed by no alarm, and little reflection on the value of liberty. And when alarm was taken at an enterprize on their own, it was not easy to carry them to the whole length of the principles which they invoked for themselves. In the first or second session of the Legislature after I became a member, I drew to this subject the attention of Col. Bland, one of the oldest, ablest, & most respected members, and he undertook to move for certain moderate extensions of the protection of the laws to these people. I seconded his motion, and, as a younger member, was more spared in the debate; but he was denounced as an enemy of his country, & was treated with the grossest indecorum. From an early stage of our revolution other & more distant duties were assigned to me, so that from that time till my return from Europe in 1789, and I may say till I returned to reside at home in 1809, I had little opportunity of knowing the progress of public sentiment here on this subject. I had always hoped that the younger generation receiving their early impressions after the flame of liberty had been kindled in every breast, & had become as it were the vital spirit of every American, that the generous temperament of youth, analogous to the motion of their blood, and above the suggestions of avarice, would have sympathized with oppression wherever found, and proved their love of liberty beyond their own share of it. But my intercourse with them, since my return has not been sufficient to ascertain that they had made towards this point the progress I had hoped. Your solitary but welcome voice is the first which has brought this sound to my ear; and I have considered the general silence which prevails on this subject as indicating an apathy unfavorable to every hope. Yet the hour of emancipation is advancing, in the march of time. It will come; and whether brought on by the generous energy of our own minds; or by the bloody process of St Domingo, excited and conducted by the power of our present enemy, if once stationed permanently within our Country, and offering asylum & arms to the oppressed, is a leaf of our history not yet turned over. As to the method by which this difficult work is to be effected, if permitted to be done by ourselves, I have seen no proposition so expedient on the whole, as that as emancipation of those born after a given day, and of their education and expatriation after a given age. This would give time for a gradual extinction of that species of labour & substitution of another, and lessen the severity of the shock which an operation so fundamental cannot fail to produce. For men probably of any color, but of this color we know, brought from their infancy without necessity for thought or forecast, are by their habits rendered as incapable as children of taking care of themselves, and are extinguished promptly wherever industry is necessary for raising young. In the mean time they are pests in society by their idleness, and the depredations to which this leads them. Their amalgamation with the other color produces a degradation to which no lover of his country, no lover of excellence in the human character can innocently consent. I am sensible of the partialities with which you have looked towards me as the person who should undertake this salutary but arduous work. But this, my dear sir, is like bidding old Priam to buckle the armour of Hector "trementibus æquo humeris et inutile ferruncingi." No, I have overlived the generation with which mutual labors & perils begat mutual confidence and influence. This enterprise is for the young; for those who can follow it up, and bear it through to its consummation. It shall have all my prayers, & these are the only weapons of an old man. But in the mean time are you right in abandoning this property, and your country with it? I think not. My opinion has ever been that, until more can be done for them, we should endeavor, with those whom fortune has thrown on our hands, to feed and clothe them well, protect them from all ill usage, require such reasonable labor only as is performed voluntarily by freemen, & be led by no repugnancies to abdicate them, and our duties to them. The laws do not permit us to turn them loose, if that were for their good: and to commute them for other property is to commit them to those whose usage of them we cannot control. I hope then, my dear sir, you will reconcile yourself to your country and its unfortunate condition; that you will not lessen its stock of sound disposition by withdrawing your portion from the mass. That, on the contrary you will come forward in the public councils, become the missionary of this doctrine truly christian; insinuate & inculcate it softly but steadily, through the medium of writing and conversation; associate others in your labors, and when the phalanx is formed, bring on and press the proposition perseveringly until its accomplishment. It is an encouraging observation that no good measure was ever proposed, which, if duly pursued, failed to prevail in the end. We have proof of this in the history of the endeavors in the English parliament to suppress that very trade which brought this evil on us. And you will be supported by the religious precept, "be not weary in well-doing." That your success may be as speedy & complete, as it will be of honorable & immortal consolation to yourself, I shall as fervently and sincerely pray as I assure you of my great friendship and respect.

To John Adams

MONTICELLO, AUGUST 1, 1816.

Dear Sir,—Your two philosophical letters of May 4th and 6th have been too long in my carton of "letters to be answered." To the question, indeed, on the utility of grief, no answer remains to be given. You have exhausted the subject. I see that, with the other evils of life, it is destined to temper the cup we are to drink.

Two urns by Jove's high throne have ever stood,
The source of evil one, and one of good;
From thence the cup of mortal man he fills,
Blessings to these, to those distributes ills;
To most he mingles both.

Putting to myself your question, would I agree to live my seventy-three years over again forever? I hesitate to say. With Chew's limitations from twenty-five to sixty, I would say yes; and I might go further back, but not come lower down. For, at the latter period, with most of us, the powers of life are sensibly on the wane, sight becomes dim, hearing dull, memory constantly enlarging its frightful blank and parting with all we have ever seen or known, spirits evaporate, bodily debility creeps on palsying every limb, and so faculty after faculty quits us, and where then is life? If, in its full vigor, of good as well as evil, your friend Vassall could doubt its value, it must be purely a negative quantity when its evils alone remain. Yet I do not go into his opinion entirely. I do not agree that an age of pleasure is no compensation for a moment of pain. I think, with you, that life is a fair matter of account, and the balance often, nay generally, in its favor. It is not indeed easy, by calculation of intensity and time, to apply a common measure, or to fix the par between pleasure and pain; yet it exists, and is measurable. On the question, for example, whether to be cut for the stone? The young, with a longer prospect of years, think these overbalance the pain of the operation. Dr. Franklin, at the age of eighty, thought his residuum of life not worth that price. I should have thought with him, even taking the stone out of the scale. There is a ripeness of time for death, regarding others as well as ourselves, when it is reasonable we should drop off, and make room for another growth. When we have lived our generation out, we should not wish to encroach on another. I enjoy good health; I am happy in what is around me, yet I assure you I am ripe for leaving all, this year, this day, this hour. If it could be doubted whether we would go back to twenty-five, how can it be whether we would go forward from seventy-three? Bodily decay is gloomy in prospect, but of all human contemplations the most abhorrent is body without mind. [. . .] I like the dreams of the future better than the history of the past,—so good night! I will dream on, always fancying that Mrs. Adams and yourself are by my side marking the progress and the obliquities of ages and countries.

To Judge Spencer Roane

POPLAR FOREST, SEPTEMBER 6, 1819.

Dear Sir,—I had read in the Enquirer, and with great approbation, the pieces signed Hampden, and have read them again with redoubled approbation, in the copies you have been so kind as to send me. I subscribe to every tittle of them. They contain the true principles of the revolution of 1800, for that was as real a revolution in the principles of our government as that of 1776 was in its form; not effected indeed by the sword, as that, but by the rational and peaceable instrument of reform, the suffrage of the people. The nation declared its will by dismissing functionaries of one principle, and electing those of another, in the two branches, executive and legislative, submitted to their election. Over the judiciary department, the constitution had deprived them of their control. That, therefore, has continued the reprobated system, and although new matter has been occasionally incorporated into the old, yet the leaven of the old mass seems to assimilate to itself the new, and after twenty years' confirmation of the federal system by the voice of the nation, declared through the medium of elections, we find the judiciary on every occasion, still driving us into consolidation.

In denying the right they usurp of exclusively explaining the constitution, I go further than you do, if I understand rightly your quotation from the Federalist, of an opinion that "the judiciary is the last resort in relation *to the other departments* of the government, but not in relation to the rights of the parties to the compact under which the judiciary is derived." If this opinion be sound, then indeed is our constitution a complete *felo de se.* For intending to establish three departments, co-ordinate and independent, that they might check and balance one another, it has given, according to this opinion, to one of them alone, the right to prescribe rules for the government of the others, and to that one too, which is unelected by, and independent of the nation. For experience has already shown that the impeachment it has provided is not even a scare-crow; that such opinions as the one you combat, sent cautiously out, as you observe also, by detachment, not belonging to the case often, but sought for out of it, as if to rally the public opinion beforehand to their views, and to indicate the line they are to walk in, have been so quietly passed over as never to have excited animadversion, even in a speech of any one of the body entrusted with impeachment. The constitution, on this hypothesis, is a mere thing of wax in the hands of the judiciary, which they may twist and shape into any form they please. It should be remembered, as an axiom of eternal truth in politics, that whatever power in any government is independent, is absolute also; in theory only, at first, while the spirit of the people is up, but in practice, as fast as that relaxes. Independence can be trusted nowhere but with the people in mass. They are inherently independent of all but moral law. My construction of the constitution is very different from that you quote. It is that each department is truly independent of the others, and has an equal right to decide for itself what is the meaning of the constitution in the cases submitted to its action; and especially, where it is to act ultimately and without appeal. I will explain myself by examples, which, having occurred while I was in office, are better known to me, and the principles which governed them.

A legislature had passed the sedition law. The federal courts had subjected certain individuals to its penalties of fine and imprisonment. On coming into office, I released these individuals by the power of pardon committed to executive discretion, which could never be more properly exercised than where citizens were suffering without the authority of law, or, which was equivalent, under a law unauthorized by the constitution, and therefore null. In the case of Marbury and Madison, the federal judges declared that commissions, signed and sealed by the President, were valid, although not delivered. I deemed delivery essential to complete a deed, which, as long as it remains in the hands of the party, is as yet no deed, it is in *posse* only, but not in *esse,* and I withheld delivery of the commissions.

They cannot issue a mandamus to the President or legislature, or to any of their officers. When the British treaty of _____ arrived, without any provision against the impressment of our seamen, I determined not to ratify it. The Senate thought I should ask their advice. I thought that would be a mockery of them, when I was predetermined against following it, should they advise its ratification. The constitution had made their advice necessary to confirm a treaty, but not to reject it. This has been blamed by some; but I have never doubted its soundness. In the cases of two persons, *ante-nati,* under exactly similar circumstances, the federal court had determined that one of them (Duane) was not a citizen; the House of Representatives nevertheless determined that the other (Smith, of South Carolina) was a citizen, and admitted him to his seat in their body. Duane was a republican, and Smith a federalist, and these decisions were made during the federal ascendancy.

These are examples of my position, that each of the three departments has equally the right to decide for itself what is its duty under the constitution, without any regard to what the others may have decided for themselves under a similar question. But you intimate a wish that my opinion should be known on this subject. No, dear Sir, I withdraw from all contests of opinion, and resign everything cheerfully to the generation now in place. They are wiser than we were, and their successors will be wiser than they, from the progressive advance of science. Tranquillity is the *summum bonum* of age. I wish, therefore, to offend no man's opinion, nor to draw disquieting animadversions on my own. While duty required it, I met opposition with a firm and fearless step. But loving mankind in my individual relations with them, I pray to be permitted to depart in their peace; and like the superannuated soldier, "*quadragenis stipendiis emeritis,*" to hang my arms on the post. I have unwisely, I fear, embarked in an enterprise of great public concern, but not to be accomplished within my term, without their liberal and prompt support. A severe illness the last year, and another from which I am just emerged, admonish me that repetitions may be expected, against which a declining frame cannot long bear up. I am anxious, therefore, to get our University so far advanced as may encourage the public to persevere to its final accomplishment. That secured, I shall sing my *nunc demittas.* I hope your labors will be long continued in the spirit in which they have always been exercised, in maintenance of those principles on which I verily believe the future happiness of our country essentially depends. I salute you with affectionate and great respect.

To John Holmes

MONTICELLO, APRIL 22, 1820.

I thank you, dear Sir, for the copy you have been so kind as to send me of the letter to your constituents on the Missouri question. It is a perfect justification to them. I had for a long time ceased to read newspapers, or pay any attention to public affairs, confident they were in good hands, and content to be a passenger in our bark to the shore from which I am not distant. But this momentous question, like a fire bell in the night, awakened and filled me with terror. I considered it at once as the knell of the Union. It is hushed, indeed, for the moment. But this is a reprieve only, not a final sentence. A geographical line, coinciding with a marked principle, moral and political, once conceived and held up to the angry passions of men, will never be obliterated; and every new irritation will mark it deeper and deeper. I can say, with conscious truth, that there is not a man on earth who would sacrifice more than I would to relieve us from this heavy reproach, in any *practicable* way. The cession of that kind of property, for so it is misnamed, is a bagatelle which would not cost me a second thought, if, in that way, a general emancipation and *expatriation* could be effected; and gradually, and with due sacrifices, I think it might be. But as it is, we have the wolf by the ears, and we can neither hold him, nor safely let him go. Justice is in one scale, and self-preservation in the other. Of one thing I am certain, that as the passage of slaves from one State to another, would not make a slave of a single human being who would not be so without it, so their diffusion over a greater surface would make them individually happier, and proportionally facilitate the accomplishment of their emancipation, by dividing the burthen on a greater number of coadjutors. An abstinence too, from this act of power, would remove the jealousy excited by the undertaking of Congress to regulate the condition of the different descriptions of men composing a State. This certainly is the exclusive right of every State, which nothing in the constitution has taken from them and given to the General Government. Could Congress, for example, say, that the non-freemen of Connecticut shall be freemen, or that they shall not emigrate into any other State?

I regret that I am now to die in the belief, that the useless sacrifice of themselves by the generation of 1776, to acquire self-government and happiness to their country, is to be thrown away by the unwise and unworthy passions of their sons, and that my only consolation is to be, that I live not to weep over it. If they would but dispassionately weigh the blessings they will throw away, against an abstract principle more likely to be effected by union than by scission, they would pause before they would perpetrate this act of suicide on themselves, and of treason against the hopes of the world. To yourself, as the faithful advocate of the Union, I tender the offering of my high esteem and respect.

To Jared Sparks

MONTICELLO, FEBRUARY 4, 1824.

Dear Sir,—I duly received your favor of the 13th, and with it, the last number of the North American Review. This has anticipated the one I should receive in course, but have not yet received, under my subscription to the new series. The article on the African colonization of the people of color, to which you invite my attention, I have read with great consideration. It is, indeed, a fine one, and will do much good. I learn from it more, too, than I had before known, of the degree of success and promise of that colony.

In the disposition of these unfortunate people, there are two rational objects to be distinctly kept in view. First. The establishment of a colony on the coast of Africa, which may introduce among the aborigines the arts of cultivated life, and the blessings of civilization and science. By doing this, we may make to them some retribution for the long course of injuries we have been committing on their population. And considering that these blessings will descend to the *"nati natorum, et qui nascentur ab illis,"* we shall in the long run have rendered them perhaps more good than evil. To fulfil this object, the colony of Sierra Leone promises well, and that of Mesurado adds to our prospect of success. Under this view, the colonization society is to be considered as a missionary society, having in view, however, objects more humane, more justifiable, and less aggressive on the peace of other nations, than the others of that appellation.

The second object, and the most interesting to us, as coming home to our physical and moral characters, to our happiness and safety, is to provide an asylum to which we can, by degrees, send the whole of that population from among us, and establish them under our patronage and protection, as a separate, free and independent people, in some country and climate friendly to human life and happiness. That any place on the coast of Africa should answer the latter purpose, I have ever deemed entirely impossible. And without repeating the other arguments which have been urged by others, I will appeal to figures only, which admit no controversy. I shall speak in round numbers, not absolutely accurate, yet not so wide from truth as to vary the result materially. There are in the United States a million and a half of people of color in slavery. To send off the whole of these at once, nobody conceives to be practicable for us, or expedient for them. Let us take twenty-five years for its accomplishment, within which time they will be doubled. Their estimated value as property, in the first place, (for actual property has been lawfully vested in that form, and who can lawfully take it from the possessors?) at an average of two hundred dollars each, young and old, would amount to six hundred millions of dollars, which must be paid or lost by somebody. To this, add the cost of their transportation by land and sea to Mesurado, a year's provision of food and clothing, implements of husbandry and of their trades, which will amount to three hundred millions more, making thirty-six millions of dollars a year for twenty-five years, with insurance of peace all that time, and it is impossible to look at the question a second time. I am aware that at the end of about sixteen years, a gradual detraction from this sum will commence, from the gradual diminution of breeders, and go on during the remaining nine years. Calculate this deduction, and it is still impossible to look at the enterprise a second time. I do not say this to induce an inference that the getting rid of them is forever impossible. For that is neither my opinion nor my hope. But only that it cannot be done in this way. There is, I think, a way in which it can be done; that is, by emancipating the afterborn, leaving them, on due compensation, with their mothers, until their services are worth their maintenance, and then putting them to industrious occupations, until a proper age for deportation. This was the result of my reflections on the subject five and forty years ago, and I have never yet been able to conceive any other practicable plan. It was sketched in the Notes on Virginia, under the fourteenth query. The estimated value of the new-born infant is so low, (say twelve dollars and fifty cents,) that it would probably be yielded by the owner gratis, and would thus reduce the six hundred millions of dollars, the first head of expense, to thirty-seven millions and a half; leaving only the expenses of nourishment while with the mother, and of transportation. And from what fund are these expenses to be furnished? Why not from that of the lands which have been ceded by the very States now needing this relief? And ceded on no consideration, for the most part, but that of the general good of the whole. These cessions already constitute one-fourth of the States of the Union. It may be said that these lands have been sold; are now the property of the citizens composing those States; and the money long ago received and expended. But an equivalent of lands in the territories since acquired, may be appropriated to that object, or so much, at least, as may be sufficient; and the object, although more important to the slave States, is highly so to the others also, if they were serious in their arguments on the Missouri question. The slave States, too, if more interested, would also contribute more by their gratuitous liberation, thus taking on themselves alone the first and heaviest item of expense.

In the plan sketched in the Notes on Virginia, no particular place of asylum was specified; because it was thought possible, that in the revolutionary state of America, then commenced, events might open to us some one within practicable distance. This has now happened. St. Domingo has become independent, and with a population of that color only; and if the public papers are to be credited, their Chief offers to pay their passage, to receive them as free citizens, and to provide them employment. This leaves, then, for the general confederacy, no expense but of nurture with the mother a few years, and would call, of course, for a very moderate appropriation of the vacant lands. Suppose the whole annual increase to be of sixty thousand effective births, fifty vessels, of four hundred tons burden each, constantly employed in that short run, would carry off the increase of every year, and the old stock would die off in the ordinary course of nature, lessening from the commencement until its final disappearance. In this way no violation of private right is proposed. Voluntary surrenders would probably come in as fast as the means to be provided for their care would be competent to it. Looking at my own State only, and I presume not to speak for the others, I verily believe that this surrender of property would not amount to more, annually, than half our present direct taxes, to be continued fully about twenty or twenty-five years, and then gradually diminishing for as many more until their final extinction; and even this half tax would not be paid in cash, but by the delivery of an object which they have never yet known or counted as part of their property; and those not possessing the object will be called on for nothing. I do not go into all the details of the burdens and benefits of this operation. And who could estimate its blessed effects? I leave this to those who will live to see their accomplishment, and to enjoy a beatitude forbidden to my age. But I leave it with this admonition, to rise and be doing. A million and a half are within their control; but six millions, (which a majority of those now living will see them attain,) and one million of these fighting men, will say, "we will not go."

I am aware that this subject involves some constitutional scruples. But a liberal construction, justified by the object, may go far, and an amendment of the Constitution, the whole length necessary. The separation of infants from their mothers, too, would produce some scruples of humanity. But this would be straining at a gnat, and swallowing a camel.

I am much pleased to see that you have taken up the subject of the duty on imported books. I hope a crusade will be kept up against it, until those in power shall become sensible of this stain on our legislation, and shall wipe it from their code, and from the remembrance of man, if possible.

I salute you with assurances of high respect and esteem.

To Henry Lee

MONTICELLO, MAY 8, 1825.

Dear Sir,— [. . .] That George Mason was author of the bill of rights, and of the constitution founded on it, the evidence of the day established fully in my mind. Of the paper you mention, purporting to be instructions to the Virginia delegation in Congress, I have no recollection. If it were anything more than a project of some private hand, that is to say, had any such instructions been ever given by the convention, they would appear in the journals, which we possess entire. But with respect to our rights, and the acts of the British government contravening those rights, there was but one opinion on this side of the water. All American whigs thought alike on these subjects. When forced, therefore, to resort to arms for redress, an appeal to the tribunal of the world was deemed proper for our justification. This was the object of the Declaration of Independence. Not to find out new principles, or new arguments, never before thought of, not merely to say things which had never been said before; but to place before mankind the common sense of the subject, in terms so plain and firm as to command their assent, and to justify ourselves in the independent stand we are compelled to take. Neither aiming at originality of principle or sentiment, nor yet copied from any particular and previous writing, it was intended to be an expression of the American mind, and to give to that expression the proper tone and spirit called for by the occasion. All its authority rests then on the harmonizing sentiments of the day, whether expressed in conversation, in letters, printed essays, or in the elementary books of public right, as Aristotle, Cicero, Locke, Sidney, &c. The historical documents which you mention as in your possession, ought all to be found, and I am persuaded you will find, to be corroborative of the facts and principles advanced in that Declaration. Be pleased to accept assurances of my great esteem and respect.

To James Madison

MONTICELLO, FEBRUARY 17, 1826.

Dear Sir,— [. . .] The friendship which has subsisted between us, now half a century, and the harmony of our political principles and pursuits, have been sources of constant happiness to me through that long period. And if I remove beyond the reach of attentions to the University, or beyond the bourne of life itself, as I soon must, it is a comfort to leave that institution under your care, and an assurance that it will not be wanting. It has also been a great solace to me, to believe that you are engaged in vindicating to posterity the course we have pursued for preserving to them, in all their purity, the blessings of self-government, which we had assisted too in acquiring for them. If ever the earth has beheld a system of administration conducted with a single and steadfast eye to the general interest and happiness of those committed to it, one which, protected by truth, can never know reproach, it is that to which our lives have been devoted. To myself you have been a pillar of support through life. Take care of me when dead, and be assured that I shall leave with you my last affections.

JAMES MADISON
1751–1836

Introduction

"The biography of an author must be a history of his writings," wrote James Madison in his autobiography. "So must that of one whose life has in a manner been a public life, be gathered from his official transactions and his manuscript papers on public subjects including letters to as well as from him."[1]

Political theorist, politician, party leader, secretary of state, president, elder statesman: Madison tells us that his writings will reveal the meaning of his life. In the meditations on government that preoccupied him for fifty years, we can discover his deepest and most creative thoughts.

To read Madison's letters and essays on constitutions, representative institutions, politics, and parties is to enter into an intellectual dialogue with him and also into the dialogue he pursued with himself, for when his thinking—or the political landscape—shifted, he was willing to revisit—and revise—his opinions.

Madison had designed a system of checks and balances that placed branches of government in adversarial relationships with one another, stressing in *Federalist* No. 51 that the members of each branch would be "as little dependent as possible on those of the others." But his warm friendship with George Washington led him to blur that separation. Although he was a member of the House of Representatives from Virginia, he served as President Washington's unofficial adviser and liaison to Congress. He not only ghostwrote Washington's inaugural address, but composed the official reply of the House to that speech and then drafted the president's replies to the House and also to the Senate! Madison was "in dialogue with himself," as the editors of the Madison papers put it,[2] but he was also trampling on the separation of powers he had so thoughtfully crafted.

The mundane reality of campaigning for office and making concessions and promises to voters also shaped Madison's political positions. In 1788, he had not considered the omission of a bill of rights from the Constitution a "material defect." Experience, he remarked, had proved the "inefficacy" of such "parchment barriers," for overbearing majorities had repeatedly violated them, even in Virginia.[3] But only a year later, none other than James Madison led the effort in Congress to add ten amendments to the Constitution, guaranteeing to the people their rights and freedoms. Why the swing? It was partly Jefferson's entreaty that "a bill of rights is what the people are entitled to against every government on earth."[4] But it was also political necessity, the price of Virginia's ratification of the Constitution as well as the price of Madison's own election to the House of Representatives.

In April 1787, a few weeks before the Constitutional Convention, Madison had sketched out for George Washington his thoughts for a constitution, stressing that the federal government should be "armed" not only with "positive and compleat authority" in matters of trade, taxation, and commerce but also with a veto on the legislative acts of the states—not to impose policies on the states but to prevent the states from encroaching on the powers of the national government. The traditional "Kingly prerogative" of a "negative" on the states appeared to him "absolutely necessary."[5] And yet, after Congress passed and President Adams signed the Sedition Act in 1798, flouting the Bill of Rights by making it a crime to malign the top elected officers of the government, Madison penned the Virginia Resolutions. Passed by the Virginia House of Delegates, the Resolutions expressed Madison's view that the states "have the right, and are in duty bound" to declare certain federal acts unconstitutional. He urged the other states to join Virginia "in maintaining unimpaired the authorities, rights, and liberties reserved" to them. Thirty-five years later, when Virginia and South Carolina, mobilized by John Calhoun, declared that they could and would nullify federal laws, he again revisited the question of national authority, now reverting to the position he first took in 1787. The Constitution and laws of the United States were "supreme," he decided, and no state had the right to unilaterally nullify congressional acts or to "withdraw its citizens" from the union.[6]

Again and again Madison would revise his thinking and his positions. From a critic of the tyranny of the majority in 1787, he came to favor government by the majority in 1833. An opponent of Hamilton's plan for the national government to assume the debts of the states, he decided in 1790 to throw his support to that plan in exchange for an agreement to locate the new federal city on the Potomac. An advocate in 1816 of a "comprehensive system of roads and canals," he vetoed a bill a few months later for just such a system.[7] Although he had argued in 1788 for elasticity in interpreting the Constitution ("Wherever the end is required, the means are authorised," he had written in *Federalist* No. 44), in his veto message of 1817 he judged that the power to construct roads and canals could not be deduced from the Constitution "without an inadmissible latitude of construction."

In one area Madison was consistent—and consistently idealistic: In the 1790s he had opposed Hamilton's vision of the United States as a powerful industrial and military state. He would oppose that vision in 1807 by opting for a trade embargo instead of a war against the European belligerents; and he would oppose it again in his arguably weak leadership during the War of 1812. "The nation can review its conduct without regret and without reproach," he told Congress at the war's end.[8] Neither the president nor the war had infringed upon citizens' political, civil, or religious rights, marveled one contemporary admirer.[9]

Madison was the most temperate and penetrating thinker among the founders. He believed that reason, not passion, ought to control government. And yet, he understood that politics was not a purely rational endeavor. It was both an art and a sport into which entered almost as much self-interest and opportunism as reason, virtue, and idealism. Madison would spend his lifetime studying, inventing, and rethinking the rules of the game.

THE WRITINGS OF JAMES MADISON

Memorial and Remonstrance Against Religious Assessments

JUNE 1785

To the Honorable the General Assembly of the
Commonwealth of Virginia
A Memorial and Remonstrance

We the subscribers, citizens of the said Commonwealth, having taken into serious consideration, a Bill printed by order of the last Session of General Assembly, entitled "A Bill establishing a provision for Teachers of the Christian Religion," and conceiving that the same if finally armed with the sanctions of a law, will be a dangerous abuse of power, are bound as faithful members of a free State to remonstrate against it, and to declare the reasons by which we are determined. We remonstrate against the said Bill,

1. Because we hold it for a fundamental and undeniable truth, "that Religion or the duty which we owe to our Creator and the manner of discharging it, can be directed only by reason and conviction, not by force or violence." The Religion then of every man must be left to the conviction and conscience of every man; and it is the right of every man to exercise it as these may dictate. This right is in its nature an unalienable right. It is unalienable, because the opinions of men, depending only on the evidence contemplated by their own minds cannot follow the dictates of other men: It is unalienable also, because what is here a right towards men, is a duty towards the Creator. It is the duty of every man to render to the Creator such homage and such only as he believes to be acceptable to him. This duty is precedent, both in order of time and in degree of obligation, to the claims of Civil Society. Before any man can be considered as a member of Civil Society, he must be considered as a subject of the Governour of the Universe: And if a member of Civil Society, who enters into any subordinate Association, must always do it with a reservation of his duty to the General Authority; much more must every man who becomes a member of any particular Civil Society, do it with a saving of his allegiance to the Universal Sovereign. We maintain therefore that in matters of Religion, no mans right is abridged by the institution of Civil Society and that Religion is wholly exempt from its cognizance. True it is, that no other rule exists, by which any question which may divide a Society, can be ultimately determined, but the will of the majority; but it is also true that the majority may trespass on the rights of the minority.

2. Because if Religion be exempt from the authority of the Society at large, still less can it be subject to that of the Legislative Body. The latter

are but the creatures and vicegerents of the former. Their jurisdiction is both derivative and limited: it is limited with regard to the co-ordinate departments, more necessarily is it limited with regard to the constituents. The preservation of a free Government requires not merely, that the metes and bounds which separate each department of power be invariably maintained; but more especially that neither of them be suffered to overleap the great Barrier which defends the rights of the people. The Rulers who are guilty of such an encroachment, exceed the commission from which they derive their authority, and are Tyrants. The People who submit to it are governed by laws made neither by themselves nor by an authority derived from them, and are slaves.

3. Because it is proper to take alarm at the first experiment on our liberties. We hold this prudent jealousy to be the first duty of Citizens, and one of the noblest characteristics of the late Revolution. The free men of America did not wait till usurped power had strengthened itself by exercise, and entangled the question in precedents. They saw all the consequences in the principle, and they avoided the consequences by denying the principle. We revere this lesson too much soon to forget it. Who does not see that the same authority which can establish Christianity, in exclusion of all other Religions, may establish with the same ease any particular sect of Christians, in exclusion of all other Sects? that the same authority which can force a citizen to contribute three pence only of his property for the support of any one establishment, may force him to conform to any other establishment in all cases whatsoever? [. . .]

11. Because it will destroy that moderation and harmony which the forbearance of our laws to intermeddle with Religion has produced among its several sects. Torrents of blood have been spilt in the old world, by vain attempts of the secular arm, to extinguish Religious discord, by proscribing all difference in Religious opinion. Time has at length revealed the true remedy. Every relaxation of narrow and rigorous policy, wherever it has been tried, has been found to assuage the disease. The American Theatre has exhibited proofs that equal and compleat liberty, if it does not wholly eradicate it, sufficiently destroys its malignant influence on the health and prosperity of the State. If with the salutary effects of this system under our own eyes, we begin to contract the bounds of Religious freedom, we know no name that will too severely reproach our folly. At least let warning be taken at the first fruits of the threatened innovation. The very appearance of the Bill has transformed "that Christian forbearance, love and charity," which of late mutually prevailed, into animosities and jealousies, which may not soon be appeased.

What mischiefs may not be dreaded, should this enemy to the public quiet be armed with the force of a law? [. . .]

To George Washington

NEW YORK, APRIL 16, 1787.

Dear Sir,

I have been honored with your letter of the 31 of March, and find with much pleasure that your views of the reform which ought to be pursued by the Convention, give a sanction to those which I have entertained. Temporising applications will dishonor the Councils which propose them, and may foment the internal malignity of the disease, at the same time that they produce an ostensible palliation of it. Radical attempts although unsuccessful will at least justify the authors of them.

Having been lately led to revolve the subject which is to undergo the discussion of the Convention, and formed *some* outlines of a new system, I take the liberty of submitting them without apology to your eye.

Conceiving that an individual independence of the States is utterly irreconcileable with their aggregate sovereignty, and that a consolidation of the whole into one simple republic would be as inexpedient as it is unattainable, I have sought for middle ground, which may at once support a due supremacy of the national authority, and not exclude the local authorities wherever they can be subordinately useful.

I would propose as the ground-work that a change be made in the principle of representation. According to the present form of the Union in which the intervention of the States is in all great cases necessary to effectuate the measures of Congress, an equality of suffrage, does not destroy the inequality of importance in the several members. No one will deny that Virginia and Massts. have more weight and influence both within & without Congress than Delaware or Rho. Island. Under a system which would operate in many essential points without the intervention of the State Legislatures, the case would be materially altered. A vote in the national Councils from Delaware, would then have the same effect and value as one from the largest State in the Union. I am ready to believe that such a change would not be attended with much difficulty. A majority of the States, and those of greatest influence, will regard it as favorable to them. To the Northern States it will be recommended by their present populousness; to the Southern by their expected advantage in this respect. The lesser States must in every event yield to the predominant will. But the consideration which particularly urges a change in the representation is that it will obviate the principal objections of the larger States to the necessary concessions of power.

I would propose next that in addition to the present federal powers, the national Government should be armed with positive and compleat authority in all cases which require uniformity; such as the regulation of trade, including the right of taxing both exports & imports, the fixing the terms and forms of naturalization, &c &c.

Over and above this positive power, a negative *in all cases whatsoever* on the legislative acts of the States, as heretofore exercised by the Kingly prerogative, appears to me to be absolutely necessary, and to be the least possible encroachment on the State jurisdictions. Without this defensive power, every positive power that can be given on paper will be evaded & defeated. The States will continue to invade the National jurisdiction, to violate treaties and the law of nations & to harass each other with rival and spiteful measures dictated by mistaken views of interest. Another happy effect of this prerogative would be its controul on the internal vicissitudes of State policy, and the aggressions of interested majorities on the rights of minorities and of individuals. The great desideratum which has not yet been found for Republican Governments seems to be some disinterested & dispassionate umpire in disputes between different passions & interests in the State. The majority who alone have the right of decision, have frequently an interest, real or supposed in abusing it. In Monarchies the sovereign is more neutral to the interests and views of different parties; but, unfortunely he too often forms interests of his own repugnant to those of the whole. Might not the national prerogative here suggested be found sufficiently disinterested for the decision of local questions of policy, whilst it would itself be sufficiently restrained from the pursuit of interests adverse to those of the whole Society. There has not been any moment since the peace at which the representatives of the Union would have given an assent to paper money or any other measure of a kindred nature.

The national supremacy ought also to be extended as I conceive to the Judiciary departments. If those who are to expound & apply the laws, are connected by their interests & their oaths with the particular States wholly, and not with the Union, the participation of the Union in the making of the laws may be possibly rendered unavailing. It seems at least necessary that the oaths of the Judges should include a fidelity to the general as well as local constitution, and that an appeal should lie to some National tribunals in all cases to which foreigners or inhabitants of other States may be parties.

The admiralty jurisdiction seems to fall entirely within the purview of the national Government.

The National supremacy in the Executive departments is liable to some difficulty, unless the officers administering them could be made appointable by the Supreme Government. The Militia ought certainly to be placed in some form or other under the authority which is entrusted with the general protection and defence.

A Government composed of such extensive powers should be well organized and balanced. The legislative department might be divided into two branches; one of them chosen every   years by the people at large, or by the Legislatures; the other to consist of fewer members, to hold their places for a longer term, and to go out in such a rotation as always to leave in office a large majority of old members. Perhaps the negative on the laws might be most conveniently exercised by this branch. As a further check, a council of revision including the great ministerial officers might be superadded.

A national Executive must also be provided. I have scarcely ventured as yet to form my own opinion either of the manner in which it ought to be constituted or of the authorities with which it ought to be cloathed.

An article should be inserted expressly guarantying the tranquillity of the States against internal as well as external dangers.

In like manner the right of coercion should be expressly declared. With the resources of Commerce in hand, the National administration might always find means of exerting it either by sea or land; But the difficulty & awkwardness of operating by force on the collective will of a State, render it particularly desirable that the necessity of it might be precluded. Perhaps the negative on the laws might create such a mutuality of dependence between the General and particular authorities, as to answer this purpose or perhaps some defined objects of taxation might be submitted along with commerce, to the general authority.

To give a new System its proper validity and energy, a ratification must be obtained from the people, and not merely from the ordinary authority of the Legislatures. This will be the more essential as inroads on the *existing Constitutions* of the States will be unavoidable.

The inclosed address to the States on the subject of the Treaty of peace has been agreed to by Congress, & forwarded to the several Executives. We foresee the irritation which it will excite in many of our Countrymen; but could not withhold our approbation of the measure. Both the resolutions and the address, passed without a dissenting voice.

Congress continue to be thin, and of course do little business of importance. The settlement of the public accounts,—the disposition of the public lands, and arrangements with Spain, are subjects which claim their particular attention. As a step towards the first, the treasury board are charged with the task of reporting a plan by which the final decision on the claims of the States will be handed over from Congress to a select set of men bound by the oaths, and cloathed with the powers of Chancellors. As to the Second article, Congress have it themselves under consideration. Between 6 & 700 thousand acres have been surveyed and are ready for sale. The mode of sale however will probably be a source of different opinions; as will the mode of disposing of the unsurveyed residue. The Eastern gentlemen remain attached to the scheme of townships. Many others are equally strenuous for indiscriminate locations. The States which have lands of their own for sale are *suspected* of not being hearty in bringing the federal lands to market. The business with Spain is becoming extremely delicate, and the information from the Western settlements truly alarming.

A motion was made some days ago for an adjournment of Congress for a short period, and an appointment of Philada. for their reassembling. The eccentricity of this place as well with regard to E. and West as to N. & South has I find been for a considerable time a thorn in the minds of many of the Southern members. Suspicion too has charged some important votes on the weight thrown by the present position of Congress into the Eastern Scale, and predicts that the Eastern members will never concur in any substantial provision or movement for a proper permanent seat for the National Government whilst they remain so much gratified in its temporary residence. These seem to have been the operative motives with those on one side who were not locally interested in the removal. On the other side the motives are obvious. Those of real weight were drawn from the apparent caprice with which Congress might be reproached, and particularly from the peculiarity of the existing moment. I own that I think so much regard due to these considerations, that notwithstanding the powerful ones on the other side, I should have assented with great repugnance to the motion, and would even have voted against it if any probability had existed that by waiting for a proper time, a proper measure might not be lost for a very long time. The plan which I shd. have judged most eligible would have been to fix on the removal whenever a vote could be obtained but so as that it should not take effect until the commencement of the ensuing federal year. And if an immediate removal had been resolved on, I had intended to propose such a change in the plan. No final question was taken in the case. Some preliminary questions shewed that six States were in favor of the motion. Rho. Island the 7th was at first on the same side, and Mr. Varnum, one of the delegates continues so. His colleague was overcome by the solicitations of his Eastern brethren. As neither Maryland nor South Carolina were on the floor, it seems pretty evident that N. York has a very precarious tenure of the advantages derived from the abode of Congress.

We understand that the discontents in Massts, which lately produced an appeal to the sword, are now producing a trial of strength in the field of electioneering. The Governor will be displaced. The Senate is said to be already of a popular complexion, and it is expected that the other branch will be still more so. Paper money it is surmised will be the engine to be played off agst. creditors both public and private. As the event of the elections however is not yet decided, this information must be too much blended with conjecture to be regarded as a matter of certainty.

I do not learn that the proposed Act relating to Vermont has yet gone through all the stages of legislation here; nor can I say whether it will finally pass or not. In truth, it having not been a subject of conversation for some time, I am unable to say what has been done or is likely to be done with it. With the sincerest affection & the highest esteem I have the honor to be, Dear Sir your devoted Servt.

The Virginia Plan: Resolutions Proposed to the Convention

MAY 29, 1787

1. Resolved that the articles of Confederation ought to be so corrected & enlarged as to accomplish the objects proposed by their institution; namely, "common defence, security of liberty, and general welfare."

2. Resd. therefore that the rights of suffrage in the National Legislature ought to be proportioned to the Quotas of contribution, or to the number of free inhabitants, as the one or the other rule may seem best in different cases.

3. Resd. that the National Legislature ought to consist of two branches.

4. Resd. that the members of the first branch of the National Legislature ought to be elected by the people of the several States every   for the term of   ; to be of the age of   years at least, to receive liberal stipends by which they may be compensated for the devotion of their time to the public service; to be ineligible to any office established by a particular State, or under the authority of the United States, except those peculiarly belong to the functions of the first branch, during the term of service, and for the space of   after its expiration; to be incapable of re-election for

the space of after the expiration of their term of service, and to be subject to recall.

5. Resold. that the members of the second branch of the National Legislature ought to be elected by those of the first, out of a proper number of persons nominated by the individual Legislatures, to be of the age of years at least; to hold their offices for a term sufficient to ensure their independency; to receive liberal stipends, by which they may be compensated for the devotion of their time to the public service; and to be ineligible to any office established by a particular State, or under the authority of the United States, except those peculiarly belonging to the functions of the second branch, during the term of service; and for the space of after the expiration thereof.

6. Resolved that each branch ought to possess the right of originating Acts; that the National Legislature ought to be empowered to enjoy the Legislative Rights vested in Congress by the Confederation & moreover to legislate in all cases to which the separate States are incompetent, or in which the harmony of the United States may be interrupted by the exercise of individual Legislation; to negative all laws passed by the several States contravening in the opinion of the National Legislature the articles of Union; and to call forth the force of the Union agst. any member of the Union failing to fulfil its duty under the articles thereof.

7. Resd. that a National Executive be instituted; to be chosen by the National Legislature for the term of years, to receive punctually at stated times, a fixed compensation for the services rendered, in which no increase or diminution shall be made so as to affect the Magistracy, existing at the time of increase or diminution, and to be ineligible a second time; and that besides a general authority to execute the national laws, it ought to enjoy the Executive rights vested in Congress by the Confederation.

8. Resd. that the Executive and a convenient number of the National Judiciary, ought to compose a Council of revision with authority to examine every act of the National Legislature before it shall operate, & every act of a particular Legislature before a Negative thereon shall be final; and that the dissent of the said Council shall amount to a rejection, unless the Act of the National Legislature be again passed, or that of a particular Legislature be again negatived by of the members of each branch.

9. Resd. that a National Judiciary be established to consist of one or more supreme tribunals, and of inferior tribunals to be chosen by the National Legislature, to hold their offices during good behaviour; and to receive punctually at stated times fixed compensation for their services, in

which no increase or diminution shall be made so as to affect the persons actually in office at the time of such increase or diminution. That the jurisdiction of the inferior tribunals shall be to hear & determine in the first instance, and of the supreme tribunal to hear and determine in the dernier resort, all Piracies & felonies on the high seas, captures from an enemy: cases in which foreigners or citizens of other States applying to such jurisdictions may be interested, or which respect the collection of the National revenue; impeachments of any national officers, and questions which may involve the national peace and harmony.

10. Resolvd. that provision ought to be made for the admission of States lawfully arising within the limits of the United States, whether from a voluntary junction of Government & Territory or otherwise, with the consent of a number of voices in the National Legislature less than the whole.

11. Resd. that a Republican Government & the territory of each State, except in the instance of a voluntary junction of Government & territory, ought to be guaranteed by the United States to each State.

12. Resd. that provision ought to be made for the continuance of Congress and their authorities and privileges, until a given day after the reform of the articles of Union shall be adopted, and for the completion of all their engagements.

13. Resd. that provision ought to be made for the amendment of the Articles of Union whensoever it shall seem necessary, and that the assent of the National Legislature ought not to be required thereto.

14. Resd. that the Legislative Executive & Judiciary powers within the several States ought to be bound by oath to support the articles of Union.

15. Resd. that the amendments which shall be offered to the Confederation, by the Convention ought at a proper time, or times, after the approbation of Congress to be submitted to an assembly or assemblies of Representatives, recommended by the several Legislatures to be expressly chosen by the people to consider & decide thereon.

The Federalist, *No. 10*

NOVEMBER 22, 1787

To the People of the State of New York:

Among the numerous advantages promised by a well-constructed Union, none deserves to be more accurately developed than its tendency to break and control the violence of faction. The friend of popular governments never finds himself so much alarmed for their character and fate as when he contemplates their propensity to this dangerous vice. He will not fail, therefore, to set a due value on any plan which, without violating the principles to which he is attached, provides a proper cure for it. The instability, injustice, and confusion introduced into the public councils, have, in truth, been the mortal diseases under which popular governments have everywhere perished; as they continue to be the favorite and fruitful topics from which the adversaries to liberty derive their most specious declamations. The valuable improvements made by the American constitutions on the popular models, both ancient and modern, cannot certainly be too much admired; but it would be an unwarrantable partiality to contend that they have as effectually obviated the danger on this side as was wished and expected. Complaints are everywhere heard from our most considerate and virtuous citizens, equally the friends of public and private faith, and of public and personal liberty, that our governments are too unstable, that the public good is disregarded in the conflicts of rival parties, and that measures are too often decided, not according to the rules of justice and the rights of the minor party, but by the superior force of an interested and overbearing majority. However anxiously we may wish that these complaints had no foundation, the evidence of known facts will not permit us to deny that they are in some degree true. It will be found, indeed, on a candid review of our situation, that some of the distresses under which we labor have been erroneously charged on the operation of our governments; but it will be found, at the same time, that other causes will not alone account for many of our heaviest misfortunes; and, particularly, for that prevailing and increasing distrust of public engagements, and alarm for private rights, which are echoed from one end of the continent to the other. These must be chiefly, if not wholly, effects of the unsteadiness and injustice with which a factious spirit has tainted our public administrations.

By a faction, I understand a number of citizens, whether amounting to a majority or minority of the whole, who are united and actuated by some common impulse of passion, or of interest, adverse to the rights of other citizens, or to the permanent and aggregate interests of the community.

There are two methods of curing the mischiefs of faction: the one, by removing its causes; the other, by controlling its effects.

There are again two methods of removing the causes of faction: the one, by destroying the liberty which is essential to its existence; the other, by giving to every citizen the same opinions, the same passions, and the same interests.

It could never be more truly said than of the first remedy, that it was worse than the disease. Liberty is to faction what air is to fire, an aliment without which it instantly expires. But it could not be less folly to abolish liberty, which is essential to political life because it nourishes faction, than it would be to wish the annihilation of air, which is essential to animal life, because it imparts to fire its destructive agency.

The second expedient is as impracticable as the first would be unwise. As long as the reason of man continues fallible, and he is at liberty to exercise it, different opinions will be formed. As long as the connection subsists between his reason and his self-love, his opinions and his passions will have a reciprocal influence on each other; and the former will be objects to which the latter will attach themselves. The diversity in the faculties of men, from which the rights of property originate, is not less an insuperable obstacle to a uniformity of interests. The protection of these faculties is the first object of government. From the protection of different and unequal faculties of acquiring property, the possession of different degrees and kinds of property immediately results; and from the influence of these on the sentiments and views of the respective proprietors, ensues a division of the society into different interests and parties.

The latent causes of faction are thus sown in the nature of man; and we see them everywhere brought into different degrees of activity, according to the different circumstances of civil society. A zeal for different opinions concerning religion, concerning government, and many other points, as well of speculation as of practice; an attachment to different leaders ambitiously contending for pre-eminence and power; or to persons of other descriptions whose fortunes have been interesting to the human passions, have, in turn, divided mankind into parties, inflamed them with mutual animosity, and rendered them much more disposed to vex and oppress each other than to co-operate for their common good. So strong is this propensity of mankind to fall into mutual animosities that, where no substantial occasion presents itself, the most frivolous and fanciful distinctions have been sufficient to kindle their unfriendly passions and excite their most violent conflicts. But the most common and durable source of factions has been the various and unequal distribution of property. Those who hold and those who are without property have ever formed distinct interests in society. Those who are creditors, and those who are debtors, fall under a like discrimination. A landed interest, a manufacturing interest, a mercantile interest, a moneyed interest, with many lesser interests, grow up of necessity in civilized nations, and divide them into different classes actuated by different sentiments and views. The regulation of these various and interfering interests forms the principal task of modern legislation, and involves the spirit of party and faction in the necessary and ordinary operations of the government.

No man is allowed to be a judge in his own cause, because his interest would certainly bias his judgment and, not improbably, corrupt his integrity. With equal, nay with greater reason, a body of men are unfit to be both judges and parties at the same time; yet what are many of the most important acts of legislation but so many judicial determinations, not indeed concerning the rights of single persons, but concerning the rights of large bodies of citizens? And what are the different classes of legislators but advocates and parties to the causes which they determine? Is a law proposed concerning private debts? It is a question to which the creditors are parties on one side and the debtors on the other. Justice ought to hold the balance between them. Yet the parties are, and must be, themselves the judges; and the most numerous party, or, in other words, the most powerful faction, must be expected to prevail. Shall domestic manufactures be encouraged, and in what degree, by restrictions on foreign manufactures? are questions which would be differently decided by the landed and the manufacturing classes, and probably by neither with a sole regard to justice and the public good. The apportionment of taxes on the various descriptions of property is an act which seems to require the most exact impartiality; yet there is, perhaps, no legislative act in which greater opportunity and temptation are given to a predominant party to trample on the rules of justice. Every shilling with which they overburden the inferior number is a shilling saved to their own pockets.

It is in vain to say that enlightened statesmen will be able to adjust these clashing interests, and render them all subservient to the public good. Enlightened statesmen will not always be at the helm. Nor in many cases can such an adjustment be made at all without taking into view indirect and remote considerations, which will rarely prevail over the immediate interest which one party may find in disregarding the rights of another or the good of the whole.

The inference to which we are brought is that the *causes* of faction cannot be removed, and that relief is only to be sought in the means of controlling its *effects*.

If a faction consists of less than a majority, relief is supplied by the republican principle, which enables the majority to defeat its sinister views by regular vote. It may clog the administration, it may convulse the society; but it will be unable to execute and mask its violence under the forms of the Constitution. When a majority is included in a faction, the form of popular government, on the other hand, enables it to sacrifice to its ruling passion or interest both the public good and the rights of other citizens. To secure the public good and private rights against the danger of such a faction, and at the same time to preserve the spirit and the form of popular government, is then the great object to which our inquiries are directed. Let me add that it is the great desideratum by which this form of government can be rescued from the opprobrium under which it has so long labored, and be recommended to the esteem and adoption of mankind.

By what means is this object attainable? Evidently by one of two only: Either the existence of the same passion or interest in a majority at the same time must be prevented, or the majority, having such coexistent passion or interest, must be rendered, by their number and local situation, unable to concert and carry into effect schemes of oppression. If the impulse and the opportunity be suffered to coincide, we well know that neither moral nor religious motives can be relied on as an adequate control. They are not found to be such on the injustice and violence of individuals, and lose their efficacy in proportion to the number combined together, that is, in proportion as their efficacy becomes needful.

From this view of the subject it may be concluded that a pure democracy, by which I mean a society consisting of a small number of citizens, who assemble and administer the government in person, can admit of no cure for the mischiefs of faction. A common passion or interest will, in almost every case, be felt by a majority of the whole; a communication and concert result from the form of government itself; and there is nothing to check the inducements to sacrifice the weaker party or an obnoxious individual. Hence it is that such democracies have ever been spectacles of turbulence and contention; have ever been found incompatible with personal security or the rights of property; and have in general been as short in their lives as they have been violent in their deaths. Theoretic politicians, who have patronized this species of government, have erroneously supposed that by reducing mankind to a perfect equality in their political rights, they would, at the same time, be perfectly equalized and assimilated in their possessions, their opinions, and their passions.

A republic, by which I mean a government in which the scheme of representation takes place, opens a different prospect, and promises the cure for which we are seeking. Let us examine the points in which it varies from pure democracy, and we shall comprehend both the nature of the cure and the efficacy which it must derive from the Union.

The two great points of difference between a democracy and a republic are: first, the delegation of the government, in the latter, to a small number of citizens elected by the rest; secondly, the greater number of citizens, and greater sphere of country, over which the latter may be extended.

The effect of the first difference is, on the one hand, to refine and enlarge the public views, by passing them through the medium of a chosen body of citizens, whose wisdom may best discern the true interest of their country, and whose patriotism and love of justice will be least likely to sacrifice it to temporary or partial considerations. Under such a regulation, it may well happen that the public voice, pronounced by the representatives of the people, will be more consonant to the public good than if pronounced by the people themselves, convened for the purpose. On the other hand, the effect may be inverted. Men of factious tempers, of local prejudices, or of sinister designs, may, by intrigue, by corruption, or by other means, first obtain the suffrages, and then betray the interest, of the people. The question resulting is, whether small or extensive republics are more favorable to the election of proper guardians of the public weal; and it is clearly decided in favor of the latter by two obvious considerations:

In the first place, it is to be remarked that, however small the republic may be, the representatives must be raised to a certain number, in order to guard against the cabals of a few; and that, however large it may be, they must be limited to a certain number, in order to guard against the confusion of a multitude. Hence, the number of representatives in the two cases not being in proportion to that of the two constituents, and being proportionally greater in the small republic, it follows that, if the proportion of fit characters be not less in the large than in the small republic, the former will present a greater option, and consequently a greater probability of a fit choice.

In the next place, as each representative will be chosen by a greater number of citizens in the large than in the small republic, it will be more difficult for unworthy candidates to practice with success the vicious arts by which elections are too often carried; and the suffrages of the people, being more free, will be more likely to center in men who possess the most attractive merit and the most diffusive and established characters.

It must be confessed that in this, as in most other cases, there is a mean, on both sides of which inconveniences will be found to lie. By enlarging too much the number of electors, you render the representative too little acquainted with all their local circumstances and lesser interests; as by reducing it too much, you render him unduly attached to these, and too little fit to comprehend and pursue great and national objects. The federal Constitution forms a happy combination in this respect; the great and aggregate interests being referred to the national, the local and particular to the State legislatures.

The other point of difference is, the greater number of citizens and extent of territory which may be brought within the compass of republican than of democratic government; and it is this circumstance principally which renders factious combinations less to be dreaded in the former than in the latter. The smaller the society, the fewer probably will be the distinct parties and interests composing it; the fewer the distinct parties and interests, the more frequently will a majority be found of the same party; and the smaller the number of individuals composing a majority, and the smaller the compass within which they are placed, the more easily will they concert and execute their plans of oppression. Extend the sphere, and you take in a greater variety of parties and interests; you make it less probable that a majority of the whole will have a common motive to invade the rights of other citizens; or, if such a common motive exists, it will be more difficult for all who feel it to discover their own strength and to act in unison with each other. Besides other impediments, it may be remarked that where there is a consciousness of unjust or dishonorable purposes, communication is always checked by distrust in proportion to the number whose concurrence is necessary.

Hence it clearly appears that the same advantage which a republic has over a democracy, in controlling the effects of faction, is enjoyed by a large over a small republic, is enjoyed by the Union over the States composing it. Does the advantage consist in the substitution of representatives whose enlightened views and virtuous sentiments render them superior to local prejudices and to schemes of injustice? It will not be denied that the representation of the Union will be most likely to possess these requisite endowments. Does it consist in the greater security afforded by a greater variety of parties against the event of any one party being able to outnumber and oppress the rest? In an equal degree does the increased variety of parties comprised within the Union increase this security. Does it, in fine, consist in the greater obstacles opposed to the concert and accomplishment of the secret wishes of an unjust and interested majority? Here, again, the extent of the Union gives it the most palpable advantage.

The influence of factious leaders may kindle a flame within their particular States, but will be unable to spread a general conflagration through the other States. A religious sect may degenerate into a political faction in a part of the Confederacy; but the variety of sects dispersed over the entire face of it must secure the national councils against any danger from that source. A rage for paper money, for an abolition of debts, for an equal division of property, or for any other improper or wicked project, will be less apt to pervade the whole body of the Union than a particular member of it; in the same proportion as such a malady is more likely to taint a particular county or district than an entire State.

In the extent and proper structure of the Union, therefore, we behold a republican remedy for the diseases most incident to republican government. And according to the degree of pleasure and pride we feel in being republicans ought to be our zeal in cherishing the spirit and supporting the character of Federalists.

PUBLIUS.

The Federalist, *No. 37*

JANUARY 11, 1788

To the People of the State of New York:

In reviewing the defects of the existing Confederation, and showing that they cannot be supplied by a government of less energy than that before the public, several of the most important principles of the latter fell of course under consideration. But as the ultimate object of these papers is to determine clearly and fully the merits of this Constitution, and the expediency of adopting it, our plan cannot be complete without taking a more critical and thorough survey of the work of the convention; without examining it on all its sides, comparing it in all its parts, and calculating its probable effects.

That this remaining task may be executed under impressions conducive to a just and fair result, some reflections must in this place be indulged, which candor previously suggests.

It is a misfortune inseparable from human affairs that public measures are rarely investigated with that spirit of moderation which is essential to a just estimate of their real tendency to advance or obstruct the public good; and that this spirit is more apt to be diminished than promoted by those occasions which require an unusual exercise of it. To those who have been led by experience to attend to this consideration, it could not appear surprising that the act of the convention, which recommends so many important changes and innovations, which may be viewed in so many lights and relations, and which touches the springs of so many passions and interests, should find or excite dispositions unfriendly, both on one side and on the other, to a fair discussion and accurate judgment of its merits. In some it has been too evident, from their own publications, that they have scanned the proposed Constitution, not only with a predisposition to censure, but with a predetermination to condemn; as the language held by others betrays an opposite predetermination or bias, which must render their opinions also of little moment in the question. In placing, however, these different characters on a level, with respect to the weight of their opinions, I wish not to insinuate that there may not be a material difference in the purity of their intentions. It is but just to remark, in favor of the latter description, that as our situation is universally admitted to be peculiarly critical, and to require indispensably that something should be done for our relief, the predetermined patron of what has been actually done may have taken his bias from the weight of these considerations, as well as from considerations of a sinister nature. The predetermined adversary, on the other hand, can have been governed by no venial motive whatever. The intentions of the first may be upright, as they may, on the contrary, be culpable. The views of the last cannot be upright, and must be culpable. But the truth is that these papers are not addressed to persons falling under either of these characters. They solicit the attention of those only who add to a sincere zeal for the happiness of their country a temper favorable to a just estimate of the means of promoting it.

Persons of this character will proceed to an examination of the plan submitted by the convention, not only without a disposition to find or to magnify faults, but will see the propriety of reflecting that a faultless plan was not to be expected. Nor will they barely make allowances for the errors which may be chargeable on the fallibility to which the convention, as a body of men, were liable; but will keep in mind that they themselves also are but men and ought not to assume an infallibility in rejudging the fallible opinions of others.

With equal readiness will it be perceived that, besides these inducements to candor, many allowances ought to be made for the difficulties inherent in the very nature of the undertaking referred to the convention.

The novelty of the undertaking immediately strikes us. It has been shown in the course of these papers that the existing Confederation is founded on principles which are fallacious; that we must consequently change this first foundation, and with it the superstructure resting upon it. It has been shown that the other confederacies which could be consulted as precedents have been vitiated by the same erroneous principles, and can therefore furnish no other light than that of beacons, which give warning of the course to be shunned, without pointing out that which ought to be pursued. The most that the convention could do in such a situation was to avoid the errors suggested by the past experience of other countries, as well as of our own; and to provide a convenient mode of rectifying their own errors, as future experience may unfold them.

Among the difficulties encountered by the convention a very important one must have lain in combining the requisite stability and energy in government with the inviolable attention due to liberty and to the republican form. Without substantially accomplishing this part of their undertaking, they would have very imperfectly fulfilled the object of their appointment or the expectation of the public; yet that it could not be easily accomplished will be denied by no one who is unwilling to betray his ignorance of the subject. Energy in government is essential to that security against external and internal danger, and to that prompt and salutary execution of the laws which enter into the very definition of good government. Stability in government is essential to national character and to the advantages annexed to it, as well as to that repose and confidence in the minds of the people, which are among the chief blessings of civil society. An irregular and mutable legislation is not more an evil in itself than it is odious to the people; and it may be pronounced with assurance that the people of this country, enlightened as they are with regard to the nature, and interested, as the great body of them are, in the effects of good government, will never be satisfied till some remedy be applied to the vicissitudes and uncertainties which characterize the State administrations. On comparing, however, these valuable ingredients with the vital principles of liberty, we must perceive at once the difficulty of mingling them together in their due proportions. The genius of republican liberty seems to demand on one side, not only that all power should be derived from the people, but that those intrusted with it should be kept in dependence on the people, by a short duration of their appointments; and that, even during this short period, the trust should be placed not in a few but a number of hands. Stability, on the contrary, requires that the hands in which power is lodged should continue for a length of time the same. A frequent change of men will result from a frequent return of elections, and a frequent change of measures from a frequent change of men; whilst energy in government requires not only a certain duration of power, but the execution of it by a single hand.

How far the convention may have succeeded in this part of their work, will better appear on a more accurate view of it. From the cursory view here taken, it must clearly appear to have been an arduous part.

Not less arduous must have been the task of marking the proper line of partition between the authority of the general and that of the State governments. Every man will be sensible of this difficulty, in proportion as he has been accustomed to contemplate and discriminate objects extensive and complicated in their nature. The faculties of the mind itself have never yet been distinguished and defined, with satisfactory precision, by all the efforts of the most acute and metaphysical philosophers. Sense, perception, judgment, desire, volition, memory, imagination, are found to be separated by such delicate shades and minute gradations that their boundaries have eluded the most subtle investigations, and remain a pregnant source of ingenious disquisition and controversy. The boundaries between the great kingdom of nature, and, still more, between the various provinces and lesser portions into which they are subdivided, afford another illustration of the same important truth. The most sagacious and laborious naturalists have never yet succeeded in tracing with certainty the line which separates the district of vegetable life from the neighboring region of unorganized matter, or which marks the termination of the former and the commencement of the animal empire. A still greater obscurity lies in the distinctive characters by which the objects in each of these great departments of nature have been arranged and assorted.

When we pass from the works of nature, in which all the delineations are perfectly accurate, and appear to be otherwise only from the imperfection of the eye which surveys them, to the institutions of man, in which the obscurity arises as well from the object itself as from the organ by which it is contemplated, we must perceive the necessity of moderating still further our expectations and hopes from the efforts of human sagacity. Experience has instructed us that no skill in the science of government has yet been able to discriminate and define, with sufficient certainty, its three great provinces—the legislative, executive, and judiciary; or even the privileges and powers of the different legislative branches. Questions daily occur in the course of practice, which prove the obscurity which reigns in these subjects, and which puzzle the greatest adepts in political science.

The experience of ages, with the continued and combined labors of the most enlightened legislators and jurists, has been equally unsuccessful in delineating the several objects and limits of different codes of laws and different tribunals of justice. The precise extent of the common law, and the statute law, the maritime law, the ecclesiastical law, the law of corporations, and other local laws and customs, remains still to be clearly and finally established in Great Britain, where accuracy in such subjects has been more industriously pursued than in any other part of the world. The jurisdiction of her several courts, general and local, of law, of equity, of admiralty, etc., is not less a source of frequent and intricate discussions, sufficiently denoting the indeterminate limits by which they are respectively circumscribed. All new laws, though penned with the greatest technical skill, and passed on the fullest and most mature deliberation, are considered as more or less obscure and equivocal, until their meaning be liquidated and ascertained by a series of particular discussions and adjudications. Besides the obscurity arising from the complexity of objects, and the imperfection of the human faculties, the medium through which the conceptions of men are conveyed to each other adds a fresh embarrassment. The use of words is to express ideas. Perspicuity, therefore, requires not only that the ideas should be distinctly formed, but that they should be expressed by words distinctly and exclusively appropriate to them. But no language is so copious as to supply words and phrases for every complex idea, or so correct as not to include many, equivocally denoting different ideas. Hence it must happen that, however accurately objects may be discriminated in themselves, and however accurately the discrimination may be considered, the definition of them may be rendered inaccurate by the inaccuracy of the terms in which it is delivered. And this unavoidable inaccuracy must be greater or less, according to the complexity and novelty of the objects defined. When the Almighty himself condescends to address mankind in their own language, his meaning, luminous as it must be, is rendered dim and doubtful by the cloudy medium through which it is communicated.

Here, then, are three sources of vague and incorrect definitions: indistinctness of the object, imperfection of the organ of conception, inadequateness of the vehicle of ideas. Any one of these must produce a certain degree of obscurity. The convention, in delineating the boundary between the federal and State jurisdictions, must have experienced the full effect of them all.

To the difficulties already mentioned may be added the interfering pretensions of the larger and smaller States. We cannot err in supposing that the former would contend for a participation in the government fully proportioned to their superior wealth and importance; and that the latter would not be less tenacious of the equality at present enjoyed by them. We may well suppose that neither side would entirely yield to the other, and consequently that the struggle could be terminated only by compromise. It is extremely probable, also, that after the ratio of representation had been adjusted, this very compromise must have produced a fresh struggle between the same parties, to give such a turn to the organization of the government, and to the distribution of its powers, as would increase the importance of the branches, in forming which they had respectively obtained the greatest share of influence. There are features in the Constitution which warrant each of these suppositions; and as far as either of them is well founded, it shows that the convention must have been compelled to sacrifice theoretical propriety to the force of extraneous considerations.

Nor could it have been the large and small States only which would marshal themselves in opposition to each other on various points. Other combinations, resulting from a difference of local position and policy, must have created additional difficulties. As every State may be divided into different districts, and its citizens into different classes, which give birth to contending interests and local jealousies, so the different parts of the United States are distinguished from each other by a variety of circumstances, which produce a like effect on a larger scale. And although this variety of interests, for reasons sufficiently explained in a former paper, may have a salutary influence on the administration of the government when formed, yet everyone must be sensible of the contrary influence, which must have been experienced in the task of forming it.

Would it be wonderful if, under the pressure of all these difficulties, the convention should have been forced into some deviations from that artificial structure and regular symmetry which an abstract view of the subject might lead an ingenious theorist to bestow on a Constitution planned in his closet or in his imagination? The real wonder is that so many difficulties should have been surmounted, and surmounted with a unanimity almost as unprecedented as it must have been unexpected. It is impossible for any man of candor to reflect on this circumstance without partaking of the astonishment. It is impossible for the man of pious reflection not to perceive in it a finger of that Almighty hand which has been so frequently and signally extended to our relief in the critical stages of the revolution.

We had occasion, in a former paper, to take notice of the repeated trials which have been unsuccessfully made in the United Netherlands for reforming the baneful and notorious vices of their constitution. The history of almost all the great councils and consultations held among mankind for reconciling their discordant opinions, assuaging their mutual jealousies, and adjusting their respective interests, is a history of factions, contentions, and disappointments, and may be classed among the most dark and degraded pictures which display the infirmities and depravities of the human character. If, in a few scattered instances, a brighter aspect is presented, they serve only as exceptions to admonish us of the general truth, and by their luster to darken the gloom of the adverse prospect to which they are contrasted. In revolving the causes from which these exceptions result, and applying them to the particular instances before us, we are necessarily led to two important conclusions. The first is that the convention must have enjoyed, in a very singular degree, an exemption from the pestilential influence of party animosities—the disease most incident to deliberative bodies, and most apt to contaminate their proceedings. The second conclusion is that all the deputations composing the convention were satisfactorily accommodated by the final act, or were induced to accede to it by a deep conviction of the necessity of sacrificing private opinions and partial interests to the public good, and by a despair of seeing this necessity diminished by delays or by new experiments.

PUBLIUS.

The Federalist, *No. 49*

FEBRUARY 2, 1788

To the People of the State of New York:

The author of the "Notes on the State of Virginia," quoted in the last paper, has subjoined to that valuable work the draught of a constitution which had been prepared in order to be laid before a convention expected to be called in 1783, by the legislature, for the establishment of a constitution for that commonwealth. The plan, like everything from the same pen, marks a turn of thinking, original, comprehensive, and accurate; and is the more worthy of attention as it equally displays a fervent attachment to republican government and an enlightened view of the dangerous propensities against which it ought to be guarded. One of the precautions which he proposes, and on which he appears ultimately to rely as a palladium to the weaker departments of power against the invasions of the stronger, is perhaps altogether his own, and, as it immediately relates to the subject of our present inquiry, ought not to be overlooked.

His proposition is "that whenever any two of the three branches of government shall concur in opinion, each by the voices of two-thirds of their whole number, that a convention is necessary for altering the constitution, or *correcting breaches of it,* a convention shall be called for the purpose."

As the people are the only legitimate fountain of power, and it is from them that the constitutional charter, under which the several branches of government hold their power, is derived, it seems strictly consonant to the republican theory to recur to the same original authority not only whenever it may be necessary to enlarge, diminish, or new-model the powers of the government, but also whenever any one of the departments may commit encroachments on the chartered authorities of the others. The several departments being perfectly co-ordinate by the terms of their common commission, none of them, it is evident, can pretend to an exclusive or superior right of settling the boundaries between their respective powers; and how are the encroachments of the stronger to be prevented, or the wrongs of the weaker to be redressed, without an appeal to the people themselves, who, as the grantors of the commission, can alone declare its true meaning and enforce its observance?

There is certainly great force in this reasoning, and it must be allowed to prove that a constitutional road to the decision of the people ought to be marked out and kept open for certain great and extraordinary occasions. But there appear to be insuperable objections against the proposed recurrence to the people as a provision, in all cases, for keeping the several departments of power within their constitutional limits.

In the first place, the provision does not reach the case of a combination of two of the departments against the third. If the legislative authority, which possesses so many means of operating on the motives of the other departments, should be able to gain to its interest either of the others, or even one-third of its members, the remaining department could derive no advantage from its remedial provision. I do not dwell, however, on this objection, because it may be thought to be rather against the modification of the principle than against the principle itself.

In the next place, it may be considered as an objection inherent in the principle that, as every appeal to the people would carry an implication of some defect in the government, frequent appeals would in a great measure deprive the government of that veneration which time bestows on every thing, and without which perhaps the wisest and freest governments would not possess the requisite stability. If it be true that all governments rest on opinion, it is no less true that the strength of opinion in each individual, and its practical influence on his conduct, depend much on the number which he supposes to have entertained the same opinion. The reason of man, like man himself, is timid and cautious when left alone, and acquires firmness and confidence in proportion to the number with which it is associated. When the examples which fortify opinion are *ancient* as well as *numerous,* they are known to have a double effect. In a nation of philosophers, this consideration ought to be disregarded. A reverence for the laws would be sufficiently inculcated by the voice of an enlightened reason. But a nation of philosophers is as little to be expected as the philosophical race of kings wished for by Plato. And in every other nation the most rational government will not find it a superfluous advantage to have the prejudices of the community on its side.

The danger of disturbing the public tranquillity by interesting too strongly the public passions is a still more serious objection against a frequent reference of constitutional questions to the decision of the whole society. Notwithstanding the success which has attended the revisions of our established forms of government, and which does so much honor to the virtue and intelligence of the people of America, it must be confessed that the experiments are of too ticklish a nature to be unnecessarily multiplied. We are to recollect that all the existing constitutions were formed in the midst of a danger which repressed the passions most unfriendly to order and concord; of an enthusiastic confidence of the people in their patriotic leaders which stifled the ordinary diversity of opinions on great national questions; of a universal ardor for new and opposite forms, produced by a universal resentment and indignation against the ancient government; and whilst no spirit of party connected with the changes to be made, or the abuses to be reformed, could mingle its leaven in the operation. The future situations in which we must expect to be usually placed, do not present any equivalent security against the danger which is apprehended.

But the greatest objection of all is that the decisions which would probably result from such appeals would not answer the purpose of maintaining the constitutional equilibrium of the government. We have seen that the tendency of republican governments is to an aggrandizement of the legislative at the expense of the other departments. The appeals to the people, therefore, would usually be made by the executive and judiciary departments. But whether made by one side or the other, would each side enjoy equal advantages on the trial? Let us view their different situations. The members of the executive and judiciary departments are few in number, and can be personally known to a small part only of the people. The latter, by the mode of their appointment, as well as by the nature and permanency of it, are too far removed from the people to share much in their prepossessions. The former are generally the objects of jealousy, and their administration is always liable to be discolored and rendered unpopular. The members of the legislative department, on the other hand, are numerous. They are distributed and dwell among the people at large. Their connections of blood, of friendship, and of acquaintance embrace a great proportion of the most influential part of the society. The nature of their public trust implies a personal influence among the people, and that they are more immediately the confidential guardians of the rights and liberties of the people. With these advantages, it can hardly be supposed that the adverse party would have an equal chance for a favorable issue.

But the legislative party would not only be able to plead their cause most successfully with the people. They would probably be constituted themselves the judges. The same influence which had gained them an election into the legislature, would gain them a seat in the convention. If this should not be the case with all, it would probably be the case with many, and pretty certainly with those leading characters on whom everything depends in such bodies. The convention, in short, would be composed chiefly of men who had been, who actually were, or who expected to be, members of the department whose conduct was arraigned. They would consequently be parties to the very question to be decided by them.

It might, however, sometimes happen that appeals would be made under circumstances less adverse to the executive and judiciary departments. The usurpations of the legislature might be so flagrant and so sudden as to admit of no specious coloring. A strong party among themselves might take side with the other branches. The executive power might be in the hands of a peculiar favorite of the people. In such a posture of things, the public decision might be less swayed by prepossessions in favor of the legislative party. But still it could never be expected to turn on the true merits of the question. It would inevitably be connected with the spirit of preexisting parties, or of parties springing out of the question itself. It would be connected with persons of distinguished character and extensive influence in the community. It would be pronounced by the very men who had been agents in, or opponents of, the measures to which the decision would relate. The *passions,* therefore, not the *reason,* of the public would sit in judgment. But it is the reason, alone, of the public, that ought to control and regulate the government. The passions ought to be controlled and regulated by the government.

We found in the last paper, that mere declarations in the written constitution are not sufficient to restrain the several departments within their legal rights. It appears in this that occasional appeals to the people would be neither a proper nor an effectual provision for that purpose. How far the provisions of a different nature contained in the plan above quoted might be adequate, I do not examine. Some of them are unquestionably founded on sound political principles, and all of them are framed with singular ingenuity and precision.

PUBLIUS.

The Federalist, *No. 51*

FEBRUARY 6, 1788

To the People of the State of New York:

To what expedient, then, shall we finally resort, for maintaining in practice the necessary partition of power among the several departments, as laid down in the Constitution? The only answer that can be given is, that as all these exterior provisions are found to be inadequate, the defect must be supplied, by so contriving the interior structure of the government as that its several constituent parts may, by their mutual relations, be the means of keeping each other in their proper places. Without presuming to undertake a full development of this important idea, I will hazard a few general observations, which may perhaps place it in a clearer light and enable us to form a more correct judgment of the principles and structure of the government planned by the convention.

In order to lay a due foundation for that separate and distinct exercise of the different powers of government, which to a certain extent is admitted on all hands to be essential to the preservation of liberty, it is evident that each department should have a will of its own, and consequently should be so constituted that the members of each should have as little agency as possible in the appointment of the members of the others. Were this principle rigorously adhered to, it would require that all the appointments for the supreme executive, legislative, and judiciary magistracies should be drawn from the same fountain of authority, the people, through channels having no communication whatever with one another. Perhaps such a plan of constructing the several departments would be less difficult in practice than it may in contemplation appear. Some difficulties, however, and some additional expense would attend the execution of it. Some deviations, therefore, from the principle must be admitted. In the constitution of the judiciary department in particular, it might be inexpedient to insist rigorously on the principle: first, because peculiar qualifications being essential in the members, the primary consideration ought to be to select that mode of choice which best secures these qualifications; secondly, because the permanent tenure by which the appointments are held in that department, must soon destroy all sense of dependence on the authority conferring them.

It is equally evident that the members of each department should be as little dependent as possible on those of the others for the emoluments annexed to their offices. Were the executive magistrate, or the judges, not independent of the legislature in this particular, their independence in every other would be merely nominal.

But the great security against a gradual concentration of the several powers in the same department consists in giving to those who administer each department the necessary constitutional means and personal motives to resist encroachments of the others. The provision for defense must in this, as in all other cases, be made commensurate to the danger of attack. Ambition must be made to counteract ambition. The interest of the man must be connected with the constitutional rights of the place. It may be a reflection on human nature that such devices should be necessary to control the abuses of government. But what is government itself, but the greatest of all reflections on human nature? If men were angels, no government would be necessary. If angels were to govern men, neither external nor internal controls on government would be necessary. In framing a government which is to be administered by men over men, the great difficulty lies in this: you must first enable the government to control the governed; and in the next place oblige it to control itself. A dependence on the people is, no doubt, the primary control on the government; but experience has taught mankind the necessity of auxiliary precautions.

This policy of supplying, by opposite and rival interests, the defect of better motives, might be traced through the whole system of human affairs, private as well as public. We see it particularly displayed in all the subordinate distributions of power, where the constant aim is to divide and arrange the several offices in such a manner as that each may be a check on the other—that the private interest of every individual may be a sentinel over the public rights. These inventions of prudence cannot be less requisite in the distribution of the supreme powers of the State.

But it is not possible to give to each department an equal power of self-defence. In republican government, the legislative authority necessarily predominates. The remedy for this inconveniency is to divide the legislature into different branches; and to render them, by different modes of election and different principles of action, as little connected with each other as the nature of their common functions and their common dependence on the society will admit. It may even be necessary to guard against dangerous encroachments by still further precautions. As the weight of the legislative authority requires that it should be thus divided, the weakness of the executive may require, on the other hand, that it should be fortified. An absolute negative on the legislature appears, at first view, to be the natural defence with which the executive magistrate should be armed. But perhaps it would be neither altogether safe nor alone sufficient. On ordinary occasions it might not be exerted with the requisite firmness, and on extraordinary occasions it might be perfidiously abused. May not this defect of an absolute negative be supplied by some qualified connection between this weaker department and the weaker branch of the stronger department, by which the latter may be led to support the constitutional rights of the former, without being too much detached from the rights of its own department?

If the principles on which these observations are founded be just, as I persuade myself they are, and they be applied as a criterion to the several State constitutions, and to the federal Constitution, it will be found that if the latter does not perfectly correspond with them, the former are infinitely less able to bear such a test.

There are, moreover, two considerations particularly applicable to the federal system of America, which place that system in a very interesting point of view.

First. In a single republic, all the power surrendered by the people is submitted to the administration of a single government; and the usurpations are guarded against by a division of the government into distinct and separate departments. In the compound republic of America, the power surrendered by the people is first divided between two distinct governments, and then the portion allotted to each subdivided among distinct and separate departments. Hence a double security arises to the rights of the people. The different governments will control each other, at the same time that each will be controlled by itself.

Second. It is of great importance in a republic not only to guard the society against the oppression of its rulers, but to guard one part of the society against the injustice of the other part. Different interests necessarily exist in different classes of citizens. If a majority be united by a common interest, the rights of the minority will be insecure. There are but two methods of providing against this evil: the one by creating a will in the community independent of the majority—that is, of the society itself; the other, by comprehending in the society so many separate descriptions of citizens as will render an unjust combination of a majority of the whole very improbable, if not impracticable. The first method prevails in all governments possessing an hereditary or self-appointed authority. This, at best, is but a precarious security; because a power independent of the society may as well espouse the unjust views of the major, as the rightful interests of the minor party, and may possibly be turned against both parties. The second method will be exemplified in the federal republic of the United States. Whilst all authority in it will be derived from and dependent on the society, the society itself will be broken into so many parts, interests, and classes of citizens that the rights of individuals, or of the minority, will be in little danger from interested combinations of the majority. In a free government the security for civil rights must be the same as that for religious rights. It consists in the one case in the multiplicity of interests, and in the other in the multiplicity of sects. The degree of security in both cases will depend on the number of interests and sects; and this may be presumed to depend on the extent of country and number of people comprehended under the same government. This view of the subject must particularly recommend a proper federal system to all the sincere and considerate friends of republican government, since it shows that in exact proportion as the territory of the Union may be formed into more circumscribed Confederacies, or States, oppressive combinations of a majority will be facilitated; the best security, under the republican forms, for the rights of every class of citizens will be diminished; and consequently the stability and independence of some member of the government, the only other security, must be proportionally increased. Justice is the end of government. It is the end of civil society. It ever has been and ever will be pursued until it be obtained, or until liberty be lost in the pursuit. In a society under the forms of which the stronger faction can readily unite and oppress the weaker, anarchy may as truly be said to reign as in a state of nature, where the weaker individual is not secured against the violence of the stronger; and as, in the latter state, even the stronger individuals are prompted, by the uncertainty of their condition, to submit to a government which may protect the weak as well as themselves; so, in the former state, will the more powerful factions or parties be gradually induced, by a like motive, to wish for a government which will protect all parties, the weaker as well as the more powerful. It can be little doubted that if the State of Rhode Island was separated from the Confederacy and left to itself, the insecurity of rights under the popular form of government within such narrow limits would be displayed by such reiterated oppressions of factious majorities, that some power altogether independent of the people would soon be called for by the voice of the very factions whose misrule had proved the necessity of it. In the extended republic of the United States, and among the great variety of interests, parties, and sects which it embraces, a coalition of a majority of the whole society could seldom take place upon any other principles than those of justice and the general good; whilst there being thus less danger to a minor from the will of a major party, there must be less pretext, also, to provide for the security of the former, by introducing into the government a will not dependent on the latter, or, in other words, a will independent of the society itself. It is no less certain than it is important, notwithstanding the contrary opinions which have been entertained, that the larger the society, provided it lie within a practical sphere, the more duly capable it will be of self-government. And happily for the *republican cause,* the practicable sphere may be carried to a very great extent, by a judicious modification and mixture of the *federal principle.*

PUBLIUS.

The Federalist, *No. 54*

FEBRUARY 12, 1788

To the People of the State of New York:

The next view which I shall take of the House of Representatives relates to the appointment of its members to the several states, which is to be determined by the same rule with that of direct taxes.

It is not contended that the number of people in each state ought not to be the standard for regulating the proportion of those who are to represent the people of each state. The establishment of the same rule for the appointment of taxes will probably be as little contested; though the rule itself in this case is by no means founded on the same principle. In the former case the rule is understood to refer to the personal rights of the people, with which it has a natural and universal connection. In the latter, it has reference to the proportion of wealth, of which it is in no case a precise measure, and in ordinary cases a very unfit one. But notwithstanding the imperfection of the rule as applied to the relative wealth and contributions of the states, it is evidently the least objectionable among the practicable rules, and had too recently obtained the general sanction of America, not to have found a ready preference with the convention.

All this is admitted, it will perhaps be said: but does it follow from an admission of numbers for the measure of representation, or of slaves combined with free citizens, as a ratio of taxation, that slaves ought to be included in the numerical rule of representation? Slaves are considered as property, not as persons. They ought therefore to be comprehended in estimates of taxation which are founded on property, and to be excluded from representation which is regulated by a census of persons. This is the objection, as I understand it, stated in its full force. I shall be equally candid in stating the reasoning which may be offered on the opposite side.

We subscribe to the doctrine, might one of our Southern brethren observe, that representation relates more immediately to persons and taxation more immediately to property, and we join in the application of this distinction to the case of our slaves. But we must deny the fact that slaves are considered merely as property, and in no respect whatever as persons. The true state of the case is, that they partake of both these qualities; being considered by our laws, in some respects, as persons, and in other respects as property. In being compelled to labor not for himself, but for a master; in being vendible by one master to another master; and in being subject at all times to be restrained in his liberty, and chastised in his body, by the capricious will of another, the slave may appear to be degraded from the human rank, and classed with those irrational animals, which fall under the legal denomination of property. In being protected on the other hand in his life and in his limbs, against the violence of all others, even the master of his labor and his liberty; and in being punishable himself for all violence committed against others; the slave is no less evidently regarded by the law as a member of the society; not as a part of the irrational creation; as a moral person, not as a mere article of property. The federal constitution therefore, decides with great propriety on the case of our slaves, when it views them in the mixed character of persons and of property. This is in fact their true character. It is the character bestowed on them by the laws under which they live; and it will not be denied that these are the proper criterion; because it is only under the pretext that the laws have transformed the negroes into subjects of property that a place is disputed them in the computation of numbers; and it is admitted that, if the laws were to restore the rights which have been taken away, the negroes could no longer be refused an equal share of representation with the other inhabitants.

This question may be placed in another light. It is agreed on all sides that numbers are the best scale of wealth and taxation, as they are the only proper scale of representation. Would the Convention have been impartial or consistent, if they had rejected the slaves from the list of inhabitants when the shares of representation were to be calculated; and inserted them on the lists when the tariff of contributions was to be adjusted? Could it be reasonably expected that the southern states would concur in a system which considered their slaves in some degree as men, when burdens were to be imposed, but refused to consider them in the same light when advantages were to be conferred? Might not some surprize also be expressed that those who reproach the southern states with the barbarous policy of considering as property, a part of their human brethren, should themselves contend that the government to which all the states are to be parties ought to consider this unfortunate race more completely in the unnatural light of property, than the very laws of which they complain?

It may be replied, perhaps, that slaves are not included in the estimate of representatives in any of the states possessing them. They neither vote themselves nor increase the votes of their masters. Upon what principle then ought they to be taken into the federal estimate of representation? In rejecting them altogether, the constitution would, in this respect, have followed the very laws which have been appealed to, as the proper guide.

This objection is repelled by a single observation. It is a fundamental principle of the proposed constitution, that, as the aggregate number of representatives allotted to the several states is to be determined by a federal rule founded on the aggregate number of inhabitants, so the right of choosing this allotted number in each state is to be exercised by such part of the inhabitants as the state itself may designate. The qualifications on which the right of suffrage depend, are not perhaps the same in any two states. In some of the states the difference is very material. In every state a certain proportion of inhabitants are deprived of this right by the constitution of the state, who will be included in the census by which the federal Constitution apportions the representatives. In this point of view the southern states might retort the complaint, by insisting, that the principle laid down by the convention required that no regard should be had to the policy of particular states toward their own inhabitants; and, consequently, that the slaves as inhabitants should have been admitted into the census according to their full number, in like manner with other inhabitants who, by the policy of other states, are not admitted to all the rights of citizens. A rigorous adherence however, to this principle, is waived by those who would be gainers by it. All that they ask is, that equal moderation be shown on the other side. Let the case of the slaves be considered, as it is in truth a peculiar one. Let the compromising expedient of the constitution be mutually adopted, which regards them as inhabitants, but as debased by servitude below the equal level of free inhabitants, which regards the *slave* as divested of two fifths of the *man.*

After all, may not another ground be taken on which this article of the Constitution will admit of a still more ready defense? We have hitherto proceeded on the idea that representation related to persons only, and not at all to property. But is it a just idea? Government is instituted no less for protection of the property, than of the persons, of individuals. The one as well as the other, therefore, may be considered as represented by those who are charged with the government. Upon this principle it is, that in several of the states, and particularly in the state of New-York, one branch of the government is intended more especially to be the guardian of property, and is accordingly elected by that part of the society which is most interested in this object of government. In the federal Constitution, this policy does not prevail. The rights of property are committed into the same hands with the personal rights. Some attention ought, therefore, to be paid to property in the choice of those hands.

For another reason, the votes allowed in the federal legislature to the people of each state, ought to bear some proportion to the comparative wealth of the states. States have not, like individuals, an influence over each other arising from superior advantages of fortune. If the law allows an opulent citizen but a single vote in the choice of his representative, the respect and consequence which he derives from his fortunate situation very frequently guide the votes of others to the objects of his choice; and through this imperceptible channel the rights of property are conveyed into the public representation. A state possesses no such influence over other states. It is not probable that the richest state in the confederacy will ever influence the choice of a single representative in any other state. Nor will the representatives of the larger and richer states possess any other advantage in the federal legislature, over the representatives of other states, than what may result from their superior number alone; as far, therefore, as their superior wealth and weight may justly entitle them to any advantage, it ought to be secured to them by a superior share of representation. The new constitution is in this respect materially different from the existing confederation, as well as from that of the United Netherlands, and other similar confederacies. In each of the latter the efficacy of the federal resolutions depends on the subsequent and voluntary resolutions of the states composing the union. Hence the states, though possessing an equal vote in the public councils, have an unequal influence, corresponding with the unequal importance of these subsequent and voluntary resolutions. Under the proposed constitution, the federal acts will take effect without the necessary intervention of the individual states. They will depend merely on the majority of votes in the federal legislature, and consequently each vote, whether proceeding from a larger or smaller state, or a state more or less wealthy or powerful, will have an equal weight and efficacy; in the same manner as the votes individually given in a state legislature, by the representatives of unequal counties or other districts, have each a precise equality of value and effect; or if there be any difference in the case, it proceeds from the difference in the personal character of the individual representative, rather than from any regard to the extent of the district from which he comes.

Such is the reasoning which an advocate for the southern interests might employ on this subject: And although it may appear to be a little strained in some points, yet on the whole, I must confess, that it fully reconciles me to the scale of representation which the convention have established.

In one respect the establishment of a common measure for representation and taxation will have a very salutary effect. As the accuracy of the census to be obtained by the congress will necessarily depend in a considerable degree on the disposition, if not on the co-operation of the states, it is of great importance that the states should feel as little bias as possible to swell or to reduce the amount of their numbers. Were their share of representation alone to be governed by this rule, they would have an interest in exaggerating their inhabitants. Were the rule to decide their share of taxation alone, a contrary temptation would prevail. By extending the rule to both objects the states will have opposite interests, which will control and balance each other and produce the requisite impartiality.

PUBLIUS.

To Thomas Jefferson

NEW YORK, OCTOBER 17, 1788.

Dear Sir,

I have written a number of letters to you since my return here, and shall add this by another casual opportunity just notified to me by Mr. St. John. Your favor of July 31 came to hand the day before yesterday. The pamphlets of the Marquis Condorcet & Mr. Dupont referred to in it have also been received. Your other letters inclosed to the Delegation have been and will be disposed of as you wish; particularly those to Mr. Eppes & Col. Lewis.

Nothing has been done on the subject of the *outfit,* there not having been a Congress of nine States for some time, nor even of seven for the last week. It is pretty certain that there will not again be a quorum of either number within the present year, and by no means certain that there will be one at all under the old Confederation. The Committee finding that nothing could be done have neglected to make a report as yet. I have spoken with a member of it in order to get one made, that the case may fall of course and in a favorable shape within the attention of the New Government. The fear of a precedent will probably lead to an allowance for a limited time of the *salary, as enjoyed originally* by *foreign ministers,* in *preference to a separate allowance for outfit.* One of the *members* of the *treasury board,* who ought, if certain facts have *not escaped his memory, to witness the reasonableness of your* calculations, *takes occasion I find to impress a contrary idea.* Fortunately *his influence will not be a very formidable obstacle to right.*

The States which have adopted the New Constitution are all proceeding to the arrangements for putting it into action in March next. Pennsylva. alone has as yet actually appointed deputies & that only for the Senate. My last mention that these were Mr. R. Morris & a Mr. McClay. How the other elections there & elsewhere will run is matter of uncertainty. The Presidency alone unites the conjectures of the public. The vice president is not at all marked out by the general voice. As the President will be from a Southern State, it falls almost of course for the other part of the Continent to supply the next in rank. South Carolina may however think of Mr. Rutledge unless it should be previously discovered that votes will be wasted on him. The only candidates in the Northern States brought forward with their known consent are *Hancock and Adams,* and *between these it seems probable the question will lie.* Both of them *are objectionable & would I think be postponed* by the *general suffrage to several others* if they *would accept the place. Hancock* is *weak ambitious a courtier of popularity, given to low intrigue,* and *lately reunited by a factious friendship with S. Adams. J. Adams* has made *himself obnoxious to many,* particularly in the *Southern States by the political principles avowed in his book.* Others *recollecting his cabal during the war against General Washington,* knowing *his extravagant self-importance,* and *considering his preference of an unprofitable dignity* to some *place of emolument* better *adapted to private fortune as a proof of his* having *an eye to the presidency, conclude* that *he would not be a very cordial second to the General,* and that *an impatient ambition* might *even intrigue for a premature advancement.* The *danger would be the greater if* particular *factious characters,* as may be the case, *should get into the public councils. Adams* it appears, is *not unaware of* some *of the obstacles to his wish,* and *thro a letter to Smith* has *thrown out popular sentiments as to the proposed president.*

The little pamphlet herewith inclosed will give you a collective view of the alterations which have been proposed for the new Constitution. Various and numerous as they appear they certainly omit many of the true grounds of opposition. The articles relating to Treaties, to paper money, and to contracts, created more enemies than all the errors in the System positive & negative put together. It is true nevertheless that not a few, particularly in Virginia have contended for the proposed alterations from the most honorable & patriotic motives; and that among the advocates for the Constitution there are some who wish for further guards to public liberty & individual rights. As far as these may consist of a constitutional declaration of the most essential rights, it is probable they will be added; though there are many who think such addition unnecessary, and not a few who think it misplaced in such a Constitution. There is scarce any point on which the party in opposition is so much divided as to its importance and its propriety. My own opinion has always been in favor of a bill of rights; provided it be so framed as not to imply powers not meant to be included in the enumeration. At the same time I have never thought the omission a material defect, nor been anxious to supply it even by *subsequent* amendment, for any other reason than that it is anxiously desired by others. I have favored it because I supposed it might be of use, and if properly executed could not be of disservice. I have not viewed it in an important light 1. because I conceive that in a certain degree, though not in the extent argued by Mr. Wilson, the rights in question are reserved by the manner in which the federal powers are granted. 2. because there is great reason to fear that a positive declaration of some of the most essential rights could not be obtained in the requisite latitude. I am sure that the rights of conscience in particular, if submitted to public definition would be narrowed much more than they are likely ever to be by an assumed power. One of the objections in New England was that the Constitution by prohibiting religious tests, opened a door for Jews Turks & infidels. 3. because the limited powers of the federal Government and the jealousy of the subordinate Governments, afford a security which has not existed in the case of the State Governments, and exists in no other. 4. because experience proves the inefficacy of a bill of rights on those occasions when its controul is most needed. Repeated violations of these parchment barriers have been committed by overbearing majorities in every State. In Virginia I have seen the bill of rights violated in every instance where it has been opposed to a popular current. Notwithstanding the explicit provision contained in that instrument for the rights of Conscience, it is well known that a religious establishment wd. have taken place in that State, if the Legislative majority had found as they expected, a majority of the people in favor of the measure; and I am persuaded that if a majority of the people were now of one sect, the measure would still take place and on narrower ground than was then proposed, notwithstanding the additional obstacle which the law has since created. Wherever the real power in a Government lies, there is the danger of oppression. In our Governments the real power lies in the majority of the Community, and the invasion of private rights is *chiefly* to be apprehended, not from acts of Government contrary to the sense of its constituents, but from acts in which the Government is the mere instrument of the major number of the Constituents. This is a truth of great importance, but not yet sufficiently attended to; and is probably more strongly impressed on my mind by facts, and reflections suggested by them, than on yours which has contemplated abuses of power issuing from a very different quarter. Wherever there is an interest and power to do wrong, wrong will generally be done, and not less readily by a powerful & interested party than by a powerful and interested prince. The difference so far as it relates to the superiority of republics over monarchies, lies in the less degree of probability that interest may prompt more abuses of power in the former than in the latter; and in the security in the former agst. an oppression of more than the smaller part of the society, whereas in the former it may be extended in a manner to the whole. The difference so far as it relates to the point in question—the efficacy of a bill of rights in controuling abuses of power—lies in this: that in a monarchy the latent force of the nation is superior to that of the Sovereign, and a solemn charter of popular rights must have a great effect, as a standard for trying the validity of public acts, and a signal for rousing & uniting the superior force of the community; whereas in a popular Government, the political and physical power may be considered as vested in the same hands, that is in a majority of the people, and, consequently the tyrannical will of the Sovereign is not to be controuled by the dread of an appeal to any other force within the community. What use then it may be asked can a bill of rights serve in popular Governments? I answer the two following which, though less essential than in other Governments, sufficiently recommend the precaution: 1. The political truths declared in that solemn manner acquire by degrees the character of fundamental maxims of free Government, and as they become incorporated with the national sentiment, counteract the impulses of interest and passion. 2. Altho' it be generally true as above stated that the danger of oppression lies in the interested majorities of the people rather than in usurped acts of the Government, yet there may be occasions on which the evil may spring from the latter source; and on such, a bill of rights will be a good ground for an appeal to the sense of the community. Perhaps too there may be a certain degree of danger, that a succession of artful and ambitious rulers may by gradual & well timed advances, finally erect an independent Government on the subversion of liberty. Should this danger exist at all, it is prudent to guard agst. it, especially when the precaution can do no injury. At the same time I must own that I see no tendency in our Governments to danger on that side. It has been remarked that there is a tendency in all Governments to an augmentation of power at the expence of liberty. But the remark as usually understood does not appear to me well founded. Power when it has attained a certain degree of energy and independence goes on generally to further degrees. But when below that degree, the direct tendency is to further degrees of relaxation, until the abuses of liberty beget a sudden transition to an undue degree of power. With this explanation the remark may be true; and in the latter sense only is it, in my opinion applicable to the Governments in America. It is a melancholy reflection that liberty should be equally exposed to danger whether the Government have too much or too little power, and that the line which divides these extremes should be so inaccurately defined by experience.

Supposing a bill of rights to be proper the articles which ought to compose it, admit of much discussion. I am inclined to think that *absolute* restrictions in cases that are doubtful, or where emergencies may overrule them, ought to be avoided. The restrictions however strongly marked on paper will never be regarded when opposed to the decided sense of the public, and after repeated violations in extraordinary cases they will lose even their ordinary efficacy. Should a Rebellion or insurrection alarm the people as well as the Government, and a suspension of the Hab. Corp. be dictated by the alarm, no written prohibitions on earth would prevent the measure. Should an army in time of peace be gradually established in our neighborhood by Britn: or Spain, declarations on paper would have as little effect in preventing a standing force for the public safety. The best security agst. these evils is to remove the pretext for them. With regard to Monopolies, they are justly classed among the greatest nuisances in Government. But is it clear that as encouragements to literary works and ingenious discoveries, they are not too valuable to be wholly renounced? Would it not suffice to reserve in all cases a right to the public to abolish the privilege at a price to be specified in the grant of it? Is there not also infinitely less danger of this abuse in our Governments than in most others? Monopolies are sacrifices of the many to the few. Where the power is in the few it is natural for them to sacrifice the many to their own partialities and corruptions. Where the power as with us is in the many not in the few the danger cannot be very great that the few will be thus favored. It is much more to be dreaded that the few will be unnecessarily sacrificed to the many.

I inclose a paper containing the late proceedings in Kentucky. I wish the ensuing Convention may take no step injurious to the character of the district, and favorable to the views of those who wish ill to the U. States. One of my late letters communicated some circumstances which will not fail to occur on perusing the objects of the proposed Convention in next month. Perhaps however there may be less connection between the two cases than at first one is ready to conjecture.

I am, Dr Sir with the sincerest esteem & Affectn Yours

To Thomas Jefferson

NEW YORK, FEBY 4. 1790.

Dear Sir,

Your favor of the 9th of Jany. inclosing one of Sepr. last did not get to hand till a few days ago. The idea which the latter evolves is a great one, and suggests many interesting reflections to legislators; particularly when contracting and providing for public debts. Whether it can be received in the extent your reasonings give it, is a question which I ought to turn more in my thoughts than I have yet been able to do, before I should be justified in making up a full opinion on it. My first thoughts though coinciding with many of yours, lead me to view the doctrine as not in *all* respects compatible with the course of human affairs. I will endeavor to sketch the grounds of my skepticism.

> "As the earth belongs to the living, not to the dead, a living generation can bind itself only: In every society the will of the majority binds the whole: According to the laws of mortality, a majority of those ripe at any moment for the exercise of their will do not live beyond nineteen years: To that term then is limited the validity of *every* act of the Society: Nor within that limitation, can any declaration of the public will be valid which is not *express.*"

This I understand to be the outline of the argument.

The Acts of a political Society may be divided into three classes:

1. The fundamental Constitution of the Government.
2. Laws involving stipulations which render them irrevocable at the will of the Legislature.
3. Laws involving no such irrevocable quality.

However applicable in Theory the doctrine may be to a Constitution, it seems liable in practice to some very powerful objections. Would not a Government so often revised become too mutable to retain those prejudices in its favor which antiquity inspires, and which are perhaps a salutary aid to the most rational Government in the most enlightened age? Would not such a periodical revision engender pernicious factions that might not otherwise come into existence? Would not, in fine, a Government depending for its existence beyond a fixed date, on some positive and authentic intervention of the Society itself, be too subject to the casualty and consequences of an actual interregnum?

In the 2d. class, exceptions at least to the doctrine seem to be requisite both in Theory and practice.

If the earth be the gift of nature to the living their title can extend to the earth in its natural State only. The *improvements* made by the dead form a charge against the living who take the benefit of them. This charge can no otherwise be satisfyed than by executing the will of the dead accompanying the improvements.

Debts may be incurred for purposes which interest the unborn, as well as the living: such are debts for repelling a conquest, the evils of which descend through many generations. Debts may even be incurred principally for the benefit of posterity: such perhaps is the present debt of the U. States, which far exceeds any burdens which the present generation could well apprehend for itself. The term of 19 years might not be sufficient for discharging the debts in either of these cases.

There seems then to be a foundation in the nature of things, in the relation which one generation bears to another, for the *descent* of obligations from one to another. Equity requires it. Mutual good is promoted by it. All that is indispensable in adjusting the account between the dead & the living is to see that the debts against the latter do not exceed the advances made by the former. Few of the incumbrances entailed on Nations would bear a liquidation even on this principle.

The objections to the doctrine as applied to the 3d. class of acts may perhaps be merely practical. But in that view they appear to be of great force.

Unless such laws should be kept in force by new acts regularly anticipating the end of the term, all the rights depending on positive laws, that is, most of the rights of property would become absolutely defunct; and the most violent struggles be generated between those interested in reviving and those interested in new-modelling the former State of property. Nor would events of this kind be improbable. The obstacles to the passage of laws which render a power to repeal inferior to an opportunity of rejecting, as a security agst. oppression, would here render an opportunity of rejecting, an insecure provision agst. anarchy. Add, that the possibility of an event so hazardous to the rights of property could not fail to depreciate its value; that the approach of the crisis would increase this effect; that the frequent return of periods superseding all the obligations depending on antecedent laws & usages, must by weakening the reverence for those obligations, cooperate with motives to licentiousness already too powerful; and that the uncertainty incident to such a state of things would on one side discourage the steady exertions of industry produced by permanent laws, and on the other, give a disproportionate advantage to the more, over the less, sagacious and interprizing part of the Society.

I find no relief from these consequences, but in the received doctrine that a tacit assent may be given to established Constitutions and laws, and that this assent may be inferred, where no positive dissent appears. It seems less impracticable to remedy, by wise plans of Government, the dangerous operation of this doctrine, than to find a remedy for the difficulties inseparable from the other.

May it not be questioned whether it be possible to exclude wholly the idea of tacit assent, without subverting the foundation of civil Society? On what principle does the voice of the majority bind the minority? It does not result I conceive from the law of nature, but from compact founded on conveniency. A greater proportion might be required by the fundamental constitution of a Society, if it were judged eligible. Prior then to the establishment of this principle, *unanimity* was necessary; and strict Theory at all times presupposes the assent of every member to the establishment of the rule itself. If this assent can not be given tacitly, or be not implied where no positive evidence forbids, persons born in Society would not on attaining ripe age be bound by acts of the Majority; and either a *unanimous* repetition of every law would be necessary on the accession of new members, or an express assent must be obtained from these to the rule by which the voice of the Majority is made the voice of the whole.

If the observations I have hazarded be not misapplied, it follows that a limitation of the validity of national acts to the computed life of a nation, is in some instances not required by Theory, and in others cannot be accomodated to practice. The observations are not meant however to impeach either the utility of the principle in some particular cases; or the general importance of it in the eye of the philosophical Legislator. On the contrary it would give me singular pleasure to see it first announced in the proceedings of the U. States, and always kept in their view, as a salutary curb on the living generation from imposing unjust or unnecessary burdens on their successors. But this is a pleasure which I have little hope of enjoying. The spirit of philosophical legislation has never reached some parts of the Union, and is by no means the fashion here, either within or without Congress. The evils suffered & feared from weakness in Government, and licentiousness in the people, have turned the attention more towards the means of strengthening the former, than of narrowing its extent in the minds of the latter. Besides this, it is so much easier to espy the little difficulties immediately incident to every great plan, than to comprehend its general and remote benefits, that our hemisphere must be still more enlightened before many of the sublime truths which are seen thro' the medium of Philosophy, become visible to the naked eye of the ordinary Politician.

I have nothing to add at present but that I remain always and most affectly. Yours

Consolidation

THE NATIONAL GAZETTE, DECEMBER 5, 1791

Much has been said, and not without reason, against a consolidation of the States into one government. Omitting lesser objections, two consequences would probably flow from such a change in our political system, which justify the cautions used against it. *First,* it would be impossible to avoid the dilemma, of either relinquishing the present energy and responsibility of a *single* executive magistrate, for some plural substitute, which by dividing so great a trust might lessen the danger of it; or suffering so great an accumulation of powers in the hands of that officer, as might by degrees transform him into a monarch. The incompetency of one Legislature to regulate all the various objects belonging to the local governments, would evidently force a transfer of many of them to the executive department; whilst the increasing splendour and number of its prerogatives supplied by this source, might prove excitements to ambition too powerful for a sober execution of the elective plan, and consequently strengthen the pretexts for an hereditary designation of the magistrate. *Second,* were the state governments abolished, the same space of country that would produce an undue growth of the executive power, would prevent that controul on the Legislative body, which is essential to a faithful discharge of its trust, neither the voice nor the sense of ten or twenty millions of people, spread through so many latitudes as are comprehended within the United States, could ever be combined or called into effect, if deprived of those local organs, through which both can now be conveyed. In such a state of things, the impossibility of acting together, might be succeeded by the inefficacy of partial expressions of the public mind, and at length, by a universal silence and insensibility, leaving the whole government to that *self directed course,* which, it must be owned, is the natural propensity of every government.

But if a consolidation of the states into one government be an event so justly to be avoided, it is not less to be desired, on the other hand, that a consolidation should prevail in their interests and affections; and this, too, as it fortunately happens, for the very reasons, among others, which lie against a government consolidation. For, in the first place, in proportion as uniformity is found to prevail in the interests and sentiments of the several states, will be the practicability of accommodating Legislative regulations to them, and thereby of withholding new and dangerous prerogatives from the executive. Again, the greater the mutual confidence and affection of all parts of the Union, the more likely they will be to concur amicably, or to differ with moderation, in the elective designation of the chief magistrate; and by such examples, to guard and adorn the vital principle of our republican constitution. Lastly, the less the supposed difference of interests, and the greater the concord and confidence throughout the great body of the people, the more readily must they sympathize with each other, the more seasonably can they interpose a common manifestation of their sentiments, the more certainly will they take the alarm at usurpation or oppression, and the more effectually will they *consolidate* their defence of the public liberty.

Here then is a proper object presented, both to those who are most jealously attached to the separate authority reserved to the states, and to those who may be more inclined to contemplate the people of America in the light of one nation. Let the former continue to watch against every encroachment, which might lead to a gradual consolidation of the states into one government. Let the latter employ their utmost zeal, by eradicating local prejudices and mistaken rivalships, to consolidate the affairs of the states into one harmonious interest; and let it be the patriotic study of all, to maintain the various authorities established by our complicated system, each in its respective constitutional sphere; and to erect over the whole, one paramount Empire of reason, benevolence, and brotherly affection.

Fashion

THE NATIONAL GAZETTE, MARCH 22, 1792

An humble address has been lately presented to the Prince of Wales by the BUCKLE MANUFACTURERS of Birmingham, Wassal, Wolverhampton, and their environs, stating that the BUCKLE TRADE gives employment to more than TWENTY THOUSAND persons, numbers of whom, in consequence of the prevailing fashion of SHOESTRINGS & SLIPPERS, are at present without employ, almost destitute of bread, and exposed to the horrors of want at the most inclement season; that to the manufactures of BUCKLES AND BUTTONS, Birmingham owes its important figure on the map of England; that it is to no purpose to address Fashion herself, she being void of feeling and deaf to argument, but fortunately accustomed to listen to his voice, and to obey his commands: and finally IMPLORING his Royal Highness to consider the deplorable condition of their trade, which is in danger of being ruined by the *mutability of fashion,* and to give that direction to the *public taste,* which will insure the lasting gratitude of the petitioners.

Several important reflections are suggested by this address.

I. The most precarious of all occupations which give bread to the industrious, are those depending on mere fashion, which generally changes so suddenly, and often so considerably, as to throw whole bodies of people out of employment.

II. Of all occupations those are the least desirable in a free state, which produce the most servile dependence of one class of citizens on another class. This dependence must increase as the *mutuality* of wants is diminished. Where the wants on one side are the absolute necessaries; and on the other are neither absolute necessaries, nor result from the habitual œconomy of life, but are the mere caprices of fancy, the evil is in its extreme; or if not,

III. The extremity of the evil must be in the case before us, where the absolute necessaries depend on the caprices of fancy, and the caprice of a single fancy directs the fashion of the community. Here the dependence sinks to the lowest point of servility. We see a proof of it in the *spirit* of the address. Twenty thousand persons are to get or go without their bread, as a wanton youth, may fancy to wear his shoes with or without straps, or to fasten his straps with strings or with buckles. Can any despotism be more cruel than a situation, in which the existence of thousands depends on one will, and that will on the most slight and fickle of all motives, a mere whim of the imagination.

IV. What a contrast is here to the independent situation and manly sentiments of American citizens, who live on their own soil, or whose labour is necessary to its cultivation, or who are occupied in supplying wants, which being founded in solid utility, in comfortable accommodation, or in settled habits, produce a reciprocity of dependence, at once ensuring subsistence, and inspiring a dignified sense of social rights.

V. The condition of those who receive employment and bread from the precarious source of fashion and superfluity, is a lesson to nations, as well as to individuals. In proportion as a nation consists of that description of citizens, and depends on external commerce, it is dependent on the consumption and caprice of other nations. If the laws of propriety did not forbid, the manufacturers of Birmingham, Wassal, and Wolverhampton, had as real an interest in supplying the arbiters of fashion in America, as the patron they have addressed. The dependence in the case of nations is even greater than among individuals of the same nation: for besides the *mutability of fashion* which is the same in both, the *mutability of policy* is another source of danger in the former.

Property

THE NATIONAL GAZETTE, MARCH 29, 1792

This term in its particular application means "that dominion which one man claims and exercises over the external things of the world, in exclusion of every other individual."

In its larger and juster meaning, it embraces every thing to which a man may attach a value and have a right; and *which leaves to every one else the like advantage.*

In the former sense, a man's land, or merchandize, or money is called his property.

In the latter sense, a man has property in his opinions and the free communication of them.

He has a property of peculiar value in his religious opinions, and in the profession and practice dictated by them.

He has property very dear to him in the safety and liberty of his person.

He has an equal property in the free use of his faculties and free choice of the objects on which to employ them.

In a word, as a man is said to have a right to his property, he may be equally said to have a property in his rights.

Where an excess of power prevails, property of no sort is duly respected. No man is safe in his opinions, his person, his faculties or his possessions.

Where there is an excess of liberty, the effect is the same, tho' from an opposite cause.

Government is instituted to protect property of every sort; as well that which lies in the various rights of individuals, as that which the term particularly expresses. This being the end of government, that alone is a *just* government, which *impartially* secures to every man, whatever is his *own.*

According to this standard of merit, the praise of affording a just security to property, should be sparingly bestowed on a government which, however scrupulously guarding the possessions of individuals, does not protect them in the enjoyment and communication of their opinions, in which they have an equal, and in the estimation of some, a more valuable property.

More sparingly should this praise be allowed to a government, where a man's religious rights are violated by penalties, or fettered by tests, or taxed by a hierarchy. Conscience is the most sacred of all property; other property depending in part on positive law, the exercise of that, being a natural and inalienable right. To guard a man's house as his castle, to pay public and enforce private debts with the most exact faith, can give no title to invade a man's conscience which is more sacred than his castle, or to withold from it that debt of protection, for which the public faith is pledged, by the very nature and original conditions of the social pact.

That is not a just government, nor is property secure under it, where the property which a man has in his personal safety and personal liberty, is violated by arbitrary seizures of one class of citizens for the service of the rest. A magistrate issuing warrants to a press gang, would be in his proper functions in Turkey or Indostan, under appellations proverbial of the most compleat despotism.

That is not a just government, nor is property secure under it, where arbitrary restrictions, exemptions, and monopolies deny to part of its citizens that free use of their faculties, and free choice of their occupations, which not only constitute their property in the general sense of the word; but are the means of acquiring property strictly so called. What must be the spirit of legislation where a manufacturer of linen cloth is forbidden to bury his own child in a linen shroud, in order to favour his neighbour who manufactures woolen cloth; where the manufacturer and wearer of woolen cloth are again forbidden the economical use of buttons of that material, in favor of the manufacturer of buttons of other materials!

A just security to property is not afforded by that government under which unequal taxes oppress one species of property and reward another species: where arbitrary taxes invade the domestic sanctuaries of the rich, and excessive taxes grind the faces of the poor; where the keenness and competitions of want are deemed an insufficient spur to labor, and taxes are again applied by an unfeeling policy, as another spur; in violation of that sacred property, which Heaven, in decreeing man to earn his bread by the sweat of his brow, kindly reserved to him, in the small repose that could be spared from the supply of his necessities.

If there be a government then which prides itself on maintaining the inviolability of property; which provides that none shall be taken *directly* even for public use without indemnification to the owner, and yet *directly* violates the property which individuals have in their opinions, their religion, their persons, and their faculties; nay more, which *indirectly* violates their property, in their actual possessions, in the labor that acquires their daily subsistence, and in the hallowed remnant of time which ought to relieve their fatigues and soothe their cares, the inference will have been anticipated, that such a government is not a pattern for the United States.

If the United States mean to obtain or deserve the full praise due to wise and just governments, they will equally respect the rights of property, and the property in rights: they will rival the government that most sacredly guards the former; and by repelling its example in violating the latter, will make themselves a pattern to that and all other governments.

The Union: Who Are Its Real Friends?

THE NATIONAL GAZETTE, APRIL 2, 1792

Not those who charge others with not being its friends, whilst their own conduct is wantonly multiplying its enemies.

Not those who favor measures, which by pampering the spirit of speculation within and without the government, disgust the best friends of the Union.

Not those who promote unnecessary accumulations of the debt of the Union, instead of the best means of discharging it as fast as possible; thereby encreasing the causes of corruption in the government, and the pretexts for new taxes under its authority, the former undermining the confidence, the latter alienating the affection of the people.

Not those who study, by arbitrary interpretations and insidious precedents, to pervert the limited government of the Union, into a government of unlimited discretion, contrary to the will and subversive of the authority of the people.

Not those who avow or betray principles of monarchy and aristocracy, in opposition to the republican principles of the Union, and the republican spirit of the people; or who espouse a system of measures more accommodated to the depraved examples of those hereditary forms, than to the true genius of our own.

Not those, in a word, who would force on the people the melancholy duty of chusing between the loss of the Union, and the loss of what the union was meant to secure.

The real FRIENDS to the Union are those,

Who are friends to the authority of the people, the sole foundation on which the Union rests.

Who are friends to liberty, the great end, for which the Union was formed.

Who are friends to the limited and republican system of government, the means provided by that authority, for the attaining of that end.

Who are enemies to every public measure that might smooth the way to hereditary government; for resisting the tyrannies of which the Union was first planned, and for more effectually excluding which, it was put into its present form.

Who considering a public debt as injurious to the interests of the people, and baneful to the virtue of the government, are enemies to every contrivance for *unnecessarily* increasing its amount, or protracting its duration, or extending its influence.

In a word, those are the real friends to the Union, who are friends to that republican policy throughout, which is the only *cement* for the Union of a republican people; in opposition to a spirit of usurpation and monarchy, which is the *menstruum* most capable of dissolving it.

A Candid State of Parties

THE NATIONAL GAZETTE, SEPTEMBER 26, 1792

As it is the business of the contemplative statesman to trace the history of parties in a free country, so it is the duty of the citizen at all times to understand the actual state of them. Whenever this duty is omitted, an opportunity is given to designing men, by the use of artificial or nominal distinctions, to oppose and balance against each other those who never differed as to the end to be pursued, and may no longer differ as to the means of attaining it. The most interesting state of parties in the United States may be referred to three periods: Those who espoused the cause of independence and those who adhered to the British claims, formed the parties of the first period; if, indeed, the disaffected class were considerable enough to deserve the name of a party. This state of things was superseded by the treaty of peace in 1783. From 1783 to 1787 there were parties in abundance, but being rather local than general, they are not within the present review.

The Federal Constitution, proposed in the latter year, gave birth to a second and most interesting division of the people. Every one remembers it, because every one was involved in it.

Among those who embraced the constitution, the great body were unquestionably friends to republican liberty; tho' there were, no doubt, some who were openly or secretly attached to monarchy and aristocracy; and hoped to make the constitution a cradle for these hereditary establishments.

Among those who opposed the constitution, the great body were certainly well affected to the union and to good government, tho' there might be a few who had a leaning unfavourable to both. This state of parties was terminated by the regular and effectual establishment of the federal government in 1788; out of the administration of which, however, has arisen a third division, which being natural to most political societies, is likely to be of some duration in ours.

One of the divisions consists of those, who from particular interest, from natural temper, or from the habits of life, are more partial to the opulent than to the other classes of society; and having debauched themselves into a persuasion that mankind are incapable of governing themselves, it follows with them, of course, that government can be carried on only by the pageantry of rank, the influence of money and emoluments, and the terror of military force. Men of those sentiments must naturally wish to point the measures of government less to the interest of the many than of a few, and less to the reason of the many than to their weaknesses; hoping perhaps in proportion to the ardor of their zeal, that by giving such a turn to the administration, the government itself may by degrees be narrowed into fewer hands, and approximated to an hereditary form.

The other division consists of those who believing in the doctrine that mankind are capable of governing themselves, and hating hereditary power as an insult to the reason and an outrage to the rights of man, are naturally offended at every public measure that does not appeal to the understanding and to the general interest of the community, or that is not strictly conformable to the principles, and conducive to the preservation of republican government.

This being the real state of parties among us, an experienced and dispassionate observer will be at no loss to decide on the probable conduct of each.

The antirepublican party, as it may be called, being the weaker in point of numbers, will be induced by the most obvious motives to strengthen themselves with the men of influence, particularly of moneyed, which is the most active and insinuating influence. It will be equally their true policy to weaken their opponents by reviving exploded parties, and taking advantage of all prejudices, local, political, and occupational, that may prevent or disturb a general coalition of sentiments.

The Republican party, as it may be termed, conscious that the mass of people in every part of the union, in every state, and of every occupation must at bottom be with them, both in interest and sentiment, will naturally find their account in burying all antecedent questions, in banishing every other distinction than that between enemies and friends to republican government, and in promoting a general harmony among the latter, wherever residing, or however employed.

Whether the republican or the rival party will ultimately establish its ascendance, is a problem which may be contemplated now; but which time alone can solve. On one hand experience shews that in politics as in war, stratagem is often an overmatch for numbers; and among more happy characteristics of our political situation, it is now well understood that there are peculiarities, some temporary, others more durable, which may favour that side in the contest. On the republican side, again, the superiority of numbers is so great, their sentiments are so decided, and the practice of making a common cause, where there is a common sentiment and common interest, in spight of circumstantial and artificial distinctions, is so well understood, that no temperate observer of human affairs will be surprised if the issue in the present instance should be reversed, and the government be administered in the spirit and form approved by the great body of the people.

Who Are the Best Keepers of the People's Liberties?

THE NATIONAL GAZETTE, DECEMBER 20, 1792

Republican.—The people themselves. The sacred trust can be no where so safe as in the hands most interested in preserving it.

Anti-republican.—The people are stupid, suspicious, licentious. They cannot safely trust themselves. When they have established government they should think of nothing but obedience, leaving the care of their liberties to their wiser rulers.

Republican.—Although all men are born free, and all nations might be so, yet too true it is, that slavery has been the general lot of the human race. Ignorant—they have been cheated; asleep—they have been surprized; divided—the yoke has been forced upon them. But what is the lesson? that because the people *may* betray themselves, they ought to give themselves up, blindfold, to those who have an interest in betraying them? Rather conclude that the people ought to be enlightened, to be awakened, to be united, that after establishing a government they should watch over it, as well as obey it.

Anti-republican.—You look at the surface only, where errors float, instead of fathoming the depths where truth lies hid. It is not the government that is disposed to fly off from the people; but the people that are ever ready to fly off from the government. Rather say then, enlighten the government, warn it to be vigilant, enrich it with influence, arm it with force, and to the people never pronounce but two words—*Submission* and *Confidence.*

Republican.—The centrifugal tendency then is in the people, not in the government, and the secret art lies in restraining the tendency, by augmenting the attractive principle of the government with all the weight that can be added to it. What a perversion of the natural order of things! to make *power* the primary and central object of the social system, and *Liberty* but its satellite.

Anti-republican.—The science of the stars can never instruct you in the mysteries of government. Wonderful as it may seem, the more you increase the attractive force of power, the more you enlarge the sphere of liberty; the more you make government independent and hostile towards the people, the better security you provide for their rights and interests. Hence the wisdom of the theory, which, after limiting the share of the people to a third of the government, and lessening the influence of that share by the mode and term of delegating it, establishes two grand hereditary orders, with feelings, habits, interests, and prerogatives all inveterately hostile to the rights and interests of the people, yet by a *mysterious* operation all combining to fortify the people in both.

Republican.—Mysterious indeed! But mysteries belong to religion, not to government; to the ways of the Almighty, not to the works of man. And in religion itself there is nothing mysterious to its author; the mystery lies in the dimness of the human sight. So in the institutions of man let there be no mystery, unless for those inferior beings endowed with a ray perhaps of the twilight vouchsafed to the first order of terrestrial creation.

Anti-republican.—You are destitute, I perceive, of every quality of a good citizen, or rather of a good *subject.* You have neither the light of faith nor the spirit of obedience. I denounce you to the government as an accomplice of atheism and anarchy.

Republican.—And I forbear to denounce you to the people, though a blasphemer of their rights and an idolater of tyranny. Liberty disdains to persecute.

Speech in Congress on "Self-Created Societies"

NOVEMBER 27, 1794

Mr. Madison—said he entirely agreed with those gentlemen who had observed that the house should not have advanced into this discussion, if it could have been avoided—but having proceeded thus far it was indispensably necessary to finish it.

Much delicacy had been thrown into the discussion, in consequence of the chief magistrate; he always regretted the circumstance, when this was the case.

This he observed, was not the first instance of difference in opinion between the President and this house. It may be recollected that the President dissented both from the Senate and this House on a particular law (he referred to that apportioning the representatives)—on that occasion he thought the President right. On the present question, supposing the President really to entertain the opinion ascribed to him, it affords no conclusive reason for the House to sacrifice its own judgment.

It appeared to him, as it did to the gentleman from Georgia, that there was an innovation in the mode of procedure adopted, on this occasion. The house are on different ground from that usually taken—members seem to think that in cases not cognizable by law, there is room for the interposition of the House. He conceived it to be a sound principle that an action innocent in the eye of the law, could not be the object of censure to a legislative body. When the people have formed a constitution, they retain those rights which they have not expressly delegated. It is a question whether what is thus retained can be legislated upon. Opinions are not the objects of legislation. You animadvert on the *abuse* of reserved rights—how far will this go? It may extend to the liberty of speech and of the press.

It is in vain to say that this indiscriminate censure is no punishment. If it falls on classes or individuals it will be a severe punishment. He wished it to be considered how extremely guarded the constitution was in respect to cases not within its limits. Murder or treason cannot be noticed by the legislature. Is not this proposition, if voted, a vote of attainder? To consider a principle, we must try its nature, and see how far it will go; in the present case he considered the effects of the principle contended for, would be pernicious. If we advert to the nature of republican government, we shall find that the censorial power is in the people over the government, and not in the government over the people.

As he had confidence in the good sense and patriotism of the people, he did not anticipate any lasting evil to result from the publications of these societies; they will stand or fall by the public opinion; no line can be drawn in this case. The law is the only rule of right; what is consistent with that is not punishable; what is not contrary to that, is innocent, or at least not censurable by the legislative body.

With respect to the body of the people, (whether the outrages have proceeded from weakness or wickedness) what has been done, and will be done by the Legislature will have a due effect. If the *proceedings* of the government should not have an effect, will this declaration produce it? The people at large are possessed of proper sentiments on the subject of the insurrection—the whole continent reprobates the conduct of the insurgents, it is not therefore necessary to take the extra step. The press he believed would not be able to shake the confidence of the people in the government. In a republic, light will prevail over darkness, truth over error—he had undoubted confidence in this principle. If it be admitted that the law cannot animadvert on a particular case, neither can we do it. Governments are administered by men—the same degree of purity does not always exist. Honesty of motives may at present prevail—but this affords no assurance that it will always be the case—at a future period a Legislature may exist of a very different complexion from the present; in this view, we ought not by any vote of ours to give support to measures which now we do not hesitate to reprobate. The gentleman from Georgia had anticipated him in several remarks—no such inference can fairly be drawn as that we abandon the President, should we pass over the whole business. The vote passed this morning for raising a force to compleat the good work of peace order and tranquility begun by the executive, speaks quite a different language from that which has been used to induce an adoption of the principle contended for.

Mr. Madison adverted to precedents—none parallel to the subject before us existed. The inquiry into the failure of the expedition under St. Clair was not in point. In that case the house appointed a Committee of enquiry into the conduct of an individual in the public service—the democratic societies are not. He knew of nothing in the proceedings of the Legislature which warrants the house in saying that institutions, confessedly not illegal, were subjects of legislative censure.

To Thomas Jefferson

PHILADA. JANY. 15. 1797.

Dear Sir

The last mail brought me your favour of Jany. 1. inclosing an unsealed one for Mr. A. & submitting to my discretion the eligibility of delivering it. In exercising this delicate trust I have felt no small anxiety, arising by no means however from an apprehension that a free exercise of it could be in collision with your real purpose, but from a want of confidence in myself, & the importance of a wrong judgment in the case. After the best consideration I have been able to bestow, I have been led to suspend the delivery of the letter, till you should have an opportunity of deciding on the sufficiency or insufficiency of the following reasons. 1. It is certain that Mr. Adams, on his coming to this place, expressed to different persons a respectful cordiality towards you, & manifested a sensibility to the candid manner in which your friends had in general conducted the opposition to him. And it is equally known that your sentiments towards him personally have found their way to him in the most conciliating form. This being the state of things between you, it deserves to be considered whether the idea of bettering it is not outweighed by the possibility of changing it for the worse. 2. There is perhaps a general air on the letter which betrays the difficulty of your situation in writing it, and it is uncertain what the impression might be resulting from this appearance. 3. It is certain that Mr. A. is fully apprized of the trick aimed at by his pseudo-friends of N.Y. and there may be danger of his suspecting in memento's on that subject, a wish to make his resentment an instrument for revenging that of others. A hint of this kind was some time ago dropped by a judicious & sound man who lives under the same roof, with a wish that even the Newspapers might be silent on that point. 4. May not what is said, of "the sublime delights of riding in the storm, &c." be misconstrued into a reflexion on those who have no distaste to the helm at the present crisis? You know the temper of Mr. A. better than I do: but I have always conceived it to be rather a ticklish one. 5. The tenderness due to the zealous & active promoters of your election, makes it doubtful whether, their anxieties & exertions ought to be depreciated by anything implying the unreasonableness of them. I know that some individuals who have deeply committed themselves, & probably incurred the political enmity at least of the P. elect, are already sore on this head. 6. Considering the probability that Mr. A.'s course of administration may force an opposition to it from the Republican quarter, & the general uncertainty of the posture which our affairs may take, there may be real embarrassments from giving written possession to him, of the degree of compliment & confidence which your personal delicacy & friendship have suggested.

I have ventured to make these observations, because I am sure you will equally appreciate the motive & the matter of them; and because I do not view them as inconsistent with the duty & policy of cultivating Mr. Adam's favorable dispositions, and giving a fair start to his Executive career. As you have, no doubt retained a copy of the letter I do not send it back as you request. It occurs however that, if the subject should not be changed in your view of it, by the reasons which influence mine, & the delivery of the letter be accordingly judged expedient, it may not be amiss to alter the date of it; either by writing the whole over again, or authorizing me to correct that part of it.

The special communication is still unmade. It is I am told to be extremely voluminous. I hope, under the sanction of the P.'s reply to our address, that it will be calculated rather to heal than irritate the wounded friendship of the two countries. Yet, I cannot look around at the men who counsel him, or look back at the snares into which he has hitherto been drawn without great apprehensions on this subject. Nothing from France subsequent to the arrival of Pinkney. The negociations for peace you will see are suspended. The accession of Spain to the war enforces the probability that its calamities are not likely yet to be terminated. The late News from the Rhine & from Italy are on the whole favorable to the French. The last battle was on the 27th Ocr. in the Hunspruck, and ended in a victory on their side. The House of Rep. are on direct taxes, which seem to be so much nauseated & feared by those who have created both the necessity & odium of them, that the project will miscarry. Hamilton, you will recollect assured the farmers that all the purposes of the Govt. could be answered without resorting to lands Houses or stock on farms. This deceptive statement with other devices of his administration, is rising up in judgment agst. him and will very probably soon blast the prospects which his ambition & intrigues have contemplated. It is certain that he has lost ground in N.Y. of late; & his treachery to Adams, will open the eyes of N. England.

Virginia Resolutions Against the Alien and Sedition Acts

IN THE HOUSE OF DELEGATES, DECEMBER 21, 1798

Resolved, That the General Assembly of Virginia doth unequivocally express a firm resolution to maintain and defend the Constitution of the United States, and the Constitution of this State, against every aggression either foreign or domestic; and that they will support the Government of the United States in all measures warranted by the former.

That this Assembly most solemnly declares a warm attachment to the Union of the States, to maintain which it pledges all its powers; and that, for this end, it is their duty to watch over and oppose every infraction of those principles which constitute the only basis of that Union, because a faithful observance of them can alone secure its existence and the public happiness.

That this Assembly doth explicitly and peremptorily declare that it views the powers of the Federal Government as resulting from the compact to which the States are parties, as limited by the plain sense and intention of the instrument constituting that compact; as no further valid than they are authorized by the grants enumerated in that compact; and that, in case of a deliberate, palpable, and dangerous exercise of other powers not granted by the said compact, the States, who are parties thereto, have the right, and are in duty bound to interpose for arresting the progress of the evil, and for maintaining within their respective limits the authorities, rights, and liberties appertaining to them.

That the General Assembly doth also express its deep regret, that a spirit has in sundry instances been manifested by the Federal Government to enlarge its powers by forced constructions of the constitutional charter which defines them; and that indications have appeared of a design to expound certain general phrases (which, having been copied from the very limited grant of powers in the former Articles of Confederation, were the less liable to be misconstrued) so as to destroy the meaning and effect of the particular enumeration which necessarily explains and limits the general phrases; and so as to consolidate the States, by degrees, into one sovereignty, the obvious tendency and inevitable result of which would be to transform the present republican system of the United States into an absolute, or, at best, a mixed monarchy.

That the General Assembly doth particularly protest against the palpable and alarming infractions of the Constitution in the two late cases of the "Alien and Sedition Acts," passed at the last session of Congress; the first of which exercises a power nowhere delegated to the Federal Government and which, by uniting legislative and judicial powers to those of [the] executive, subverts the general principles of free government, as well as the particular organization and positive provisions of the Federal Constitution; and the other of which acts exercises, in like manner, a power not delegated by the Constitution, but, on the contrary, expressly and positively forbidden by one of the amendments thereto,—a power which more than any other, ought to produce universal alarm, because it is levelled against the right of freely examining public characters and measures, and of free communication among the people thereon, which has ever been justly deemed the only effectual guardian of every other right.

That this State having by its Convention which ratified the Federal Constitution expressly declared "that, among other essential rights, the liberty of conscience and of the press cannot be cancelled, abridged, restrained or modified by any authority of the United States," and from its extreme anxiety to guard these rights from every possible attack of sophistry or ambition, having, with other States, recommended an amendment for that purpose, which amendment was in due time annexed to the Constitution,—it would mark a reproachful inconsistency and criminal degeneracy, if an indifference were now shown to the palpable violation of one of the rights thus declared and secured, and to the establishment of a precedent which may be fatal to the other.

That the good people of this Commonwealth, having ever felt and continuing to feel the most sincere affection for their brethren of the other States, the truest anxiety for establishing and perpetuating the union of all and the most scrupulous fidelity to that Constitution, which is the pledge of mutual friendship, and the instrument of mutual happiness, the General Assembly doth solemnly appeal to the like dispositions of the other States, in confidence that they will concur with this Commonwealth in declaring, as it does hereby declare, that the acts aforesaid are unconstitutional; and that the necessary and proper measures will be taken by each for co-operating with this State, in maintaining unimpaired the authorities, rights, and liberties reserved to the States respectively, or to the people.

That the Governor be desired to transmit a copy of the foregoing resolutions to the Executive authority of each of the other States, with a request that the same may be communicated to the Legislature thereof; and that a copy be furnished to each of the Senators and Representatives representing this State in the Congress of the United States.

To Robert R. Livingston and James Monroe

DEPARTMENT OF STATE, JULY 29TH—1803.

Gentlemen,

Your dispatches, including the Treaty and two conventions signed with a French Plenipotentiary on the 30th of April, were safely delivered on the 14th by Mr. Hughes, to whose care you had committed them.

In concurring with the disposition of the French Government to treat for the whole of Louisiana, altho' the western part of it was not embraced by your powers, you were justified by the solid reasons which you give for it, and I am charged by the President to express to you his entire approbation of your so doing.

This approbation is in no respect precluded by the silence of your Commission and instructions. When these were made out, the object of the most sanguine was limited to the establishment of the Mississippi as our boundary. It was not presumed that more could be sought by the United States either with a chance of success, or perhaps without being suspected of a greedy ambition, than the Island of New Orleans and the two Floridas, it being little doubted that the latter was or would be comprehended in the Cession from Spain to France. To the acquisition of New Orleans and the Floridas, the provision was therefore accommodated. Nor was it to be supposed that in case the French Government should be willing to part with more than the Territory on our side of the Mississippi, an arrangement with Spain for restoring to her the territory on the other side would not be preferred to a sale of it to the United States. It might be added, that the ample views of the subject carried with him by Mr. Monroe and the confidence felt that your judicious management would make the most of favorable occurrences, lessened the necessity of multiplying provisions for every turn which your negotiations might possibly take.

The effect of such considerations was diminished by no information or just presumptions whatever. The note of Mr. Livingston in particular stating to the French Government the idea of ceding the Western Country above the Arkansa and communicated to this Department in his letter of the 29th January, was not received here till April 5 more than a month after the Commission and instructions had been forwarded. And besides that this project not only left with France the possession and jurisdiction of one bank of the Mississippi from its mouth to the Arkansa, but a part of West Florida, the whole of East Florida, and the harbours for ships of war in the Gulph of Mexico, the letter inclosing the note intimated that it had been treated by the French Government with a decided neglect. In truth the communications in general between Mr. Livingston and the French Government, both of prior and subsequent date, manifested a repugnance to our views of purchase which left no expectation of any arrangement with France by which an extensive acquisition was to be made, unless in a favorable crisis of which advantage should be taken. Such was thought to be the crisis which gave birth to the extraordinary commission in which you are joined. It consisted of the state of things produced by the breach of our deposit at New Orleans, the situation of the French Islands, particularly the important Island of St. Domingo; the distress of the French finances, the unsettled posture of Europe, the increasing jealousy between G Britain and France, and the known aversion of the former to see the mouth of the Mississippi in the hands of the latter. These considerations it was hoped, might so far open the eyes of France to her real interest and her ears to the monitory truths which were conveyed to her thro' different channels, as to reconcile her to the establishment of the Mississippi as a natural boundary to the United States; or at least to some concessions which would justify our patiently waiting for a fuller accomplishment of our wishes under auspicious events. The crisis relied on has derived peculiar force from the rapidity with which the complaints and questions between France and Great Britain ripened towards a rupture, and it is just ground for mutual and general felicitation, that it has issued under your zealous exertions, in the extensive acquisition beyond the Mississippi.

With respect to the terms on which the acquisition is made, there can be no doubt that the bargain will be regarded as on the whole highly advantageous. The pecuniary stipulations would have been more satisfactory, if they had departed less from the plan prescribed; and particularly if the two millions of dollars in cash, intended to reduce the price or hasten the delivery of possession had been so applied, and the assumed payments to American claimants on the footing specified in the instructions. The unexpected weight of the draught now to be made on the Treasury will be sensibly felt by it, and may possibly be inconvenient in relation to other important objects.

The President has issued his proclamation convening Congress on the 17th of October, in order that the exchange of the ratifications may be made within the time limitted. It is obvious that the exchange, to be within the time, must be made here and not at Paris; and we infer from your letter of   that the ratifications of the Chief Consul are to be transmitted hither with that view.

I only add the wish of the President to know from you the understanding which prevailed in the negotiation with respect to the Boundaries of Louisiana, and particularly the pretensions and proofs for carrying it to the River Perdigo, or for including any lesser portion of West Florida.

With high respect, &c.

First Inaugural Address

MARCH 4, 1809

Unwilling to depart from examples, of the most revered authority, I avail myself of the occasion now presented, to express the profound impression made on me, by the call of my Country to the station, to the duties of which I am about to pledge myself, by the most solemn of sanctions. So distinguished a mark of confidence, proceeding from the deliberate and tranquil suffrage of a free and virtuous nation, would, under any circumstances, have commanded my gratitude and devotion; as well as filled me with an awful sense of the trust to be assumed. Under the various circumstances which give peculiar solemnity to the existing period, I feel that both the honor and the responsibility allotted to me are inexpressibly enhanced.

The present situation of the world is indeed without a parallel, and that of our own Country full of difficulties. The pressure of these too is the more severely felt, because they have fallen upon us at a moment, when the national prosperity being at a height not before attained, the contrast resulting from the change, has been rendered the more striking. Under the benign influence of our Republican institutions, and the maintenance of peace with all nations, whilst so many of them were engaged in bloody and wasteful wars, the fruits of a just policy were enjoyed in an unrivalled growth of our faculties and resources. Proofs of this were seen in the improvements of agriculture; in the successful enterprizes of commerce; in the progress of manufactures, and useful arts; in the increase of the public revenue, and the use made of it in reducing the public debt; and in the valuable works and establishments every where multiplying over the face of our land.

It is a precious reflection that the transition from this prosperous condition of our Country to the scene which has for some time been distressing us, is not chargeable on any unwarrantable views, nor, as I trust, on any involuntary errors in the public Councils. Indulging no passions, which trespass on the rights or the repose of other nations, it has been the true glory of the United States to cultivate peace by observing justice, and to entitle themselves to the respect of the nations at war, by fulfilling their neutral obligations, with the most scrupulous impartiality. If there be candor in the world, the truth of these assertions will not be questioned. Posterity at least will do justice to them.

This unexceptionable course could not avail against the injustice and violence of the Belligerent powers. In their rage against each other, or impelled by more direct motives, principles of retaliation have been introduced equally contrary to universal reason, and acknowledged law. How long their arbitrary edicts will be continued, in spite of the demonstrations that not even a pretext for them has been given by the United States, and of the fair and liberal attempt to induce a revocation of them, can not be anticipated. Assuring myself, that under every vicissitude, the determined spirit and united Councils of the nation will be safeguards to its honor and its essential interests, I repair to the post assigned me with no other discouragement, than what springs from my own inadequacy to its high duties. If I do not sink under the weight of this deep conviction, it is because I find some support in a consciousness of the purposes, and a confidence in the principles which I bring with me into this arduous service.

To cherish peace and friendly intercourse with all nations having correspondent dispositions; to maintain sincere neutrality toward belligerent nations; to prefer in all cases amicable discussion and reasonable accommodation of differences to a decision of them by an appeal to arms; to exclude foreign intrigues and foreign partialities, so degrading to all Countries and so baneful to free ones; to foster a spirit of independence too just to invade the rights of others, too proud to surrender our own, too liberal to indulge unworthy prejudices ourselves and too elevated not to look down upon them in others; to hold the Union of the States as the basis of their peace and happiness; to support the Constitution, which is the cement of the Union, as well in its limitations as in its authorities; to respect the rights and authorities reserved to the States and to the people, as equally incorporated with, and essential to the success of, the general system; to avoid the slightest interference with the rights of conscience, or the functions of religion, so wisely exempted from civil jurisdiction; to preserve in their full energy the other salutary provisions in behalf of private and personal rights, and of the freedom of the press; to observe œconomy in public expenditures; to liberate the public resources by an honorable discharge of the public debts; to keep within the requisite limits a standing military force, always remembering that an Armed and trained militia is the firmest bulwark of Republics; that without standing Armies their liberty can never be in danger; nor with large ones, safe; to promote by authorized means, improvements friendly to agriculture, to manufactures, and to external as well as internal commerce; to favor, in like manner, the advancement of science and the diffusion of information as the best aliment to true liberty; to carry on the benevolent plans which have been so meritoriously applied to the conversion of our aboriginal neighbors from the degradation and wretchedness of savage life, to a participation of the improvements of which the human mind and manners are susceptible in a civilized state: As far as sentiments and intentions such as these can aid the fulfillment of my duty, they will be a resource which can not fail me.

It is my good fortune, moreover, to have the path in which I am to tread, lighted by examples of illustrious services, successfully rendered in the most trying difficulties by those who have marched before me. Of those of my immediate predecessor, it might least become me here to speak. I may, however, be pardoned for not suppressing the sympathy with which my heart is full, in the rich reward he enjoys in the benedictions of a beloved Country, gratefully bestowed for exalted talents, zealously devoted, thro' a long career, to the advancement of its highest interest and happiness.

But the source to which I look for the aids which alone can supply my deficiencies, is in the well tried intelligence and virtue of my fellow citizens, and in the Councils of those representing them, in the other Departments associated in the care of the national interests. In these my confidence will under every difficulty be best placed, next to that which we have all been encouraged to feel in the guardianship and guidance of that Almighty Being whose power regulates the destiny of nations, whose blessings have been so conspicuously dispensed to this rising Republic, and to whom we are bound to address our devout gratitude for the past, as well as our fervent supplications and best hopes for the future.

Veto Message

FEBRUARY 21, 1811.

To the House of Representatives of the United States:

Having examined and considered the bill entitled "An Act incorporating the Protestant Episcopal Church in the town of Alexandria, in the District of Columbia," I now return the bill to the House of Representatives, in which it originated, with the following objections:

Because the bill exceeds the rightful authority to which governments are limited by the essential distinction between civil and religious functions, and violates in particular the article of the Constitution of the United States which declares that "Congress shall make no law respecting a religious establishment." The bill enacts into and establishes by law sundry rules and proceedings relative purely to the organization and polity of the Church incorporated, and comprehending even the election and removal of the minister of the same, so that no change could be made therein by the particular society or by the general church of which it is a member, and whose authority it recognizes. This particular Church, therefore, would so far be a religious establishment by law, a legal force and sanction being given to certain articles in its constitution and administration. Nor can it be considered that the articles thus established are to be taken as the descriptive criteria only of the corporate identity of the society, inasmuch as this identity must depend on other characteristics, as the regulations established are generally unessential and alterable according to the principles and canons by which churches of that denomination govern themselves, and as the injunctions and prohibitions contained in the regulations would be enforced by the penal consequences applicable to a violation of them according to the local law.

Because the bill vests in the said incorporated Church an authority to provide for the support of the poor and the education of poor children of the same, an authority which, being altogether superfluous if the provision is to be the result of pious charity, would be a precedent for giving to religious societies as such a legal agency in carrying into effect a public and civil duty.

Second Inaugural Address

MARCH 4, 1813

About to add the solemnity of an oath to the obligations imposed by a second call to the station in which my country heretofore placed me, I find in the presence of this respectable assembly an opportunity of publicly repeating my profound sense of so distinguished a confidence and of the responsibility united with it. The impressions on me are strengthened by such an evidence that my faithful endeavors to discharge my arduous duties have been favorably estimated, and by a consideration of the momentous period at which the trust has been renewed. From the weight and magnitude now belonging to it I should be compelled to shrink if I had less reliance on the support of an enlightened and generous people, and felt less deeply a conviction that the war with a powerful nation, which forms so prominent a feature in our situation, is stamped with that justice which invites the smiles of Heaven on the means of conducting it to a successful termination.

May we not cherish this sentiment without presumption when we reflect on the characters by which this war is distinguished?

It was not declared on the part of the United States until it had been long made on them, in reality though not in name; until arguments and expostulations had been exhausted; until a positive declaration had been received that the wrongs provoking it would not be discontinued; nor until this last appeal could no longer be delayed without breaking down the spirit of the nation, destroying all confidence in itself and in its political institutions, and either perpetuating a state of disgraceful suffering or regaining by more costly sacrifices and more severe struggles our lost rank and respect among independent powers.

On the issue of the war are staked our national sovereignty on the high seas and the security of an important class of citizens, whose occupations give the proper value to those of every other class. Not to contend for such a stake is to surrender our equality with other powers on the element common to all and to violate the sacred title which every member of the society has to its protection. I need not call into view the unlawfulness of the practice by which our mariners are forced at the will of every crushing officer from their own vessels into foreign ones, nor paint the outrages inseparable from it. The proofs are in the records of each successive Administration of our Government, and the cruel sufferings of that portion of the American people have found their way to every bosom not dead to the sympathies of human nature.

As the war was just in its origin and necessary and noble in its objects, we can reflect with a proud satisfaction that in carrying it on no principle of justice or honor, no usage of civilized nations, no precept of courtesy or humanity, have been infringed. The war has been waged on our part with scrupulous regard to all these obligations, and in a spirit of liberality which was never surpassed.

How little has been the effect of this example on the conduct of the enemy!

They have retained as prisoners of war citizens of the United States not liable to be so considered under the usages of war.

They have refused to consider as prisoners of war, and threatened to punish as traitors and deserters, persons emigrating without restraint to the United States, incorporated by naturalization into our political family, and fighting under the authority of their adopted country in open and honorable war for the maintenance of its rights and safety. Such is the avowed purpose of a Government which is in the practice of naturalizing by thousands citizens of other countries, and not only of permitting but compelling them to fight its battles against their native country.

They have not, it is true, taken into their own hands the hatchet and the knife, devoted to indiscriminate massacre, but they have let loose the savages armed with these cruel instruments; have allured them into their service, and carried them to battle by their sides, eager to glut their savage thirst with the blood of the vanquished and to finish the work of torture and death on maimed and defenseless captives. And, what was never before seen, British commanders have extorted victory over the unconquerable valor of our troops by presenting to the sympathy of their chief captives awaiting massacre from their savage associates.

And now we find them, in further contempt of the modes of honorable warfare, supplying the place of a conquering force, by attempts to disorganize our political society, to dismember our confederated Republic. Happily, like others, these will recoil on the authors; but they mark the degenerate counsels from which they emanate: and if they did not belong to a series of unexampled inconsistencies, might excite the greater wonder, as proceeding from a Government which founded the very war in which it has been so long engaged, on a charge against the disorganizing and insurrectional policy of its adversary.

To render the justice of the war on our part the more conspicuous, the reluctance to commence it was followed by the earliest and strongest manifestations of a disposition to arrest its progress. The sword was scarcely out of the scabbard, before the enemy was apprized of the reasonable terms on which it would be resheathed. Still more precise advances were repeated, and have been received in a spirit forbidding every reliance not placed on the military resources of the nation.

These resources are amply sufficient to bring the war to an honorable issue. Our nation is, in number, more than half that of the British isles. It is composed of a brave, a free, a virtuous, and an intelligent people. Our country abounds in the necessaries, the arts, and the comforts of life. A general prosperity is visible in the public countenance. The means employed by the British Cabinet to undermine it, have recoiled on themselves; have given to our national faculties a more rapid development; and draining or diverting the precious metals from British circulation and British vaults, have poured them into those of the United States. It is a propitious consideration, that an unavoidable war should have found this seasonable facility for the contributions required to support it. When the public voice called for war, all knew and still know, that without them it could not be carried on through the period which it might last; and the patriotism, the good sense, and the manly spirit of our fellow-citizens, are pledges for the cheerfulness with which they will bear each his share of the common burden. To render the war short, and its success sure, animated, and systematic exertions alone are necessary; and the success of our arms now may long preserve our country from the necessity of another resort to them. Already have the gallant exploits of our naval heroes proved to the world our inherent capacity to maintain our rights on one element. If the reputation of our arms has been thrown under clouds on the other, presaging flashes of heroic enterprise assure us that nothing is wanting to correspondent triumphs there also, but the discipline and habits which are in daily progress.

Special Message to Congress

WASHINGTON, FEBRUARY 18, 1815.

To the Senate and House of Representatives of the United States:

I lay before Congress copies of the treaty of peace and amity between the United States and His Britannic Majesty, which was signed by the commissioners of both parties at Ghent on the 24th of December, 1814, and the ratifications of which have been duly exchanged.

While performing this act I congratulate you and our constituents upon an event which is highly honorable to the nation, and terminates with peculiar felicity a campaign signalized by the most brilliant successes.

The late war, although reluctantly declared by Congress, had become a necessary resort to assert the rights and independence of the nation. It has been waged with a success which is the natural result of the wisdom of the legislative councils, of the patriotism of the people, of the public spirit of the militia, and of the valor of the military and naval forces of the country. Peace, at all times a blessing, is peculiarly welcome, therefore, at a period when the causes for the war have ceased to operate, when the Government has demonstrated the efficiency of its powers of defense, and when the nation can review its conduct without regret and without reproach.

I recommend to your care and beneficence the gallant men whose achievements in every department of the military service, on the land and on the water, have so essentially contributed to the honor of the American name and to the restoration of peace. The feelings of conscious patriotism and worth will animate such men under every change of fortune and pursuit, but their country performs a duty to itself when it bestows those testimonials of approbation and applause which are at once the reward and the incentive to great actions.

The reduction of the public expenditures to the demands of a peace establishment will doubtless engage the immediate attention of Congress. There are, however, important considerations which forbid a sudden and general revocation of the measures that have been produced by the war. Experience has taught us that neither the pacific dispositions of the American people nor the pacific character of their political institutions can altogether exempt them from that strife which appears beyond the ordinary lot of nations to be incident to the actual period of the world, and the same faithful monitor demonstrates that a certain degree of preparation for war is not only indispensable to avert disasters in the onset, but affords also the best security for the continuance of peace. The wisdom of Congress will therefore, I am confident, provide for the maintenance of an adequate regular force; for the gradual advancement of the naval establishment; for improving all the means of harbor defense; for adding discipline to the distinguished bravery of the militia, and for cultivating the military art in its essential branches, under the liberal patronage of Government.

The resources of our country were at all times competent to the attainment of every national object, but they will now be enriched and invigorated by the activity which peace will introduce into all the scenes of domestic enterprise and labor. The provision that has been made for the public creditors during the present session of Congress must have a decisive effect in the establishment of the public credit both at home and abroad. The reviving interests of commerce will claim the legislative attention at the earliest opportunity, and such regulations will, I trust, be seasonably devised as shall secure to the United States their just proportion of the navigation of the world. The most liberal policy toward other nations, if met by corresponding dispositions, will in this respect be found the most beneficial policy toward ourselves. But there is no subject that can enter with greater force and merit into the deliberations of Congress than a consideration of the means to preserve and promote the manufactures which have sprung into existence and attained an unparalleled maturity throughout the United States during the period of the European wars. This source of national independence and wealth I anxiously recommend, therefore, to the prompt and constant guardianship of Congress.

The termination of the legislative sessions will soon separate you, fellow-citizens, from each other, and restore you to your constituents. I pray you to bear with you the expressions of my sanguine hope that the peace which has been just declared, will not only be the foundation of the most friendly intercourse between the United States and Great Britain, but that it will also be productive of happiness and harmony in every section of our beloved country. The influence of your precepts and example must be every where powerful; and while we accord in grateful acknowledgments for the protection which Providence has bestowed upon us, let us never cease to inculcate obedience to the laws, and fidelity to the union, as constituting the palladium of the national independence and prosperity.

To Robert J. Evans

MONTPELLIER, JUNE 15, 1819

Sir,

I have recd. your letter of the 3d instant, requesting such hints as may have occurred to me on the subject of an eventual extinguishment of slavery in the U.S.

Not doubting the purity of your views, and relying on the discretion by which they will be regulated, I cannot refuse such a compliance as will at least manifest my respect for the object of your undertaking.

A general emancipation of slaves ought to be 1. gradual. 2. equitable & satisfactory to the individuals immediately concerned. 3. consistent with the existing & durable prejudices of the nation.

That it ought, like remedies for other deep-rooted and wide-spread evils, to be gradual, is so obvious that there seems to be no difference of opinion on that point.

To be equitable & satisfactory, the consent of both the Master & the slave should be obtained. That of the Master will require a provision in the plan for compensating a loss of what he held as property guarantied by the laws, and recognised by the Constitution. That of the slave, requires that his condition in a state of freedom, be preferable in his own estimation, to his actual one in a state of bondage.

To be consistent with existing and probably unalterable prejudices in the U.S. the freed blacks ought to be permanently removed beyond the region occupied by or allotted to a White population. The objections to a thorough incorporation of the two people are, with most of the Whites insuperable; and are admitted by all of them to be very powerful. If the blacks, strongly marked as they are by Physical & lasting peculiarities, be retained amid the Whites, under the degrading privation of equal rights political or social, they must be always dissatisfied with their condition as a change only from one to another species of oppression; always secretly confederated agst. the ruling & privileged class; and always uncontroulled by some of the most cogent motives to moral and respectable conduct. The character of the free blacks, even where their legal condition is least affected by their colour, seems to put these truths beyond question. It is material also that the removal of the blacks be to a distance precluding the jealousies & hostilities to be apprehended from a neighboring people stimulated by the contempt known to be entertained for their peculiar features; to say nothing of their vindictive recollections, or the predatory propensities which their State of Society might foster. Nor is it fair, in estimating the danger of Collisions with the Whites, to charge it wholly on the side of the Blacks. There would be reciprocal antipathies doubling the danger.

The colonizing plan on foot, has as far as it extends, a due regard to these requisites; with the additional object of bestowing new blessings civil & religious on the quarter of the Globe most in need of them. The Society proposes to transport to the African Coast all free & freed blacks who may be willing to remove thither; to provide by fair means, &, it is understood with a prospect of success, a suitable territory for their reception; and to initiate them into such an establishment as may gradually and indefinitely expand itself.

The experiment, under this view of it, merits encouragement from all who regard slavery as an evil, who wish to see it diminished and abolished by peaceable & just means; and who have themselves no better mode to propose. Those who have most doubted the success of the experiment must at least have wished to find themselves in an error.

But the views of the Society are limited to the case of blacks already free, or who may be *gratuitously* emancipated. To provide a commensurate remedy for the evil, the plan must be extended to the great Mass of blacks, and must embrace a fund sufficient to induce the Master as well as the slave to concur in it. Without the concurrence of the Master, the benefit will be very limited as it relates to the Negroes; and essentially defective, as it relates to the U. States; and the concurrence of Masters, must, for the most part, be obtained by purchase.

Can it be hoped that voluntary contributions, however adequate to an auspicious commencement, will supply the sums necessary to such an enlargement of the remedy? May not another question be asked? Would it be reasonable to throw so great a burden on the individuals distinguished by their philanthropy and patriotism?

The object to be obtained, as an object of humanity, appeals alike to all; as a National object, it claims the interposition of the nation. It is the nation which is to reap the benefit. The nation therefore ought to bear the burden.

Must then the enormous sums required to pay for, to transport, and to establish in a foreign land all the slaves in the U.S. as their Masters may be willg. to part with them, be taxed on the good people of the U.S. or be obtained by loans swelling the public debt to a size pregnant with evils next in degree to those of slavery itself?

Happily it is not necessary to answer this question by remarking that if slavery as a national evil is to be abolished, and it be just that it be done at the national expence, the amount of the expence is not a paramount consideration. It is the peculiar fortune, or, rather a providential blessing of the U.S. to possess a resource commensurate to this great object, without taxes on the people, or even an increase of the public debt.

I allude to the vacant territory the extent of which is so vast, and the vendible value of which is so well ascertained.

Supposing the number of slaves to be 1,500,000, and their price to average 400 drs, the cost of the whole would be 600 millions of dollrs. These estimates are probably beyond the fact; and from the no. of slaves should be deducted 1. those whom their Masters would not part with. 2. those who may be gratuitously set free by their Masters. 3. those acquiring freedom under emancipating regulations of the States. 4. those preferring slavery where they are, to freedom in an African settlement. On the other hand, it is to be noted that the expence of removal & settlement is not included in the estimated sum; and that an increase of the slaves will be going on during the period required for the execution of the plan.

On the whole the aggregate sum needed may be stated at about 600 Mils. of dollars.

This will require 200 mils. of Acres at 3 dolrs. per Acre; or 300 mils. at 2 dollrs. per Acre a quantity which tho' great in itself, is perhaps not a third part of the disposable territory belonging to the U.S. And to what object so good so great & so glorious, could that peculiar fund of wealth be appropriated? Whilst the sale of territory would, on one hand be planting one desert with a free & civilized people, it would on the other, be giving freedom to another people, and filling with them another desert. And if in any instances, wrong has been done by our forefathers to people of one colour, by dispossessing them of their soil, what better atonement is now in our power than that of making what is rightfully acquired a source of justice & of blessings to a people of another colour?

As the revolution to be produced in the condition of the negroes must be gradual, it will suffice if the sale of territory keep pace with its progress. For a time at least the proceeds wd. be in advance. In this case it might be best, after deducting the expence incident to the surveys & sales, to place the surplus in a situation where its increase might correspond with the natural increase of the unpurchased slaves. Should the proceeds at any time fall short of the calls for their application, anticipations might be made by temporary loans to be discharged as the land should find a Market.

But it is probable that for a considerable period, the sales would exceed the calls. Masters would not be willing to strip their plantations & farms of their laborers too rapidly. The slaves themselves, connected as they generally are by tender ties with others under other Masters, would be kept from the list of emigrants by the want of the multiplied consents to be obtained. It is probable indeed that for a long time a certain portion of the proceeds might safely continue applicable to the discharge of the debts or to other purposes of the Nation. Or it might be most convenient, in the outset, to appropriate a certain proportion only of the income from sales, to the object in view, leaving the residue otherwise applicable.

Should any plan similar to that I have sketched, be deemed eligible in itself no particular difficulty is foreseen from that portion of the nation which with a common interest in the vacant territory has no interest in slave property. They are too just to wish that a partial sacrifice shd. be made for the general good; and too well aware that whatever may be the intrinsic character of that description of property, it is one known to the constitution, and, as such could not be constitutionally taken away without just compensation. That part of the Nation has indeed shewn a meritorious alacrity in promoting, by pecuniary contributions, the limited scheme for colonizing the Blacks, & freeing the nation from the unfortunate stain on it, which justifies the belief that any enlargement of the scheme, if founded on just principles would find among them its earliest & warmest patrons. It ought to have great weight that the vacant lands in question have for the most part been derived from grants of the States holding the slaves to be redeemed & removed by the sale of them.

It is evident however that in effectuating a general emancipation of slaves, in the mode which has been hinted, difficulties of other sorts would be encountered. The provision for ascertaining the joint consent of the masters & slaves; for guarding agst. unreasonable valuations of the latter; and for the discrimination of those not proper to be conveyed to a foreign residence, or who ought to remain a charge on Masters in whose service they had been disabled or worn out and for the annual transportation of such numbers, would Require the mature deliberations of the National Councils. The measure implies also the practicability of procuring in Africa, an enlargement of the district or districts, for receiving the exiles, sufficient for so great an augmentation of their numbers.

Perhaps the Legislative provision best adapted to the case would be an incorporation of the Colonizing Society or the establishment of a similar one, with proper powers, under the appointment & superintendence of the National Executive.

In estimating the difficulties however incident to any plan of general emancipation, they ought to be brought into comparison with those inseparable from other plans, and be yielded to or not according to the result of the comparison.

One difficulty presents itself which will probably attend every plan which is to go into effect under the Legislative provisions of the National Govt. But whatever may be the defect of existing powers of Congress, the Constitution has pointed out the way in which it can be supplied. And it can hardly be doubted that the requisite powers might readily be procured for attaining the great object in question, in any mode whatever approved by the Nation.

If these thoughts can be of any aid in your search of a remedy for the great evil under which the nation labors, you are very welcome to them.

You will allow me however to add that it will be most agreeable to me, not to be publickly referred to in any use you may make of them.

To Spencer Roane

SEPTR. 2; 1819.

Dear Sir

I have recd. your favor of the 22d Ult inclosing a copy of your observations on the Judgment of the Supreme Court of the U.S. in the case of M'Culloch agst. the State of Maryland; and I have found their latitudinary mode of expounding the Constitution, combated in them with the ability and the force which were to be expected.

It appears to me as it does to you that the occasion did not call for the general and abstract doctrine interwoven with the decision of the particular case. I have always supposed that the meaning of a law, and for a like reason, of a Constitution, so far as it depends on Judicial interpretation, was to result from a course of particular decisions, and not these from a previous and abstract comment on the subject. The example in this instance tends to reverse the rule and to forego the illustration to be derived from a series of cases actually occurring for adjudication.

I could have wished also that the Judges had delivered their opinions seriatim. The case was of such magnitude, in the scope given to it, as to call, if any case could do so, for the views of the subject separately taken by them. This might either by the harmony of their reasoning have produced a greater conviction in the Public mind; or by its discordance have impaired the force of the precedent now ostensibly supported by a unanimous & perfect concurrence in every argument & dictum in the judgment pronounced.

But what is of most importance is the high sanction given to a latitude in expounding the Constitution which seems to break down the landmarks intended by a specification of the Powers of Congress, and to substitute for a definite connection between means and ends, a Legislative discretion as to the former to which no practical limit can be assigned. In the great system of Political Economy having for its general object the national welfare, everything is related immediately or remotely to every other thing; and consequently a Power over any one thing, if not limited by some obvious and precise affinity, may amount to a Power over every other. Ends & means may shift their character at the will & according to the ingenuity of the Legislative Body. What is an end in one case may be a means in another; nay in the same case, may be either an end or a means at the Legislative option. The British Parliament in collecting a revenue from the commerce of America found no difficulty in calling it either a tax for the regulation of trade, or a regulation of trade with a view to the tax, as it suited the argument or the policy of the moment.

Is there a Legislative power in fact, not expressly prohibited by the Constitution, which might not, according to the doctrine of the Court, be exercised as a means of carrying into effect some specified Power?

Does not the Court also relinquish by their doctrine, all controul on the Legislative exercise of unconstitutional powers? According to that doctrine, the expediency & constitutionality of means for carrying into effect a specified Power are convertible terms; and Congress are admitted to be Judges of the expediency. The Court certainly cannot be so; a question, the moment it assumes the character of mere expediency or policy, being evidently beyond the reach of Judicial cognizance.

It is true, the Court are disposed to retain a guardianship of the Constitution against legislative encroachments. "Should Congress," say they, "under the pretext of executing its Powers, pass laws for the accomplishment of objects not entrusted to the Government, it would become the painful duty of this Tribunal to say that such an act was not the law of the land." But suppose Congress should, as would doubtless happen, pass unconstitutional laws not to accomplish objects not specified in the Constitution, but the same laws as means expedient, convenient or conducive to the accomplishment of objects entrusted to the Government; by what handle could the Court take hold of the case? We are told that it was the policy of the old Government of France to grant monopolies, such as that of Tobacco, in order to create funds in particular hands from which loans could be made to the Public, adequate capitalists not being formed in that Country in the ordinary course of commerce. Were Congress to grant a like monopoly merely to aggrandize those enjoying it, the Court might consistently say, that this not being an object entrusted to the Governt. the grant was unconstitutional and void. Should Congress however grant the monopoly according to the French policy as a means judged by them to be necessary, expedient or conducive to the borrowing of money, which is an object entrusted to them by the Constitution, it seems clear that the Court, adhering to its doctrine, could not interfere without stepping on Legislative ground, to do which they justly disclaim all pretension.

It could not but happen, and was foreseen at the birth of the Constitution, that difficulties and differences of opinion might occasionally arise in expounding terms & phrases necessarily used in such a charter; more especially those which divide legislation between the General & local Governments; and that it might require a regular course of practice to liquidate & settle the meaning of some of them. But it was anticipated I believe by few if any of the friends of the Constitution, that a rule of construction would be introduced as broad & as pliant as what has occurred. And those who recollect, and still more those who shared in what passed in the State Conventions, thro' which the people ratified the Constitution, with respect to the extent of the powers vested in Congress, cannot easily be persuaded that the avowal of such a rule would not have prevented its ratification. It has been the misfortune, if not the reproach, of other nations, that their Govts. have not been freely and deliberately established by themselves. It is the boast of ours that such has been its source and that it can be altered by the same authority only which established it. It is a further boast that a regular mode of making proper alterations has been providently inserted in the Constitution itself. It is anxiously to be wished therefore, that no innovations may take place in other modes, one of which would be a constructive assumption of powers never meant to be granted. If the powers be deficient, the legitimate source of additional ones is always open, and ought to be resorted to.

Much of the error in expounding the Constitution has its origin in the use made of the species of sovereignty implied in the nature of Govt. The specified powers vested in Congress, it is said, are sovereign powers, and that as such they carry with them an unlimited discretion as to the means of executing them. It may surely be remarked that a limited Govt. may be limited in its sovereignty as well with respect to the means as to the objects of his powers; and that to give an extent to the former, superseding the limits to the latter, is in effect to convert a limited into an unlimited Govt. There is certainly a reasonable medium between expounding the Constitution with the strictness of a penal law, or other ordinary statute, and expounding it with a laxity which may vary its essential character, and encroach on the local sovereignties with wch. it was meant to be reconcilable.

The very existence of these local sovereignties is a controul on the pleas for a constructive amplification of the powers of the General Govt. Within a single State possessing the entire sovereignty, the powers given to the Govt. by the People are understood to extend to all the Acts whether as means or ends required for the welfare of the Community, and falling within the range of just Govt. To withhold from such a Govt. any particular power necessary or useful in itself, would be to deprive the people of the good dependent on its exercise; since the power must be there or not exist at all. In the Govt. of the U.S. the case is obviously different. In establishing that Govt. the people retained other Govts. capable of exercising such necessary and useful powers as were not to be exercised by the General Govt. No necessary presumption therefore arises from the importance of any particular power in itself, that it has been vested in that Govt. because tho' not vested there, it may exist elsewhere, and the exercise of it elsewhere might be preferred by those who alone had a right to make the distribution. The presumption which ought to be indulged is that any improvement of this distribution sufficiently pointed out by experience would not be withheld.

Altho' I have confined myself to the single question concerning the rule of interpreting the Constitution, I find that my pen has carried me to a length which would not have been permitted by a recollection that my remarks are merely for an eye to which no aspect of the subject is likely to be new. I hasten therefore to conclude with assurances &c &c.

To Robert Walsh

MONTPELLIER, NOVR. 27 1819.

Dear Sir,

Your letter of the 11th was duly recd. and I should have given it a less tardy answer, but for a succession of particular demands on my attention, and a wish to assist my recollections, by consulting both Manuscript & printed sources of information on the subjects of your enquiry. Of these, however, I have not been able to avail myself but very partially.

As to the intention of the framers of the Constitution in the clause relating to "the migration and importation of persons, &c" the best key may perhaps be found in the case which produced it. The African trade in slaves had long been odious to most of the States, and the importation of slaves into them had been prohibited. Particular States however continued the importation, and were extremely averse to any restriction on their power to do so. In the convention the former States were anxious, in framing a new constitution, to insert a provision for an immediate and absolute stop to the trade. The latter were not only averse to any interference on the subject; but solemnly declared that their constituents would never accede to a Constitution containing such an article. Out of this conflict grew the middle measure providing that Congress should not interfere until the year 1808; with an implication, that after that date, they might prohibit the importation of slaves into the States then existing, & previous thereto, into the

States not then existing. Such was the tone of opposition in the States of S. Carolina & Georgia, & such the desire to gain their acquiescence in a prohibitory power, that on a question between the epochs of 1800 & 1808, the States of N. Hampshire, Masstts. & Connecticut, (all the eastern States in the Convention,) joined in the vote for the latter, influenced however by the collateral motive of reconciling those particular States to the power over commerce & navigation; against which they felt, as did some other States, a very strong repugnance. The earnestness of S. Carolina & Georgia was farther manifested by their insisting on the security in the V article, against any amendment to the Constitution affecting the right reserved to them, & their uniting with the small states, who insisted on a like security for their equality in the Senate.

But some of the States were not only anxious for a Constitutional provision against the introduction of slaves. They had scruples against admitting the term "slaves" into the Instrument. Hence the descriptive phrase, "migration or importation of persons;" the term migration allowing those who were scrupulous of acknowledging expressly a property in human beings, to view *imported* persons as a species of emigrants, while others might apply the term to foreign malefactors sent or coming into the country. It is possible tho' not recollected, that some might have had an eye to the case of freed blacks, as well as malefactors.

But whatever may have been intended by the term "migration" or the term "persons," it is most certain, that they referred exclusively to a migration or importation from other countries into the U. States; and not to a removal, voluntary or involuntary, of slaves or freemen, from one to another part of the U. States. Nothing appears or is recollected that warrants this latter intention. Nothing in the proceedings of the State conventions indicates such a construction there. Had such been the construction it is easy to imagine the figure it would have made in many of the states, among the objections to the constitution, and among the numerous amendments to it proposed by the State conventions not one of which amendments refers to the clause in question. Neither is there any indication that Congress have heretofore considered themselves as deriving from this Clause a power over the migration or removal of individuals, whether freemen or slaves, from one State to another, whether new or old: For it must be kept in view that if the power was given at all, it has been in force eleven years over all the States existing in 1808, and at all times over the States not then existing. Every indication is against such a construction by Congress of their constitutional powers. Their alacrity in exercising their powers relating to slaves, is a proof that they did not claim what they did not exercise. They punctually and unanimously put in force the power accruing in 1808 against the further importation of slaves from abroad. They had previously directed their power over American vessels on the high seas, against the African trade. They lost no time in applying the prohibitory power to Louisiana, which having maritime ports, might be an inlet for slaves from abroad. But they forebore to extend the prohibition to the introduction of slaves from other parts of the Union. They had even prohibited the importation of slaves into the Mississippi Territory from *without the limits of the U.S.* in the year 1798, without extending the prohibition to the introduction of slaves from *within those limits;* altho' at the time the ports of Georgia and S. Carolina were open for the importation of slaves from abroad, and increasing the mass of slavery within the U. States.

If these views of the subject be just, a power in Congress to controul the interior migration or removals of persons, must be derived from some other source than Sect 9, Art. 1; either from the clause giving power "to make all needful rules and regulations respecting the Territory or other property belonging to the U.S. or from that providing for the admission of New States into the Union."

The terms in which the 1st. of these powers is expressed, tho' of a ductile character, cannot well be extended beyond a power over the Territory as property, & a power to make the provisions really needful or necessary for the Govt. of settlers until ripe for admission as States into the Union. It may be inferred that Congress did not regard the interdict of slavery among the needful regulations contemplated by the constitution; since in none of the Territorial Governments created by them, is such an interdict found. The power, however be its import what it may, is obviously limited to a Territory whilst remaining in that character as distinct from that of a State.

As to the power of admitting new States into the federal compact, the questions offering themselves are; whether congress can attach conditions, or the new States concur in conditions, which after admission, would abridge or *enlarge* the constitutional rights of legislation common to the other States; whether Congress can by a compact with a new member take power either to or from itself, or place the new member above or below the equal rank & rights possessed by the others; whether all such stipulations, expressed or implied would not be nullities, and so pronounced when brought to a practical test. It falls within the Scope of your enquiry, to state the fact, that there was a proposition in the convention to discriminate between the old and new States, by an Article in the Constitution declaring that the aggregate number of representatives from the States thereafter to be admitted should never exceed that of the States originally adopting the Constitution. The proposition happily was rejected. The effect of such a discrimination, is sufficiently evident.

In the case of Louisiana, there is a circumstance which may deserve notice. In the Treaty ceding it, a privilege was retained by the ceding party, which distinguishes between its ports & others of the U.S. for a special purpose & a short period. This privilege however was the result not of an ordinary legislative power in Congress; nor was it the result of an arrangement between Congress & the people of Louisiana. It rests on the ground that the same entire power, even in the nation, over that territory, as over the original territory of the U.S. never existed; the privilege alluded to being in the deed of cession carved by the foreign owner, out of the title conveyed to the purchaser. A sort of necessity therefore was thought to belong to so peculiar & extraordinary a case. Notwithstanding this plea it is presumable that if the privilege had materially affected the rights of other ports, or had been of a permanent or durable character, the occurrence would not have been so little regarded. Congress would not be allowed to effect through the medium of a Treaty, obnoxious discriminations between new and old States, more than among the latter.

With respect to what has taken place in the N.W. Territory, it may be observed, that the ordinance giving its distinctive character on the Subject of Slaveholding proceeded from the old Congress, acting, with the best intentions, but under a charter which contains no shadow of the authority exercised. And it remains to be decided how far the States formed within that Territory & admitted into the Union, are on a different footing from its other members, as to their legislative sovereignty.

For the grounds on which 3/5 of the slaves were admitted into the ratio of representation, I will with your permission, save trouble by referring to No. 54 of the Federalist. In addition, it may be stated that this feature in the Constitution was combined with that relating to the power over Commerce & navigation. In truth these two powers, with those relating to the importation of slaves, & the Articles establishing the equality of representation in the Senate & the rule of taxation, had a complicated influence on each other which alone would have justified the remark, that the Constitution was "the result of mutual deference & Concession."

It was evident that the large States holding slaves, and those not large which felt themselves so by anticipation, would not have concurred in a constitution, allowing them no more Representation in one legislative branch than the smallest States, and in the other less than their proportional contributions to the Common Treasury.

The considerations which led to this mixed ratio which had been very deliberately agreed on in Apl., 1783, by the old Congress, make it probable that the Convention could not have looked to a departure from it, in any instance where slaves made a part of the local population.

Whether the Convention could have looked to the existence of slavery at all in the new States is a point on which I can add little to what has been already stated. The great object of the Convention seemed to be to prohibit the increase by the *importation* of slaves. A power to emancipate slaves was disclaimed; Nor is anything recollected that denoted a view to controul the distribution of those within the Country. The case of the N. Western Territory was probably superseded by the provision agst. the importation of slaves by S. Carolina & Georgia, which had not then passed laws prohibiting it. When the existence of slavery in that territory was precluded, the importation of slaves was rapidly going on, and the only mode of checking it was by narrowing the space open to them. It is not an unfair inference that the expedient would not have been undertaken, if the power afterward given to terminate the importation everywhere, had existed or been even anticipated. It has appeared that the present Congress never followed the example during the twenty years preceding the prohibitory epoch.

The *expediency* of exercising a supposed power in Congress, to prevent a diffusion of the slaves actually in the Country, as far as the local authorities may admit them, resolves itself into the probable effects of such a diffusion on the interests of the slaves and of the Nation.

Will it or will it not better the condition of the slaves, by lessening the number belonging to individual masters, and intermixing both with greater masses of free people? Will partial manumissions be more or less likely to take place, and a general emancipation be accelerated or retarded? Will the moral & physical condition of slaves, in the mean time, be improved or deteriorated? What do experiences and appearances decide as to the comparative rates of generative increase, in their present, and, in a dispersed situation?

Will the aggregate strength security tranquillity and harmony of the whole nation be advanced or impaired by lessening the proportion of slaves to the free people in particular sections of it?

How far an occlusion of the space now vacant, agst. the introduction of slaves may be essential to prevent compleatly a smuggled importation of them from abroad, ought to influence the question of expediency, must be decided by a reasonable estimate of the degree in which the importation would take place in spight of the spirit of the times, the increasing co-operation of foreign powers agst. the slave trade, the increasing rigor of the

Acts of Congress and the vigilant enforcement of them by the Executive; and by a fair comparison of this estimate with the considerations opposed to such an occlusion.

Will a multiplication of States holding slaves, multiply advocates of the importation of foreign slaves, so as to endanger the continuance of the prohibitory Acts of Congress? To such an apprehension seem to be opposed the facts, that the States holding fewest slaves are those which most readily abolished slavery altogether; that of the 13 primitive States, Eleven had prohibited the importation before the power was given to Congs., that all of them, with the newly added States, unanimously concurred in exerting that power; that most of the present slaveholding States cannot be tempted by motives of interest to favor the reopening of the ports to foreign slaves; and that these, with the States which have even abolished slavery within themselves, could never be outnumbered in the National Councils by new States wishing for slaves, and not satisfied with the supply attainable within the U.S.

On the whole, the Missouri question, as a constitutional one, amounts to the question whether the condition proposed to be annexed to the admission of Missouri would or would not be void in itself, or become void the moment the territory should enter as a State within the pale of the Constitution. And as a question of expediency & humanity, it depends essentially on the probable influence of such restrictions on the quantity & duration of slavery, and on the general condition of slaves in the U.S.

The question raised with regard to the tenor of the stipulation in the Louisiana Treaty, on the subject of its admission, is one which I have not examined, and on which I could probably throw no light if I had.

Under one aspect of the general subject, I cannot avoid saying, that apart from its merits under others, the tendency of what has passed and is passing, fills me with no slight anxiety. Parties under some denominations or other must always be expected in a Govt. as free as ours. When the individuals belonging to them are intermingled in every part of the whole Country, they strengthen the Union of the Whole, while they divide every part. Should a State of parties arise, founded on geographical boundaries and other Physical & permanent distinctions which happen to coincide with them, what is to controul those great repulsive Masses from awful shocks agst. each other?

The delay in answering your letter made me fear you might doubt my readiness to comply with its requests. I now fear you will think I have done more than these justified. I have been the less reserved because you are so ready to conform to my inclination formerly expressed, not to be drawn from my sequestered position into public view.

Since I thanked you for the copy of your late volume I have had the pleasure of going thro' it; and I should have been much disappointed, if it had been recd. by the public with less favor than is everywhere manifested. According to all accounts from the Continent of Europe, the American character has suffered much there by libels conveyed by British Prints, or circulated by itinerant Calumniators. It is to be hoped the truths in your book may find their way thither. Good translations of the Preface alone could not but open many eyes which have been blinded by prejudices against this Country.

To W.T. Barry

AUG 4, 1822.

Dr Sir,

I recd. some days ago your letter of June 30, and the printed Circular to which it refers.

The liberal appropriations made by the Legislature of Kentucky for a general system of Education cannot be too much applauded. A popular Government, without popular information, or the means of acquiring it, is but a Prologue to a Farce or a Tragedy; or, perhaps both. Knowledge will forever govern ignorance: And a people who mean to be their own Governors, must arm themselves with the power which knowledge gives.

I have always felt a more than ordinary interest in the destinies of Kentucky. Among her earliest settlers were some of my particular friends and Neighbors. And I was myself among the foremost advocates for submitting to the Will of the "District" the question and the time of its becoming a separate member of the American family. Its rapid growth & signal prosperity in this character have afforded me much pleasure; which is not a little enhanced by the enlightened patriotism which is now providing for the State a Plan of Education embracing every class of Citizens, and every grade & department of Knowledge. No error is more certain than the one proceeding from a hasty & superficial view of the subject: that the people at large have no interest in the establishment of Academies, Colleges, and Universities, where a few only, and those not of the poorer classes can obtain for their sons the advantages of superior education. It is thought to be unjust that all should be taxed for the benefit of a part, and that too the part least needing it.

If provision were not made at the same time for every part, the objection would be a natural one. But, besides the consideration when the higher

Seminaries belong to a plan of general education, that it is better for the poorer classes to have the aid of the richer by a general tax on property, than that every parent should provide at his own expence for the education of his children, it is certain that every Class is interested in establishments which give to the human mind its highest improvements, and to every Country its truest and most durable celebrity.

Learned Institutions ought to be favorite objects with every free people. They throw that light over the public mind which is the best security against crafty & dangerous encroachments on the public liberty. They are the nurseries of skilful Teachers for the schools distributed throughout the Community. They are themselves schools for the particular talents required for some of the Public Trusts, on the able execution of which the welfare of the people depends. They multiply the educated individuals from among whom the people may elect a due portion of their public Agents of every description; more especially of those who are to frame the laws; by the perspicuity, the consistency, and the stability, as well as by the just & equal spirit of which the great social purposes are to be answered.

Without such Institutions, the more costly of which can scarcely be provided by individual means, none but the few whose wealth enables them to support their sons abroad can give them the fullest education; and in proportion as this is done, the influence is monopolized which superior information every where possesses. At cheaper & nearer seats of Learning parents with slender incomes may place their sons in a course of education putting them on a level with the sons of the Richest. Whilst those who are without property, or with but little, must be peculiarly interested in a System which unites with the more Learned Institutions, a provision for diffusing through the entire Society the education needed for the common purposes of life. A system comprizing the Learned Institutions may be still further recommended to the more indigent class of Citizens by such an arrangement as was reported to the General Assembly of Virginia, in the year 1779, by a Committee* appointed to revise laws in order to adapt them to the genius of Republican Government. It made part of a "Bill for the more general diffusion of knowledge" that wherever a youth was ascertained to possess talents meriting an education which his parents could not afford, he should be carried forward at the public expence, from seminary to seminary, to the completion of his studies at the highest.

But why should it be necessary in this case, to distinguish the Society into classes according to their property? When it is considered that the

*The report was made by Mr. Jefferson, Mr. Pendleton, and Mr. Wythe.

establishment and endowment of Academies, Colleges, and Universities are a provision, not merely for the existing generation, but for succeeding ones also; that in Governments like ours a constant rotation of property results from the free scope to industry, and from the laws of inheritance, and when it is considered moreover, how much of the exertions and privations of all are meant not for themselves, but for their posterity, there can be little ground for objections from any class, to plans of which every class must have its turn of benefits. The rich man, when contributing to a permanent plan for the education of the poor, ought to reflect that he is providing for that of his own descendants; and the poor man who concurs in a provision for those who are not poor that at no distant day it may be enjoyed by descendants from himself. It does not require a long life to witness these vicissitudes of fortune.

It is among the happy peculiarities of our Union, that the States composing it derive from their relation to each other and to the whole, a salutary emulation, without the enmity involved in competitions among States alien to each other. This emulation, we may perceive, is not without its influence in several important respects; and in none ought it to be more felt than in the merit of diffusing the light and the advantages of Public Instruction. In the example therefore which Kentucky is presenting, she not only consults her own welfare, but is giving an impulse to any of her sisters who may be behind her in the noble career.

Throughout the Civilized World, nations are courting the praise of fostering Science and the useful Arts, and are opening their eyes to the principles and the blessings of Representative Government. The American people owe it to themselves, and to the cause of free Government, to prove by their establishments for the advancement and diffusion of Knowledge, that their political Institutions, which are attracting observation from every quarter, and are respected as Models, by the new-born States in our own Hemisphere, are as favorable to the intellectual and moral improvement of Man as they are conformable to his individual & social Rights. What spectacle can be more edifying or more seasonable, than that of Liberty & Learning, each leaning on the other for their mutual & surest support?

The Committee, of which your name is the first, have taken a very judicious course in endeavouring to avail Kentucky of the experience of elder States, in modifying her Schools. I enclose extracts from the laws of Virginia on that subject; though I presume they will give little aid; the less as they have as yet been imperfectly carried into execution. The States where such systems have been long in operation will furnish much better answers to many of the enquiries stated in your Circular. But after all, such is the diversity of local circumstances, more particularly as the population varies in density & sparseness, that the details suited to some may be little so to others. As the population however, is becoming less & less sparse, and it will be well in laying the foundation of a Good System, to have a view to this progressive change, much attention seems due to examples in the Eastern States, where the people are most compact, & where there has been the longest experience in plans of popular education.

I know not that I can offer on the occasion any suggestions not likely to occur to the Committee. Were I to hazard one, it would be in favour of adding to Reading, Writing, & Arithmetic, to which the instruction of the poor, is commonly limited, some knowledge of Geography; such as can easily be conveyed by a Globe & Maps, and a concise Geographical Grammar. And how easily & quickly might a general idea even, be conveyed of the Solar System, by the aid of a Planatarium of the Cheapest construction. No information seems better calculated to expand the mind and gratify curiosity than what would thus be imparted. This is especially the case, with what relates to the Globe we inhabit, the Nations among which it is divided, and the characters and customs which distinguish them. An acquaintance with foreign Countries in this mode, has a kindred effect with that of seeing them as travellers, which never fails, in uncorrupted minds, to weaken local prejudices, and enlarge the sphere of benevolent feelings. A knowledge of the Globe & its various inhabitants, however slight, might moreover, create a taste for Books of Travels and Voyages; out of which might grow a general taste for History, an inexhaustible fund of entertainment & instruction. Any reading not of a vicious species must be a good substitute for the amusements too apt to fill up the leisure of the labouring classes.

I feel myself much obliged Sir by your expressions of personal kindness, and pray you to accept a return of my good wishes, with assurances of my great esteem & respect.

P.S. On reflection I omit the extracts from the laws of Virga., which it is probable may be within your reach at home. Should it be otherwise, and you think them worth the transmission by the mail, the omission shall be supplied.

To Nicholas P. Trist

MONTPELLIER, DECR 23, 1832.

Dr Sir

I have received yours of the 19th, inclosing some of the South Carolina papers. There are in one of them some interesting views of the doctrine of secession; one that had occurred to me, and which for the first time I have seen in print; namely that if one State can at will withdraw from the others, the others can at will withdraw from her, and turn her, nolentem, volentem, out of the union. Until of late, there is not a State that would have abhorred such a doctrine more than South Carolina, or more dreaded an application of it to herself. The same may be said of the doctrine of nullification, which she now preaches as the only faith by which the Union can be saved.

I partake of the wonder that the men you name should view secession in the light mentioned. The essential difference between a free Government and Governments not free, is that the former is founded in compact, the parties to which are mutually and equally bound by it. Neither of them therefore can have a greater right to break off from the bargain, than the other or others have to hold them to it. And certainly there is nothing in the Virginia resolutions of —98, adverse to this principle, which is that of common sense and common justice. The fallacy which draws a different conclusion from them lies in confounding a *single* party, with the *parties* to the Constitutional compact of the United States. The latter having made the compact may do what they will with it. The former as one only of the parties, owes fidelity to it, till released by consent, or absolved by an intolerable abuse of the power created. In the Virginia Resolutions and Report the *plural* number, *States,* is in *every* instance used where reference is made to the authority which presided over the Government. As I am now known to have drawn those documents, I may say as I do with a distinct recollection, that the distinction was intentional. It was in fact required by the course of reasoning employed on the occasion. The Kentucky resolutions being less guarded have been more easily perverted. The pretext for the liberty taken with those of Virginia is the word *respective,* prefixed to the "rights" &c to be secured within the States. Could the abuse of the expression have been foreseen or suspected, the form of it would doubtless have been varied. But what can be more consistent with common sense, than that all having the same rights &c, should unite in contending for the security of them to each.

It is remarkable how closely the nullifiers who make the name of Mr. Jefferson the pedestal for their colossal heresy, shut their eyes and lips, whenever his authority is ever so clearly and emphatically against them. You have noticed what he says in his letters to Monroe & Carrington Pages 43 & 203, vol. 2, with respect to the powers of the old Congress to coerce delinquent States, and his reasons for preferring for the purpose a naval to a military force; and moreover that it was not necessary to find a right to coerce in the Federal Articles, that being inherent in the nature of a compact. It is high time that the claim to secede at will should be put down by the public opinion; and I shall be glad to see the task commenced by one who understands the subject.

I know nothing of what is passing at Richmond, more than what is seen in the newspapers. You were right in your foresight of the effect of the passages in the late Proclamation. They have proved a leaven for much fermentation there, and created an alarm against the danger of consolidation, balancing that of disunion. I wish with you the Legislature may not seriously injure itself by assuming the high character of mediator. They will certainly do so if they forget that their real influence will be in the inverse ratio of a boastful interposition of it.

If you can fix, and will name the day of your arrival at Orange Court House, we will have a horse there for you; and if you have more baggage than can be otherwise brought than on wheels, we will send such a vehicle for it. Such is the state of the roads produced by the wagons hurrying flour to market, that it may be impossible to send our carriage which would answer both purposes.

To William Cabell Rives

MONTPR., MARCH 12, 1833.

Dear Sir

I have recd. your very kind letter of the 6th, from Washington, and by the same mail a copy of your late Speech in the Senate for which I tender my thanks. I have found as I expected, that it takes a very able and enlightening view of its subject. I wish it may have the effect of reclaiming to the doctrine & language held by all from the birth of the Constitution, & till very lately by themselves, those who now Contend that the States have never parted with an Atom of their sovereignty; and consequently that the Constitutional band which holds them together, is a mere league or partnership, without any of the characteristics of sovereignty or nationality.

It seems strange that it should be necessary to disprove this novel and nullifying doctrine; and stranger still that those who deny it should be denounced as Innovators, heretics & Apostates. Our political system is admitted to be a new Creation—a real nondescript. Its character therefore must be sought within itself; not in precedents, because there are none; not in writers whose comments are guided by precedents. Who can tell at present how Vattel and others of that class, would have qualified (in the Gallic sense of the term) a Compound & peculiar system with such an example of it as ours before them.

What can be more preposterous than to say that the States as united, are in no respect or degree, a Nation, which implies sovereignty; altho' acknowledged to be such by all other Nations & Sovereigns, and maintaining with them, all the international relations, of war & peace, treaties, commerce, &c, and, on the other hand and at the same time, to say that the States separately are compleatly nations & sovereigns; although they can separately neither speak nor harken to any other nation, nor maintain with it any of the international relations whatever and would be disowned as Nations if presenting themselves in that character.

The nullifiers it appears, endeavor to shelter themselves under a distinction between a delegation and a surrender of powers. But if the powers be attributes of sovereignty & nationality & the grant of them be perpetual, as is necessarily implied, where not otherwise expressed, sovereignty & nationality according to the extent of the grant are effectually transferred by it, and a dispute about the name, is but a battle of words. The practical result is not indeed left to argument or inference. The words of the Constitution are explicit that the Constitution & laws of the U.S. shall be supreme over the Constitution & laws of the several States; supreme in their exposition and execution as well as in their authority. Without a supremacy in those respects it would be like a scabbard in the hand of a soldier without a sword in it. The imagination itself is startled at the idea of twenty four independent expounders of a rule that cannot exist, but in a meaning and operation, the same for all.

The conduct of S. Carolina has called forth not only the question of nullification; but the more formidable one of secession. It is asked whether a State by resuming the sovereign form in which it entered the Union, may not of right withdraw from it at will. As this is a simple question whether a State, more than an individual, has a right to violate its engagements, it would seem that it might be safely left to answer itself. But the countenance given to the claim shows that it cannot be so lightly dismissed. The natural feelings which laudably attach the people composing a State, to its authority and importance, are at present too much excited by the unnatural feelings, with which they have been inspired agst. their brethren of other States, not to expose them, to the danger of being misled into erroneous views of the nature of the Union and the interest they have in it. One thing at least seems to be too clear to be questioned; that whilst a State remains within the Union it cannot withdraw its citizens from the operation of the Constitution & laws of the Union. In the event of an actual secession without the Consent of the Co-States, the course to be pursued by these involves questions painful in the discussion of them. God grant that the menacing appearances, which obtruded it may not be followed by positive occurrences requiring the more painful task of deciding them!

In explaining the proceedings of Virga. in 98–99, the state of things at that time was the more properly appealed to, as it has been too much overlooked. The doctrines combated are always a key to the arguments employed. It is but too common to read the expressions of a remote period thro' the modern meaning of them, & to omit guards agst. misconstruction not anticipated. A few words with a prophetic gift, might have prevented much error in the glosses on those proceedings. The remark is equally applicable to the Constitution itself. [. . .]

On Majority Governments

[1833]

Dear Sir,—You justly take alarm at the new doctrine that a majority Government is of all other Governments the most oppressive. The doctrine strikes at the root of Republicanism, and if pursued into its consequences, must terminate in absolute monarchy, with a standing military force; such alone being impartial between its subjects, and alone capable of overpowering majorities as well as minorities.

But it is said that a majority Government is dangerous only where there is a difference in the interest of the classes or sections composing the community; that this difference will generally be greatest in communities of the greatest extent; and that such is the extent of the U.S. and the discordance of interests in them, that a majority cannot be trusted with power over a minority.

Formerly, the opinion prevailed that a Republican Government was in its nature limited to a small sphere; and was in its true character only when the sphere was so small that the people could, in a body, exercise the Government over themselves.

The history of the ancient Republics, and those of a more modern date, had demonstrated the evils incident to popular assemblages, so quickly formed, so susceptible of contagious passions, so exposed to the misguidance of eloquent & ambitious leaders; and so apt to be tempted by the facility of forming interested majorities, into measures unjust and oppressive to the minor parties.

The introduction of the representative principle into modern Governments particularly of Great Britain and her colonial offsprings, had shown the practicability of popular Governments in a larger sphere, and that the enlargement of the sphere was a cure for many of the evils inseparable from the popular forms in small communities.

It remained for the people of the U.S., by combining a federal with a republican organization, to enlarge still more the sphere of representative Government and by convenient partitions & distributions of power, to provide the better for internal justice & order, whilst it afforded the best protection against external dangers.

Experience & reflection may be said not only to have exploded the old error, that republican Governments could only exist within a small compass, but to have established the important truth, that as representative Governments are necessary substitutes for popular assemblages; so an association of free communities, each possessing a responsible Government under a collective authority also responsible, by enlarging the practicable sphere of popular governments, promises a consummation of all the reasonable hopes of the patrons of free Government.

It was long since observed by Montesquieu, has been often repeated since, and, may it not be added, illustrated within the U.S. that in a confederal system, if one of its members happens to stray into pernicious measures, it will be reclaimed by the frowns & the good examples of the others, before the evil example will have infected the others.

But whatever opinions may be formed on the general subjects of confederal systems, or the interpretation of our own, every friend to Republican Government ought to raise his voice against the sweeping denunciation of majority Governments as the most tyrannical and intolerable of all Governments. [. . .]

[. . .] It has been said that all Government is an evil. It would be more proper to say that the necessity of any Government is a misfortune. This necessity however exists; and the problem to be solved is, not what form of Government is perfect, but which of the forms is least imperfect; and here the general question must be between a republican Government in which the majority rule the minority, and a Government in which a lesser number or the least number rule the majority. If the republican form is, as all of us agree, to be preferred, the final question must be, what is the structure of it that will best guard against precipitate counsels and factious combinations for unjust purposes, without a sacrifice of the fundamental principle of Republicanism. Those who denounce majority Governments altogether because they may have an interest in abusing their power, denounce at the same time all Republican Government and must maintain that minority governments would feel less of the bias of interest or the seductions of power. [. . .]

It may be objected to majority governments, that the majority, as formed by the Constitution, may be a minority when compared with the popular majority. This is likely to be the case more or less in all elective governments. It is so in many of the States. It will always be so where property is combined with population in the election and apportionment of representation. It must be still more the case with confederacies, in which the members, however unequal in population, have equal votes in the administration of the government. In the compound system of the United States, though much less than in mere confederacies, it also necessarily exists to a certain extent. That this departure from the rule of equality, creating a political and constitutional majority in contradistinction to a numerical majority of the people, may be abused in various degrees oppressive to the majority of the people, is certain; and in modes and degrees so oppressive as to justify ultra or anti-constitutional resorts to adequate relief is equally certain. Still the constitutional majority must be acquiesced in by the constitutional minority, while the Constitution exists. The moment that arrangement is successfully frustrated, the Constitution is at an end. The only remedy, therefore, for the oppressed minority is in the amendment of the Constitution or a subversion of the Constitution. This inference is unavoidable. While the Constitution is in force, the power created by it, whether a popular minority or majority, must be the legitimate power, and obeyed as the only alternative to the dissolution of all government. It is a favourable consideration, in the impossibility of securing in all cases a coincidence of the constitutional and numerical majority, that when the former is the minority, the existence of a numerical majority with justice on its side, and its influence on public opinion, will be a salutary control on the abuse of power by a minority constitutionally possessing it: a control generally of adequate force, where a military force, the disturber of all the ordinary movements of free governments, is not on the side of the minority.

The result of the whole is, that we must refer to the monitory reflection that no government of human device and human administration can be perfect; that that which is the least imperfect is therefore the best government; that the abuses of all other governments have led to the preference of republican government as the best of all governments, because the least imperfect; that the vital principle of republican government is the *lex majoris partis*, the will of the majority; that if the will of a majority cannot be trusted where there are diversified and conflicting interests, it can be trusted nowhere, because such interests exist everywhere; that if the manufacturing and agricultural interests be of all interests the most conflicting in the most important operations of government, and a majority government over them be the most intolerable of all governments, it must be as intolerable within the States as it is represented to be in the United States; and, finally, that the advocates of the doctrine, to be consistent, must reject it in the former as well as in the latter, and seek a refuge under an authority master of both.

Advice to My Country

[1834]

As this advice, if it ever see the light will not do it till I am no more it may be considered as issuing from the tomb, where truth alone can be respected, and the happiness of man alone consulted. It will be entitled therefore to whatever weight can be derived from good intentions, and from the experience of one who has served his country in various stations through a period of forty years, who espoused in his youth and adhered through his life to the cause of its liberty, and who has borne a part in most of the great transactions which will constitute epochs of its destiny.

The advice nearest to my heart and deepest in my convictions is that the Union of the States be cherished and perpetuated. Let the open enemy to it be regarded as a Pandora with her box opened; and the disguised one, as the Serpent creeping with his deadly wiles into Paradise.

Chronologies

GEORGE WASHINGTON

1732 Born February 22 in Bridges Creek, Virginia.

1753 Governor Robert Dinwiddie of Virginia sends him west to demand that the French stop encroaching on land in the Ohio Valley.

1754–1758 Serves as lieutenant colonel in the French and Indian Wars.

1754 Surrenders Fort Necessity.

1758 Captures Fort Duquesne.

1759 Marries Martha Dandridge Custis, wealthy widow with two children. Elected to the Virginia House of Burgesses; will serve as a burgess until 1775.

1761 Inherits Mount Vernon from his half-brother Lawrence.

1774 Chosen to be a delegate from Virginia to the First Continental Congress.

1775 Chosen to be a delegate to the Second Continental Congress; elected commander in chief of the Continental Army.

1776 Defends New York, retreats to New Jersey; has success in Trenton.

1777 Has success in Princeton; defeated at Brandywine.

1781 Leads secret, rapid march from the Hudson River to the Chesapeake Bay; defeats British troops and Lord Charles Cornwallis at Yorktown.

1782 Denounces suggestions made in Newburgh, New York, by Colonel Lewis Nicola that he crown himself monarch.

1783 Retires to Mount Vernon.

1787 Though reluctant to attend the Constitutional Convention in Philadelphia, he yields to the entreaties of his friends—and is elected president of the Convention.

1789 Unanimously elected president of the United States. Appoints heads of executive departments of state, treasury, war; sets up executive branch of government.

1791 Signs bill chartering Bank of the United States. Selects site for new capital city on the Potomac River.

1792 Unanimously reelected to a second presidential term. Tries to mediate feud between Jefferson and Hamilton.

1793 Proclaims American neutrality after France declares war on Great Britain, Spain, and the Netherlands.
1794 Leads troops to put down the Whiskey Rebellion in western Pennsylvania—the only American president ever to lead troops in the field.
1795 Signs the Jay Treaty, a commercial treaty with Great Britain.
1796 Signs the Treaty of San Lorenzo with Spain, giving Americans access to navigation on the Mississippi River. Publishes his Farewell Address.
1798 Leaves retirement to accept post as lieutenant general and commander in chief of the army.
1799 Dies December 14. Leaves instructions to free his slaves upon his death, or upon Martha's death, should she outlive him.

ALEXANDER HAMILTON

1755 Born January 11 in Nevis, British West Indies.
1766 Works as a shipping clerk in Saint Croix.
1773 Travels to New York; attends King's College. Writes pamphlets for the Patriot cause.
1775 Appointed captain in the Provincial Company of Artillery.
1777–1781 Appointed aide-de-camp to Washington with rank of lieutenant-colonel.
1780 Marries Elizabeth Schuyler, daughter of General Philip Schuyler.
1781 Fights at Yorktown.
1782 Serves in Congress; practices law in New York.
1784 Founds and becomes director of the Bank of New York.
1785 Joins group in creating the New York Society for Promoting the Manumission of Slaves.
1786 Attends Annapolis Convention; drafts resolution that leads to the Constitutional Convention in Philadelphia.
1787 Serves as delegate to the New York State Assembly. Elected delegate to the Constitutional Convention in Philadelphia, which he attends sporadically. Urges strong, energetic, centralized national government; writes many of the *Federalist* essays.
1788 Leads the fight for ratification of the Constitution in New York.
1789–1795 Appointed secretary of the treasury by George Washington; lays the foundation for American economic and fiscal strength.
1790–1791 Issues a Report on Public Credit, a Report on a National Bank, and a Report on Manufactures.
1792 His policies, called the "Hamiltonian system," as well as his pro-British, anti-French positions, are supported by Federalists and opposed by the Jeffersonian Republicans.
1795 Resigns from Washington's Cabinet; practices law in New York.
1796 Helps draft Washington's Farewell Address.
1798 Appointed major-general of the army during the "Quasi War" with France.
1800 Publishes pamphlet attacking the character of John Adams; opposes election of Aaron Burr after Burr ties with Jefferson in the Electoral College.
1801 Founds the New York *Evening Post.*

1801 His oldest son, Philip, is killed in a duel.
1804 After making hostile comments about Burr, he accepts Burr's challenge to a duel. The duel takes place on July 11. Hamilton dies from his wounds on July 12 in New York City.

JOHN ADAMS

1735 Born October 30 in Braintree, Massachusetts.
1751–1755 Attends Harvard College.
1756–1758 Studies law and is admitted to the Massachusetts bar.
1764 Marries Abigail Smith, with whom he will have five children.
1765 Protests against the Stamp Act.
1774 Chosen as a delegate from Massachusetts to the First Continental Congress.
1775 Serves as delegate to the Second Continental Congress; recommends Washington as commander in chief of the Continental Army.
1776 Serves on the committee that drafts the Declaration of Independence.
1778 Serves as commissioner to France, joining Benjamin Franklin in trying to secure French aid for the American war of independence.
1779 Returns to Massachusetts; drafts a constitution for Massachusetts.
1779–1784 Returns to Europe; along with Benjamin Franklin and John Jay, negotiates peace treaty with Great Britain; arranges for loans from the Netherlands.
1785 Serves as American minister to Great Britain.
1789 Elected vice president of the United States.
1792 Reelected vice president.
1797 Inaugurated as second president of the United States; tries, unsuccessfully, to conciliate the Hamiltonian Federalists and the Jeffersonian Republicans.
1798 Resists pressure from his own Federalist Party to enter into war with France. Signs Alien and Sedition Acts, prohibiting criticism of government officials.
1800 Loses presidential election to Thomas Jefferson.
1801 Just before leaving office, appoints John Marshall as chief justice of the U.S. Supreme Court.
1812 Heals rift with Jefferson and begins correspondence once again with him.
1826 Dies in Quincy, Massachusetts, July 4, 1826, the same day as Jefferson, on the fiftieth anniversary of the signing of the Declaration of Independence.

THOMAS JEFFERSON

1743 Born April 13 in Shadwell, Virginia.
1760–1762 Studies at William and Mary College in Williamsburg, Virginia.
1762–1767 Studies law with his mentor George Wythe; begins practicing law.
1768–1775 Serves in Virginia House of Burgesses.
1770 Begins construction of Monticello.
1772 Marries Martha Wayles Skelton; they will have three daughters.
1774 Publishes "A Summary View of the Rights of British America."
1775 Attends Continental Congress.

1776 Drafts the Declaration of Independence; elected to Virginia House of Burgesses.

1777 Drafts Virginia Statute for Religious Freedom; supports abolition of primogeniture and entails, separation of church and state, and establishment of a public school system; advocates termination of the slave trade and gradual emancipation.

1779–1781 serves as governor of Virginia for a two-year term. Not particularly successful in resisting the British advance.

1782 His wife dies.

1783–1784 Serves in Continental Congress; proposes decimal monetary system and a plan for organizing the western territories.

1784–1789 Serves as minister to France.

1785 Publishes *Notes on the State of Virginia.*

1789 Is an enthusiastic witness to the beginning of the French Revolution. Helps his friend Lafayette draft a Charter of Rights for France. Returns to the United States.

1790–1793 Serves as secretary of state under President Washington.

1791–1792 Supports Hamilton's plan for the national government to fund the debt and assume the debts of the states in exchange for Hamilton's agreement to locate the new national capital on the Potomac.

1793 Resigns from Washington's Cabinet in protest against Hamilton's energetic, modernizing economic policies and his pro-British anti-French stance. Returns to Monticello.

1796 Defeated by John Adams in the presidential election but is elected vice president.

1797–1801 Serves as vice president under Adams.

1798 Opposing the Alien and Sedition Acts, he drafts the Kentucky Resolutions, which suggest that a state can nullify federal legislation it considers unconstitutional.

1800 Defeats John Adams in the presidential election but ties with his own vice-presidential running mate, Aaron Burr.

1801 Defeats Burr in a tense tie-breaking vote in the House of Representatives.

1801–1809 Serves as third president of the United States. Stands for small, frugal, limited government.

1803 Purchases Louisiana Territory, doubling the size of the United States. Sends Meriwether Lewis and William Clark on a three-year journey to explore the western portion of the continent.

1807 Calls for the Embargo Act to curtail American trade with Europe in order to preserve American neutrality.

1809 Retires to Monticello.

1812 Heals breach with Adams; they resume correspondence.

1819 Begins effort to found the University of Virginia, which opens in 1825.

1820 Opposes the Missouri Compromise, which prohibited the spread of slavery in new western states north of the 36°30' latitude.

1826 Dies on July 4, the fiftieth anniversary of the Declaration of Independence.

JAMES MADISON

1751 Born March 16 in Port Conway, Virginia.

1769–1771 Studies at College of New Jersey, which later became Princeton University.

1775 Serves as chairman of the committee of public safety for Orange County, Virginia.

1776 Elected to the Virginia General Assembly in Williamsburg. Helps draft new state constitution; supports Jefferson's proposals for reform.

1778–1779 Serves on Virginia Council of State.

1779–1783 Serves in Continental Congress. Drafts instructions for John Jay's mission to demand free navigation on the Mississippi from Spain. Realizes that the nation needs a stronger centralized government.

1784–1786 Serves in Virginia House of Delegates; successfully pushes passage of Jefferson's Statute for Religious Liberty.

1786 Calls for and attends the Annapolis Convention. Urges that another convention be held to amend the Articles of Confederation. That convention will be the Constitutional Convention, held in Philadelphia in 1787.

1787 Leads the Virginia delegation to the Constitutional Convention; advocates stronger, more unified government. His theories about checks and balances are central in crafting the new government; he was the single most influential member at the Convention.

1787–1788 Writes twenty-nine *Federalist* essays along with Hamilton and John Jay; leads struggle for ratification of the Constitution in Virginia.

1789–1797 Serves in U.S. House of Representatives. Proposes and drafts the first ten amendments to the Constitution, the Bill of Rights. Opposes Hamilton's economic policies; breaks with Hamilton, becomes congressional leader of the Republican opposition party.

1794 Marries Dolley Payne Todd.

1798 Retires to Montpelier. Drafts Virginia Resolves opposing the Alien and Sedition Acts and declaring the right of states to reject federal laws they consider unconstitutional.

1801–1809 Serves as secretary of state under President Jefferson.

1808 Defeats South Carolinian C.C. Pinckney in presidential election.

1809–1817 Serves as fourth president of the United States.

1812 Defeats De Witt Clinton in presidential election. Conducts War of 1812 against Great Britain. Although judged a weak wartime leader, he believes in limited government and does not want the United States to become a powerful fiscal-military nation-state like Great Britain.

1814 The Capitol building and the White House are burned by the British. The Hartford Convention discusses disunion. Peace talks are held in Ghent, Belgium.

1815 Peace treaty ratified.

1816 Signs bill establishing Second Bank of the United States.

1817 Retires to Montpelier, Virginia.

1828 After Jefferson's death, becomes rector of the University of Virginia.

1829 Participates in Virginia Constitutional Convention.

1830 Writes public letter defending the supremacy of federal law and attacking South Carolina's new doctrine of "nullification," that is, the right of one state to nullify federal laws.

1836 Dies on June 18 in Montpelier, Virginia.

Notes

INTRODUCTION

1. Washington to Henry Knox, 1 April 1789, in Washington, *Writings,* ed. John Rhodehamel (New York: Library of America, 1997), 726.

2. Garry Wills, *Cincinnatus: George Washington and the Enlightenment* (Garden City, NY: Doubleday, 1984), 23, 3.

3. Hamilton to Elizabeth Hamilton, 6 September 1781, in *The Papers of Alexander Hamilton,* ed. Harold C. Syrett, 27 vols. (New York: Columbia University Press, 1962), 2:675.

4. Adams to John Quincy Adams, 5 May 1796, in Page Smith, *John Adams,* 2 vols. (Garden City, N.Y.: Doubleday, 1962), 2:885.

5. Adams to Abigail Adams, 15 February 1796, in *Letters of John Adams Addressed to His Wife,* ed. Charles Francis Adams, 2 vols. (Boston: C.C. Little and J. Brown, 1841), 2:202.

6. Adams to Abigail Adams, 9 April 1796, in *Letters of John Adams Addressed to His Wife,* ed. Adams, 2:217.

7. Jefferson to James Monroe, 20 May 1782, in Jefferson, *Writings,* ed. Merrill Peterson (New York: Library of America, 1984), 777–779.

8. Jefferson to Madison, 28 December 1794, in *The Republic of Letters: The Correspondence Between Thomas Jefferson and James Madison, 1776–1826,* ed. James Morton Smith, 3 vols. (New York: W.W. Norton, 1995), 2:868.

9. Jefferson to Madison, 28 December 1794, in *Republic of Letters,* ed. Smith, 2:868.

10. Gordon S. Wood, "The Democratization of Mind in the American Revolution," in *Leadership in the American Revolution* (Washington, D.C.: Library of Congress, 1974), 67, 64.

11. John Adams, *Diary and Autobiography of John Adams,* ed. L.H. Butterfield et al., 2 vols. (Cambridge: Harvard University Press, 1961), 1:78, 95.

12. Hamilton to Edward Stevens, 11 November 1769, in Hamilton, *Writings,* ed. Joanne B. Freeman (New York: Library of America, 2001), 3.

13. Hamilton to Washington, 22 November 1780, in *Papers of Alexander Hamilton,* ed. Syrett, 2:509.

14. Washington to John Augustine Washington, 28 May 1755, in Washington, *Writings,* ed. Rhodehamel, 52.

15. Washington to Warner Lewis, 14 August 1755, in *The Writings of George Washington from the Original Manuscript Sources, 1745–1799,* ed. John C. Fitzpatrick, 39 vols. (Washington, D.C.: U.S. Government Printing Office, 1931–1944), 1:159–163.

16. Washington to John Augustine Washington, 28 May 1755, in Washington, *Writings,* ed. Rhodehamel, 52.

17. John Adams, "Thoughts on Government" [1776], in *The Revolutionary Writings of John Adams,* ed. C. Bradley Thompson (Indianapolis: Liberty Fund, 2000), 293.

18. Niccolò Machiavelli, *The Discourses,* Bk. 1, ch. 10.

19. Hamilton to James Bayard, 16 January 1801, in *Papers of Alexander Hamilton,* ed. Syrett, 25:323.

20. Douglass Adair, *Fame and the Founding Fathers: Essays by Douglass Adair,* ed. Trevor Colbourn (New York: W.W. Norton, 1974), 24.

21. Machiavelli, *The Discourses,* Bk. 3, ch. 28.

22. Adams to Abigail Adams, 3 July 1776, in *Works of John Adams,* ed. Charles Francis Adams, 10 vols. (Boston: Little, Brown, 1850–1856), 1:230–231.

23. Washington to John Thomas, 23 July 1775, in *Writings of George Washington,* ed. Fitzpatrick, 3:359.

24. Washington to William Gordon, 23 December 1788, in *Writings of George Washington,* ed. Fitzpatrick, 30:169.

25. Madison, *Federalist* No. 37.

26. "Universal Peace," *National Gazette,* 31 January 1792, in James Madison, *Writings,* ed. Jack N. Rakove (New York: Library of America, 1999), 505.

27. James Madison, in Jonathan Elliot, ed., *Debates in the Several State Conventions on the Adoption of the Federalist Constitution,* 3 vols. (Philadelphia: Lippincott, 1937), 3:394, 399.

28. Madison, *Federalist* No. 14.

29. Jefferson to Martha Jefferson, 28 March 1787, in *The Family Letters of Thomas Jefferson,* ed. Edwin Betts and James Bear (Charlottesville: Published for the Thomas Jefferson Memorial Foundation by the University Press of Virginia, 1966), 35.

30. Hamilton, *Federalist* No. l.

31. Madison, *Federalist* No. 14.

32. Madison, *Debates in the Several State Conventions,* ed. Elliot, 3:616.

33. William Pierce, in Max Farrand, *The Framing of the Constitution* (New Haven, Conn.: Yale University Press, 1930), 17.

34. Wood, "The Democratization of Mind in the American Revolution," 67, 64.

35. Jefferson to Diodati, 3 August 1789, in Jefferson, *Writings,* ed. Peterson, 958.

36. Jefferson to David Humphreys, 18 March 1789, in *Papers of Thomas Jefferson,* ed. Julian Boyd et al., 32 vols. (Princeton, N.J.: Princeton University Press, 1950–), 14:677.

37. Jefferson to Madison, 6 September 1789, in *Republic of Letters,* ed. Smith, 1:635.

38. Madison to Jefferson, 14 February 1790, in *Republic of Letters,* ed. Smith, 1:650–652.

39. Madison, *Federalist* No. 49.

40. Hamilton to Lafayette, 6 October 1789, in *Papers of Alexander Hamilton,* ed. Syrett, 5:425.

41. Hamilton to Washington, 15 September 1790, in *Papers of Alexander Hamilton,* ed. Syrett, 7:51.

42. Hamilton, *Federalist* No. 6.

43. John Adams, "A Dissertation on the Canon and Feudal Law" [1765], in *The Political Writings of John Adams,* ed. George W. Carey (Washington, D.C.: Regnery, 2000), 19–20.

44. Adams to Jefferson, 2 March 1816, in *The Adams-Jefferson Letters,* ed. Lester Cappon, 2 vols. (Chapel Hill: University of North Carolina Press, for the Institute of Early American History and Culture, 1959), 2:464.

45. John Adams, *Discourses on Davila: A Series of Papers on Political History,* in *The Works of John Adams,* ed. Adams, 6:276.

46. Adams, Letters to John Taylor, Letter 8, in *Works of John Adams,* ed. Adams, 6:464.

47. Washington, "Circular to the States," 8 June 1783, in *Writings of George Washington,* ed. Fitzpatrick, 26:485.

48. Washington, Eighth Annual Message to Congress, 7 December 1796, in Washington, *Writings,* ed. Rhodehamel, 985.

49. Jefferson, "The Anas," in *Writings of Thomas Jefferson,* ed. Paul Leicester Ford, 10 vols. (New York: G.P. Putnam's Sons, 1892–1899), 1:155.

50. Washington to George Steptoe Washington, 23 March 1789, in Washington, *Writings,* ed. Rhodehamel, 721, italics added.

51. Jefferson to Peter Carr, 19 August 1785, in Jefferson, *Writings,* ed. Peterson, 815, italics added.

52. Jefferson to Thomas Jefferson Randolph, 24 November 1808, in Jefferson, *Writings,* ed. Peterson, 1194–1195.

53. Alexander Hamilton, "A Letter from Phocion," January 1784, in Hamilton, *Writings,* ed. Freeman, 127–129.

54. Washington to Lafayette, 19 January 1788, in Washington, *Writings,* ed. Rhodehamel, 683–684.

55. Washington, Fragments of a Draft of the First Inaugural Address, in Washington, *Writings,* ed. Rhodehamel, 707.

56. Washington, "Draft of Farewell Address," in Washington, *Writings,* ed. Rhodehamel, 947.

57. Jefferson to Thomas Jefferson Randolph, 24 November 1808, in Jefferson, *Writings,* ed. Peterson, 1195.

58. Madison, *Federalist* No. 37.

59. See Drew McCoy, *The Last of the Fathers: James Madison and the Republican Legacy* (New York: Cambridge University Press, 1989), 63.

60. Edmund S. Morgan, "Conflict and Consensus in the American Revolution," in *Essays on the American Revolution,* ed. Stephen G. Kurtz and James H. Hutson (Chapel Hill: The University of North Carolina Press for the Institute of Early American History and Culture, 1973), 307.

61. Jefferson to Destutt de Tracy, 26 January 1811, in *Writings of Thomas Jefferson,* ed. Ford, 9:307.

62. Hamilton, *Americanus No. 1,* 31 January 1794, in *Papers of Alexander Hamilton,* ed. Syrett, 15:671.

63. Madison, "A Candid State of Parties," *National Gazette,* 26 September 1792, in Madison, *Writings,* ed. Rakove, 531.

64. Hamilton, *Federalist* No. 11.

65. Hamilton, "Camillus," 1795, in *Papers of Alexander Hamilton,* ed. Syrett, 19:53–57.

66. Washington to Hamilton, 26 August 1792, in *Writings of George Washington,* ed. Fitzpatrick, 32:132–134.

67. Madison, *Federalist* No. 37.

68. Jefferson to Francis Hopkinson, 13 March 1789, in Jefferson, *Writings,* ed. Peterson, 941.

69. Adams to Jefferson, 9 July 1813, in *The Adams-Jefferson Letters,* ed. Cappon, 2:351.

70. Madison, Note to his Speech on the Right of Suffrage [1821], in Max Farrand, ed., *Records of the Federal Convention of 1787,* 4 vols. (New Haven, Conn.: Yale University Press, 1966), 3:452.

71. Washington to Bryan Fairfax, 24 August 1774, in Washington, *Writings,* ed. Rhodehamel, 158.

72. Washington to John Francis Mercer, 9 September 1786, in *Writings of George Washington,* ed. Fitzpatrick, 29:5.

73. Washington to David Stuart, 28 March 1790, in Washington, *Writings,* ed. Rhodehamel, 757–758.

74. Thomas Jefferson, *Notes on the State of Virginia,* ed. William Peden (Chapel Hill: University of North Carolina Press, 1982), Query 18, "Manners," 163.

75. Jefferson to Albert Gallatin, 26 December 1820, in Jefferson, *Writings,* ed. Peterson, 1449–1450.

76. Jefferson to William Short, 18 January 1826, in *Writings of Thomas Jefferson,* ed. Ford, 10:362. See D.B. Davis, *Was Thomas Jefferson an Authentic Enemy of Slavery?* (Oxford: Clarendon, 1970).

77. Jefferson, Second Inaugural Address, 4 March 1805, in *Writings of Thomas Jefferson,* ed. Ford, 8:344.

78. Jefferson to William H. Harrison, 27 February 1803, in Jefferson, *Writings,* ed. Peterson, 1118.

79. Abigail Adams to John Adams, 31 March 1776, in *Adams Family Correspondence,* ed. L.H. Butterfield, 7 vols. (Cambridge: Belknap Press of Harvard University Press, 1963–1993), 1:370.

80. Jefferson to Nathaniel Burwell, 14 March 1818, in *Writings of Thomas Jefferson,* ed. Ford, 10:104.

81. Jefferson to Albert Gallatin, 13 January 1807, in *The Writings of Albert Gallatin,* ed. Henry Adams, 3 vols. (Philadelphia: J.B. Lippincott, 1879), 1:328.

82. Madison, *Debates in the Several State Conventions,* ed. Elliot, 5:242.

83. Madison, "Majority Governments," in Marvin Meyers, ed., *The Mind of the Founder: Sources of the Political Thought of James Madison* (Hanover, N.H.: University Press of New England, 1983), 409–417.

84. Ralph Lerner, *The Thinking Revolutionary: Principle and Practice in the New Republic* (Ithaca, N.Y.: Cornell University Press, 1987).

GEORGE WASHINGTON

1. Washington to Hamilton, 1 September 1796, in *The Writings of George Washington from the Original Manuscript Sources, 1745–1799,* ed. John C. Fitzpatrick, 39 vols. (Washington, D.C.: U.S. Government Printing Office, 1931–1944), 35:199–200.

2. Washington to George Mason, 5 April 1769, in *Writings of George Washington,* ed. Fitzpatrick, 2:500–501.

3. Ibid.

4. Adams to John Jebb, 10 September 1785, in *Works of John Adams,* ed. Charles Francis Adams, 10 vols. (Boston: Little, Brown, 1850–1856), 9:541.

5. Washington to Sir Newenham, 29 August 1788, in *Writings of George Washington,* ed. Fitzpatrick, 30:73.

6. "Draft of First Inaugural Address," in George Washington, *Writings,* ed. John Rhodehamel (New York: Library of America, 1997), 714.

7. Washington to Lafayette, 29 January 1789, in Washington, *Writings,* ed. Rhodehamel, 717.

8. Madison, Memorandum on Washington's Retirement, 5 May 1792, in Madison, *Writings,* ed. Jack N. Rakove (New York: Library of America, 1999), 519–523.

9. Jefferson to Washington, 23 May 1792, in *Writings of Thomas Jefferson,* ed. Paul Leicester Ford, 10 vols. (New York: G.P. Putnam's Sons, 1892–1899), 6:5.

10. Hamilton to Washington, 30 July 1792, in Hamilton, *Writings,* ed. Joanne B. Freeman (New York: Library of America, 2001), 752.

ALEXANDER HAMILTON

1. Hamilton to Robert Morris, 30 April 1781, in *The Papers of Alexander Hamilton,* ed. Harold C. Syrett, 27 vols. (New York: Columbia University Press, 1962), 2:635.

2. *The Continentalist No. V,* 8 April 1782, in *The Papers The of Alexander Hamilton,* ed. Syrett, 3:76.

3. Max Farrand, ed., *Records of the Federal Convention of 1787,* 4 vols. (New Haven, Conn.: Yale University Press, 1966), 1:467.

4. Conversation with George Beckwith, October 1789, in *The Papers of Alexander Hamilton,* ed. Syrett, 5:483.

5. Hamilton to Gouverneur Morris, 29 February 1802, in *The Papers of Alexander Hamilton,* ed. Syrett, 25:544.

6. Hamilton to C.C. Pinckney, 29 December 1802, in *The Papers of Alexander Hamilton,* ed. Syrett, 26:71.

7. Hamilton to Theodore Sedgwick, 10 July 1804, in *The Papers of Alexander Hamilton,* ed. Syrett, 26:309.

8. Hamilton, "Statement on Impending Duel with Aaron Burr" [28 June–10 July 1804], in *Papers of Alexander Hamilton,* ed. Syrett, 26:280.

9. Gouverneur Morris to Robert Walsh, 5 February 1811, in *The Life of Gouverneur Morris, with Selections from His Correspondence and Miscellaneous Papers,* ed. Jared Sparks, 3 vols. (Boston: Gray and Bowen, 1832), 3:260–268, italics added.

JOHN ADAMS

1. Adams to Jefferson, 10 June 1813, in *The Adams-Jefferson Letters,* ed. Lester Cappon, 2 vols. (Chapel Hill: University of North Carolina Press, for the Institute of Early American History and Culture, 1959), 2:327.

2. Jefferson to Adams, 15 June 1813, in *The Adams-Jefferson Letters,* ed. Cappon, 2:332.

3. John Adams, "To the Young Men of the City of Philadelphia, 7 May 1798," in *Works of John Adams,* ed. Charles Francis Adams, 10 vols. (Boston: Little, Brown, 1850–1856), 9:188.

4. John Adams, "Thoughts on Government" [1776], in *The Political Writings of John Adams,* ed. George W. Carey (Washington, D.C.: Regnery, 2000), 490.

5. Adams to Benjamin Hichborn, 29 May 1776, in *Papers of John Adams,* ed. Robert J. Taylor, vols. 1–13 (Cambridge: The Belknap Press of Harvard University Press, 1979), 4:218.

6. Adams to Abigail Adams, 3 July 1776, in *Works of John Adams,* ed. Adams, 1:230–231.

7. Adams to James Warren, 9 January 1787, in *Warren-Adams Letters,* 2 vols. (Boston: Massachusetts Historical Society, 1925), 2:280. See also Gordon S. Wood, *The Creation of the American Republic, 1776–1787* (Chapel Hill: The University of North Carolina Press for the Institute of Early American History and Culture, 1969), 571.

8. Adams to Jefferson, 15 July 1813, in *The Adams-Jefferson Letters,* ed. Cappon, 2:358.

9. Madison, *Federalist* No. 10.

10. Madison, *Federalist* No. 49.

11. John Adams to Samuel Adams, 18 October 1790, in *Works of John Adams,* ed. Adams, 6:414–420.

12. Adams to Jefferson, 6 December 1787, in *The Adams-Jefferson Letters,* ed. Cappon, 1:214.

13. Adams to Benjamin Rush, 9 June 1789, in *Old Family Letters: Copied from the Originals for Alexander Biddle,* Series A (Philadelphia: J.B. Lippincott, 1892), 38.

14. Wood, *The Creation of the American Republic, 1776–1787,* ch. 14, "The Relevance and Irrelevance of John Adams," 567–592.

THOMAS JEFFERSON

1. Jefferson to John Taylor, 14 February 1821, in Jefferson Papers, *Collections of the Massachusetts Historical Society,* 7th ser., vol. 1 (Boston: Published by the Society, 1900), 305–306.

2. Jefferson to General Breckenridge, 15 February 1821, in *The Writings of Thomas Jefferson,* ed. Andrew Lipscomb and Albert Bergh, 20 vols. (Washington, D.C.: The Thomas Jefferson Memorial Association, 1904), 15:315, italics added.

3. Madison to Samuel Smith, 4 November 1826, in *Writings of James Madison,* ed. Gaillard Hunt, 9 vols. (New York: G.P. Putnam's Sons, 1900–1910), 9:257.

4. Jefferson to Madison, 17 February 1826, in *The Republic of Letters: The Correspondence Between Thomas Jefferson and James Madison, 1776–1826,* ed. James Morton Smith, 3 vols. (New York: W.W. Norton, 1995), 3:1965.

5. Jefferson to Isaac McPherson, 13 August 1813, in Jefferson, *Writings*, ed. Merrill Peterson (New York: Library of America, 1984), 1291.

6. Jefferson to Joshua Dodge, 3 August 1823, in Jefferson Papers, *Collections of the Massachusetts Historical Society*, 7th ser., vol. 1, 327.

7. Jefferson to Crawford, 20 June 1816, in *Writings of Thomas Jefferson*, ed. Paul Leicester Ford, 10 vols. (New York: G.P. Putnam's Sons, 1892–1899), 10:34–35.

8. Jefferson to Abigail Adams, 22 February 1787, in Jefferson, *Writings*, ed. Peterson, 890.

9. Jefferson to William Short, 3 January 1793, in Jefferson, *Writings*, ed. Peterson, 1004.

10. Adams to Jefferson, 13 July 1813, in *The Adams-Jefferson Letters*, ed. Lester Cappon, 2 vols. (Chapel Hill: University of North Carolina Press, for the Institute of Early American History and Culture, 1959), 2:355.

11. Jefferson to Adams, 8 April 1816, in Jefferson, *Writings*, ed. Peterson, 1382.

JAMES MADISON

1. Douglass Adair, "James Madison's Autobiography," in *The William and Mary Quarterly*, 3rd ser., vol. 2, no. 2 (April 1945), 209.

2. *The Papers of James Madison*, ed. Charles F. Hobson, et al. (vols. 1–17) (Charlottesville: University Press of Virginia, 1979), 12:120.

3. Madison to Jefferson, 17 October 1788, in *The Republic of Letters: The Correspondence Between Thomas Jefferson and James Madison, 1776–1826*, ed. James Morton Smith, 3 vols. (New York: W.W. Norton, 1995), 1:564.

4. Jefferson to Madison, 20 December 1787, in *Republic of Letters*, ed. Smith, 1:513.

5. Madison to Washington, 16 April 1787, in James Madison, *Writings*, ed. Jack N. Rakove (New York: Library of America, 1999), 81.

6. Madison to William Cabell Rives, 12 March 1833, in Madison, *Writings*, ed. Rakove, 864–865.

7. "8th Annual Message to Congress," 3 December 1816, in *Writings of James Madison*, ed. Gaillard Hunt, 9 vols. (New York: G.P. Putnam's Sons, 1900–1910), 8:379.

8. "Message to Congress on Peace Treaty," 18 February 1815, in Madison, *Writings*, ed. Rakove (New York: Library of America, 1999), 708.

9. Irving Brant, *James Madison, Commander in Chief*, 6 vols. (Indianapolis: Bobbs-Merrill, 1961), 6:419.

Sources

Texts by the founders are taken from *The Writings of George Washington,* ed. Worthington Chauncey Ford, 14 vols. (New York: G.P. Putnam's Sons, 1889–1893); *The Writings of George Washington,* ed. Jared Sparks, 12 vols. (Boston: Little, Brown, 1855); *The Writings of George Washington,* ed. John C. Fitzpatrick, 39 vols. (Washington, D.C.: U.S. Government Printing Office, 1931–1944); *Works of Alexander Hamilton,* ed. Henry Cabot Lodge, 12 vols. (New York: Putnam, 1903); *Works of Alexander Hamilton,* ed. John C. Hamilton, 7 vols. (New York: J.F. Trow, Printer, 1850–1851); *The Works of John Adams,* ed. Charles Francis Adams, 10 vols. (Boston: Little, Brown, 1850–1856); *Writings of Thomas Jefferson,* ed. Paul Leicester Ford, 10 vols. (New York: G.P. Putnam's Sons, 1892–1899); *The Writings of Thomas Jefferson,* ed. Andrew A. Lipscomb and Albert E. Bergh, 20 vols. (Washington, D.C.: Issued under the Auspices of the Thomas Jefferson Memorial Association of the United States, 1905); *The Writings of James Madison,* ed. Gaillard Hunt, 9 vols. (New York: G.P. Putnam's Sons, 1900–1910).

The letter from Washington to John Adams, 10 May 1789, is taken from *The Papers of George Washington: Presidential Series,* ed. Dorothy Twohig (Charlottesville: University Press of Virginia, 1987). The following letters are taken from *The Papers of Alexander Hamilton,* ed. Harold C. Syrett, 26 vols. (New York: Columbia University Press, 1961–1987): Hamilton to Elizabeth Schuyler, August 1780; Hamilton to James Duane, 3 September 1780; Memorandum by George Beckwith, October 1789; Hamilton to John Laurens, 8 January 1780; Hamilton to Washington, 9 September 1792; Hamilton to Theodore Sedgwick, 10 July 1804; William P. Van Ness's account of Hamilton's death, 21 July 1804. The letter from Abigail Adams to John Adams, 31 March 1776, is taken from *Adams Family Correspondence,* ed. L.H. Butterfield, 7 vols. (Cambridge: Belknap Press of Harvard University Press, 1963–1993). The letter from John Adams to Thomas Brand Hollis, 5 April 1788, is taken from John Disney, *Memoirs of Brand-Hollis* (London: 1808). The letter from John Adams to Benjamin Rush, 19 June 1789, is taken from *Old Family Letters: Copied from the Originals for Alexander Biddle,* Series A (Philadelphia: J.B. Lippincott, 1892).

I have mostly maintained the style of capitalization, punctuation, spelling, and the like that was used in the source materials listed here. These sources updated the original handwritten texts to various degrees, and those differences are therefore reflected in the reprinted pieces.

Index